THE EMERGENCE OF THE EASTERN WORLD

THE EMERGENCE OF THE EASTERN WORLD

Seven Essays on Political Ideas

by

G. L. SEIDLER

Rector of Marie Curie-Skłodowska University,
Lublin, Poland

with a Foreword by

SIR ISAIAH BERLIN

THE QUEEN'S AWARD
TO INDUSTRY 1966

PERGAMON PRESS

OXFORD · LONDON · EDINBURGH · NEW YORK

TORONTO · SYDNEY · PARIS · BRAUNSCHWEIG

Pergamon Press Ltd., Headington Hill Hall, Oxford
4 & 5 Fitzroy Square, London W.1
Pergamon Press (Scotland) Ltd., 2 & 3 Teviot Place, Edinburgh 1
Pergamon Press Inc., 44–01 21st Street, Long Island City, New York 11101
Pergamon of Canada Ltd., 207 Queen's Quay West, Toronto 1
Pergamon Press (Aust.) Pty. Ltd., Rushcutters Bay, Sydney, N.S.W.
Pergamon Press S.A.R.L., 24 rue des Écoles, Paris 5ᵉ
Vieweg & Sohn GmbH, Burgplatz 1, Braunschweig

First edition 1968

Library of Congress Catalog Card No. 68-22329

PRINTED IN GREAT BRITAIN BY A. WHEATON AND CO., EXETER
08 003500 0

There are more things in heaven and earth,
Horatio, than are dreamt of in your philosophy

SHAKESPEARE

CONTENTS

FOREWORD

I AM not qualified to comment on the essays on the Emergence of the Eastern World of the Rector of the University of Lublin, but I welcome the appearance of a book by this distinguished Polish scholar whom, since his visit to Oxford some years ago, I have held in admiration and respect and am glad to call a personal friend. Western historians of political theory have confined themselves, naturally perhaps but regrettably, to a somewhat narrow preoccupation with social and political thought only in Western Europe: this is the canon, and few scholars look or see beyond it. It is a service to scholarship and to the widening of the historical horizon, largely due to the growing power of the Soviet Union and the Chinese Republic, that these perspectives should begin to seem outdated.

That a Polish work on the social ideas of a great empire which affected the development of Eastern Europe should now appear in English is a sign (it is to be hoped) of a return to a freer circulation of ideas, and the destruction of walls in the world of learning. Like Marie Curie-Skłodowska, after whom his university is named, Dr. Seidler is a champion of humanity and reason, and I wish him and his work very well indeed.

Oxford, 1967   ISAIAH BERLIN

PREFACE

EUROPE's contact with the East has been mainly on the battlefield and the market-place. There has been little interest in political systems, still less in political ideas. Interest has been centred mainly on the European tradition. In my studies on the history of political ideas, I have endeavoured to go beyond this European centrism. *The Emergence of the Eastern World* is part of my broader studies; it comprises seven essays on Eastern political thought, which are normally outside the traditional course of teaching.

My aim is to present a general synthesis of concepts, some of which gave rise to world-wide changes, e.g. the Mongol belief.

Against the broad social–economic background, I should like not only to describe the content of the ideas, but also to try to explain why they arose and how they affected history.

If this book can contribute a little to changing the European-centric approach in the teaching of history of political ideas, it will have fulfilled its purpose.

G. L. SEIDLER

THE POLITICAL THOUGHT
OF THE ANCIENT EAST

THE beginnings of political thought in the world should be sought in the history of the Eastern states, since the political doctrines of the peoples of the East, entangled as they were with religious beliefs, preceded the Hellenic theories of social economy.

Many centuries before the formation of the states of Greece, great theocratic monarchies came into being in the East, where there also emerged the first political doctrines. These as a rule were contained within the framework of the prevailing creeds. The will of the god explained the existence and vicissitudes of states. Belief in the intervention of the divinity in state affairs was linked with the conviction either that the ruler expresses directly the will of the god, that he is the viceroy of the god or even the god himself on earth, or else, as in the State of Israel, that the god reveals his will to the people through his priests and prophets. However the relationship between the state authorities and the god was conceived, the dominating social concepts of the Eastern states as a rule constituted an integral part of the religious systems; hence the Eastern theories of social economy may be defined as religious–political doctrines. The typical feature of almost all the doctrines of the East, in spite of their specific distinctions, is a fatalistic obedience to the will of heaven, humble submission to one's destiny, and indifference to questions of social economy.

Amidst the rocky wastes of the deserts which stretched from the Sahara towards Central Asia, human settlements could only be maintained in the basins of the great rivers. On those fertile oases, the hearts of which were such rivers as the Nile, the Tigris, the Euphrates, the Ganges, or the Hwang-ho, state organizations sprang up.

The most characteristic feature of the states of the Ancient East, both Near and Far, was the dominating role of the great rivers, constituting the central axes of these states. The river was regarded as a god, arbitrarily distributing punishment or favours to the people settled on its banks. At one time, flood destroyed all hope; at another, harm was wrought by drought. At first, people took refuge in prayer, but in time experience taught them to regulate the state of the water by means of dykes, dams, and canals. Links were formed between the separate villages on the banks of the river, since they gave each other help in their mutual struggle against the external enemy. It is by no means an accident that almost all the great states of antiquity in the East lay on mighty rivers; Egypt on the Nile and Mesopotamia on the Euphrates and Tigris; while India possessed two vast water arteries in the Indus and the Ganges, the germ of the Chinese State should be sought in the Hwang-ho, and the further spread of China occupied territory on both banks of the Yangtze-kiang. The Nile joined the separate parts of Egypt into one whole, and linked Egypt with the tropical countries of Africa and the Mediterranean. The Euphrates and the Tigris brought Mesopotamia closer to the Persian Gulf and to the neighbouring countries. The Indus and the Ganges played and still play a great role in the life of India.

The material foundation of the power of the great states of the East was the regulation of the water supply for the rural population. "The necessity for the calculation of the flood periods of the Nile," says Marx, "gave birth to Egyptian astronomy, and together with this the reign of the priestly caste as directors of agriculture." In this way the ruling castes, by gaining mastery over the rivers, made the life and very existence of the people dependent on them. Hence, too, the interest of the population was concentrated on the problem of the regular floods, whereas the problems of power remained beyond their field of vision.

The great rivers formed centres of crystallization for the states of the Ancient East. State organisms occupying vast territories in the river confluences, often peopled by various races, formed far-stretching states, governed by despotic rulers. In these states, subject to normal development, any process of change came to pass very slowly, in consequence of the indifference to questions of social economy fostered by the religious creeds. The divinity of the ruler stifled all signs of rebellion and dissatisfaction. The internal contradictions of these states were manifested with difficulty, and were but little affected by external impulses on account of the weak mutual bonds between the Eastern powers. A process of slow change brought about a confusion of the old and the new elements of social economy in the theocratic monarchies of the East. Hence, too, in these slave-type states, social economies of family property held in common, or even feudalism, were co-existent with slavery, e.g. in China.[1]

Both the social economies and the political systems of the Eastern states diverged from the classical example of the slave state in Ancient Greece and Rome. In the East, all the land was owned by the state, to which in principle the slaves also belonged; in this way the economic basis of the despotic rule of the Eastern monarchs was founded. In spite of the concentration of the land in the hands of the state, in reality a considerable part of the land was always in the hands of the agricultural community and was cultivated by free farmers. It is significant that the whole burden of production was not cast on the shoulders of slaves, as was the case in Ancient Greece and Rome. Slaves and freemen worked side by side; hence there also arose a marked social differentiation among the freemen in the Eastern states. Slavery in the Eastern states did not advance beyond the first stage of development. Besides domestic slavery, there existed a collective ownership of slaves, who were the property of the temples or of the state itself.

The social antagonisms between rich and poor on the one hand, and the class antagonism between slave-owners and slaves on the other, led to the rise of a state serving the rich in their subjugation of the free farmers and slaves. Moreover, the people's continual fear of disaster by flood or drought, and the vital necessity for the central regulation of the river, strengthened the despotic power of the state apparatus. The highest power belonged to the autocratic monarch, whose position was made stronger by a religion founded on humble obedience to divine authority.

In the same way as in the various states of the Ancient East the typical form of organization was a theocratic monarchy, so the principle of passive submission was the typical feature of the various religious and political doctrines. This principle runs through all the doctrines of the East, although they arose out of various social conflicts when the ruling classes were declining and the old structural forms no longer answered to the new social relations.

Since it is the political doctrines of China which show the greatest heterogeneity, let us begin our considerations with these, which will bring us to a discussion of the doctrines of India, Babylon, Israel and Egypt.

1. ON THE THRESHOLD OF CHINESE HISTORY

The banks of the Yellow River were the cradle of China. The people cultivated with care the fertile river valley, covered with a thick layer of loess dust, hundreds of thousands of hectares in extent. The burning winds from the Mongolian deserts, bringing the disaster of drought, were combated by the regular irrigation of the fields. The threat of inundation was opposed by a system of canals, carrying the water away from the fields in time of flood. The need for the regulation of the river brought about the development of the irrigation system; here is the beginning of astronomy in connection with the establishment of the dates of the dry seasons, the floods, seed-time and harvest. On this loess plain, man very early cultivated the land, and knew the use of plough and cart.

Chinese legends tell of hero-emperors, such as Yao, Shun, and Yü, whose rule was characterized by their providence for the good of their subjects.[2] This remote period, veiled in myth and called "The Age of Gold", is linked with man's struggles to obtain mastery over the Yellow River. Legends tell of a famine caused by river floods during the reign of Emperor Yao the Just. Mencius, one of the chroniclers who came after Confucius, wrote:

In the time of Yao, when the state had not yet been put into order, the waters rose from their beds and caused a great flood. Plants and trees were strewn over the earth, and everywhere there were hosts of birds and wild beasts. The five fruits of the field did not grow, and the birds and wild beasts drove out the humans. Paths trodden by the feet of animals and the tracks of birds' feet made a network everywhere in the Middle Kingdom.

The next two legendary emperors Shun and Yü—masters of astronomy and geometry—dominated the river and removed the threat of floods, so that the heroic Emperor Yü is said to have declared of himself: "I have made a way for the streams through nine provinces and directed the waters to the rivers, while together with Chih I have sown grain and shown the people how to gain food by the use of nets."

The power of the state became crystallized around the river, and the struggle to conquer it was the theme of the legends of the three hero-emperors. From these legends we can form a picture of the social concepts of the remote past in China. This information is contained in the two Confucian books, *Shu Ching*, the *Canon of History*, which hands down legends and myths, and *Shih Ching*, the *Canon of Odes*, containing 305 songs, the majority from the period after 1200 B.C. These books have been re-edited and altered many times, and express the opinions of the ruling classes at the turn of the second millennium before our era.

What is especially striking in the *Canon of History* is the outlook on nature, the expression of man's struggle with natural forces. Here are described the successive seasons of the year, the elements of earth and heaven, the points of the compass, the course of the sun and moon; to all these phenomena are attributed numbers in order to establish the conviction of their stability and regularity. Problems of social economy are also connected with this outlook on nature. The incarnation of God on earth was Ti, the Son of Heaven, the ruler whose knowledge of the celestial laws laid the foundation for his good rule on earth. He was the mediator between heaven and earth; he also brought about harmony between heaven and earth, and by virtue of this he induced the regularity of atmospheric phenomena, ensuring good harvests for the people. The paths traced by the planets in their courses led to the picturesque conception of a principle of universal regularity penetrating heaven and earth—hence also the definition of this principle as the "path of Heaven" (Tao), which lies at the root of Chinese philosophy.

The chief task of the ruler was to ensure on earth the harmony delineated in the Great Plan (Hung Fan). In social matters, harmony was to be ensured by observing the eight elements of government, viz. provision of food, a guarantee of articles for use, the meticulous observance of sacrifices, attention to public works, care of learning, the introduction of just punishments, and finally careful protection of guests and of the army. The Great Plan mentions justice, severity, and mildness as the three means which a good ruler should use in order to ensure a fivefold happiness to his subjects: long life, health, riches, love of virtue, and a death crowning life. Contact between earth and heaven took place by means of sacrifices minutely regulated by formal pre-scriptions, failure in the observance of which invalidated the offerings.

The social relations, consecrated by tradition and religion through long centuries, were made more conspicuous by these ceremonial sacrifices. From this most remote period date the five relations, namely, that of the son to the father, the wife to the husband, the younger brother to the elder, the subject to the ruler, and lastly, the friend to the friend. The rites of the cult, however, were carried out only by the ruling class, while the people strove only to win the favour of good or bad spirits. Ancestor-worship was the only cult common to all the Chinese; by this the conviction was established that the past models the future and the present, and that the sacred obligation of every man is to continue the work of his ancestors. In this way, a religious faith in the wisdom of the past was born to deepen the spirit of conservatism.

From the Confucian Canon, we know only the religious and social views of the ruling classes. A deep chasm divided these classes from the working people, of whose daily toil one of the oldest songs tells:

> We rise at dawn of day,
> We rest at dusk.
> We dig wells and we drink,
> We cultivate the soil and we eat.
> In what then can help us
> The might of the emperor?

In the middle of the eleventh century B.C. the Chou dynasty came to power in China, beginning the feudal era in that country. China's period of family communism and slavery was over.[3]

2. THE SOURCES OF THE NEW DOCTRINES

During the rule of the Chou dynasty, feudal relations became established in China, composed as it was of many vassal principalities. A system of feudal dependencies was built up, subject to many conventions, which were strictly observed both in state and religious activities as well as in private life.

In those times the land belonged to the gentry, who spent most of their time in hunting or warfare, while the rural population supported their lords by their labour, supplying them with the fruits of their toil. There was little intercourse between the feudal gentry and the people cultivating the soil. In the country, the power was wielded by the fathers of the families, the eldest of whom was the head of the village. The chief occupation of the populace was the regular cultivation of the soil. As handicrafts developed, the craftsmen became differentiated from the rural population. Whole families devoted themselves to certain crafts, so that even the organization of craftmanship in China bore the mark of a patriarchal family occupation.

The feudal system of China was formed during the reign of the Chou dynasty, whose princes took a royal title and subordinated the very numerous, though territorially not large, principalities lying in the valley of the Yellow River. Thus by the middle of the ninth century B.C. the Chou dynasty had linked up these numerous fiefs by feudal bonds, exercising direct power over the principality lying in the centre of the feudal state. After 100 years, however, i.e. from the middle of the eighth century B.C., the principalities began a period of continuous warfare among themselves. This led to the fall of the feudal state of the Chou dynasty, and in 221 B.C. to the union of all China under the absolute central power of an emperor. The five-century period of quarrels among the fiefs falls into two phases. The first ends about the middle of the fifth century B.C., when the larger principalities won hegemony over the smaller fiefs as a result of treaties, and the second begins about the middle of the fifth century B.C., when the rapacious policy of the large principalities led to the liquidation of the small fiefs. In this second phase, called "the Period of Contending States", the number of principalities steadily diminished, so that out of well over a hundred, only seven remained by the middle of the third century B.C. As the principalities lying on the frontiers of China increased their territories at the expense of their barbarian neighbours, their bonds with the Chou dynasty weakened. Since the principality of the Chou dynasty lay in the centre of the feudal state, however, it could not expand outwards, while the political growth of vassal principalities weakened its importance, making its power over them illusory.

The five centuries of struggle among the fiefs, on the one hand, brought about the weakening of the central authority, wars devastating the populace, and pauperization, while the aristocracy of those states which were conquered in battle by the stronger principalities lost their privileges; on the other hand, an apparatus of power was built up by the principalities in process of becoming independent. The impoverished gentry found occupation in the courts of the feudal principalities, holding posts in administration, the army, or diplomacy. The principalities, loosely federated with the central government, mingled war by force of arms with a policy of reciprocal pacts and treaties, and so built up diplomacy, administration, and an army. In this way, new political doctrines arose in official circles in the courts of the princes, as here there was lively discussion on concepts of the model ruler, good methods of government, and ways of emerging from confusion.

Besides the symptoms of political fermentation perceived and experienced by the China of the Chou dynasty, changes of an economic nature shook the traditional system much more strongly. Bronze, which had been known to the Chinese from about 2000 B.C., gave place to iron, which spread all over China between the sixth and third centuries B.C. The introduction of iron implements influenced the development of handicrafts, and trade became brisk as a result of a goods–money economy. In the last phase of the reign of the Chou dynasty, the means of payment which had hitherto been used, such as shells, silk, or jade, were replaced by easily distributable metal coins. The traditional feudal relations did not correspond to the economic changes in the more advanced principalities, and the need was felt for a uniform law, the protection of private property, and security for trade.

However, the economic changes did not take place to the same extent in all the principalities. We know of some economic development in the fiefs of Cheng and Tsi; the most striking, however, was that in the principality of Ch'in, of which the ruler in 221 B.C. united seven fiefs—Ch'in, Chu, Wei, Han, Chao, Tsi and Yen—giving rise to the Chinese Empire.

As early as the fourth century B.C. in the principality of Ch'in, private ownership of land by the peasants was recognized on the basis of the reform of 350 B.C. The peasants were obliged to pay a land-tax, but could freely dispose of their land. The state gave rewards for good husbandry. Old feudal customary norms were replaced by a uniform law guaranteeing the rigorous protection of private property. The law was unified in order to facilitate trade, as were the weights and measures. The prevailing doctrine in the principality of Ch'in was founded on the views of the School of Legalists, whose adherents, combating the last vestiges of feudalism, declared themselves for absolute obedience to the written law for the general good of the state. The economic successes of the principality of Ch'in were accompanied in the fourth and third centuries B.C. by successes in foreign policy. From the year 325 B.C. its rulers assumed the title of kings. Ch'in had not only an economic but also a military advantage over the other principalities, for in this fief the unwieldy war-chariots had been replaced by a mobile cavalry.

On the forcing-bed of the strong politico-economic ferment, new doctrines arose. The doctrine of cosmic harmony, put into force by the virtuous hero-rulers, already belonged to the past. Wars, infertility, social changes, and oppression by victorious princes, gave birth to pessimism and doubt. The nominal power of the last kings of the Chou dynasty, the unceasing conflicts with vassal states, internal confusion, the menace of raids by barbarian tribes, all disposed thinking people towards pessimism. Publications censuring the lack of authority and the misery of the toiling masses appeared. In written criticism, the poets are especially distinguished for their denunciations of the difficult situation of the people, of their misery, and of the decline of traditional manners and customs in the whole community. A literature of censure thus preceded the new political doctrines. The ruling classes at this period of confusion sought new social solutions, while the hitherto humble people expressed their revolt and remonstrances in doleful songs, exalting death over the heavy toil of life.

The picture of political thought arising from the profound changes during the reign of the Chou dynasty gives us four politico-social schools of thought.[4] The first is represented by the followers of Lao Tse, who declared themselves against any intervention of the ruler in social matters. The second is represented by the followers of Confucius, who, idealizing the past, believed in the excellence of the feudal system. The third is represented by the followers of Mo Ti, who desired to base social relations on all-embracing love. The last is represented by the School of Legalists, who fought against the feudal past and expressed a doctrine corresponding to the economic changes, declaring themselves in favour of a strong ruler.

3. LAO TSE AND HIS SCHOOL

Not very much is known about the life of Lao Tse. We know that this name means the Venerable Sage, and that his family name was Li. The exact date of his birth is unknown, but he was born during the reign of the twenty-first emperor of the Chou dynasty, Tsing Wang (606–585 B.C.). Lao Tse, living aloof from political affairs, spent a tranquil life as librarian of the state archives in Lo-Yong. In spite of his inconspicuous position, he must have been famous, since Confucius, who was younger by a generation, turned to him for information in his search for ancient principles. During this meeting, Lao Tse must have been very sceptical of the Confucian cult of the past. "How can you continually speak of men," said he to Confucius, "whose limbs have long been scattered in dust? Indeed, those sayings of theirs which have come down to us were surely appropriate in their own times, but they are now mere words; the wheel of time does not stand still, and we must keep pace with it, adapting our ideas to the changed conditions."

A return to a primitive state of nature, an escape from life and culture, were—in the opinion of Lao Tse—the best means of preventing all social deficiencies. Faithful to this wisdom, Lao Tse towards the end of his life resigned his post in the Royal Archives, and retired into complete solitude, where unknown and alone he ended his days. During his last journey, while crossing a mountain pass, he wrote down his philosophy in 5000 or so characters, at the request of the Warden of the Gate, Yin Hsî. By writing down his wisdom, the Venerable Sage was faithless to his own precepts of teaching without words, but thanks to this, posterity has knowledge of his doctrine.

Without entering into the disputed problems of the authenticity of this work, we know Lao Tse's doctrine from a book from the third century B.C. bearing the title of *Tao-te-King*. Lao Tse's philosophical system, in accordance with the title, is divided into two parts, the first of which treats of Tao, the supreme principle of the universe, and the second of virtue. The whole consists of eighty-one chapters.

The foundation of Lao Tse's system is "Tao"; in European literature this word has not always the same significance.[5] Lao Tse speaks of Tao as something invisible, inaudible, intangible, without substance, yet at the same time creating, penetrating, and completing all phenomena and things. Man can approach Tao by completely separating himself from practical life and turning inwards towards his own nature. Tranquillity and happiness may be attained by the cessation of all effort and all activity. "Tao never acts, yet still achieves everything." From this arises the supreme principle of Taoism—the conception of abstinence from action. Lao Tse's teaching on the inner life was taken up in later ages by various mystic schools. The original Taoism of Lao Tse, however, contained elements of primitive materialism, manifested in his acknowledgement of the material unity of the world, which is expressed in the impersonal order of nature—in Tao.

Lao Tse taught that in the world of reality there prevails a struggle between contraries, that all phenomena and things condition their opposites. It is only Tao that expresses the natural regularity and ensures perfection, and any action is only a disturbance of the natural order. Lao Tse's followers were therefore opposed to any norms regulating social life, since they considered any attempt at social reform as a grave offence, inevitably doomed to failure. By forbidding any intervention in social affairs, Lao Tse attempted to save the state from chaos. In his doctrine, he attempted to explain the necessity for the passive subordination of man to fate and for behaviour according to Tao; for otherwise the life of man would be full of passion, disappointment, and sorrow. By abstinence from action, that is, by a total surrender to the natural course of things, man attains inner peace and happiness. The thought of a total surrender to fate was attributed before Lao Tse to the half-mythical Emperor Shun, who made it a fundamental principle of his rule.

Lao Tse was antagonistic to all government rules and regulations, considering that law brings in its train trespasses and law-breaking, which in their turn cause disorder and unrest in the state. "The State is a product of the spirit," he says, "and cannot be influenced. Any attempt at interference is always doomed to failure and disrupts the unity." A ruler should not intervene in the affairs of his people. "The Sacred One by ruling purges hearts and fills bellies, weakens the will and strengthens the bones. He strives always that the people should know nought and desire nought, and that those who have knowledge should not dare to act. If abstinence from action is cultivated, then the government is good."

The ruling emperor, according to the doctrine of Lao Tse, is one of the four supreme magnitudes of the universe. "Great is Tao, great are the heavens, great is the earth, and great is the emperor." The Taoist doctrine tells of the divine origin of the imperial ruler: "He who is emperor is united with heaven; he who is united with heaven will be like Tao, which has existed from time everlasting."

However, the emperor should rule without any compulsion, without any apparatus of power, without any army. "The greater the number of prohibitions issued in the world, the more the people become impoverished.... The greater the number of laws and orders passed, the more thieves and robbers there will be." Any violence provokes reaction and unrest among the people. Armies leave misery behind them. Therefore the ruler should comport himself with humility towards his subjects, and his yielding to their wishes is the best method of government.

> If the ruler is tranquil and unobtrusive, then the people are righteous and noble ....
> If the people go hungry, this means that the taxes are too great a burden, and this is the cause of their misery ....
> If the people are hard to command, this means that their work is too great a burden, and this is the cause of their disobedience ....
> If the people look up on death with indifference, this means that they suffer too much to care for life—this is why they die without regret ....

In one of the last chapters of *Tao-te King*, the Venerable Sage sketches his ideal social system in a few lines. Is is a small principality ruled without any bureaucracy or army. The state is self-sufficient and does not menace its neighbours. The people in the ideal state live according to nature, and are happy, for they have returned to the idyllic harmony of the primeval community. The coexistence of small principalities unfitted to wage war was Lao Tse's ideal in that period of internal conflicts which rent China.[6]

The doctrine of Lao Tse is a criticism of the prevailing social relations. His followers believed that any community stricken with a grave disease might recover only by complete peace, that is, that by abstinence from action the strength of the community might be regenerated. The Taoists considered any procedure, any intervention in social affairs, as a cause intensifying the disease.

Lao Tse's doctrine might have appealed to those classes which felt most heavily the burden of waging war, pestered as they were by the load of taxes and the formalistic bureaucracy of the feudal rulers. But this was too abstract a doctrine to spread widely among the Chinese people, and moreover, it was penetrated by a fatalistic passivity and a complete disbelief in the the man for whom the ideal was to be abstinence from action.

Among the successors of Lao Tse, the two philosophers Chuang Tzu and Yang Chu deserve attention. The first, living in the fourth century B.C., is the author of a work in which he combats Confucianism and preaches the principles of Taoism. This volume has been known since 742 A.C. under the name of *The Genuine Book of the Southern Flower*.[7] The world in which we live, taught Chuang Tzu, is full of contradictions, hence human judgements on it differ and change. Since it is not possible to establish an absolute criterion for the assessment of phenomena, one should retire from the world, and by means of abstinence from action and the indifference brought about by inner peace, attain Tao, i.e. perfect knowledge. "Abstinence from action effects the fulfilment of one's duty. Abstinence from action leads to sweet content, and then there is no room for care and worry...." Chuang Tzu also expresses the conviction that man has no influence upon the events of the world surrounding him, and it is only by means of Tao that he achieves unity with nature. The attainment of this oneness which begins and ends all phenomena and things was the ideal of Chuang Tzu. "He who comprehends unity, may do anything. To him who has no aims of his own, even ghosts and spirits are obedient." The Taoist sage, a man of royal virtues, walks unknown, and blushes for his knowledge. Chuang Tzu saw a natural order in society:

> If in heaven and earth, which are indeed the most divine, there are degrees of high and low, how much more is this necessary for the order of humanity! In the ancestral shrines, it is the degrees of relationship which come first. At the court, dignity has precedence. In the country, age is given priority. Judgement is of most importance in the ordering of affairs. And this is the order of the great Tao.

Through the understanding of Tao, a ruler attains to an understanding of the social order; he is not bound by any law but only Tao. It is only subjects who are bound by laws and customs.

Yang Chu, many years older than Chuang Tzu, and also a Taoist, reached quite different conclusions. He did not leave any works, and so we have the picture of his doctrine only from the remarks of other writers. He too regards all effort and endeavour to improve and reconstruct social relations as vain. The road to happiness according to him does not lead through inner contemplation, as was taught by the Taoists, but through the fulfilment of egoistic desires. Yang Chu recommends that we should make the most of our lives, since in the face of death we are all equal, both the good and the evil, the just and the unjust, the wise and the foolish. Full of scepticism as to any recovery from the social chaos, the doctrine of Yang Chu propagates egoism, contending against the traditional creeds, conventions, and prevailing ethics. Deriding the Confucianists, who were passionately opposing the reversal of the old order, Yang Chu tauntingly asks: "For what more need care he who has a comfortable dwelling, fine clothes, delicious food, and fair women?"

The political doctrine of Confucius, however, was different, although the divergences between the two schools only became sharply apparent in the course of centuries. The Taoistic teaching expounded by the followers of Lao Tse on desistance from intervention, on not attempting to influence social questions, and on not opposing oneself to evil, aroused criticism on the part of the disciples of Confucius, who put forward a positive programme for the restoration of the former feudal relations.

4. CONFUCIUS AND HIS DOCTRINE

The doctrine of Confucius arose and gained followers amongst the official circles which played no small role during the period when China was broken up into many small states.[8] In these circles, good birth was highly regarded and the common people held in contempt. The atmosphere in these circles was also favourable for the cultivation of formalism, ceremony, and ritual. Here also tradition, which served the officials to justify the mutual demands and claims of their mandators, was esteemed and studied. The official circles shaped a doctrine to suit the ruling class. The essence of this doctrine was a return to past times, the resurrection of feudalism with its formalism, etiquette, and ritual, and above all the restoration of humble submissiveness in the people. "The virtue of power", repeated the followers of Confucius after their master, "is like a breath of wind, and the virtue of the common people is like grass. When the wind blows, the grass must bend."

Confucius was born in 551 B.C. of the official classes, as his father was a minor military functionary. K'ung, for this was the surname of Confucius, prepared himself for a clerk's position, and as he says of himself, turned all his thoughts towards knowledge from his fifteenth year onwards. It was not, however, granted to Confucius to realize his doctrine in practical politics. Beyond a short period in office in the state of Lu, where the results of his political activity are said to have been extraordinary, K'ung had to restrict himself to lecturing to his pupils on his doctrine. He was called K'ung the Master, K'ung Fu-tse, which in Europe was latinized into Confucius.

We see Confucius surrounded by his disciples, commenting on ancient documents and tradition. "I hand down, I do not create", he told them. "I believe in the past, and I love it." The conversations of the Master with his disciples, the *Lun Yi*, written about 100 years after the death of Confucius in 479 B.C., give us a picture of his lively activity as a teacher. His personality must have had a strong influence on those who surrounded him, since a numerous band of his disciples accompanied their master on his wanderings in search of a ruler who would put his doctrine into practice. Confucius tried in vain to influence politics by the knowledge and interpretation of ancient texts. Since he was unable to carry out his intentions, he spent his declining years, undiscouraged by his failures, in editing ancient documents in order to hand them down to his disciples.

The chief aim of Confucius was to restore the old order of society, which had become distorted, especially during the period described by Mencius, the follower of Confucius: "The world has departed from its tracks, and laws and rights are held in slight esteem. Impious speech is heard on every side, and cruel deeds are perpetrated everywhere." It was therefore the ardent desire of Confucius to reform society according to the traditional models, and to bring back the peace and order which had departed from both family and state. Confucius once questioned three of his disciples on their political ambitions; one desired the fame of a military leader and the courage of a hero; the second wished to educate the people by the power of his words. The dream of the third was to hold the position of counsellor to a wise monarch, through whom he could influence the social system and the people. "It would be my care," said this disciple, "that the towns and market-places should no longer be surrounded by walls, and that the people should beat their swords into ploughshares and pasture their cattle in the valleys and woods without fear or dread. I should try to keep the peace for a thousand years, and then of what use would it be to have the courage of a hero, or to sway the mob with oratory?" Confucius accepted this answer as his own. But how could the lost order of society be restored?

Confucius thought that the shaken equilibrium of state and family could be restored by perfecting human personality. He taught that the Holy Ones and heroes are creators of culture simply by means of their inborn characteristics. On the other hand, anyone may acquire culture by studying tradition, ritual, music; in brief, man becomes ennobled by continually improving himself, taking example from the models of the past. And those who possessed ethical culture and knowledge, the noble men, were to bring about the correction of the social system. Holding very varied posts, they were to influence both the family and the state. In this way the ruling classes, with the support of official circles trained in tradition, could maintain their power, opposing all progress in the name of the idealized past. The state officials who were to rule the unlettered commons were to be recruited from among noble men of the Confucian type. Decorum, virtue, moderation, faith in word and deed, loyalty, exactitude, logical behaviour—these are the characteristics distinguishing the noble man from the mob.

Confucius gave utterance to his aristocratic gospel when he said to his disciples that the conditions of moral behaviour were "personal dignity, greatness of soul, responsibility, zeal, and virtue. He who possesses personal dignity has self-control; greatness of soul wins the people; from responsibility is born confidence; zeal guarantees success; finally, by virtue man can be elevated and his nature altered."

Adequately trained, these noble men were to bring about a metamorphosis of society, beginning with the family, which Confucius regarded as the natural unit. There should be a return to hallowed traditions and old relationships, and above all a restoration of the supremacy of the father over his wife and children. The doctrine decreed the restoration of relationships in the state on the model of the family, a natural and stable relationship between the rulers and the ruled. An active part in the reconstruction of order in the state was to be played by educated officials, whose task it would be to restore to the people their lost confidence in authority. The power of the state, Confucius taught, cannot be based solely on commands and a penal system, as order and peace in the state are guaranteed by a voluntary and conscious acknowledgement of authority. Carefully trained officials are of particular importance in the doctrine of Confucius. Hence, when asked about the art of governing, the Master replied, "Take heed to choose virtuous and suitable officials, condone small faults, and finally distinguish those with talent and character." Officials trained in such a tradition were to revive the old institutions both in the family and in the state.

As the years passed, the doctrine of Confucius began to affect social relations; under its influence there was created a system of examinations, which it was necessary to pass before an official appointment could be obtained.

These officials were reared in a spirit of formalism, while the cult of the past inculcated in them hampered all progress.

After the death of Confucius his successors in a certain sense modified the political doctrine of their master. Many schools arose where the new doctrine was cultivated. The parent foundation was that carried on for some time in Lu by Tzu Ssu, a grandson of Confucius. It is from this school that, among other works, there comes the treatise on government, the *Great Learning*. The leading thought of this treatise is also the Confucian conception of perfecting the personality, with this addition, that the development of personal ethics should keep equal pace with the development of social ethics. Besides the perfecting of the individual consciousness, which conditioned clear thinking and the premeditated activity of man, the *Great Learning* indicates the duty of the individual towards his family, the state, and humanity. In this way, an endeavour was made to unite the process of individual perfection with social activity.

The most ardent and talented advocate of the Confucian doctrine was Meng Tzu (372–289 B.C.), who is better known under the Latin form of his name, Mencius. Full of unparalleled admiration for the Master, whom he considered as the greatest of mankind, he successfully combated the adversaries of Confucius. The clarity and colourfullness of his style rendered him the leading teacher of the new doctrine. It seems that in the same way as Chuang Tzu had championed Lao Tse, bringing fame and renown, so the optimistic Mencius vindicated the fame of Confucius. It was he who used to say that man is by nature good and inclined to noble deeds, and that it was only bad environment and improper upbringing which depraved and violated human nature; hence it was a duty to foster the development of the inborn virtues of man. At the summit of all virtues, Mencius placed the need for mutual help, life in common, co-operation, and sympathy for one's neighbours. Since he believed that these virtues of human nature are the foundation of human society, the social interpretation of the Master's doctrine did not weaken the basic Confucian thesis of the restoration of a healthy life in family and state. Mencius taught that "without a prince and a father, without a state and a family, man would return to the status of an animal".

Among those who continued the thought of Confucius may also be counted Hsün Tzu (315–253 B.C.), in spite of his lapses from orthodoxy. He had one of the soundest and most realistic intellects among the followers of Confucius. His comprehension of Confucianism, and especially of its fundamental conceptions, however, entirely differed from that of Mencius. Hsün Tzu revealed the animal nature of man, and saw the need for its subjugation; "Every man has inborn lusts, which seek an object for their satisfaction. Strife and confusion will prevail, if human lusts are not kept at bay by the law. The saints held disorder in contempt, so they set up customs and laws, in order to bridle the people." Hsün Tzu considered that the egoistic human nature, tending towards evil, can only gain noble traits by a scrupulous observation of etiquette and standards of law and morality. Goodness is therefore an artificial product of upbringing, and the observance of ritual, ceremony, decorum, and law, like music, should be treated as a means of education.

In the course of time, the new doctrine gained followers, so that towards the end of the Chou dynasty it was widely spread. Not long afterwards, however, at the time of the union of China in 221 B.C., the doctrine of Confucius was officially condemned and its followers persecuted. The period of disgrace for the adherents of Confucius was short, as a few decades afterwards a splendid renascence of Confuciansim was to come to pass.

5. MO TI IN THE STRUGGLE AGAINST THE CONFUCIAN DOCTRINE

The exaggerated ceremonial advocated by the followers of Confucius was bound to evoke criticism. More sober spirits thought the strict observance of the rules of courtesy to be empty and burdensome. Confucius had laid down that "Respect, when not based on courtesy, becomes a fatiguing bustle; solicitude without courtesy becomes timidity; courage without courtesy turns into disobedience; energy without the restraint of courtesy becomes lack of refinement ...."; could such a statement have a general appeal?

The Confucian etiquette and external ceremonial were sharply criticized by the creator of a third political doctrine, Mo Ti. Two generations younger than Confucius, Mo Ti proclaimed his opinions at a time when the first disciples of the former were already dead. There is no doubt that he had a deeper and more original mentality than Confucius, although his doctrine, at first popular because of certain Utopian features, was only maintained in China for not quite two centuries. Towards the beginning of the second century B.C., his adherents were no longer found.[9]

Again, Mo Ti's doctrine was formed amid a social ferment, during the struggle with the Confucian views. It seems that on the one hand Mo Ti's mathematical and technical studies, and on the other the military environment in which he moved, were not without influence on the formation of his doctrine. He was engaged in the strengthening of military fortifications, and the fact that the last chapters of his reflections on religious and social doctrine contain suggestions on methods of waging a defensive war and on the principles of the technique of fortification, is a proof of his interest in technical military questions. The formalism of the Confucian doctrine found itself under fire from Mo Ti's sharp criticism. Ancestor-worship, funeral ceremonies, and costly etiquette were treated as unnecessary extravagances; these formal activities were considered as completely redundant and only for calculated effect, burdening the unpropertied classes with expense. For the sake of accuracy, Mo Ti objected to the ambiguity, fluidity, and lack of clarity in such Confucian terms as "virtue" or "morality". He strove against the

Confucian conception of the natural character of the family and state. In Mo Ti's political doctrine, state and family were not ethical and natural links binding society together, as Confucius had imagined. Mo Ti wished to see society as an association of units, reciprocally bestowing universal love on one another, capable of conscious and deliberate organization. Although this conception of a social system is permeated by a theistic *Weltanschauung*, Mo Ti attempted to give his views a logical foundation. The starting-point of his doctrine was the recognition of one personal Deity, who as the highest authority for men, should command universal love. The reign of God on earth was to be realized by a specific kind of theocracy.

The forms of social organization in Mo Ti's doctrine diverged from the traditional models. People were to be bound together by unconditional and universal love, and this society, united by feelings of love, was to form a system organized in a hierarchic and deliberate manner, recalling a military organization. Those directing social life were to devote themselves without reserve to social service. At the top of the social hierarchy was a "great ruler", carrying into effect the will of the Deity; according to the doctrine he was responsible only to God. Independently of the basic principle of universal and unconditional love, Mo Ti's doctrine required of society simplicity of life, moderation, economy, and obedience. Thus the principle of universal love, obedience, and an ascetic mode of life were to permeate this new, artificially organized society; this intended organization of society became the model for the school which Mo Ti founded for his disciples. In order to justify his views, Mo Ti sometimes made use of utilitarian arguments. He taught that self-interest commands people to accept and observe the principle of universal love; Mo Ti believed that such a behest would be carried out, since the citizens were obedient to the much more exacting commandments issued by their rulers.

But Mo Ti did not ground his views solely on utilitarian motives; his doctrine demanded a disinterested readiness for self-sacrifice for the good of society. Even Mo Ti's enemies and critics acknowledged that he himself was ready to lay down his life for the salvation of the world. From the general principle of love he derived his unconditional condemnation of aggressive wars, desiring to guide strife-ridden China to universal peace. He supplemented his thesis of the prohibition of offensive warfare, however, by pointing out the necessity of preparing the country for defence against any aggression. This logically-thinking philosopher desired to create an actual basis for a guarantee of peace; hence follows his prohibition only of offensive wars. Mo Ti attempted to give a rational justification of his views, and did not recognize arguments based on tradition; he denied the natural character of family and state, and did not make use of any ethical arguments in his political doctrine. He wished to see a social system resulting from deliberate and conscious human action. He made no attempt to arrest the decline of social relations by recalling the models of the past, as had been done by the followers of Confucius. On the contrary, he advanced a new and daring conception of a social system, not entirely free from Utopian features, which the society of that time was not yet sufficiently mature to accept.

6. THE LEGALIST DOCTRINE

While Mo Ti had attempted to combat the doctrine of Confucius by means of logical argumentation, setting against it in a certain sense a Utopian social organization, the adherents of the so-called Legalist School fought against the Confucian views from the standpoint of practical politics. The ruling classes used the doctrine of the School of Legalists, which had come into being as a result of the economic and social changes, to fight against the useless relations of declining feudalism, already failing to correspond to the goods–money economy then beginning to arise, or to the consolidation of private property, or to the increasing commercial turnover. In states in which the new economic life was breaking down the obstacles of the past, the need arose for an efficient administration, a uniform legal order, and the protection of private property. The School of Legalists was the ideological reflection of the social changes and the needs of practical politics, so that in its ranks we find men of action as well as theorists.

The beginnings of the legalist doctrine are linked with the history of the principality of Tsi, which played a dominating role among the feudal states of China in the sixth and fifth centuries B.C. In this state, the prince Suan, faced by the decline of feudal relations, appointed an Academy for the scientific elaboration of the principles of the new centralized system. This Academy was the ground for the mutual antagonism between the adherents of the doctrines of Lao Tse, Confucius, and Mo Ti, and provided a framework for the formulation of the legalist doctrine.[10]

Contrary to the opinions of Confucius, who made the value of a system dependent on the ethical values of the ruler and his officials, the adherents of the legalist doctrine saw the chief source of a good system in political and legal institutions. A conversation between three members of the Academy characterizes the views prevailing in this institution:

> Tien Tsi, during his studies on the Canon of History, observed that when Yao was ruler, universal peace reigned. Yung Tsi then asked whether this state of affairs was caused by the edicts of the Sacred Ruler. Pong Mong replied in explanation that universal peace was brought not by the government of the Sacred One, but by the sacred laws.

The legal system then in force was regarded in the Academy as a central social problem; according to the Legalist School, the supreme role of legal institutions overshadowed that of the ruler. The Academicians did not intend to improve the world morally. Their aim was merely to introduce order into the social relations by appropriate legal regulations, acting on the assumption that the amount of good and evil in the world is constant. The desired social system was to be achieved by putting eight ideas into practice in the state: love, justice, precision of definitions, morality, music, law, reward and punishment. According to these opinions, the realization of these ideas would guarantee the efficient functioning of the state, regardless of the personal qualifications of the ruler. The theoretical formulations of the legalist doctrine in the State of Tsi became indications for the political activities of the principality of Ch'in. The further history of the legalist doctrine is connected with that of the State of Ch'in in the fourth and third centuries B.C. This period was a series of successes for Ch'in, crowned by the union of all China under the ruler of the state. The official political doctrine of Ch'in was that of the Legalist School. Its chief representative was Wei Yang, who was at the same time an excellent organizer of economic and political life. It was he who granted land to the peasants, unified the weights and measures, reconstructed the taxation system, introduced a police organization, promulgated laws, built roads, drained marshes—in brief, with the help of authority and law, he built up social relations anew.

The adherents of the legalist doctrine fought against the Confucian apotheosis of the past. They considered that the only guarantee for the power of the state was a disposition adapted to the actual situation, i.e. they advocated the need for a strong government and an efficient administration, keeping watch over law and order. Legal norms, in the legalist doctrine, were the fundamental factor in the struggle against the feudal system, hence analytical considerations on the subject of law, its universality, sanction, publication, and efficiency.[11]

When Ch'eng, the ruler of the fief of Ch'in, united all China in 221 B.C., there began a period of ruthless struggle, based on the principles of the legalist doctrine, against the feudal system of division. With the intention of making a complete break with the past history of China, Ch'eng called himself the First Yellow Ruler—Shih Huang-ti.

Having concentrated absolute power in his own hands, the new Emperor liquidated the feudal principalities, and in their place set up thirty-six administrative districts under the charge of officials responsible to the central authority. Taking Ch'in and the reforms of Wei Yang as his model, the Emperor aimed at the complete unification of the state, and issued a series of laws. He introduced a uniform handwriting, a uniform faith, and for the sake of ethnic uniformity transported hundreds of thousands of people from one end of the country to the other, forming settlements in the south confines of China in particular. On the north, from fear of the raids of the nomad Huns, Shih Huang-ti protected his uniform state by a wall, joining up fragments of the defensive embankments built at various times by the individual principalities into one unbroken fortification extending for nearly 1500 miles. In 213 B.C., in his struggle against the feudal tradition, the Emperor issued a decree ordering the burning of books, in this way aiming his chief blow against the doctrine of Confucius and his adherents. All his subjects had to give up all their books at the nearest office, only excepting treatises on agriculture, medicine, or divination. Piles of books on the teaching of Confucius and his followers, written on narrow bamboo tablets, were consigned to the flames. Shih Huang-ti did not hesitate in his unyielding struggle against feudalism, depriving the adherents of Confucius of their freedom and even putting them to death in the ruthless carrying out of his aim of unifying all China.

The fame of the Emperor Shih Huang-ti and of his native principality must have been great, since Europe called the whole united state by the name of Ch'in, changing the corresponding Greek sound to China.

The practical successes of the legalist doctrine were also accompanied by theoretical elaborations. As a representative of the Legalist School we may cite Han Fei-tzu, the author of fifty-five works distinguished for their clarity and precision, but reproached for their complete lack of love of mankind.[12] Han Fei differentiated in man natural and unchanging qualities, and others which were acquired and variable. These variable qualities are formed by an appropriate legal order; above all, the law should strengthen the feeling for discipline, duty, and obedience. The ruler set above the apparatus of government was to be regarded as the highest source of punishment and reward. In Han Fei's doctrine, fear of punishment was the chief motive for human activity, so that sanctions regulated by law were the surest guarantee of the good behaviour both of the governed and the governing. He connected the efficiency of legal norms with the need for continuous adjustment of the law to changing social conditions, and by this showed himself in decided opposition to the traditional feudal norms.

Han Fei came into touch with the Emperor Shih Huang-ti while the latter was still the ruler of Ch'in. It was in that state that the leading representative of the Legalist School ended his days, committing suicide in 233 B.C. The influence and development of the legalist doctrine are connected with the history of Ch'in and the Emperor Shih Huang-ti, who in his struggle for the unification of China, strove against Confucian traditionalism and the customary norms.

7. THE HAN DYNASTY AND THE RENASCENCE
OF CONFUCIANISM

The persecution of the Confucians did not last long. The death of Shih Huang-ti in 211 B.C. and the ensuing period of anarchy, which lasted for some years, gave rise to a new dynasty which was to reign in China for more than four centuries, from 206 B.C. to A.D. 220. Under the rule of the Han dynasty there was a renascence of Confucianism, which then became the official doctrine, while its creator was elevated to the status of a hero and even of a god.

While the government of the Han dynasty held power, there reigned an atmosphere of tolerance for all religious and social doctrines, but Confucianism, crowned by the halo of martyrdom, now expressed the feeling of opposition against the despotic government of the late ruler, who had burnt the Confucian books and imprisoned the followers of the Master and condemned them to death. So the founder of the new dynasty, Liu Pang, a peasant from southern China, suspicious and distrustful of all philosophizing, made a gesture of reconciliation with Confucianism, in spite of the fact that personally Taoism, which was already imbued with mysticism, made a greater appeal to him. The first emperor of the Han dynasty offered up a great sacrifice of a bull, a sheep, and a swine at the tomb of Confucius in 195 B.C.

Now began some decades of assiduous work on the reconstruction of the Confucian books. Not only were texts that had escaped the fire of the censors unearthed from their hiding-places, but the wisdom of Confucius was also reproduced from oral tradition. The books recovered were given the name of the "Old Text", while those reconstructed from oral tradition were called the "New Texts", since they were written in the new alphabet. Profiting by the tolerant policy of the Han dynasty, Chinese scholars assiduously worked at the reconstruction of the burnt Confucian writings, introducing changes and alterations with no less zeal.

In A.D. 79, a commission of scholars was appointed by order of the government to establish the authentic text. Nearly 100 years later, in A.D. 175, the supposedly authentic text of the writings of Confucius, the so-called *Canon of Confucius*, was carved on the stone portals of the State Academy. This was to be the standard for all time, which did not, however, preclude the possibility of later modifications of the texts.

The re-born doctrine of Confucius shows considerable deviations from its original assumptions. Confucianism had become the theoretical foundation of the bureaucratic system of the Chinese State; it was the doctrine of a bureaucratic monarchy. The rulers of the Han dynasty did not intend to resuscitate the previous form of the feudal system, as Confucius himself had recommended. On the contrary, they did what they could to obtain a uniform and efficient apparatus of government and to strengthen the central authority. This is why, in spite of their recognition of the doctrine of Confucius, the rulers of the Han dynasty continued their struggle against the remains of military feudalism, and with the help of officials trained in Confucianism they built up a centralized bureaucratic apparatus of government. Official posts were filled by those who had mastered the Confucianistic literature. In place of the feudal aristocracy, there appeared an aristocracy of Confucian scholars, occupying the highest posts in the state hierarchy. A system of difficult examinations brought about the use, up to the beginning of the twentieth century, of the dead language of Confucian literature as the official language, incomprehensible to the common people. Thus in spite of the fact that the rulers of the Han dynasty endeavoured to revive the tradition of the old, mild priest–

emperors, in accordance with the doctrine of Confucius, yet in practical politics they were advocates of a central and absolute power. It was owing to this policy that China had gained her position as a great power towards the end of the old era and the beginning of the new. Especially during the reign of the Emperor Wu-ti, who came to the throne in 140 B.C., there came about a distinct consolidation of the central authority and a decisive dispute with feudalism. The Emperor opposed the feudal gentry, abolishing their right of entail and causing family possessions to be broken up; he abolished local monopolies, introducing at the same time state monopolies in salt and iron; he got rid of the local monetary systems and introduced a uniform currency with a fixed value.

Towards the turn of the era, China considerably extended her possessions, having at her disposal excellent squadrons of cavalry. In 101 B.C. Fergana, the crossroads between East and West, fell to China. The road was opened to the West; the Chinese army stood on the threshold of Persia and India. In this way China came into contact with the outposts of the Graeco-Roman world and with India. Persia, on the other hand, played the role of an inter-mediary between the three centres of culture, as a gangway between the Graeco-Roman world, China, and India. At this time the roads of the cara-vans carrying Chinese silk crossed the vast expanses of Asia. There began a period of animated commercial expansion, lasting for three centuries.

At this time Rome of the Caesars learnt of the delicate Chinese fabrics through the Parthians, without knowing the people who wove these luxurious silks. This unknown people dwelling on the eastern limits of the world, the Romans called the Seres, saying of them that "they knew their textiles, but not their faces".

Externally expansive and internally coherent, the state under the Han dynasty transformed the doctrine of Confucius into the official opinion of a bureaucratic monarchy. The adherents of Confucius at that time did not criticize the state system from the point of view of the past, as had formerly been the case in the times of the warring kingdoms. Now in the name of the doctrine of the Master, the Confucian sages carried into effect the policy of a unified monarchy, adapting the past to the needs of the present.

The official character of the doctrine of Confucius did not hinder theoreti-cal considerations, although most of the Confucians limited themselves to commentaries on the works of the Master.

The problem of good and evil, *yin* and *yang*, was dealt with by Tung Chung-shu (170–90 B.C.), one of the leading representatives of the Confucian school. He considered that light and shade express the most profound sense of the world. Light corresponds to the spiritual life of man, whereas shade corres-ponds to his lusts. Tung Chung-shu did not see any leaning towards good or evil in human nature. In consequence, he thought that the commands of heaven to do good and to avoid evil were directed towards the neutrality of human nature. Hence he also treated ethical principles as heteronomic commands, originating in external sources, and not in human nature itself. The majority of the philosophical disputes in the Confucian schools were concentrated on ethical problems. Yang Hsiung (53 B.C.–A.D. 18), who published his opinions in the form of conversations and aphorisms, also referred to these problems. In his ethics, Yang Hsiung contrasted an ethical ideal of an absolute character with the possibility of a comparative realization of the ideal. It is true that Confucius had also distinguished between the innate ethics of the Holy Ones and the human ethics acquired by the way of perfection; he taught, however, that man might achieve perfection by dint of working on himself. Yang Hsiung, on the contrary, speaks only of the endeavour to attain perfection, without prejudice to the realization of the ethical ideal.

A third Confucian, Wang Ch'ung (A.D. 27–97), possessed a very penetrating and independent intellect. Only some fragments of his work *Lung Hong*, which contained a critique of mystical thought, divination, and magic, have come down to our times. The comprehension of natural and deterministic phenomena in the thought of Wang Ch'ung is striking. Compared with the background of the ethical and ritual considerations of the Confucian schools, Wang Ch'ung's rational thought, rejecting all mysticism, is a really extraordinary phenomenon. He considered it his mission to teach people how to think rationally, and so, attaching great importance to clearness of style and attempting to gain a wide circulation for his writings, he frequently wrote in feuilleton form.

The primeval, undifferentiated entity, according to Wang Ch'ung, is divided between heaven and earth in such a way that heaven contains the pure parts which tend to fly upwards, whereas the impure parts fall downwards and are absorbed by the earth. The whole universe is penetrated by a *vis vitalis*, the sole cause of eternal and incessant change. In his system Wang Ch'ung rejected the existence of any supreme intelligence initiating change, since as a result of inner necessity all phenomena pass into their opposites after having attained their plenitude. He treated human consciousness as a transitory phenomenon, conditioned by the coexistence of soul and body. He taught that just as before birth consciousness does not exist, so the death of a man puts an end to his consciousness. In agreement with the point of view of natural determinism, he considered that every man comes into the world with innate qualities which decide the future course of his life. In spite of his fatalistic convictions of the innate qualities of man, Wang Ch'ung stressed the need of educating the young, recognizing the role of pedagogy.

This daring thinker, who saw into the essence of phenomena, tried in vain to purify the Confucian doctrine from magic and mysticism. But his doctrine was both inaccessible to any bolder thought and little understood by the common people. The doctrine of Confucius was foreign to the masses, as became evident when China, after the reign of the Han dynasty (which fell in A.D. 220), entered a period of several centuries of complete economic and political confusion. Then the Chinese people, hard hit by the gloomy reality as well as by the consequences of economic decay, wars, the breaking-up of the state, and the ruin of the treasury, flocked to Buddhism, which advocated a flight from life. The new religion penetrated to China from India through Persia, beginning from the first century A.D.

Buddha was teaching in India more or less at the same time as Confucius was teaching in China, when the Indian philosophers were establishing their natural philosophy in Asia Minor.

India was therefore the cradle of a religious and social doctrine of world-wide range, which conquered the Ancient East.

8. THE POLITICAL DOCTRINES OF INDIA

India, a land almost entirely cut off from the rest of the world, seemed full of mystery to the ancients. Separated from the rest of Asia by high ranges of mountains, surrounded by sea, the Indian peninsula formed a world of its own. In the remote past the only gates giving access to India were the mountain passes in the north-west, opening a road through the Punjab into the interior. The fundamental history of India, as it unfolded in the northern part of the peninsula, in the plain between the Himalayas and the river Narbada, is linked with these paths. The fertile mud brought down by the Indus and the Ganges with their tributaries, and the abundant rains brought by the south-west winds after the dry season, caused the inhabitants of the plain to pass quickly from pasturing their flocks to tilling the soil. In comparison with the sun-scorched expanses of Central Asia, India with her subtropical climate, luxuriant vegetation, and two harvests a year, is quite exceptional.

But it was not only nature which aroused amazement in India; the way of life of the people inhabiting this land seemed strange and incomprehensible to the ancients. Their beliefs, opinions, behaviour, and social organization diverged from the established patterns.

When Alexander the Great, after subduing Asia Minor, Syria, Egypt and Persia, crossed the Indus in 326 B.C., and marched northwards through the Punjab, he heard of sages leading an ascetic life, whose extraordinary spiritual powers were recognized and admired by the Indians. Wishing to know more of these strange people, the fearless Macedonian commanded his officer Onesikritus, a follower of the cynics, to gather more accurate information. As a result, an Indian ascetic found himself in Alexander's retinue. He was called Kalanos, because he usually greeted his compatriots with the Sanscrit word *Kalyana*. This ascetic, however, cannot have felt at his ease amid the splendour of Alexander's court, since when the latter was in Persia he astounded everyone by his decision to make an end of his life. A funeral pyre was prepared, and on to this Kalanos stepped, after having distributed all his belongings.

The flames enveloped the praying sage, who to the amazement of the army chose death, despising earthly happiness.

A similar event took place some centuries later in Athens, when during the reign of Augustus the ascetic Zarmanochegos, who had been one of the envoys sent from India to Rome, sought a voluntary death on the pyre. In the first century, when mysticism was spreading in Rome, the interest in the Hindu doctrines must have been much more lively. It is said that the leading mystic in Rome, Apollonius of Tyana, probed the secret lore of India. The concepts of the Indian sages reached Rome at that time through the colony of Hindus in Alexandria.

A more accurate picture of the prevailing creeds and the ancient teachings of India was gained by Europe only towards the end of the eighteenth century. In 1786 an Englishman, Sir William Janes, in a discourse showed that the Latin, Celtic, and Germanic languages are related to Sanskrit and that all these languages can be traced back to a common stock. Further investigations on the history of India led to the conviction that about 2000 B.C. Aryan tribes speaking a pre-Indo-European language occupied the Persian plain. At some later time part of the Aryans left this plain to invade the Punjab through the mountain passes on the north-west. About 1500 B.C. we find the Aryans on the Indus and in the Punjab. They gradually advanced towards the south-east, until at last after continual successful warfare against the aboriginal population, they took possession of the whole basin of the Ganges. Here, in the early part of the first millennium B.C., ended the migration of the Aryans in India.

The history of the political thought of India is connected with the religious cult and the beliefs of the Aryans; the *Vedas*, the books of "holy lore", are the source of our knowledge of these remote times.[13] The *Vedas* form a religious literature very wide in range, arising in the course of centuries. They contain religious songs, sacrificial formulae, charms, theological speculations, rituals —in brief, all that was connected with the beliefs of the Aryans in those days. The *Vedas*, which have been handed down to our times, consist of four collections *Sanhita*. The first and oldest is the *Rig-Veda*, containing hymns in honour of the gods. The second is the *Sama-Veda*, with priestly songs. The third is the *Yajur-Veda*, a collection of prayers and sacrificial formulae, and the fourth, the *Atharva-Veda*, gives the prayers and formulae uttered during incantations.

Other sacred writings are linked with the *Vedas*, for instance the *Brahmanas* describing sacrifices, or the later religious and philosophical *Upanishads*, which was written to explain the most profound meaning of sacrifice. The supplementation of the sacred lore by the priests lasted for centuries, and came to an end only in 500 B.C. Although Indian literature is religious in character, it yet shows the social and political ideas of the priests, who expressed their outlook, aspirations, and interests in the guise of theology. The content of the *Vedas*, growing through the centuries, reveals the change in the political opinions of their creators. Changes in the social conditions of the Aryans, economic differentiation, the struggle between the castes, changes in the social system, in a word all the transformations which took place during 1000 years found their reflection in the constantly supplemented *Vedas*. The political opinions contained in these books are defined as Brahmanism, because they express the outlook of the Brahmans, the priestly caste.

The next religious and social doctrine to arise was Buddhism. About 500 B.C., a wave of opposition arose against the dominating role of the Brahmans and their privileged standing. At that time, India was seething with ferment; continuous wars between the numerous states, acute controversies between the castes, and the growth of the influence of the military aristocracy, shook the authority of the priests and of the *Vedas*. The time had arrived for criticism of the old religious social doctrine, and new opinions and beliefs were born. Of these, Buddhism attracted the greatest number of adherents. Buddhism spread beyond the confines of India; the new religious social doctrine extended its range over the vast expanses of Asia; it became a world religion.

Brahmanism contained the political opinions of the priests, whereas Buddhism expressed under the cloak of religion the outlook of the military aristocracy. The separation of the priestly and warrior castes and the contradiction of their interests was manifested in both these religious social doctrines.

The picture of the political thought of ancient India, however, is found in other works besides those of Vedic and Buddhist literature. The sources of our knowledge of political opinions are the *Book of Manu*, the two Indian epics *Mahabharata* and *Ramayana*, and a political tractate of which the authorship is attributed to the Brahman Kautilya.

In Ancient India it was believed that the *Book of Laws* was revealed by the creator of the world to his son Manu, the guardian of social order, and he in turn spread it amongst men. The *Book of Manu* is not a uniform collection of precepts, but often contains contradictory norms. It cannot be treated as a collection of laws as we understand the word today. The *Book of Manu* is the work of priests, who at the end of the old and the beginning of the new era collected various rules tending to maintain the social order. Hence it contains norms regulating religious cults, as well as the duties of fathers of families, priests, and ascetics, besides the legal norms. There are also rules for the art of governing.

In both the epics we find evaluations of good and bad rulers, opinions on the social system, and thoughts on the art of government. Both epics are the work of several generations of poets. The *Mahabharata* took longer to grow, while the *Ramayana* was finished in a shorter time, but both belong to the centuries when the old era was drawing to its end and our era beginning. The *Mahabharata* is a heroic epic in 100,000 double verses on the great war between the Kuru and Pandu tribes. The action of the poem is interrupted by many episodes from the lives of the gods and the heroes. The *Ramayana* narrates the heroic deeds and struggles of the noble ruler Rama with the wicked king of the giants, Ravana.

The *Arthasastra* (the *Book of Profits*), of which the authorship is attributed to Kautilya, a minister of the Emperor Chandragupta, is a valuable illustration of political concepts. About 300 B.C. Chandragupta united many previously independent small states into one kingdom in northern India. From the indirectly preserved account of Magastenes, who stayed for a long time at the court of Chandragupta as an envoy from Syria, we learn that the Indian Emperor governed by means of excellent ministers who knew the art of government. We do not know if Kautilya was reckoned among the Emperor's best politicians, but in any case the *Arthasastra* contains valuable information on the political doctrine of Ancient India.

Thus the information extracted from the Ancient Indian literature which has been preserved supplements the political concepts contained in Brahmanism and Buddhism. The whole of the political doctrine of Ancient India may be therefore dealt with in three sections; the first is devoted to Brahmanism, the second to Buddhism, and the third to secular political thought.

9. BRAHMANISM

"Brahma" means prayer, which was supposed to give strength to gods and men. In the *Vedic Hymns* this expression is used to define the act of piety, of prayer and sacred song. The whole of the later theological literature supplementing the *Vedas* is called *Brahmanas*. In time the impersonal and abstract concept came to be personified, so that in the *Upanishads* the god creating the world from primeval matter bears the name of Brahma.

In the sense in which we use the word, Brahmanism is a religious social doctrine which was taking shape in India from the time when the Aryans marched into the Punjab until the appearance of Buddhism. Brahmanism is not synonymous with the acknowledgement of Brahma as the supreme deity. The word is taken to mean the acknowledgement by society in Ancient India of a religious social doctrine, created and imposed upon that society by the Brahman priests, who by means of the general belief in their supernatural powers succeeded in directing the social consciousness during many centuries. The history of Brahmanism, closely connected with the appearance of the *Vedas*, lasted for about 1000 years, and falls into two almost equal periods, that of the earlier *Vedas* and that of the later *Vedas*.

The first period begins when the tall, slender Aryans marched into India from the north-west. Fighting fiercely with the aboriginal population, they advanced southwards and eastwards. This was about 1500 B.C. The aborigines, the small black-skinned Dravidians, who knew neither the language nor the beliefs of their conquerors, were taken as slaves by the Aryans, who scornfully called them *dasa warnah*—nigger slaves.

The difference in appearance between the conquerors and the subjugated aborigines deepened the gulf between the old and the new populations. The Aryans lived in complete isolation from the aboriginal population. Separating themselves from the Dravidians as by a wall, they made the first sharp division of society. In the distant future, when differences of wealth had arisen among the Aryans, this was to become the model for the segregation of society into castes.

In the first period, the organization of the state on the banks of the Indus, in the Land of the Five Rivers, where the Aryans had settled, was only in the initial phase. Hardly had differences in wealth become apparent, when the Aryans crossed the threshold of patriarchal and familial organization, and the land cultivated became the property of the family. Their chief occupations were the pasturing of their flocks and military crafts. Their knowledge of metals was limited to bronze and copper, and cattle were their standard value in barter. Government was carried on by the heads of the families, who were at the same time the leaders; in their retinues we find priests and inspired bards, who lost no opportunity of gaining the confidence of the Indian elders. By their prayers and hymns, the priests were supposed to gain the grace of the gods for their lords. A life lasting for "a hundred autumns", wealth, and many male descendants—these were all that those warrior-shepherds desired. Since the Aryans were advancing amidst continual warfare, their standard of morality was simple: courage, obedience, and loyalty to their leader.

A spirit of strife permeated the life and creeds of the Aryans; the whole world seemed to them a field of struggle between the forces of good and evil, between darkness and light, between day and night, between fair and foul weather. Their gods stood sentinel for the forces of virtue and light; Mithras, the god of day, Varuna, the defender of truth, Ushas, the guardian of youth and light, Indra, the god of war, holding the demon of darkness at bay.

The leaders and their troops must have played a dominating part in the period of unceasing and victorious warfare. Even at this time, when fighting was the chief occupation of the Aryans, there began to be a conviction that without sacral offerings and without hymns the gods could not act, and that it was the priestly sacrifices that gave the gods their supernatural strength. Thus their favourite god Indra, the lord of war and guardian of the troops, the god of battles and victories over the black-skinned aborigines, was dependent on the priestly sacrifices which created his power and strength. The standing of the priests gradually rose in proportion to the spread of the view that their offerings and prayers ensured the order of the universe, manifested both in the invariable order of natural phenomena and in the order of the social organization. The martial fame of the leaders in the period of the militant migrations, however, still overshadowed the position of the priests. Even at that time the ideal was Shukravatin, the ruler of kings, who governed the four quarters of the world, and whose kingdom was bounded by the path of the sun. It is possible that the idea of a divine ruler of the world came to India from Mesopotamia, where it had become the inspiration for martial deeds.

Soon, however, the priests were to gain supremacy in the Aryan society; this was the second period of Brahmanism, at the turn of the second millennium B.C. In their victorious march, the Aryans reached the basin of the Ganges. When they migrated to the banks of the sacred river Sarasvati, which they crossed in order to occupy the damp, hot, fertile plains of the Ganges, the songs of the *Rig-Veda* changed. The methods of production changed, the castes crystallized, the creeds and concepts changed. New crafts were mastered, pasturage was replaced by agriculture, and the use was learnt of iron, silver, tin, lead, and gold besides bronze and copper. Even the political system changed. The patriarchal and familial organization was replaced by a community divided into castes. The Aryan tribes formed state organizations with kings at their head, who ruled with the support of troops of warriors. Differences in wealth, ill-defined in the old days, now became sharp, since they were the source of the division of society into castes. The transition to a settled life accelerated the process of social differentiation into priests, a military aristocracy, farmers, craftsmen, and merchants.

Three hereditary castes arose from the differences in wealth and in work within the Aryan community. These formed separate social groups with special obligations, rights, and moralities, with different manners and customs and occupations. About the king were grouped chosen warriors and the descendants of the princely families, forming the Aryan aristocracy—the Kshatriya or warrior caste. The majority of Aryans, who had exchanged the sword for the ploughshare, or a craft, or a trade, formed the Vaisya caste. The priests were isolated from the rest of the community, and formed the ruling Brahman caste. The idea that the priestly sacrifices animated the gods led to the belief that the priests themselves, by virtue of their sacred power through offerings, became masters of divine and earthly forces. The priests immured themselves in the highest caste, favoured by special privileges as compared with other castes. They were treated with special reverence, subject to lower taxes, and liable to lesser penalties for infringement of the law. It was thought that the world depended on the gods, the gods on the sacrificial formulae, and these again on the Brahmans, so that the Brahmans were equal to the gods. At the same time it was declared that only birth made a man a Brahman, who by his innate qualities could but deepen his knowledge of the sacred lore.

The social structure of the Aryans was thus crowned by the Brahman caste, while the despised aboriginal population formed its foundation. The dark-skinned Dravidians were confined within the separate framework of the lowest and despised "unclean" Sudra caste, debarred from the knowledge of the *Vedas* and the wisdom of the Brahmans.[14]

The division of society was manifested by a change in the religious social doctrine, which was fostered by the priests for their own benefit. Having achieved a dominating position in the community, they endeavoured to pettrify the social relations they had formed. In their hands, Brahmanism became an instrument which sanctioned and established the division into castes. On the other hand, the special system of education built up by the priests effectively strengthened the influence of Brahmanism on social relations. The priests must have spared no effort to consolidate the authority of Brahmanism, if having no organization or means of power at their disposal, they yet acquired their privileged position solely by means of their doctrine. The Brahmans established the belief that the sacred lore and its earthly teachers were set above the armed forces of the warriors, above the wealth of the Vaisyas, above the daily toil of the common man. In order to justify the division of the community, the Brahmans cited the divine order of the universe and the will of the gods, expressed in the very formation of the castes. We know, from the famous *Purusa Sukta* (*Rig-Veda* X. 90), that the priests came forth from the mouth of the Primeval Being, the Kshatriyas from his shoulders, the Vaisyas from his loins, and lastly the Sudras from his feet.[15]

At the time of the struggle for social supremacy, the priests introduced the dogma of transmigration of souls into their religion. It is indisputable that in the original Vedic religion this dogma did not yet exist. If the hypothesis that the source of this conception should be sought in the beliefs of the Dravidians is correct, then the beliefs of the conquered people themselves served their conquerors to subjugate them.

The old beliefs that life after death depended on the behaviour preceding death underwent changes in the *Upanishads*. The Brahmans now taught that in the chain of incarnations each life was only one link depending on the position and behaviour in the preceding life, while the conduct of a being in each of its lives decided the next link, and so the next incarnation. The Brahman religious social doctrine in this way on the one hand justified the earthly situation of each individual, and on the other gave a prospect of a better life in the next incarnation on condition of complete obedience to the order in force.

The Sudras and the Brahmans received special treatment in the dogma of transmigration of souls. If the members of the first three castes could close the circle of reincarnation by the power of sanctity and the fullness of wisdom, and by divesting themselves of their individuality could reach complete union with the infinite, then the Sudras had not even the hope that the torment of their lives would end with death, for the doctrine of the Brahmans condemned them to a perpetual transmigration of souls. "Those who led a godly life on earth will be found in the womb of a good Brahman or Kshatriya mother, or even a Vaisya. But those who led an impure life on earth will be found in the womb of an unclean mother, in the body of a dog or of a swine, or in the womb of a woman belonging to the despised castes." (Chandogya, *Upanishads* 5. 10. 3).

From the *Upanishads* we also learn that only a sage may attain infinite immortality, and then he is above prayers and sacrifices, above justice and injustice, above the future and the present, above the transmigration of souls. In this stage of highest perfection, the sage is united with eternity, and then he thinks without thinking, he sees without looking, he hears without listening. It is of him that the *Upanishads* says: "As a river flows, until losing shape and name, it is lost in the depths, so losing his shape and his name, the wise man changes into divinity."

We must remember, however, that the all-powerful influence of Brahman ideology on society could be effective first and foremost by the system of education developed and directed by the priests. In principle all Aryans were under the system of Brahman education throughout their lives. After childhood, the young boys of the first three castes were handed over to the Brahmans for schooling. For several years they learnt the sacred lore, in complete dependence on their masters. The first period of education lasted from 12 to 48 years. Then the mature man entered the second phase of his life (*qrhastha*). He set up house, and as the head of a household, besides his chosen occupation, he continued to study the sacred lore. When he had brought up his children and grandchildren, the father of the family entered the third stage. He relinquished his home to give himself up to meditation and prayer in solitude and asceticism. Finally, at the end of his life, the Brahmans prescribed wandering as a mendicant, when at last the man thus freed from earthly needs became mature for salvation. Naturally, not all Aryans went through all four stages. There were interruptions in the process of education; many remained merely fathers of families; others at once became ascetics. Nevertheless, the system of education included all members of the three higher castes, and their lives were under the constant control of the Brahmans. Under the influence of their doctrine, the desires and ideals of the ancient Aryans changed. Humble prayer, asceticism, and meditation now took precedence over the active life.

Life, however, proved to be stronger than the prevailing religious social doctrine. In the middle of the millennium, India passed through a strong ferment. The controversies between the priests and the warriors became acute, the wars between the many states brought misery in their train, the priests were criticized, and the authority of the *Vedas* was questioned. New concepts and ideas arose, among which Buddhism was to take the place of Brahmanism.

10. BUDDHISM

We have not much actual material on the events which took place in India about 500 B.C. The Brahman and Buddhist books reaching back to that time delineate the ideological struggles which were then being waged in that country. Voices were raised in revolt against the pretensions of the Brahman priests and their superior position. This opposition came mainly from the warrior caste. Some of the songs from the *Upanishads* bear the mark of the strife amid which they were composed, and traces of the inveterate feuds between the priests and the warriors. In the song of the king Adzatasatra, the Brahman priests humbly acknowledge the superiority of the monarch's wisdom and beg to be admitted to the circle of royal pupils.

In north-eastern India, there gathered a wave of opposition to the Brahmans. About 500 B.C., in a territory of animated commerce, and many towns and states, the struggle with the priestly caste became acute.[16]

According to Buddhist sources, at the time when Buddha was teaching in northern India, there existed sixteen states, of which the largest were Magadha and Koshala, besides independent town republics, as for instance Buddha's birthplace, Kapilavastu. Benares seems to have been the town where there was the busiest trade at that time. In this very important industrial and commercial centre, where the production of cloth was especially developed and where the backward west of India came into contact with the economically developed east, where the caste barriers had become unsettled by wealth, Buddha is supposed to have preached his famous first sermon.

This land of animated commerce and developing industry was the cradle of new doctrines and concepts.

The caste system must have hampered economic life in the north-eastern regions of India, in spite of the fact that the Brahman tyranny was comparatively weaker there than elsewhere. In this part of the country the warriors, in alliance with the energetic merchants and their fortunes, successfully opposed the Brahmans. In the circles of warriors and merchants, new ideas came to birth, opposition to the observance of the *Vedas* increased, new philosophical and religious concepts were formed, and a wave of philosophical disputation began. The prevailing Brahman doctrine, with its insistence on ritual ceremonies, rendered it possible for many sects and schools to arise. About the middle of the period many of these schools were engaged in mutual disagreement; some proclaimed the inner necessity and regularity of nature, others raised chance to the status of a ruling principle; besides the materialists, there were theists of varying shades; the determinists disputed with the indeterminists; some regarded the world as eternal and infinite, others rejected this standpoint. Besides these quarrelling schools, there were again agnostics and sceptics.[17] From the literature combating the opponents of Buddhism, we make the acquaintance of the ardent disciple of determinism, Gonsala, who taught that the conduct of every man is determined by innate necessity and by his environment. The leader of the materialistic school seems to have been Charvak, of whose concepts and person little is known.[18]

From references in the Buddhist literature the impression is gained that materialism had many adherents, and that both these views were treated as the greatest heresy, in spite of the fact that the sources of the ideas of the materialistic schools lay in Brahmanism itself. The Brahman priests' picture of the universe was rather vague; in the song *Nasadya Sukta* there is a reference to the eternal primordial matter, when: "There was darkness, and the universe, an ocean without change, was plunged in this darkness."

In the Brahman cosmogony, some materialistic elements can be found among the various legends. The Brahmans believed that the world, born of indestructible and eternal primordial matter, was constantly undergoing change. As a result of the union of the five elements, fire, water, earth, air, and aether, the world and the gods had come into being, and when the life of the gods came to an end—for their existence was thought to be finite—the elements would return to the primordial matter, until after a long period of peace a new cycle of life began spontaneously. We do not know today to what extent the materialistic schools were connected with the Brahman cosmogony, for the extant data are too few to establish the whole content and class essence of all the contradictory doctrines of the period. Of all these trends, the best known to us are the concepts of the warrior caste, which are contained in Buddhism and in the slightly earlier Jainism. The cradle of both doctrines was the land of Magadha. Both doctrines were proclaimed at about the same time by the representatives of the warriors; both were opposed to Brahmanism, both rejected the authority of the *Vedas*, both strove against the Brahman priests.

It is said that the founder of Jainism, Mahavira, the "great hero", came from royal stock. Legend says that at the age of thirty he left his wife and daughter to devote himself to ascetic practices. For 12 years he suffered scorn and humiliation in patience, until at last he achieved by his asceticism "Jaina", the complete victory over the world and his salvation.[19] The followers of Mahavira pessimistically regarded the history of mankind as being in the declining stages. They thought that social inequality and the need of introducing legal standards, kings, authority, judges, the caste system, and other political institutions, had arisen as a result of the general decadence.[20] It was not Jainism, however, but Buddhism which became the prevailing doctrine. The new religion was embraced by the whole community. Buddhism expressed the aspirations and hopes of the warriors, while not forgetting the merchants, and at the same time gave the lowest castes, bowed down under the burden of life, illusive hopes.

Of the two warrior doctrines born of the social and economic ferment which north-eastern India was going through at this time, Buddhism became the victor.

The town of Kapilavastu, an independent oligarchic republic, was the birthplace of Buddha; there Gautama Siddartha was born into an old aristocratic family, he who was called Buddha, the "Enlightened One", when he revealed his doctrine. Legend connected the current of opposition to

Brahmanism with the person of Gautama, dubbing him the founder of Buddhism. The dates of his life, from 560 to 480 B.C., became of fundamental importance in the history of India. According to the legend, the 29-year-old Buddha left his family and his princely wealth to seek perfection amongst the Brahman ascetics. When he saw that ascetic self-torment was in vain, he gave up asceticism, and in his further wanderings, after having attained the four truths of wisdom—suffering, the origin of suffering, the annihilation of suffering, and finally the path to the liquidation of suffering—he began to preach his doctrine. Buddha accepted the ancient Indian conception that life is a period of suffering between past and future existences. Contrary to the Brahmans, who attempted to quench the desire for life by asceticism, Buddha taught that it is enough merely to bring to a minimum all that attaches a man to life. It is not necessary to be an ascetic to attain the state of perfection, it is enough to become a mendicant monk. Even laymen who have charity are already on the way to salvation, although in contradistinction to the hermit monks they keep their family life and possessions. Again contrary to the Brahman priests, the new doctrine proclaimed that every man should save himself, and by opening a number of brotherhoods for all people regardless of their caste, the doctrine of Buddha weakened the rigid structure of Indian society and the hegemony of the priests.

The new religion naturally obtained popularity both among the warriors and the merchants. The legend says that the first disciples of the Master were two merchants, Trapusha and Bhalika, who formed the first circle of lay believers, and only afterwards were there added the five ascetics who started the Buddhist brotherhood. Buddhism set up two standards for its followers. The hermit monks were to live in celibacy without any property of their own, but the laity were bound only by the fivefold prohibition of murder, theft, falsehood, the use of intoxicating liquors, and profligacy. By opening the doors of the monasteries to all people, Buddha raised the morality of his hermits above the particularism of the castes. He rejected Brahman ritualism, for he taught that anyone could attain perfection, not as the result of sacral formulae, but by self-reformation and by a proper life. He opposed to the Brahman asceticism the life of the hermit monks, in which his followers, rejecting the authority of the *Vedas*, meditated together on the teaching of the Master in order to propagate it amongst the people. The monks left their hermitage to proclaim the teaching of the Master. Unlike the Brahmans, who kept themselves apart, these Buddhist monks taught amongst the people, and the people flocked to them, for they spoke of love and pity, of liberation from poverty and suffering. In its struggle against Brahmanism, Buddhism at the same time propagated a philosophy of pessimism, clad as religion, among the masses. On the one hand, Buddha's doctrine justified the aspirations and victory of the warrior and merchants castes over the Brahman priests, but on the other it paralysed the masses by its ideal of passiveness. Buddha taught that the highest wisdom lies in indifference to life and in its abnegation; this leads to eternal peace, to the state of Nirvana, bringing the migration of souls to an end.

Buddha included "the wisdom of compromise and pessimism" in his famous sermon in Benares,[21] saying:

> These two extremes, O monks, are not to be practised by one who has gone forth from the world. What are the two? That conjoined with the passions, low, vulgar, common, ignoble, and useless, and that conjoined with self-torture, painful, ignoble, and useless. Avoiding these two extremes the Tathagata has gained the knowledge of the Middle Way, which gives sight and knowledge, and tends to calm, to insight, enlightenment, nirvana.
>
> What, O monks, is the Middle Way, which gives sight ... ? It is the noble Eightfold Path, namely, right views, right intention, right speech, right action, right livelihood, right effort, right mindfulness, right concentration. This, O monks, is the Middle Way ....
>
> 1. Now this, O monks, is the noble truth of pain: birth is painful, old age is painful, sickness is painful, death is painful, sorrow, lamentation, dejection, and despair are painful. Contact with unpleasant things is painful, not getting what one wishes is painful. In short the five khandhas of grasping are painful.
> 2. Now this, O monks, is the noble truth of the cause of pain: that craving which leads to rebirth, combined with pleasure and lust, finding pleasure here and there, namely, the craving for passion, the craving for existence, the craving for non-existence.
> 3. Now this, O monks, is the noble truth of the cessation of pain: the cessation without a remainder of that craving, abandonment, forsaking, release, non-attachment.
> 4. Now this, O monks, is the noble truth of the way that leads to the cessation of pain: this is the noble Eightfold Path, namely, right views, right intention, right speech, right action, right livelihood, right effort, right mindfulness, right concentration . . .

For 40 years Buddha taught in north-eastern India, and departing this life as an old man of 80, he left his disciples a last injunction: "All that exists will pass away, and it is the duty of the disciples to perfect themselves unceasingly."

The new religion gained many followers in India; towards the end of the old era and the beginning of the new, Buddhism penetrated through Iran to China. According to Ancient Chinese legend, the Emperor Ming Ti of the Han dynasty brought Buddhism to China in A.D. 61 after a prophetic dream. At first the new doctrine made little progress, but from the third century A.D. Buddhism marched victoriously through China. This was the time when the official state character of Confucianism proved to be powerless against the internal economic and social crises which China experienced for four centuries, from the fall of the Han dynasty (in A.D. 220) to the reunion of China under the sceptre of the Sui dynasty (A.D. 589).

11. POLITICAL THOUGHT IN THE LITERATURE OF INDIA

The political thought of Ancient India was not expressed in the religious systems only. The opinions of the ruling classes on the juristic and political institutions are contained in two epics, the *Mahabharata* and the *Ramayana*. In these, amongst different views on good and bad rulers, are found some considerations on the art of government.[22] In the twelfth book of the *Maha-bharata* especially, the warrior statesman Bhima, in conversation with a king, Juddhisthira, who has been exiled from his kingdom, gives utterance to a series of thoughts on authority, the state, and the law. Social problems are more precisely comprehended in the *Ramayana*, of which the sixth book merits special attention.

Besides the epics, many chapters of the *Laws of Manu* contain political doctrines, and so does a textbook on the art of government attributed to Kautilya the Brahman, who in 325 B.C. helped Chandragupta to bring about a revolution and seize power in the state of Magadha. For 24 years Chandra-gupta reigned, ruthless towards his subjects and menacing towards his neighbours. At his court in Pataliputra, Kautilya fulfilled the function of a minister. Megasthenes, the envoy of Seleucus, also stayed there for some years, and the accounts he dispatched thence acquainted Ancient Europe with the Indies.[23]

Behind its legendary adornments, the literature of Ancient India reveals the concepts of the groups in power, and thoughts emerge which are sur-prising in the sobriety of their conception of the essence of social and juristic phenomena. It follows from the disputes cited by Kautilya that much atten-tion was devoted to political affairs, of which authority forms the fundamen-tal theme. There even existed a school limiting knowledge of political life to studies on the actual art of governing, so that one Usana, the leader of such a trend, denied any value whatsoever to other political problems.

According to the *Laws of Manu*, and also to Kautilya, a state consists of seven elements: the king, the ministers, the territory, the capital city, the state treasury, the army, and finally international alliances.

We do not meet with any concept of an eternally existing state in Indian doctrine. The genesis of state organization is associated with the corruption of morality.

In the texts there is a constant repetition of the questions of how the rule of a king over other people can be justified, and how his title to authority can be accounted for. We find the answer in the utterance of Bhima, who explains that human weaknesses have put an end to those times when people were subject only to law and when there was no government. "People, overcome by the lust of possession, seized the property of others, became slaves to their passions, did not know what they should do and what they should not do, could not distinguish between permissible and impermissible actions, did not perceive the difference between virtue and vice, between good words and evil, between forbidden food and what is permitted ... all order was des-troyed." Then the gods in terror turned for help to Brahma, who would lead the people back from chaos, restore order and establish the authority of government.

The ruling groups saw the guarantee of order in the government of kings, of which Kautilya said, "it ensures a tranquil existence to philosophy, to the sacred *Vedas* and to economic life ... for when there is no government, the stronger devours the weaker".

In the *Laws of Manu* and the *Mahabharata* the power to govern is treated as a most important element, without which social life would not exist. Naturally, these poems sing the power of the king and the highest castes.

> Authority watches over the sleeping, rules the creatures, cares for them, guards the universal harmony; it is the eye of order, it protects wealth and corn ....
>
> If there were no obedience to authority, wild beasts and birds would destroy the offerings and tear people to pieces, the *Vedas* would not be studied, the cows would not be milked, maidens would not enter into wedlock, all bonds would be broken, and there would be robbery everywhere.

The doctrine therefore justified the authority standing sentinel over the caste system, which was part of the general order, the *tri-varga*.[24]

According to the concepts of the Indian theorists, the principles of co-existence were involved in the general order, the *tri-varga*, composed of three elements, *dharma*, *artha*, and *kama*. By *dharma* is meant the sacred order; the word afterwards serves for the definition of law. It was thought that *dharma* was the standard of order, which "maintained harmony in the universe, gave power to the gods, and was the foundation of people's practical behaviour". The term was used to mean both legal and moral standards, as well as sacral duties. The sphere of people's practical action was regulated by *artha*, establishing at the same time aims for artistic activity, and for domestic occupations, stockbreeding, craftsmanship, trade, etc. *Kama*, on the other hand, meant human endeavours directed towards the fulfilment of definite purposes. In this way the *tri-varga*, comprising *dharma*, *artha*, and *kama*, was to conclude the whole order, beginning from general regularities, proceeding through the regulation of human action, to the fulfilment of concrete aims. From the controversies on the subject of the three elements of the *tri-varga*, it follows that the prevailing doctrine recognized the fundamental importance of *dharma*. In the *Mahabharata* we read: "*Dharma* is the highest value of the world, from it there comes what is favourable and what gives happiness; by *dharma* we may attain all things, it is the essence of the world ...."

In Indian doctrine, order is identified with sacred truth. In the *Rig-Veda* religious truths are the law, and in the *Ramayana* we read that "the proclamation of law is the proclamation of truth".

However, in deciding quarrels between people beyond the precepts of the law, Kautilya recommends that evidence, tradition, and royal commands should be taken into account. Law, *dharma*, expresses the sacred truth, the witnesses justify the evidence, tradition consists in the strict observance of the principles of the past, and finally the royal commands should be respected when giving a decision.

The doctrine goes realistically to the heart of authority and law, since we read that "a king is supported by his treasury and his might; the might by the treasury; law by the might; and eventually the people by the law". Kautilya knew that a monarch acquires unshaken power only when he keeps the treasury and the army in his own hands.[25] The Indian doctrine places ruthless men of action at the head of the state; according to Bhima, "one cannot rule a State with vacuous kindness. The world does not value those who in spite of their wisdom are at the same time submissive, unduly sensitive, unmanly, full of virtues and compassion". Indian kings should, in the interests of the state, break the law and use a double morality, since "human faults may be kingly virtues".

The ruling classes had their own ideal of a good monarch, whom they contrasted with a base ruler. Ravana, for instance, is a bad ruler, giving himself up to pleasure, lacking in self-control, disregarding danger, and neglecting his royal duties. "When misfortune comes, people do not hasten to help the king who is unwise, rash, proud, and wicked." But blessed is the good ruler, like the model Rama, taking counsel of the wisest men in his state, acting only after due thought, calm and contained, consequent in action, quick in performance, vigilant in danger. Such a monarch, says the Laws of Manu, "possesses divinity in a human body".

For Kautilya, the means leading to good rule was the education of the monarchs. In future rulers, this was to join theoretical knowledge with practical action, as a king "who possessed only book-learning and kept aloof from practical activity might fall into doubt".

As was demanded by the prevailing doctrine, Kautilya ends his chapter on government by asserting the necessity of maintaining the caste system. The division of society into castes constituted the immutable basis of the political concepts of the ruling castes. In the Mahabharata as in the Laws of Manu, the happiness of society is bound up with the strict observance of division into castes. "If the activity of the four castes is established and the boundaries between the castes are not erased, then the ruler guarantees peace, and society is not threatened by any danger; if the three upper castes fulfil their duties according to the precepts, then the happiness of the people is well-founded."

The three upper castes approved of the caste system, which became an inseparable part of their political doctrines. Friction between the castes weakened the caste barriers, but did not upset the system itself, which became bound up with the history of the Aryans in India. The history of the Aryans, however, does not exhaust the whole of the history of Ancient India. Excavations in Mesopotamia and India have shown that in the latter country before the Aryans came there existed towns with a high degree of culture, in constant contact with Babylon.[26] In Tel Asmar in Mesopotamia a seal dating from 2500 B.C. has been excavated, the workmanship of which shows that it had been brought from India. There must therefore have been contact between Mesopotamia and pre-Aryan India, where, as again excavations in north-western India, near Mohenjo Daro and Harappa have proved, 2500 years before our era there existed towns which were most probably linked by trade with the towns of Mesopotamia.[27]

12. THE BABYLONIAN THEOCRACY

Almost 4000 years before our era, in the basin of the Tigris and Euphrates, in the fertile land called Mesopotamia—the Land between the Rivers—there existed communities with well-developed forms of society.[28] Among the earliest dwellers in this region were the Sumerians, who tamed the rivers, possessed the art of draining marshes, knew how to construct reservoirs for water to last through the dry seasons, and built independent towns. The mighty lords of the Sumerian towns, such as Nippur, Ur, Uruk, or Lagash, were either at war with one another or had friendly trade relations.

About 2750 B.C. the ambitious ruler of Akkad, Sargon I, united all Mesopotamia by force of arms. On the south, Babylon came under his rule, on the east he took Elam, and on the west his might approached Cyprus. Sargon did not come to such power without opposition. History tells us of revolts which the King of Akkad crushed by force in order to maintain his might. The successors of Sargon continued his policy for a certain time, but after 197 years, the reign of the kings of Akkad came to an end, and a new period of mutual strife and invasions began. About 2100 B.C., the towns of southern Mesopotamia appear on the scene. When Hammurabi sat on the throne of Babylon (1730–1685 B.C.), a united state was again formed, centring round Babylon, which lay in the lower basin of the Tigris and the Euphrates, and was called by the Semitic name of Bab-ibi—the Rich Gate.

The new united state, enclosing the Sumerian towns within its borders, was divided by Hammurabi into provinces and towns under royal governors. He strove to maintain his extensive kingdom and his power, and took heed of efficient administration, the treasury, and the army. An epic on the creation of the world, the *Enuma-elis*, of which the origin dates back to the times of Hammurabi, expresses the idea of the preservation of an immutable social system and the domination of the world by Babylon. Praising Marduk, the god of gods, the epic gives utterance to the desire of the rulers to make the political and social situation of Babylon unchanging. "I shall determine fate," says Marduk, "let nothing that I create undergo any change, let not the word from my mouth fall in vain."[29]

In his care for the preservation of the system, in which the whole weight rested on slaves and peasants and leaseholders in a state of semi-servitude, Hammurabi issued laws to secure the immutability of social relations.[30] The monarch ordered the laws given to him by the sun god, Samas, as we see from the carving underneath the text, to be cut on a block of diorite 7 ft^2. In the introduction to the codex, Hammurabi refers to the will of the gods Anu and Enlil, who had ordered him to proclaim the laws, "so that justice should be enlightened in the land, and so that I should stamp out evil men and criminals, so that the strong should not violate the weak, and so that, like Samas, I should rise above the black-headed people and shine on the whole country".

Hammurabi transferred the realization of the legal system to the priests who gave judgement in the shrines. They also were to guard the immutable divine laws. Hammurabi gave warning against any change or infringement of the law. "He of my successors who will observe these laws, will be loaded with favours by Samas; he who will act against them will encounter a series of the most frightful disasters and penalties .... Let Enlil himself, he who is unchanging, curse him aloud by the sentence from his mouth, and let his curse reach him right speedily."

The thoughts on the divine origin of the law contained in the introduction to the codex are in harmony with the official political doctrine of the Mesopotamian states concerning the divine origin of the monarch.

In these states, the idea of the divinity of the ruler took form gradually. In the original Sumerian terminology, the ruler is still called "lugal", the great man. This term was used to define powers, whether physical, mental, or of wealth, greater than those of other citizens. Soon the priests were to drop the lay explanations of power. They treated the gods as the owners of the towns, they asked them to ratify treaties and pacts in the name of the towns. Thus we learn that "the god of the town Lagash, Ningirsu, and the god of Unna have fixed the frontiers". The kings became the plenipotentiaries of the gods, and were marked out by the gods when still in their mothers' wombs, so that they should be cared for and educated. The gods fed the elect on sacred milk, endowed them with strength, taught them prudence— in short, formed the monarchs in their own image. As the concept of the divinity of the ruler became established, altars and even shrines were raised to the deified monarchs. The process of deification of the kings proceeded most intensively during the reign of the Akkad dynasty. The kings coming from this state were called the gods from Akkad; the word "god" was placed before the name of the king from this time onwards. The kings wore the insignia of the gods, with horns on their headgear. Shrines were built in their honour, offerings were made to them while they were alive, and after their deaths the divine cult of the monarch was continued. The Babylonian king Hammurabi used the designations "Brother of the god Zaman", "the Sun-god of Babylon who casts his rays over all Sumeria and Akkad", "Hammurabi the god, king of the town", and "the god of kings". Rulers of single towns were called kings, those who ruled over several towns were given the epithet of "the great shepherd", while the ruler under whose sceptre fell at least Babylon, Elam, Amurru and Subari, received the title of "king of the four quarters of the earth".

Independently of the official doctrine proclaiming the divine origin of kings, the ruler at all times endeavoured to justify his authority. When there was a change in the dynasty, the new rulers also desired to pass as favourites of the gods, and the learned men of the court worked out divine genealogies for them. The rulers gave good heed both to justifying the legality of their authority, and to the divine cult of their persons.[31]

The spread of the theocratic doctrine to some extent brought about a change in religious beliefs. The gods and goddesses of the ancient pantheon, personifying the forces of nature, were transformed into the guardians of the royal authority and the state, affirming and sanctifying the rule of the rich. The gods symbolized the concepts of justice and power, becoming the protectors of warriors and kings. Samas the sun god became the guardian of law and justice; Marduk, the god of husbandry, tillage and cattle-breeding, "the lord of fertility and abundance", undertook to protect the Babylonian State, changing his insignia, for the hoe of the tiller of the soil was turned into a bow and arrows, the symbol of violence; Ishtar, the goddess of love and fertility, took kings and wars under her care.

The doctrine of royal authority had a different content in Babylon, as there kings were treated either as gods administering power on earth, or else were regarded as mouthpieces for the will of the gods. For instance, the divinity of Hammurabi was proclaimed and acknowledged. Fifteen centuries later, Nebuchadnezzar II was regarded only as a representative of the gods to whom he was subject, and he said of himself that "... the god Marduk has confided authority over the country and the care of its people to me ... I, god-fearing, gave ear unto him, I bent my neck unto the yoke of the gods".

In spite of the differences in the Babylonian theocratic doctrine, it was generally considered that only the ruling king might mediate between gods and men, and that only he could ensure the favours of heaven to his people. The secular power of the king was fused with the power of the god, and the political power with the religious. Hence the commands of the kings were treated as divine laws, and any resistance to their authority was regarded as an insult to the gods.

The prevailing doctrine justified the power of the kings, social inequalities, and the exploitation of slaves, by the authority of the gods. The principle proclaimed and recognized by the ruling classes was the belief that "a man is the shadow of a god, a slave the shadow of a man, but a king is equal to a god".

On the other hand, those who felt the wrongs of the poor, and the misery of the social system, began to doubt; they questioned the wisdom of the gods, complained of their indifference, fell into pessimism. Some of the psalms dating from the end of the third or the beginning of the second millennium are full of bitterness and disillusionment, expressing the pain and despair of the lowest classes, to whom the official doctrine was foreign.

Wherever I turn, there is evil everywhere;
My torment increases, I see no hope.
When I called upon my god, he uncovered not his face;
When I wept unto my goddess, she raised not her head.
The soothsayer did not prophecy my future by his divinations;
The prophet did not save my rights by his sacrifices ....
O what perversity rules in this world!

What an accusation against the theocratic doctrine and system is contained in
this poem!

In 1775 B.C. Babylon lost her independence, and came under the rule of the
Kassites for nearly six centuries. Then, after continuous warfare with her
neighbours, she fell into the power of the Assyrians, who began their expansion from the northern parts of Mesopotamia about the tenth century before
our era, and had become a world power by the eighth century B.C. The
Assyrian kings by that time had widened the boundaries of their state from
the Tigris to the sands of the Sahara, from the Armenian mountains to the
Persian Gulf. Their excellent military organization, militant policy, and
successes in warfare had an effect on the Assyrian political doctrine. In
contradistinction to the deification and the sacral character of the Babylonian
kings, the Assyrian kings, though fulfilling the highest priestly functions,
owed their power to the army and officially stressed their military force.
Thus the powerful Tiglath Pilesar (745–727 B.C.) boasted above all of his
military position.

> I am Tiglath Pilesar, a mighty king, set over an unvanquished army, lord of the four
> quarters of the world, king of all rulers, lord of lords, the prince-shepherd, king of kings,
> and an inspired prophet .... I have conquered sixty kings, and have extended my
> power over them. None has dared to meet me in battle—I have had no rival. I have
> joined new lands to Assyria, I have increased the number of my people's slaves, I have
> expanded the boundaries of my State.

The power of Assyria did not last long; in 612 B.C. Nineveh was taken by
the Babylonian and Median armies, which put an end to this powerful military kingdom. This was the time when the Jews were led into captivity by the
Babylonians.

13. JEWISH MESSIANISM

When Nebuchadnezzar's hosts entered Jerusalem in 586 B.C., the Jews had
already over 1000 years of history behind them. Towards the end of the
second millennium before our era, a people who called themselves "the
warriors of God" (*Iisra 'el*) or "the children of Israel" (*bene Iisra'el*) began to
stream from the north-eastern steppes and deserts of the Near East towards
the south-eastern shores of the Mediterranean.

The Israelites passed through the lands of the Edomites, Moabites, and
Amorites, and settled in the country between the Mediterranean and the
Dead Sea. Even at that time they believed that this exodus was guided by the

almighty eternal god Yahveh. We read in the subsequently written book of Judges (1.17, 19, 22): "And Judah went with Simeon his brother, and they slew the Canaanites that inhabited Zephath .... And the Lord was with Judah; and he drave out the inhabitants of the mountain .... And the house of Joseph, they also went up against Beth-el; and the Lord was with them."

For nearly 100 years the Jews carried on fierce warfare with the warlike tribes of the Philistines, who hindered them from completely dominating all Palestine. During David's long fight for mastery (about 1000 B.C.), the Jewish tribes were finally united under one sceptre, and this enabled them to gain the victory over the Philistines. The Jewish Kingdom reached the peak of its power under David's successor, King Solomon, who caused the Jewish people to toil at many great buildings, including the splendid temple to Jehovah in Jerusalem. After the death of Solomon (c. 930 B.C.), the Jewish State broke up into the northern kingdom of Israel and the southern kingdom of Judah.

When the Jews were in Canaan, they had after the death of Joshua at first no common leader, and each generation chose its own chief and judge. Only in times of imminent danger did the several generations give the power into the hands of one judge. It was only during the struggle with the Philistines that the patriarchs turned to Samuel the priest, asking him to name them a king. "Then all the elders of Israel gathered themselves together, and came to Samuel . . . and said unto him, Behold, thou art old, and thy sons walk not in thy ways; now make us a king to judge us like all the nations . . . . And the Lord said unto Samuel, Hearken unto the voice of the people in all that they say unto thee ..." (1 Samuel 8. 4, 5, 7).

In spite of the establishment of a monarchy, the Jews believed that their god Jehovah exercised direct government over the people, while the king and the priests were merely the agents of his will. They called their god "the Lord of the Hosts of Israel, Yahveh Sabaoth", and diligently listened for his voice in times of trouble. Their god spoke to the Jews when they were slaves in Babylon through the mouth of his prophet Isaiah:

> Now saith the Lord God, who created thee, O Jacob, and who has created Israel; fear not, for I have redeemed thee and called thee by my name; thou art mine .... When thou goest by water I shall be with thee, and the rivers shall not swallow thee up; when thou goest through fire, it shall not scorch thee and thou shalt not feel the heat of the flames; for I am the Lord thy God, I am thy Saviour .... Fear not, for I am with thee. Thus saith Jehovah, thy Redeemer and the Giver of thy life.

The concept of the direct rule of the god did not prevent the king from being called "the Lord's Anointed", "the Consecrated", or "the Son of God". Neither did it prevent the people from believing that the authority of the king was under the special protection of God, nor, in the Book of Psalms, Jehovah from addressing the king in the words: "Thou art my son, this day I myself have begotten thee."

The political conceptions of the Jews did not differ from those of other peoples in the Ancient East, since the political thought was entangled with religious belief. In time, after the settlement of Palestine, the idea of Messianism came to play a dominating role in Jewish political doctrine, as a result of the special economic and political conditions. The Jews came to have a firm belief that their god had chosen them in order to rule over them and take them under his special care. The idea that other peoples remained in darkness, and that they, the Jews, alone were called upon to show their faith and fullness of love for their god became a strong link binding the Jewish people together. The idea of Messianism was born of the struggle of the Jews with powerful enemies against whose might and whose gods they set their god, the leader who took especial care of the Jewish people. They took misfortunes and defeats as temporary punishments for disobedience, after which the appeased god would grant full victory to his chosen people.

In times of the greatest humiliation and despondency, the Chosen People were not beset by pessimism, for they believed that their god would send them a Messiah, who would restore the splendour of the Jewish Kingdom on earth. As this conception of the raising of the Jewish people above the rest of humanity became established, it had distinct consequence within the Jewish community. The messianic character of the doctrine caused the people to stand up for their rights, to set themselves against authority, and to criticize their rulers through the mouths of their prophets. At the same time, the idea that the god ruled directly weakened the position of the king in favour of the priesthood, which endeavoured to bring both monarch and people under its sway. The aristocratic–priestly and the popular tendencies beginning to appear in Jewish doctrine correspond to the controversies then being carried on in the Jewish community between the people, the aristocracy, the priesthood, and the king.[32]

The expounder of the priestly doctrine is the prophet Ezekiel, priest of Jerusalem, son of Buzi, led into bondage in Babylon in 597 B.C. Ezekiel consoled his countrymen, slaves to the Babylonians, with the hope of returning to their own country and of the restoration of the Jewish State; he told them of the dominating role which the priests were to play in the future Jewish State. The king was to be merely the representative of the people and the protector of religion, while the priests were to keep full power in their own hands. The king, limited in power and deprived of the leadership of the army, is called the prince of the people, for "the Lord himself will lead Israel and will fight for his people". Ezekiel desired to assign the highest power to the priests of Jerusalem, while lesser priests were to occupy the lower rungs of the ladder of power. In this way the all-powerful organization of the priests was to govern a submissive people in Ezekiel's priest-ruled state. Tendencies to limit the power of the king in favour of the priests are found in Deuteronomy (dating from c. 621 B.C.), which is supposed to contain the last will of Moses, thus justifying the claims of the priests.[33]

The doctrine of priestly rule over a passive people could not have appealed to the Jews, who had a conscious conviction that they were the Chosen of God. And although the Jewish masses without property were constantly threatened with bondage for debt, although they carried the burden of the rule of the propertied classes, although they supported the wealthy by their work, the Jewish people knew how to demand their rights, conscious of their mission. The struggle of the Jewish people for their rights and the appearance of their defenders the prophets, established the idea of Messianism. This enabled them to endure the days of bondage, while when they had their own state the thought of the divine protection for the people caused the ruling classes to take more care of the masses. Hence the social situation of the lowest classes was better amongst the Jews as compared with that in other ancient states.[34]

In this way the concepts of the Jewish people had some influence on the shaping of the juristic institutions on the one hand, and on the other the idea of Jewish Messianism inspired the prophets' defence of the people. In the laws of Moses we read that if a man should beat his slave or servant to death, the crime should be avenged by the death penalty, and if a slave or servant should be struck on the eye so that the eye was injured, then he must be set free in recompense.

The law dealt particularly with slaves of Jewish origin, who in contradistinction to those of other communities, were not treated as mere chattels. The Jewish law allowed the owner of a slave to dispose only of "the hand" of the slave, i.e. his work. In Leviticus it is laid down that a Jew should not be looked upon as a bondsman, as a subject being in thrall to his owner, but as an impoverished and unfortunate brother of the same faith. In the tractate *Kidushin* the idea of Messianism even annuls the idea of a Jew as a slave: "God, who led Israel forth from Egypt, who made a people of free men out of wild hordes of slaves, who called his nation the servants of God, this God could not suffer a man to put his person at the mercy of another, and become the slave of man instead of the servant of God."

Even the *Torah* attempted to weaken the ruthlessness of the wealthy towards those of the same faith; its precepts warn the propertied classes against any financial exploitation of the Jewish people: "If thou lendest money to a poor man, take no interest. If thou takest from him as a pledge his outer garment, give it back to him before the sun sets, since it is his covering, and how then shall he sleep?"

The *Torah* also provided for moratoria in the case of the needy. According to the Law, every seventh year should be a sabbatical year, when all tillers of the soil were to give up their fields and orchards for the use of the poor, while the rich were not to demand money from their poorer debtors.

The prevailing conviction of the special care of God over the Jewish people did not only influence the shaping of juristic institutions but also gave pretext for the rise of prophets, who spoke for the people in the name of God.

Beginning from the second half of the eighth century B.C. the voice of the prophets makes itself heard, a voice stigmatizing evil rulers, the exploitation of the people, the arrogance of the rich, and unjust laws. Associated with the poor, the prophets accused the rich. These unofficial representatives of the priesthood expounded the demands of the people. It was the universal conviction that God spoke through the mouths of his prophets, who said of themselves that they were the mouths of God, that God inspired them and put his words into their mouths.

The prophet Amos (*c.* 750 B.C.), a tiller of the soil from a little town in Judah, said of himself (Amos 7. 14, 15): "I was an herdsman and a gatherer of sycomore fruit. And the Lord took me as I followed the flock, and the Lord said unto me, Go prophecy unto my people Israel." If God commands, who may refuse? Amos denounced the arrogance and the dissolute way of life of the propertied classes (Amos 4. 1, 2, and 5. 11, 12): "Hear this word, ye kine of Bashan, that are in the mountains of Samaria, which oppress the poor, which crush the needy, which say to their masters, Bring, and let us drink. The Lord God hath sworn by his holiness, that lo, the days shall come upon you, that he will take you away with hooks and your posterity with fishhooks ... Forasmuch therefore as your treading is upon the poor, and ye take from him burdens of wheat, ye have built houses of hewn stone, but ye shall not dwell in them."

The prophets did not hesitate to denounce the king, the functionaries, and lawlessness in general. The prophet Hosea (*c.* 740) condemned the kings, saying (Hosea 8. 4, 5): "They have set up kings, but not by me; they have made princes, and I knew it not . . . mine anger is kindled against them."

About the turn of the seventh century, the prophet Jeremiah defended the poor against the oppression and wilfulness of those in power, lamenting that the holy city of Jerusalem had become blasphemous, and where righteousness and justice had once ruled, now murderers governed. The princes were apostates and friends of thieves, running after money and precious gifts. Why did such people come to the temple to offer up sacrifices to the Almighty, who could not hear their prayers, for their hands were stained with blood? They must first renounce unclean things, learn virtue and endeavour to be just. The prophet Isaiah in the first half of the seventh century B.C. also denounced lawlessness and thundered at the rich. "Woe unto them who set up unjust laws to deprive the needy of their rights," he cries; "Woe unto you who rise in the morning to pass the time in drinking and tope until evening, to heat yourselves with strong waters. The zither, the lute, the drum, and the pipe ye have at your revels and wine in plenty, but ye look not on the things of the Lord, holding the deeds of his hands lightly. Thy leaders, O Israel, are debauched, and companions of thieves."

The prophet Samuel criticized Saul the king in a similar manner, as Nathan did David, as Isaiah did Ashaz, as Jeremiah did Jehoiakim and Zedekiah. The voices of these prophets criticizing the kings and the rich found hearers among the people. The ruling classes, on their side, opposed these prophets with their own soothsayers, who defended the existing system. Ezekiel was condemning the prophets of the people when he cried woe unto those foolish prophets who prophesied although they had seen nothing, for the hand of the Lord would be against them who saw but vanity and told but falsehood.

In this way, the class struggle emerges out of the messianic idea. The concept of Messianism could not veil the actuality; on the contrary, the actuality was contained in the idea. The interpretation of Messianism also varied; it served both the non-propertied classes to express their social aspirations and the propertied classes to express their political aspirations.

14. THE EGYPTIAN THEOCRACY

"In Egypt there are more wonders than in all the rest of the world", wrote Herodotus. When the Semitic tribes migrating from Asia stopped at the Nile, they were surprised at the fertility of the black soil from which the land took its name (Kamit or Kemi) in contrast to their sun-faded wastes.

The annual flooding of the Nile in July bringing moisture and fertile mud changed Egypt into a fecund oasis amidst the deserts.

In the eyes of the ancients, Egypt was the gift of the Nile, to which they devoted songs and the honours of divinity. "Honour be to thee, O Nile," run the words of a hymn, "Praise be to thee, O Nile, Thou who rulest over our land, and bringest life abounding to Egypt . . . . Greeting unto thee, O Nile, Thou descendest upon this land, comest in peace, to give life unto Egypt."

To master the river demanded a collective effort, hence the rapid growth of about forty districts, called nomes, ruled by monarchs, set over the patriarchal organization.[35] As early as about 3500 B.C. these districts were collected into two states, Lower Egypt in the delta of the Nile and Upper Egypt in the middle reaches of the river. Three hundred years later, under the rule of Menes, a single state was created with its capital at Memphis.[36]

When domination over the people became a most important question in the class society, the Egyptian gods, who had originally personified natural powers, began to change their characters, becoming protectors of authority and the state. Osiris became the guardian of the monarchic government, and gave up the care of the eternal law of re-birth and death in nature. The former sun god Horus, whose name was taken as the official title of the ruler of Egypt, also became the guardian of the king. Later, all the districts and indeed the whole state came under the care of the sun god Ra; but when in the period of the Middle Empire the capital was transferred from Memphis to

Thebes, the cult of the local Theban god Amen or Ammon was joined to that of Ra, leading to the creation of the god Amen-Re, the maker of the world and the guardian of Egypt, a deity for the whole state.

As despotic rule came to be established, the idea of a god–ruler, the pharaoh, emerged beside the concept of divine protection for the government and the state.[37] Pharaoh was regarded as a god, who at the same time bore the dignity of a high priest, a leader in war, and a judge. The theocratic doctrine of the divinity of the monarch, proclaimed incessantly in Egypt for some thousands of years, was manifested with unusual strength in that country.

The pharaoh was recognized as a "good and great God, Lord of Eternity, the Source of Life, Health and Joy of Heart, who dies not, but sets beyond his own eternal horizon". The homage due to the gods was paid to the divine rulers in temples built for this purpose. Both in art and in literature, pharaoh was imagined as a supreme being directly descended from the gods. The pyramids from the Ancient Empire were meant to symbolize by their dimensions the divine power of the pharaohs, while the texts found in these edifices dating from the fifth and sixth dynasties tell of the happy life of the pharaohs who had been received into the celestial company of the gods.[38]

The official titles of the pharaoh sang his divinity. He was called Horus, i.e. the heir of the god Horus on the Egyptian throne; the Lord of Diadems, i.e. the holder of the crowns of Upper and Lower Egypt; the Vanquisher of Seth (the god of darkness and evil); the King of Lower and of Upper Egypt; and finally the Son of the sun god.

In the theocratic doctrine of Egypt the gods spoke to the pharaohs as to deities, even acknowledging their superiority. An inscription from the wall of the temple at Abu-Simbel contains a message from the sun god to Ramesses II of the nineteenth dynasty:

> I have created thee as a god. All thy members are divine. Taking the shape of the ram Mendes, I went in unto thy noble mother. Thinking of thee, I gave thee shape that thou shouldst be my comfort. I brought thee forth as a rising sun and raised thee to be among the gods, O Ramesses the King. . . . Gods and goddesses were delighted by thy beauty and gave thee praise, telling me of their admiration, saying, "Thou art our father, who called us into life, but Ramesses the King is a god like thee . . . . I distinguished thee, I chose thee, I perfected thee, thou are most good of heart and thy words are a pattern unto us . . . . Thou givest life to the dwellers upon earth by thy will, O King Ramesses. I have made thee King to all eternity, a prince who will endure for all time . . . . I have appointed the dignity of a divine crown for thee . . . . I have given thee the Nile, which for thee fills Egypt with abundance of riches and health . . . . I shall give thee heaven with all that it contains . . . ."

Aware of his greatness, the Pharaoh Ramesses II, Maker of the World, replies: "Father of the gods, I am thy son, thou hast set me on my throne, thou hast given unto me thy royal power. Thou hast made me in thine own likeness, thou hast bestowed upon me all that thou hast created. I in return for all this will perform all those praiseworthy deeds which thou desirest . . . ."

Apparently during the nineteenth dynasty, when the Hittites threatened Egypt, the cult of the pharaoh was specially instilled into the people.[39] A hymn to Menephtah, the son and successor of Ramesses II, dates from this time:

> Turn thy face upon me, thou who risest to light the earth by thy goodness. O sunny sphere of thy people, lighting the darkness of Egypt, thou art the countenance of the Sun thy father, who rises in the sky. Thy rays penetrate the secret places of the earth. There is no place without thy goodness. Thy words are law to all nations. Reposing in thy palace, thou canst hear the words that sound through all lands. Thou hast millions of ears and the brightness of thine eye outshines the stars in the sky . . . .

It was the custom to fall on the face before pharaoh, and to kiss the dust off his feet. To hold conversation with him was a very high honour.[40]

The belief in the divinity of the ruler, and that every command of pharaoh was an order from a god, aroused respect and fear in his subjects, especially since the pharaohs deliberately based their power on violence and terror. The dying Pharaoh Amenemhet I (*c.* 2000 B.C.) gave practical advice to his co-regent Sesostris I: "That thou mayest be a good king on earth, that thou mayest valiantly rule the nations, and propagate their welfare, harden thy heart towards all thy subjects. The people respect him whom they fear. Never approach them alone. Let thy heart love no brother. Never take unto thee any friend, make no soul thy confidant, for therein lies naught good. . . . "

The officials were to be guided by a similar principle of ruthlessness. In the admonitions of Tuthmosis III to his newly appointed vizier, he recommended the observance of the law, with violence towards the subjects. " . . . Remember that a high official such as thou art liveth in the public eye. Wind and water tell of all that he doeth, which will never remain hidden. The only protection for such an official is the strict observance of the law, and the careful performance of what is laid down. Let the people stand in fear before thee, for only he whom the people fear is as a ruler should be."

The political ideal was to keep the people in lowliness and obedience.

The thoughts of the minister Ptahhotep (who lived about 2000 B.C.) which have come down to us, express the views of the classes ruling in Egypt, whose greatest care was to maintain the existing system and the subjection of the people.[41] Ptahhotep took social inequality as an immutable principle, at the same time denying any virtues to the lower classes, who "should not raise their hands against their superiors, but should bow themselves down". He taught that the happiness of the people depends only on the grace of the rich, since "the noble give when they wish to and to those whom they favour . . . for the power of graciousness is greater than the power of force."

"Bow thy back humbly", says Ptahhotep, "before those set over thee ... and thy house will be lasting and all thy goods also, and thy reward will be fitting. To resist one's superiors is bad. Only he may live at peace to whom his superior is merciful. If thou art indeed humble in obedience toward thy superior, thou doest well in the sight of the gods."

Apparently the chief endeavour of Ptahhotep was to establish a belief in the excellence of the social system handed down by tradition from father to son. "A son who is obedient to his father follows in the footsteps of Horus. Good fortune will come to him if he gives ear unto the teaching and the counsels of his father, and when he himself becomes old he will be held in veneration. Then let him say the same to his son also, renewing and repeating the teaching of his father, which he heard in his youth."

The perpetuation of a spirit of humility in the non-propertied classes and of faith in the perfection of the social system lay within the interests of the ruling classes, especially as the barbarously treated slaves kept rising in hopeless despair. They found allies among the exploited craftsmen and peasants, in whom the priests instilled the principle that "as soon as a man comes forth from the womb, he stands before his superior, and must abase himself. As a child he must be obedient to his preceptor, as a young man to some official, as an old man to those lesser than himself, for man is created only to bow his neck".

The risings of the slaves and the poor more than once caused the fall of a hated dynasty, bringing fear and terror to the propertied classes. From papyri dating from the eighteenth century B.C., we learn of the situation which reigned in Egypt during a great insurrection of slaves and peasants.

> The earth has whirled round like a potter's wheel, and what was low has become high. The country is full of armed bands, and men carry shields when ploughing . . . . All say it is impossible to understand what is going on in the land . . . . Men of low condition now live in splendour; those who once were without sandals now possess treasures . . . . Each town says, 'Let us drive out the wealthy from among us' . . . . One cannot recognize the son of a rich man, the child of a lady becomes the son of a servant girl . . . . Architects and the captains of the king's ships have become labourers in the fields . . . . The mob have dashed the heads of the children of princes against the walls . . . . Wealthy folk have been set to grinding corn at the mill-stones, those who went in fine linen robes have been under the lash . . . . Servitors have become lords . . . ."

However, these revolts of slaves and the poor could not change the essentials of the system, which corresponded to the contemporary level of productive forces. After a hated dynasty had been overthrown, new rulers came upon the scene to continue the theocratic system of exploitation.

In the periods of social chaos, hedonistic ideas were set up against views in which death was regarded as the only means of release from the too-heavy burden of life.

The *Harper's Song*, which dates from the fifteenth century B.C., contains a hedonistic doctrine praising a carefree existence.

> Some beings pass away and perish, while others are born in their place and live; so it is and so it has been from the time of our earliest forebears. The earthly gods, the kings, who were once alive, have long rested in their pyramids; in like manner have other great men been buried in their tombs . . . . Lift up thy heart therefore, that thou mayest forget what awaits thee, and think only of what thou findest fair upon earth. Satisfy thy desires to the full whilst thou livest. Anoint thy head with myrrh and robe thyself in delicate attire,

scented with the costliest perfumes, with the true odour of the gods. Let the joys of thy life be multiplied more and more, and let not thy heart grow weary. Satisfy thy wishes, take heed for thy pleasures, and order thine affairs according to the desires of thine own heart . . . . Give up thy days to merriment, cease not to be joyful, mourn not, and spare not, for none has yet carried his wealth to the grave, and none of those who have gone thither has yet returned.

The propertied classes could replace the official religious and political doctrine by hedonistic ideas in the face of rioting and dynastic weakness, but the poor could only oppose to the sad reality a pessimistic desire for death.

To whom shall I turn today? [says a song from the eighteenth century B.C.]; Brother is set against brother, nowadays love is lost between friends. To whom shall I turn today? Hearts are false . . . . The gentle fall by the way, but the strong prevail in every place. To whom shall I turn today? The fair face is vile, virtue is everywhere neglected . . . crimes are committed everywhere. Death now stands before me, like the health longed for by a sick man . . . . Death now stands before me, like the yearning for home in the soul of him who has spent long years in prison.

The strophes of the song are imbued with a complete lack of faith in the world and in men; the masses, overwhelmed with the burden of the theocratic system in this life full of inequality, saw in death a true and ideal equality. "Neither the coward nor the brave can escape the grave; there the needy and the great are equal."

The complaints of the poor in these sad songs on death were veiled by the splendour of the court of the divine pharaoh; hence only the theocratic system of Egypt and its history of thousands of years made any impression on the men of ancient Hellas and Rome.

NOTES

1. One cannot agree with J. Pirenne: *Civilisations antiques*, 1951, pp. 125 ff., who, e.g., discussing Babylon or the Achaic civilization, gives the name of feudalism to the rule of aristocracy in ancient times, co-existent with slavery. Pirenne in principle accepts the structure of power as the basis of his division into historical periods, disregarding the nature of ancient states.

2. In *Propyläen Weltgeschichte*, vol. I: *Das Erwachen der Menschheit. Die Kulturen der Urzeit Ostasiens und des vorderen Orients*, Ed. H. Freyer *et al.*, 1931, pp. 177 ff., and *Weltgeschichte. Die Entwicklung der Menschheit in Staat und Gesellschaft in Kultur und Geistesleben*, vol. III: *Geschichte des Orients*, Ed. C. Bezold *et al.*, Berlin, 1910, pp. 521 ff., a comprehensive survey of the earliest history of China is found.

3. Mao Tse-tung: *Izbrannyje proizwiediennija*, 1953, III, p. 138; the line dividing slavery from feudalism as accepted here, is drawn from Mao Tse-tung's studies.

4. A discussion of philosophic trends, in which political views are reflected, may be found in E. V. Zenker: *Geschichte der Chinesischen Philosophie*, Breslau, 1929, Richard Wilhelm, *Chinesische Philosophie*, Breslau, 1929, H. Hackmann, *Chinesische Philosophie*, München, 1927.

5. H. Haas: *Das Sprachgut K'ung tszes und Lao-tszes in gedanklicher Zusammenordnung*, Leipzig, 1920, p. 48, contains a translation of the word "Tao" into various European languages, e.g. *Weg, Grande Voie du Monde, Lauf der Dinge, Weltordnung, Weltgesetz, Natur, Great Creating Nature, Gottnatur, Naturlauf, Naturgesetz, Macht, Wort, Logos, Vernunft, Ratio, La Raison, Raison Suprême Universelle, Reason, Weltvernunft, Urvernunft, Weltseele, Allseele, Vernunftprinzip, Sinn, Wahrheit, Wisdom, Right, The Principle of Right, Vorsehung, Providence, Clarity, Love.*

6.   Richard Wilhelm: *Lao-Tse und der Taoismus*, Stuttgart, 1948, pp. 67 ff., while discussing Lao Tse's political doctrines is pointing out that the philosopher recognized a hierarchical structure of the society in which the individual starts the ladder to be followed by the family, the community, the state, humanity constituting a unit of the highest rank. Thus the state is seen as one of the elements of which humanity is composed. As particular individuals are members of families, so are states members of humanity. The author is pointing out that this idea made Lao Tse condemn aggressive wars, achieving peace having been his highest ideal.

7.   W. Jabłoński, J. Chmielewski and O. Wojtasiewicz prepared a Polish translation of Chuang Tzu, 1953. Attention should be drawn to the introduction written by W. Jabłoński in which a scholarly analysis of Taoism, as thrown against the background of other trends of ancient China, is presented.

8.   Richard Wilhelm, in *Kung-Tse, Leben und Werk*, Stuttgart, 1925, and the reprinted study under the same title, 1950, is trying to demonstrate that Confucius' doctrine is a consistent and thorough system. Analogies with European political ideas are the author's own innovations. These, however, should not lead us to an underestimation of his merits as translator and textual commentator. Treatments of the rise, development and changes of Confucius' doctrine, as thrown against other trends or viewed from the aspect of utility of the doctrine for the ruling classes, may be found in F. Biallas: *Konfuzius und sein Kult*, 1928, O. Franke: *Studien zur Geschichte des konfuzianischen Dogmas u. der chinesischen Staatsreligion*, 1920, and G. Maspero: *La Chine antique*, 1927.

9.   In European literature there exist erroneous tendencies of treating Mo Ti as a precursor of socialism. Cf., e.g., A. David: *Socialisme chinois*, 1907, or A. Forke: *Mo-Ti*, 1922.

10.   The Confucian idea of natural order carried out by people (*yen-che-chou-yi*) was opposed by the idea of the rules of law (*fa-che-chou-yi*), whose adherents, the Legalists, were grouped round the Fa-Kia law school. The Legalists, who tended towards active attitudes, represented the view that human nature was weak and evil. Hence their cult of strong authority. According to J. Escarre: *La conception chinoise du droit*, "Archives de philosophie du droit et de sociologie juridique", 1935, No. 1–2, pp. 1–73, the oldest representative of the Legalist School is Kuang Chung (died in 643 B.C.), the author of the Cheng penal code. Further names of Legalists include that of Li-Kusi (424–387 B.C.), the author of the code which was the first to extend over the whole legislation of the Chinese Empire. In the middle of the fourth century the two greatest figures of the School appear: Che-Kiao and Shen Pu-hai, the latter having greatly influenced the development of law in the spirit of the Legalist School. The last representatives of the Legalist School, Li Ssu and Han-fei-tzu, live in the third century, the latter being most famous of all. His prominence in Chinese philosophy is compared to that of Confucius, Lao Tse and Mo Ti. These topics are discussed in Wu-Kuo-Cheng: *Ancient Chinese Political Theories*, 1928, and Ling-Ki-Chao: *Conception du droit et théories des légistes*, 1926.

11.   In the third century Yin-Wen-Tsen, a representative of the Legalist School, applied the old Chen-ming doctrine concerning the precise meaning of words to legal norms. In critical literature Yin Wen-Tsen's merit in the introduction of precision to legal terms is particularly stressed. Cf. M. Granet: *La pensée chinoise*, 1934, and the same author's *Quelques particularités de la langue et de la pensée chinoise*, "Rev. philos.", 1920, pp. 45, 98, 181.

12.   Han-fei-tzu's doctrine is discussed by Lin-You-Tang: *Han-Fei as a Cure for Modern China*, to be found in *China's Own Critics*, 1931, p. 68.

13.   Among early studies mention should be made of the somewhat obsolete book by A. Ludwig: *Die philosophischen und religiösen Anschauungen des Veda in ihrer Entwicklung*, 1875, and the sources collected in J. Muir's *Original Sanscrit Texts*, 1872, among more recent studies G. Courtillier: *Les anciennes civilisations de l'Inde*, 1930, S. Schayer: *Indie starożytne w świetle zródel*, Kraków, 1926.

14.   E. Słuszkiewicz: *Państwo i społeczeństwo w dawnych Indiach*, Warszawa, 1949, discusses, basing on most recent investigations, the social and political relations in ancient India.

15.   S. Schayer: *Indie starożytne w świetle źródeł*, Pieśń Rygwedy X, 90, 11 and 12, Kraków, 1926.

The oldest text referring to castes is the hymn on the emergence of the world out of the "cosmic pre-man" (*purusa*). The gods make an offering of the *purusa*; out of the body, cut into pieces, liturgical substances, living beings, the sun, the moon, etc., emerge. "When did the gods divide purusa, how many parts did they make? What emerged from his mouth? What emerged from his shoulders, his loins? What was called what emerged from his feet? The Brahman caste was his mouth, his shoulders became the Kshatriyas, his loins the Vaisyas, his feet became the Sudras."

16.   W. I. Awdijew: *Istoria Drewniego Wostoka*, 1948, p. 504, writes: "The Brahman religion and the caste system was opposed by Buddhism which, according to tradition, goes back to the sixth century B.C., and which, as follows from the Aśoka edicts, was widely spread in the third century B.C. At a time of economic, and to some extent commercial development of enslaved India, Buddhism arose as an ideological protest against Brahmanism and the petri-fied caste system which was inhibiting social and economic development of India. Buddhism was particularly strongly opposed to the caste of the Brahmans. The teachings of Buddha contain a protest against considering everybody born in the Brahman caste to be a priest."

17.   H. Glasenapp: *Brahma u. Buddha*, Berlin, 1926, pp. 138 ff., presents the philosophical orientations which were opposed to each other towards the middle of the millennium B.C., while O. Strauss: *Indische Philosophie*, München, 1925, pp. 116 ff., discusses Gonsala's fatalism. Other materials can be found in P. Regnaud: *Materiaux pour servir à l'histoire de la philosophie de l'Inde*, Paris, 1878, while a complete bibliographical guide is contained in C. Ragamey: *Buddhistische Philosophie*, 1950.

18.   S. Chatterjee and D. Datta: *An Introduction to Indian Philosophy*, 1954. (Russian trans-lation, p. 64.)

19.   S. Chatterjee and D. Datta: *op. cit.*, p. 105.

20.   In the cult of Jainism sculptures of completely naked saints are not infrequently encountered. It seems that the adherents to Mahavira were imitating Greek sculptures. The sculpture of the archaic Apollo (520 B.C.) could have inspired Jainist art. It has been esta-blished that in the cities of Asia Minor cross-influences of Greece and India were a fact.

21.   The text of Buddha's sermon is found in *A Source Book in Indian Philosophy*, Ed. S. Radhakrishnan and C. A. Moore, 1957, pp. 274-5.

22.   M. Winternitz: *Geschichte der indischen Literatur*, Leipzig, vol. I, 1909, vol. II, 1920, and H. Glasenapp: *Die Literaturen Indiens*, 1929. Especially compare pp. 80 ff.

23.   Megasthenes' observations of India are known indirectly, namely from the accounts of Strabon and Arrian, as the original accounts got lost. The relations at Chandragupta's court are discussed in O. Stein: *Megasthenes u. Kauti-lya*, Wien, 1921, where some differences in the dress of Kautilya and Megasthenes are pointed out.

24.   A. Hillebrandt, Altindische Politik, 1923, pp. 16 ff., discusses elements of *tri-varga*, as well as the problem of legal order as seen against the background of the ancient Indian socio-political structure.

25.   This problem is dealt with by B. Kumar Sarkar: *The Political Institutions and the Hindus*, 1922, pp. 88 ff., and E. Washburn Hopkins: *The Social and Military Positions of the Ruling Caste in Ancient India*.

26.   B. Hroźny's investigations have revealed cultural and economic contacts between India and Mesopotamia to have existed already in the pre-Indian period, i.e. between 2400 and 2100. This especially in his study *Histoire de l'Asie Antérieure*, 1947, pp. 226 ff.

27.   Commercial contacts between the cities of Mesopotamia and those of the Indus region are discussed by V. Gordon Childe: *Postęp a archeologia*, Warsaw, 1954, p. 106.

28.   Chronology is according to Soviet authors.

29.   J. Pirenne, *op. cit.*, pp. 66 ff., is demonstrating that the growth of Babylon at the time of Hammurabi and the country's superior position in relation to other countries is connected with the superior position of the god Marduk in relation to regional deities. "The hegemony of Babylon", Pirenne writes, "thoroughly changes the character of the god Marduk. Political centralization and religious centralization . . . were being materialized simultaneously."

30.   The Hammurabi *Codex* was found in 1901 and many works have been written on the codex since that time. Polish studies embrace among others: St. Estreicher: *Kodeks Ham-murabiego*, Kraków, 1905, and *Najstarsze kodeksy pisane świata*, rocznik PAU, 1930-31, pp. 89-173, M. Schorr: *Kodeks Hammurabiego a ówczesna praktyka prawa*, Kraków, 1907. All the documents of the Hammurabi epoch found up to the year 1923 were edited in the four volume publication *Hammurabis Gesetz 1909-1923*. The organization of the juridical system during the rules of Hammurabi is discussed in M. C. Cölgecen: *Le Code d'Hammurabi*, 1949, pp. 67 ff.

31. B. Meissner: *Babylonien und Assyrien*, 1920, pp. 46 ff., deals with the process of the formation of the theocratic doctrine in Babylon. A monographic treatment of the problem may be found in Christliebe Jeremias: *Die Vergöttlichung der babyl. assyr. Köonige*, 1929.

32. The social differentiation of the Jews and its causes are discussed in M. Weber: *Wirtschaftsgeschichte*, München, 1923, pp. 60 ff., E. Meyer, *Die Israeliten und ihre Nachbarstämme*, Halle, 1906, p. 504, is demonstrating the dominating role of rich land-owners who were subjugating poorer land owners during the time of the Philistine wars.

33. Contrary to Gressmann's opinion, I do not think that the Deuteronomy was considered by the Jews as "something binding", nor that it was the expression of the "Nation's genius" (*Josia und das Deuteronomium*, 1924, p. 337). Neither do I share the conviction (K. Galling: *Die Israelitische Staatsverfassung in ihrer vorderorientalischen Umwelt*, 1929, p. 63) that the Deuteronomy marks the transition from absolute rules to a "constitutional, democratic monarchy".

34. St. Estreicher: *Najstarsze kodeksy prawne świata*, 1931, pp. 51 ff., is pointing out that ethical concepts have penetrated the Jewish law: "In no nation, including Persia and India, do the literary and legal documents reveal such a supremacy of ethics over law, a feature so clearly characteristic of the chosen nation . . . ." (p. 53).

35. K. Koranyi: *Powszechna historia państwa i prawa*, vol. I, Warsaw, 1951, p. 5, points to the role of the Nile for the creation of the state.

36. A few miles south of the present capital city of Egypt are the ruins of the ancient city of Men-nofer. This city was devoted to the god Ptah, hence it was also called Hikuptah (Ptah's stead). The Greeks modified the former into Memphis, the latter into Aigyptos, which names were then associated with the city alone and the whole country respectively.

37. The political structure which had developed in Egypt was a despotic, theocratic monarchy, with the pharaoh as the highest priest, legislator, commander in chief and the highest judge. The term pharaoh denotes a kind of title and is composed of two words: Per-o, meaning great house, and Phar-ga, great seat. The royal palace was the centre of the whole state and its name became the title of the ruler himself. The name, however, was not used by the Egyptians; it is first encountered in Hebrew books.

38. In texts of the first half of the third millennium we may read: "It gives delight to watch king Mer-en-Re fly into the sky, adorned with the crown of the god Re. His armour is like the armour of Hathor, his feathers like the feathers of Horus the hawk. Thus clad he enters into heaven to join his two brothers the gods. Flying into the sky, into the country of sunshine, the deceased king becomes like Hathor, the goddess of heaven, and Re, the god of the sun."

39. W. I. Awdijew: *op. cit.*, p. 256, is demonstrating that while Egypt was fighting to keep its military and economic positions at the large markets and commercial tracts of Asia Minor, while the pharaohs of the nineteenth dynasty were fighting against the Hittite invasions, the divine character of the pharaoh and the cult of his person were emphatically promoted among the people. Inscriptions on numerous plates dating back to this period and found in the eastern part of the Nile delta seem to be indicative of this.

40. Sinuhe, an Egyptian subject, thus relates his conversation with the Pharaoh (a document of the eighteenth century B.C.): "God spoke to me in a friendly way . . . . My body became weak, my heart was not in my body any more and I could not know whether I was alive or dead. What is my Lord saying to me? I cannot answer this question. I feel the hand of god over me . . . ."

41. Ptahhotep served as minister to one of the last monarchs of the fifth dynasty. The fact is that the minister is credited with the work of a number of people and generations. In the form in which the collection is known, it goes back to, roughly, the year 2000 (beginning of twelfth dynasty). Ptahhotep's ideas are contained in the Prisse Papyrus, so named after the French archeologist E. Prisse.

2

ISLAM AS A POLITICAL DOCTRINE

1. ARABIA BEFORE MOHAMMED

The countries situated around the Arabian peninsula—Egypt, Syria, Persia, and India—already had a long history behind them when at length the Arabs came upon the scene of world history. A thousand years after the birth of Buddhism and more than five hundred after the birth of Christianity, a new religious doctrine arose in the Arabian peninsula—Islam, whose believers were shortly to set up a political world power.

The Ancients had little knowledge of Arabia, although by her favour the Greeks and Romans profited through the importation of goods from far-off India; reports that were only fragmentary revolved about her wealth and the beautiful Yemen, and about the eternal spring in the land lying to the south-west of the peninsula. It seems, however, that the reports of great riches, which the imagination of the Ancients linked with the Yemen, came from Egyptians, who directed the attention of the Greeks and Romans to the transit country of the Yemen, passing over in silence the true sources of these riches, namely India and the south-east coast of Africa. Since Ptolemy, Arabia had been divided into Desert—Arabia Deserta, Rocky—Arabia Petrea, and Fortunate —Arabia Felix. Desert Arabia comprised the sandy area stretching from Syrian Palmyra to the south. Rocky Arabia was the north-west portion of the peninsula, which was also called Arabia Petrea from the town of Petra, situated to the east of the Sinai peninsula. This province included the Sinai peninsula and the eastern massif. It was the south-western part of the peninsula that was known as Arabia Felix.

Their somewhat forbidding land was always the object of the burning love of its inhabitants. Long before Mohammed the Arab had heard the words of a song telling with love and admiration of the earth scorched by the live coals of the sun's fires, and of the teeming infinity of glittering stars in the sky of the desert night. With pride he listened to his poets who sang of the untamed elements, endurance in battle, and passionate love. The pathos of the poetry must have spoken to the restless nature of the tent-dwelling Arabs, who long before Mohammed listened every year to the poets in the markets at Okaz, a town in the Hejaz province, where the title of the best poet in Arabia was contested for.

The population of Arabia was of Semitic origin, the legends telling that it had sprung from Kathan the descendant of Sem, the son of Noah, or from Ishmael the son of Abraham and Hagar. The stories had it that Kathan's son Jarab formed the state of Yemen on a fertile strip of land in the south-west part of the peninsula, and that from the name Jarab came the name Arabia.

The population of Arabia was divided into nomads and settlers. The nomads led a wandering life; they were Bedouins, making their living in the desert lands by internecine wars and brigandage. The other part of the population lived in the fertile valleys tilling the land and raising cattle. Part of the settled population set up towns and ports, employing themselves in business and sailing. Such was the greater part of the population of the Yemen. They were most enterprising sailors—their ships brought myrrh and balsam from African shores, gold and spices from India. The imported merchandise together with their own produce was sent by the Arabs from the Yemen across the desert to the north to reach its destination—the towns of Persia, Phoenicia, Syria, and later Greece and Rome. The goods transported by the Arabs had to travel a long way: first by ship, then across the sands. Caravans made of scores and hundreds of camels crossed the desert, forming links between India, Ethiopia, the Yemen, and Syria and Palestine.

The Yemen must have been known since the Jewish prophets speak of this state. Isaiah addressing Jerusalem said: "The multitude of camels shall cover thee, the dromedaries of Midian and Ephah; all they from Sheba shall come: they shall bring gold and incense."[1]

Ezekiel weeping over the fall of Tyre similarly cried out: "The merchants of Sheba and Raamah, they were thy merchants: they occupied in thy fairs with chief of all spices, and with all precious stones, and gold. Haran, and Canneh, and Eden, the merchants of Sheba, Asshur, and Chilmad, were thy merchants."[2]

The Arab merchants were distinguished by their great liveliness and enterprise. They had to make use of their wandering brothers for their desert transport, and these desert brethren held their fellows from the settlements in contempt. The wandering tribes proudly repeated the story of how the Creator of the world changed the wind into the free Bedouin and made the desert steeds from arrows. Another story contemptuously tells at the same time of the creation of the settler population: "Now God, loving the Arabs of the desert, changed the clods of the earth into an ass, so that from his dung He might make town-dwellers and peasants." This legend, however, did not prevent the co-operation of the tent-dwellers with the settlers. The wandering desert-dwellers supplied camels, armed and guarded the merchants' caravans, and often added their only merchandise—fleeces of thin wool—to the desert convoys. These Arabs spent their lives in tents, roaming the desert far and wide in search of springs and pasturage for their herds, and when in time they had stripped the land they occupied, would move on seeking suitable countryside. The wandering Arabs were divided into tribes and families. At the head of the tribe stood the sheikh, chosen by the tribe; a spear placed before his tent signified his authority. The sheikh's rule had to be upheld by the unwavering confidence of the tribe, which ruthlessly removed incapable chiefs. Personal character, wisdom, and experience of life were considered by the desert people better qualifications for chieftainship than family traditions. In the sphere of government the sheikh's duty was first and foremost the direction of the life of the tribe; he chose the places for halts and for camps, led the tribe to battle, made war, negotiated with the tribal enemies, was, indeed, the guardian of harmony and of tribal traditions expressed in customs, songs and poetry. Sometimes the tribal chiefs created a supreme chief of sheikhs, who would, in times of common danger, unite the troubled tribes normally in a permanent state of conflict among themselves.

The desert demanded great versatility of the Arabs. It formed their personalities, insisting on great sensitivity and adaptability in action. The Bedouins had to join courage with cunning, excitability and a lively imagination with prudent moderation and reflection, pride and hate with noble hospitality. The Arab of the desert was a warrior and brigand, despising the merchants, who according to his ideas were engaged in unworthy occupations; at the same time he negotiated with them, led and guarded their caravans, although he preferred to watch out for caravans on their principal toilsome routes, so as to plunder them, rather than to guard them.

The life of the tent-dwelling Arabs depended on unwritten rules, the observance of which virtually determined the existence or the death of the Bedouins. They were principles compulsory within the tribe as well as unwritten rules making possible the co-existence of the tribes in the desert. The Arab could not exist outside his tribe, his life was conditioned by the life of the tribe, which in a virtually unrestricted way disposed of people, livestock and property. Whoever transgressed the tribal laws was threatened with exclusion from the commonwealth, which was equivalent to death. The status of every Arab depended on strength, wealth and the number of his family in the tribe. The fathers of several sons enjoyed particular respect, being called wise and fortunate. The Bedouin would repeat with conviction: "That man is wise who can have as many children as he pleases—he is blessed by God." Wealth lay in having sons—the future warriors, elders, poets, sheikhs; on the other hand, the tent-dwellers treated the birth of a daughter as a burden—for women did not go to war, did not capture pasturage, and did not rob caravans. If warriors from another tribe killed a man, the law of revenge bade the tribe to which the dead man belonged to take a bloody revenge. At the source of the bloody revenge, besides emotional motives and feelings of solidarity, lay the longing to create conditions for existence in the desert. Fear of this revenge kept a brittle peace between quarrelsome tribes, a temporary equilibrium, and counteracted anarchy. The obligatory laws of bloody revenge and the idea of tribal solidarity were interwoven with the anxious preservation of an equilibrium of strength among the tribes.

On the limitless sands of the desert the unwritten laws forbade the destruction of trees and water cisterns, even where these were situated on territories occupied by an enemy tribe. In the desert lived the free people of Arabia, who, despite their mutual quarrels and disputes in an atmosphere of battle and tribal hatred, observed the principles that imposed respect for trees and the wells of the enemy. Hence arose a duty, respected by all, of hospitality. Every Arab regarded as sacred the compulsion to shelter a wanderer, even if he were his mortal enemy. The unwritten laws made the observance of peace among tribes for one-third of the year obligatory; for the duration of 4 months he abandoned the noise of war, the most quarrelsome tribes broke off their disputes, held markets, pilgrimages and religious rites. The life of the tribes then continued peacefully; the Arabs took off their armour, so as to go in pilgrim's robes to the holy places. For many centuries before Mohammed the Arabs journeyed to Mecca in the Hejaz province, a town which was a crossroads for the merchants' routes and the holy goal of the Arab pilgrims. There was to be found the famous shrine of the Kaaba which held a black stone venerated by all the Arab tribes. Near the Kaaba ran the sacred fountain Zamzan. The legends tell that originally the stone was white and even transparent, and that it was the sinful mouths of the pilgrims humbly kissing the stone which eventually gave it its black colour. The peace observed among the tribes for a time made possible universal pilgrimages to Mecca: belief in the miraculous stone for a short while united the disputants.

The Arabs of the south were different from the other Arabs in language, writing, beliefs and above all in their settled tribal life. From the tradition of the kingdom of Saba which existed until the tenth century B.C., and played an important role in the life of southern Arabia, they bore the name of Sabians. In their beliefs they gave life to the stars of the firmament, the sun and moon, paying them the adoration due to gods, turning to them with feelings of awe and hope, and erecting to these their gods shrines and altars.

In the rest of Arabia stones were venerated in addition to the star-gods cult, stirring the sensitive imagination of the nomads by their shape, while trees, springs, and streams were recognized as the homes of gods in the desert land.

A legend describes how the nomads of a tribe offered their own children on altars to their gods, and how Mohammed abolished a terrible ritual which permitted the burial in sand of new-born daughters, that they might not suck the milk intended for boys. In the pantheon of Arab gods the three daughters of Allah, al-Lat, al-Uzza and al-Manat, had the most venerated position and enjoyed the most general worship. It was their cult that Mohammed fought against, gradually and over a long period of time.[3]

Before Mohammed the Arabic language united the divided tribes to an even greater degree than the pilgrimages to the Kaaba. The beliefs of the tribes were too disparate for the cult of the black stone of Mecca to unite them. This task was to a certain extent performed by poetry. The wild tribes were connected by the words of songs and poetry, which, as it were, lorded it over the desert. With their feeling for fine words, their sound and substance, the Arabs formed a language of rare richness. The Arab knew and loved to use rich language in which he might express many shades and nuances of meaning; for designating his comrade in his wanderings, the camel, or for naming a sword, he had over a 100 synonyms. He greatly appreciated eloquence, believing in the power and efficacy of the word. The Arabs compared utterances spoken rhythmically to pearls strung on a cord, while they compared the speaking of prose to scattered pearls. According to Arab ideas the poor man worthy of sympathy was he to whom nature had denied the gift of speech. The simple Bedouin woman taught her children to glorify speech, for language was to this people of the desert the greatest gift of God, a sacred treasure. One of the oldest Arabic poems says: "God in His goodness gave the Arab four treasures: the simple turban, which serves him as a crown, the tent, more comfortable than an apartment in a palace, the sword, which replaces for him the highest wall; and lastly God gave the Arab as the fourth gift heaven's greatest treasure, poetry and song."

Poetry in particular was held in great esteem among the Arabs, the poet being regarded as a person gifted with superhuman knowledge. The poetic pathos, play on words, and literary vision suited these desert folk, and thus to everyday speech they brought the phrases and comparisons of the poets. The form of Arab lyric poetry, the *kasida*, had already become fixed 100 years before Mohammed. These poems were divided into three parts: in the first the poet described the erotic feelings of the Arab in love, in the second he praised the road to the town of the beloved, describing here the beauty and terror of the desert, and in the third part he praised or accused the tribe of the person to whom the *kasida* was dedicated. The poet was regarded as the fame and pride of the tribe. Every year in Okaz meetings of the tribes took place which lasted a month, and during this time the poets competed for the champion's palm. The poem chosen as the best was put into the Kaaba beside the seven famous poems—the golden verses (*Mu'allakat*).

For many centuries life in Arabia did not change. In the deep lonely desert, which no army of riders reached, intertribal warfare took place. The word "Kaaba" and its cult were too weak to unite the scattered tribes, deprived of a strong political and religious tie. It was at length in the sixth century, when Arabia became decidedly isolated from mediation in intercontinental business, which brought about a marked weakening of the economy, and this at the same time created objective reasons in support of the concept of unity of the Arab tribes. At that time the differences between the nomadic and the settled Arabs became sharper; within the town the economic difficulties affected the poorer families above all, among whom arose a feeling of hatred and jealousy of the rich; at length antagonism arose and developed against the economic background between the Arab and Jewish merchants. (There were many Jews who had found shelter in various towns on the Peninsula after the fall of Jerusalem.)

Various occurrences, for tens and hundreds of years, had prepared the economic situation of Arabia in the sixth century. The Roman emperors, particularly Augustus, had tried to destroy Arab trade, removing the Yemen from the dominating position in trade with India. Elius Galius, regent of Egypt, undertook in this connection an expedition to southern Arabia, which ended in the utter defeat of the Roman expedition. The trade position of Arabia Felix began to weaken from the second century, for the Romans managed to link up the sea trade-routes to India without resorting to the desert convoys. From the fourth century the economic situation grew even worse, for at this time invasions of the Ethiopian armies devastated south-western districts of the Peninsula, trade fell away and the settler-people left the destroyed area and wandered to the north. In the year 570 the Persian armies controlled south-western Arabia and the Yemen, driving out the invaders. The new rulers were interested in the absolute limitation of the Arab trade, and the Persian merchants had the chance to get rid of their rivals. When the Persian armies entered the Yemen, Mohammed was born, and Arabia entered a difficult economic period.

2. THE PROPHET AND HIS DOCTRINE

From the earliest times the object generally venerated by the Arabs was the black stone at Mecca. The shrine built for it was in the form of a great cube called the Kaaba, of which Diodorus Siculus speaks half a century before the birth of Christ, saying it was the most well-known and the oldest of all shrines. Combating its natural surroundings, far from the sea, amid bare and barren hills, forced to bring in food for its inhabitants, lay Mecca, the heart of Arabia. Not only religious motives, but also earthly impulses inclined people to visit Mecca. Here the caravan route, leading from north to south, to the Yemen, crossed the road from the south going north-west towards Syria. The sacred stone at the crossroads of the trade routes added lustre to Mecca, which was first and foremost a market-town, a mid-point for the great trade between India and the West. Besides the merchants pious pilgrims made their way to Mecca, known as "the mother of towns". The tribe exercising power in Mecca was the political power in Arabia, thanks to the key position of the town both from a business and religious point of view. From the fifth century Mecca had been in the hands of the Koreishite tribe, which for scores of years maintained its rule in the holy town. The richest families, to which the Omayyads belonged who were later to produce the successors of Mohammed, directed this tribe. The families formed organizational units in the town, exercised authority over their members, pursued their separate interests, had their households in common, and their influence and significance was estimated by the distance of their homes from the Kaaba. Thus the richest merchants, living in the Batha district, near the Kaaba, in fact ruled Mecca. The town also had its tribal political institution (*Mala*)—a council which included all male inhabitants of Mecca over the age of 40, and whose work was to decide on matters of common interest. Twice every year the inhabitants organized a great trade caravan; those taking part brought in more than 100% profit. For almost 6 months there were several thousand camels outside Mecca, guarded by several hundred armed inhabitants. Mecca was a sacred aristocratic republic, supported by blood ties. According to the ideas of the townsmen, prosperity and the business of the town were linked with the traditional beliefs, multiplicity of gods, the Kaaba pilgrimages; thus they had to maintain a somewhat sceptical attitude towards the Jewish and Christian merchants discussing their own religion and god. Those who doubted the prevailing creed and the value of the temporal laws left Mecca. Hanifs, sceptics seeking truth, met in the desert, and expressed the growing religious unrest of the Arabs in the time of Mohammed.

Through the mists of legend the face of the creator of a new politico-religious doctrine can be seen, drawn in blurred outline; here fantasy is interwoven with truth, facts with the pious intention of his followers. It seems his name was Kutam, one of the many members of the Koreishite tribe, and that till he was a grown man there was nothing peculiarly distinctive about him. Precise in business, provident, observant of the obligatory ritual, the inhabitants of Mecca called him "Respectable", "Worshipful"—Mohammed, which suited him very well, so much so that he gladly used this designation in place of his former name. We do not know the exact date of Mohammed's birth; it is accepted that he saw the light of day in 570 in Mecca, lost his parents very early and was put under the care of first his grandfather and later his uncle Abu-Talib. He grew up in the business atmosphere of Mecca, lived his merchant's life, accompanied caravans on journeys to Syria and Abyssinia and got to know new people, their customs and beliefs. The journeys to Syria had an influence on his spiritual development; the sensitive and lively nature of Mohammed actively responded to the fabulous aspect of monotheistic beliefs. It seems, however, that the proofs taught by the Christian and Jewish theologians were hardly accessible to this practical Arab merchant, who was not blessed with the ability to write.[4]

At the age of twenty Mohammed undertook the handling of the business affairs of the rich widow Khadija, some years later marrying her and becoming a respectable and rich inhabitant of Mecca. It was as a grown man that he voiced his new politico-religious doctrine, believing that he personified several prophets of whom the Jewish religion had spoken. In the loneliness of the mountain valleys not far from Mecca, where he had gone to give full rein to his nervous and sickly imagination, the 40-year-old merchant felt himself called by God to save the Arab nation from evil and ruin. Hallucinations became, for him, evidence of a divine calling, bringing at times conversations with God and angels. Mohammed's contact with Jewish, Christian and Persian beliefs helped in the formation of his outlook, for a characteristic of the Arab prophet was the eclectic combination of various religious impressions, with which he had met on his mercantile travels. The Christian and Jewish creeds particularly influenced Mohammed's doctrine.[5]

Mohammed did not at once have a finished politico-religious doctrine; at first he was more of a moralizer and not a political reformer.[6] Neither did he at once come into conflict with the compulsory tradition, even yielding in the matter of plurality of gods; for a time he tolerated the cult of the three goddesses known as al-Lat, al-Uzza, and al-Manat, the supposed daughters of Allah (a cult rooted in Mecca); soon, however, he started to preach a radical monotheism.

At first tolerated in Mecca for 10 years by his relations, he branded with words the evil and corruption of his fellow countrymen. His speeches were angry and inflammatory and in them he threatened sinners with the Last Judgement, promising the devout the reward of Paradise. He painted in violent colours the end of the world, the Last Judgement, the cruel fate of those who disregarded their prophets and strayed from the one God. He ordered the Arabs to break with their cults and beliefs, to give up such customs as the killing of their daughters—he branded this as frightful barbarism (*Jahilija*).[7]

The moralizing tone characteristic of the Prophet could not convince the sober merchants of Mecca, but it provoked the opposition of those who saw in the criticism of traditional beliefs economic danger for the town. If he had not belonged to the powerful Koreishite tribe, Mohammed would have had to put an end quickly to his missionary career. However, the moralizing prophet and the inconsiderable number of his followers were tolerated, perhaps so as not to start an intratribal quarrel and disputes.

In the thirteenth year of his mission, reaching his fiftieth year, after the death of his wife Khadija and uncle Abu-Talib, he left Mecca with a few followers to settle in Yathrib. It was A.D. 622, the year of the famous flight (*Hijra*) of Mohammed, from which Muslims begin their calendar.[8] Scorned by his fellow-countrymen, he left his native town to go to Yathrib, a town about 400 km to the north of Mecca, to find a lively welcome. There he was treated as an opposer of the mercantile oligarchy in Mecca. The Jews especially gave him warm support, seeing in Mohammed a man whose mission was linked with their beliefs.

The inhabitants of Yathrib, who gave support to the Prophet (who had been so far unlucky) and his followers, called their town the fortress of the Prophet: Medina en-Nabi—Medina for short. It had been a former Jewish colony dependent on the Aus and Khazraj tribes. Against the background of trade, antagonism between Mecca and Medina developed, and within the town differences between Jews and Arabs showed themselves of which Mohammed skilfully took advantage.

One of his first public actions in Medina was the preparation of a legal agreement between Arabs and Jews. Soon the prophet became omnipotent in Medina and 10 years later the ruler of Arabia. His word, supported by the sword, now persuaded the robber tribes that the time was ripe for the uniting of the scattered tribes quarrelling among themselves, in the name of the mono-theism preached by Mohammed. In these new conditions the substance of his revelation was changed, and he now spoke like a statesman knowing his own strength and problems. "God has sent various prophets", said Moham-med. "Moses possessed the grace of Providence, Solomon wisdom and glory, Jesus righteousness, omniscience and power . . . . And what was the use of it? The miracles of Moses and Jesus were not believed. So I, the last of God's prophets, am sent with His sword. Let not my followers meddle in quarrels with infidels, let their stubbornness be broken by the sword. Whoever fights for his creed, whether he fails or wins, will receive a wonderful reward." Faithful to the Prophet, the refugees from Mecca united with the inhabitants of Medina under the concept of brotherhood, a concept which is, according to the words of Mohammed, stronger than true blood-ties. "Those who be-lieved and fled from their country, risking their lives and property, and fought for their faith, will be joined closer than blood-relations with those who gave shelter to the Prophet" (VIII. 75). The refugees from Mecca, familiar with the business secrets of their native town, undertook merchants' business in Medina, sometimes resorting to the sword in the fight with their rival. Mo-hammed's believers robbed the Meccan caravans, plundered the rich Jewish colonies and broke the ancient laws of the desert, calling their fights "God's business". Besides religious motives, there was a noticeable longing to enrich themselves on the part of the followers of the new doctrine. We know that the close companion of Mohammed, Zubair, as a result of business transactions and wars, left property worth 50 million dirhems (a dirhem is three grams of silver); and another friend of the Prophet, one of the most faithful believers, Talha, accumulated property worth more than 30 million dirhems. Just as in Mecca family affairs were intertwined with traditional beliefs, so in Medina the followers of Mohammed, independent of blood-ties, could combine their material affairs with the new religious doctrine.

In the year 624, by the stream called Badr, 300 followers of the Prophet defeated three times as many warriors of the Koreishite tribe. During this battle Mohammed encouraging his followers in the fight, shouted: "Fight! Fear not! The gates of Paradise are in the shadow of the sword! He who can reliably fight for his faith will infallibly taste the delights of Heaven". The victory made Mohammed and his followers into a political power which the Prophet's temporary defeats and lack of success could not now weaken.[9]

After many struggles Mohammed made himself master of his native town and in March A.D. 632 performed his last solemn pilgrimage to the Kaaba. A few months later the Prophet died.

Mohammed's personality must have been full of contradictions and very complex: sensual, oversensitive, uncontrolled, regarding himself as God's elect, he combined these characteristics at the same time with great realism, and sobriety of behaviour. His mode of life, of which his followers speak with such devotion, compels us to see in Mohammed a man who experienced great hardships, and who was capable of self-denial—a man who had to patch his shoes and coat with his own hands. At the same time the Prophet was prone to human weaknesses, notably susceptibility to women. This he justified by saying it was a privilege accorded him by God. "O Prophet!" we read in the Koran, "it is permitted to you to take as your wives the slaves who have been given dowry by you, and who fell into your hands; the daughters of your mother's brothers and sisters, as well as your cousins on your father's side, who followed you and every woman believer who consecrates her heart to you. This is a privilege bestowed upon you" (XXXIII. 49).

There is no doubt about his great individuality. He knew, as no one else, how to express in his doctrine and actions the longings of the eloquent and restless Arab tribes, those longings which, in the moving utterances of the Prophet, could be expanded on a firm foundation.

Islam was not at once a complete body of religio-political doctrine—it changed and was tempered in the fire of the practical activity of the Prophet and his successors.

Mohammed was already convinced in Mecca that thanks to divine grace he had emerged from the darkness of ignorance and penetrated all secrets. Therefore he announced with the deepest conviction that there is one great God: there is nothing as great outside Him; one ought to give oneself unreservedly to Him, whatever destiny He might ordain for man. He taught: "God is great—Allah akbar, and to Him complete and unlimited surrender should be made—islam." Throughout the centuries since Mohammed's time, every Arab has repeated several times daily in war or peace: "Away with other gods! There is no god but Allah, and Mohammed is his Prophet."[10]

In Mohammedan doctrine the fatalistic command to surrender to divine necessity, linked with the idea of monotheism, had already become the substantial meaning of Islam in the period of Mecca, although it was only in Medina that Islam at length formed itself into an institution and an organization of warriors. The modest prophet of yesterday, scorning temporal affairs, mocked at by the merchants of Mecca, organized in Medina armed expeditions, laid down the rules for dividing the plunder, dealt with problems of ownership, inheritance and family affairs—in a word, the whole life of the community of the faithful—in an orderly manner. His decisions, sayings, verdicts, handed down by tradition from the time of his stay in Medina, were to become (besides the Koran) the model and basis for future regulation of intercourse in the great Arab state.

The Koran, the holy book of Islam, in which are put together the chief Mohammedan religio-political ideals, reflects the changes in outlook which took place in Medina. Over a period of 23 years Mohammed dictated the sacred book in fragments, in various situations and environments, convinced all the time that the Koran was a divine manifestation revealed to the people through his medium.[11] In the book the lively reactions of the emotional nature of the Prophet to various happenings can be felt—those happenings caused by his own stormy life. Among the ideas crowding in tedious disorder can be separated the logically developed idea of monotheism which was to unite the Arabs. The Koran is considered a model of Arab style, experts holding that it is written with the utmost elegance and purity in the dialect of the Koreishite tribe. A considerable portion of the book has a musicality and rhythm completely untranslatable. It is divided into 114 chapters (sur) in which the pronouncements of the Prophet are collected. The fact that the order of the chapters depended on their length meant that the most extensive are at the beginning and the least at the end. The longer utterances of the Prophet derive from the time of his stay in Medina, when he ruled the town and afterwards the whole of Arabia. For this reason the sur of Medina are put at the beginning of the Koran. In the sur of Mecca feverish vision can be perceived, the emotional atmosphere of the fanatic communicating to his hearers convictions of the greatness of God, His infinite power, and the end of the world. In the sur of Medina, however, we rather sense the tone of a thoughtful statesman, who, conscious of his strength, announces to his warriors and submissive hearers that his words create the principles behind the temporal organization set up for his followers.

The religious doctrine of Islam depends on five basic principles which were given their final form in Medina. First and foremost Islam requires the believer to recognize one god, and Mohammed as his prophet. The second religious canon is the duty of reading the Koran, the repetition several times daily of prayers preceded by washing the body and performed with carefully outlined movements and gestures—in a word, the rigorous observance of the ritualistic duty. The third principle, which is at the root of Mohammed's religious doctrines, calls on the believer to give alms; this was first conceived as a free-will gift. In time, freely-given alms were distinguished from obligatory: the first were given to the poor according to one's own ideas on the subject, the second were paid compulsorily to the state. Thus the idea of alms became tax (zakat) and constituted 2·5% of the movable and immovable property of the Muslim. The zakat was not only treated as the means of support for the poor but as a reward for those defending the faith, and was also used for the other needs of the state. The fourth principle of Islam is the duty of observing the fasts, especially in the ninth lunar month of the year, called Ramadan. Finally, the last religious canon is the duty of making a pilgrimage to Mecca. In these basic principles of Islam, elements from various creeds may be observed. The prayer ritual and fasting derives from Judaism and Christianity, pilgrimage to the Kaaba from pre-Mohammedan Arab tradition; the sabbath was abolished according to Persian custom, with the establishment of communal ceremonies on Friday for the faithful, after which the Arabs returned to their ordinary occupations.

The religious principles of Islam noticeably penetrate the political ideas, for Mohammed had to wage a real war to gain recognition for his mission. Fighting and victory are the means and end of his religious activity. Mohammed's God is not only full of love (*vadud*) but he is simultaneously the god of war, ruthless and cunning. All the political ideals of the Prophet are reflected in the attributes of the Arab God. Mohammed's God insists on constant battle, faith, and the unrestricted surrender of the self to Him and the Prophet. At the same time the justification of all methods for the destruction of an opposition permits fraud, intrigue, and lying; indeed waging a war, as old Arab proverbs say, is continuous trickery. The Almighty, the powerful God of Islam, who determined in advance the fate of the world, things and people, expects humility, unity, and battle with the infidels from the faithful. The Prophet, in the pages of the Koran, says, "O God, King of Kings! Thou givest and takest away crowns according to Thy will, Thou raisest and lowerest the things of the people as Thou pleasest; wealth lies within Thy hands. Thou art all-powerful" (III. 25). "Thou changest night into day and day into night; Thou bringest life from the bosom of death and death from the bosom of life; Thou pourest out infinite treasures upon those who please Thee" (III. 26). Accordingly: "Believe in God and His Prophet! Fight beneath the standards of the holy faith, make wonderful sacrifices of your lives and fortunes! That way lies happiness for you . . . O, if you but knew this truly" (LXI. 11). "Obey God and His Prophet, fear lest discord hath not taken away your courage. Be persevering. God is with those who preserve their endurance in sufferings" (VIII. 48). "Faithful, curb your curiosity. The knowledge of things, that you wish for, may harm you; try to ask for those things which are shown you in the Koran, they will be discovered unto you" (V. 101). In the doctrine of Islam the Arabs are regarded as chosen people called to a total war with infidels. "You are the chosen people of the world, be obedient, eschew your transgressions, and believe in God" (III. 106). "God loves those who fight in battle order for the faith and are like a steady wall" (LX. 4). "Young and old, go ye to war, consecrate your lives and fortunes in the defence of the faith, there is nothing more worthy of you than united service . . ." (IX. 41). "Kill the enemies of your faith wherever you meet them . . ." (II. 187). "If they fall on you in the holy month and in holy places, use your right to retaliate; let their laws be broken by you, since they do not observe any towards you . . ." (II. 190). "If you die or are killed defending the Faith, remember that divine compassion means more than the riches you collected on earth and left behind" (III. 151).

The severe command for total war on infidels is not in conflict with the principle of tolerance and liberality towards them, if when conquered they loyally recognize the authority of the followers of Islam and pay tribute.[12] The combating of the infidels had as its goal not so much conversion as the spread of Islamic influence and the submission of the unbelievers. Says the Prophet in the Koran: "You are to uphold faithfully any alliance with the infidels so long as they do not break it nor give help to your enemies against you . . ." (IX. 4) "Exterminate those who do not believe in God and the Last Day, unless they pay tribute with their own hands and become completely submissive" (IX. 29).

The God of Mohammed insisted on unity among the Arabs but at the same time he recognized the existence of social inequalities due to the difference in material possessions among the faithful. "Do not strive to be the equal of him whom God has placed above you; each will reap his harvest according to his own deeds . . ." (IV. 8). "Cut off the hands of thieves, men or women, as punishment for their crime; this is a punishment such as God has destined for them, He is mighty and wise" (V. 42). They say that Mohammed was asked to pardon a theft committed by a young Arab, and said "We do what the sacred law commands us. If my favourite daughter Fatima took one thread secretly from one of you, I swear before God that her hand would be cut off." Anxious about possible haughtiness and too dazzling material differences, the Prophet ordered care for the poor to be provided from the compulsory religious alms. Questioned on the most important thing in Islam he replied "The most important thing is to feed the hungry . . . . No one will find himself in heaven who has harmed his neighbour." It seems that after the death of the Prophet, when differences of wealth among the followers of Islam were more powerfully disrupting unity, humanitarianism and compassion were to put an end to this process. Then the teachings of the Prophet were applied to the disputants. Abu Warr, one of those distinguished in the circle about Mohammed, said "My friend Mohammed gave me seven precepts: (1) Love the poor and live close to them. (2) Always have an eye for those beneath you and do not look on those above you. (3) Never ask for anything from anybody. (4) Be true to your relations even when they anger you. (5) Always speak the truth even if it is bitter. (6) When fighting for God's purposes do not let yourself be discouraged by the contempt of scoffers. (7) Repeat the words from the divine treasury, that there is no power or strength greater than that of Allah." This same Abu Warr also said, in the name of the Prophet: "Gold and silver collected for an unfruitful end will be a burning coal for the possessor." The call for compassion, however, did not have an influence on the widening rifts between the faithful on the question of property.

For full knowledge of the doctrines of Islam, knowledge of the Koran does not suffice, as the substance of the holy book changed even in Mohammed's lifetime: he modified his viewpoint in accordance with new situations, referring this to the will of God. When Islam reached beyond the confines of the Arab world, the Koran was not enough. Then the sayings and decisions of the Prophet that had been handed down by tradition were referred to, and were re-formed or even created for the needs of current policy. The successors of Mohammed had to solve practical problems resulting from the world-wide spread of Islam. In the fatherland as well as in conquered lands the formulation of the principles of government had to be appropriate to the new problems.[13] Life called for the regulation of the politico-economic situation of the victorious and the vanquished, the more so as the Arabs had formed closed social groups in the conquered lands for some time. The highest authority that could be invoked for the solution of current problems could only be the will of the Prophet. This was therefore called to mind by those who had lived in the Prophet's circle, seen his behaviour, heard his words and decisions. In time when the companions of Mohammed died, their family tradition (*hadith*) handed on the sacred customs of the Prophet (*sunna*).[14] In this way, besides the Koran, the basis for the construction of rules of procedure was custom (*sunna*), the significance of which is shown by the words of Ali, said to one of the leaders dealing with rebellious clans: "Do not fight them with the words of the Koran, because the book may be variously interpreted and has many meanings. Rather use the arguments of the *sunna* and they will not have a leg to stand on." Tradition was a wonderful way to disentangle the doctrines of Islam, a path meandering among ideas of Greek philosophy, Indian and Persian thought and even principles of Roman jurisprudence. *Hadith* made possible the development of new outlooks and opinions even if unsupported by facts. The Arabs make use of a fiction in all seriousness and with full knowledge, referring beforehand to the words of the Prophet: "When I am gone the number of sayings ascribed to me will increase, as is the case with former prophets who are credited with many sayings they actually never uttered. Thus, when anyone refers to my words, check them in the divine book and if they agree with it, then they are my words, in fact it will be all the same whether I actually did say them or not." Only in the third century after Mohammed's death was a codification of the sacred customs attempted. In A.D. 870 the collection of Buchari was published, in A.D. 875 Muslim's collection, and in 888 Abu Dawud's collection appeared. Independent of the elastic attitude of tradition there developed a loose interpretation of the texts in which new material appeared, which enabled legal formulae suitable for the new social intercourse to be made; Roman jurisprudence was not without influence on the law-making activities of the followers of Islam.

In the political doctrine of Mohammed two tendencies can be delineated: the first is the effort to unite the warring Arab tribes, the second the struggle to establish order in the world. The second tendency persevered with the growth of influence and strength. "Allah speaks as the lord of the whole world" (*rabb al-allamin*): these words repeated in the Koran contain the seeds of the future policy of conquest. We know that Mohammed before his death already demanded the recognition of his doctrines by Byzantium and Persia, convinced of Islam's role in the world.[15]

3. ARAB EXPANSION

The economic difficulties of Arabia—which had ceased to play its intermediary role in trade at the beginning of the seventh century—were reflected in the organization of life in Mecca. The sharp differences in prosperity among the inhabitants of the holy town, the pressure of the nomadic tribes on the settled population and the bitter rivalry between the different places of business contributed to the strengthening of the authority of aristocratic families in the town.

While in Mecca, Mohammed was not yet interested in authority. His one aim was to smooth away the suffering and injustice inflicted on the poor: he appealed for help for the destitute, alms for their use, yet at the same time he considered private property and slavery to be divinely authorized institutions. The situation underwent a complete change in Medina—there the Prophet thoughtfully, skilfully and consistently managed to obtain the reins of government; there the first contours of the future state emerged. On the town lands a theocratic government was set up over the people who professed the Islamic faith. Mohammed cleverly took advantage, for his own ends and to the profit of the exiles from Mecca, of the hostility existing in the town between Arabs and Jews, nomads and townsmen; he adroitly removed the conflicts between the immigrant population, that had come with him from Mecca, and the established inhabitants.

In Medina, Mohammed was at first merely the leader of a religious movement, but although he had no authority, the townspeople had to remember his position; this was fairly powerful, since he was surrounded by emigrants from Mecca, the faithful (*muhadjirun*) who had been tried in suffering and battle, who had moreover left their native town and followed the Prophet to share his fortune whether good or ill. In Medina they were obliged to keep close together, lest they be oppressed by the clannish organization of the town—an organization to which the only right of entry was blood-relationship. Since they did not belong to the clan community, the emigrants created their own religio-militarist commonwealth, which was directed by Allah through the person of Mohammed. Their merchants' lore, which they had brought from business in Mecca, served them well, quickly putting them into an important position economically. Tradition hands down a tale from this time, which characterizes the economic enterprise of the emigrants. When a poor exile from Mecca met, for the first time, his rich friend from Medina, who was willing to come to his aid with material help, the exile let fall these words: "O best of friends, only show me the way to the market place, I'll take care of the rest myself." The story runs that the man from Mecca soon took an active part in business and became a powerful figure.

Gradually the townspeople, as well as the emigrants, began to assemble round Mohammed. By contrast with the emigrants (*muhadjirun*) they were called the converts of the Prophet (*ansar*). The greater part were young people eager for adventure and quick profits, who without opposition recognized the authority of their new lord. The attainment of unity among the believers must have been Mohammed's chief problem; indeed among the adherents of the Prophet in Medina, who were composed of emigrants and townspeople, tribal differences and regional antagonisms caused divisions of such a kind that, under the outward appearance of a common faith, former antipathies were finding voice. The new politico-religious structure created by Mohammed could not fit into the traditional system of clannish organization. His efforts to make the converts in the town take the exiles from Mecca into their families proved fruitless. Mohammed then attempted to unite his adherents by the idea of brotherhood, and the commonwealth of their creed, interests and struggles, which were to show themselves stronger than blood-ties and hinder the process, which was then going on, of the creating of a class society in the country. Mohammed formed a united disciplined army of the faithful, ready for anything, to oppose those who stood against him. He then possessed full power in the town, and felt himself to be the unrestricted lord of the new theocratic republic, in which all followers of Islam had full civic rights. The Prophet, in the name of God, decided on matters of war and peace, judged, pronounced, urged the ransoming of fellow-believers from slavery, commanded alms-giving so that there should be no paupers among the faithful. The doctrine of Islam demanded mutual help, as well as an unquestioning obedience to the orders of the Prophet. In creating his religio-political structure, Mohammed left the family the right to punish private transgressions and guaranteed protection to unbelievers at the price of recognizing his law and paying tribute. But whoever opposed Islam and rebelled against the sacred law lost all protection, even from his own family. Making his new rules for living, Mohammed loosened the chains of the clannish system, unaware that he was the man in whom the objective development of Arabia was mirrored, and that Arabia had gone beyond the early stage of merely clannish unions.[16] Mohammed did not meddle much in family and tribal affairs, leaving them to the traditional laws of custom (*adat*). But at the same time he strove to regulate the whole private and public life of his followers according to the precepts of the holy law (*sari'a*). In practice, Islam penetrated every aspect of the life of the faithful; *sari'a* contained defined norms as well as problems of belief, and thus principles of property law, family law, inheritance, norms of punishment, and it regulated the duties and obligations of servants and masters; in a word, it decided on the destiny of the faithful on earth and in the future life. In Mohammed's theocratic republic, if we leave out inequality caused by the possession of property, all the faithful were equal in the sight of God; they were dependent on the same standards. They paid taxes at an identical rate and fulfilled the same obligations. However, the unbelievers who were loyal to Islam, and enjoyed full toleration provided they paid taxes, were freed from the duty of fighting for Allah. Islam brought unity to the Arab tribes, giving the free Arabs the rules of the divine law and fiscal and military discipline simultaneously. Alms were now given regularly in the form of taxes, the commands of the Prophet were fulfilled, holy wars were supported by all, and the necessary rites and prayers were performed. As the authority of Islam spread, the country was already, in the lifetime of Mohammed, divided into parts where the closest companions of the Prophet, whose endurance had been proved and whom war had tried, represented his authority. Mohammed himself, at the head of the state, felt that an earthly government ought to put into practice the divine calling of Islam; he thought that God alone is the unrestricted lord of the state, while the Prophet only filled the role of mediator for the divine manifestations. Conscious of his divine mission, he turned to contemporary rulers, to have them acknowledge Islam. The reaction of the ruler of Persia, Chosroes II, to Mohammed's letter was courageous. In a fit of anger he sent the following to his governor in the Yemen: "I hear there is a madman in Medina giving himself out to be a prophet. Bring him to his senses, and if this does not help, send me his head." However, the Emperor Heraclius treated the message rather better, since he gave liberal presents to the messengers of the barbarian prophet, heaping politenesses on his strange proposition.

After Mohammed's death Arabia experienced fierce upheavals, many tribes breaking their links with Medina, and the tendency to self-rule (*ridda*) much weakened the unity of the state.[17] Besides this, many prophets appeared, all endeavouring to step into Mohammed's shoes. Confusion became worse as the Prophet had not forseen any way of finding a successor; only the enterprise of Abu Bekr, and especially Omar, made possible the normal running of the state. Abu Bekr became the successor of the Prophet, and after his 2-year rule he was followed by Omar in A.D. 634. During Omar's 10-year period in office the formation of Arabia into a great nation took place. The idea of Islam became the watchword for organizing all the Arabs into aggressive warfare.[18] The conversion of infidels was not the concern of the followers of Islam; their aim was expansion, the conquest of the rich territories of their neighbours. For scores of years the dynamic Arab tribes had spent their energies in internecine feuds, but the sallies of certain strictly frontier tribes had for long threatened the borders of Persia and Byzantium. The domestic economic troubles of Arabia made it imperative to unite the scattered tribes; Islam did this, giving, for some years after Mohammed's death, unprecedented power and authority to its followers. Islam became a power for order and organizing the elemental movements of the nomadic tribes, which lived in a state of permanent readiness for war.[19]

Wisdom and knowledge had decided the election of a successor to the Prophet. However, the relationship with Mohammed had not been taken into consideration. In this way the courageous Ali, married to the Prophet's daughter Fatima, and his sons Hassan and Hussein, the grandsons of the Prophet, were ignored. The procedure of the election of a caliph, while ignoring blood-ties, began endless religio-political disputes among the Arabs. However, the first successors of the Prophet showed themselves to be men who had grown mature enough to direct the forces of liberation through their experience in Islam. They finished the fight with *ridda*, bringing order to the rebellious tribes. They began a systematic conquest of neighbouring states, created frameworks for the organization of Muslim power, choosing educated chiefs and administrators for the running of the state. In the first battles of conquest the unrivalled military genius of Khalid ibn al-Walid shone forth —he threw in Arab divisions with unheard-of speed, surprised the enemy, and cut into the opposition at its weakest points. He besieged the town of Hira in Iraq with scarcely 3,000 volunteers from central Arabia, and after extorting 60,000 dirhems withdrew his divisions like lightning to Syria, which more than anywhere else lay within the caliphs' sphere of interest. The Arabs brought off fine victories in Syria against the Byzantine armies, occupied Damascus, and took over the whole country finally from A.D. 636–8. The conquerors, since they respected the customs and religious beliefs of the indigenous population, were everywhere welcomed as the swordsmen of freedom, which gave them advantage over the armies of the Byzantine rulers and Persian satraps, who brought religious, fiscal and political oppression with them. The Arabs did not give civil power to their victorious generals in the conquered lands; contrary to expectations, Omar did not appoint the heroic Ibn Walid to the regency in Syria, but the experienced politician Abu-Obaid. The third governor of Syria was Muawiya ibn Abi Sufiyan, later chief representative of the Omayyad dynasty. In principle, conquered Syria kept her former institutions, both political and legal, and the town-dwellers enjoyed self-government by merely paying their taxes regularly. But the Arabs living in conquered territories preserved their religious, political and legal differences, thus becoming an exclusive, aristocratic group. After A.D. 630 the Arab armies defeated the Persian armies and took all of Mesopotamia. The fertile land of Iraq lay open to the followers of Islam, and the town of Ktesiphon surrendered, whose treasures had enticed the imaginations of the sons of the desert. However, after the capture of Iraq the seat of central and military government was Kufa—a military camp, for the caliphs feared lest the eastern luxuries demoralize the victorious armies. Besides Kufa, the second military centre on the Euphrates was the camp in the town of Basra. Almost at the same time, in A.D. 640, the swift conquest of Egypt began, the experienced strategist Amr ibn al-Asi being at the head of the Arab troops. Similarly, after the fall of Alexandria in A.D. 642 the caliphs put into action their policy of military isolation; the victorious soldiers were to erect a camp like that in Kufa, on the eastern shores of the Nile. It bore the name *Phostat* after the Greek word Φόσσατο. As in Syria, the governor of the conquered land was the politician and financier Abdallah ibn S'ad and not the conqueror. The first caliphs kept these leaders away from the government of the conquered lands; the army, separated from the civil administration and concentrated at special points, formed the real strength in the occupied territories.

To control the Mediterranean basin, the militarists from Syria and Egypt went on to build a fleet, so that in the second half of the seventh century the Arabs had considerable sea power, which was a threat from the sea to Byzantium.

When in a foreign country the Arabs were subject to the sacred law of Islam; they might buy land, profiting by freedom from taxes. From the time of Omar onwards, they invariably received soldiers' pay; thus the religious duty of sharing in war received material compensation. It appears that Omar had his own ideas on organization for the conquered territories; he treated Islam as a religious doctrine for Arabs, and, while treating the conquered peoples with the utmost toleration, made his Arabs into a privileged aristocracy.[20] He was unable to form any newly organized apparatus of government but continued to uphold the existing system, and was particularly interested in fiscal problems. In the style of the Romans and Persians he set up treasury offices, permanent accountancy and inspection and finally an exchequer for the whole country. In the captured lands of Syria, Persia, Iraq, and Egypt the Muslims came into contact with the spirit of Hellenistic culture. The conquered lands had long been used to political organization and the population of the towns helped to raise the level of knowledge and standard of living of the conquerors. The first caliphs found ready-made political and legal institutions on the conquered territories, and took high taxes from the indigenous population without troubling about their beliefs or way of life. In time the people were converted to Islam, to rid themselves of taxes and enjoy all the privileges of their conquerors.

With the death of Omar, murdered in 644 by a Persian slave, began the nepotic rule of Caliph Othman who put members of the Omayyad family into all the possible important positions. After Othman's death quarrels occurred between the followers of the Omayyads, at whose head was the remarkable and skilful administrator of Syria, Muawiya, and their opponents grouped around the person of Ali, the Prophet's son-in-law. Thanks to his cunning policy Muawiya achieved the caliphate in A.D. 660, while Ali died

6 months later, murdered in Kufa. Ali had been the most important candidate for the caliphate. Ali's son, Hussein, died 20 years later in the battle of Kerbel, near Kufa, becoming a symbol of the martyrdom of all who had fought for the Prophet's family and its claims to power. In Muawiya's time, Syria became the heart of the Arab state, and Damascus its capital, where for nearly 100 years the government was to be carried on by the Omayyad dynasty. The rulers of this clan treated Islam as a political tool, useful for uniting the Arabs, and simultaneously giving them world power. The opponents of the Omayyads were the orthodox believers of Mohammed, who regarded the leaders of Islam as usurpers; they thought the Omayyads followed Satan's wishes rather than God's.

Internal strife over the government did not, however, prevent the Arabs from furthering their conquests. In the middle of the seventh century, the Arab fleet gradually gained control of the Mediterranean, pillaged Cyprus, Crete, Rhodes, and, although at first without success, attacked Byzantium. The conquest of northern Africa, carried out at this time, met, at first, the resistance of the Berber tribes, which the Arabs shortly won over to Islam so that they might strike a blow together at Spain. In 711, Muslims, led by Tarik, landed on the shores of Spain, near the rock which today still bears the name of the Arab leader, Gibraltar—Gabal al Tariq. In 718 the Arabs crossed the Pyrenees, beginning systematic sorties on the land on the other side; they were stopped only by a defeat inflicted on them by the army of Charles Martel at Tours and Poitiers in 732. The victorious advance of the Arabs in the west was checked largely by the fact that bitter antagonism had flared up between the Berbers and the Arabs in the army. The Arabs had tried to maintain an ascendancy over their comrades-in-arms from North Africa, although they too had embraced Islam. At the same time Arabs in the east had penetrated into western Chinese Turkestan; crossing the Oxus they had captured Bokhara, Samarkand, and Fergana. So it was that in the first half of the eighth century Islam reached the peak of its strength under the Omayyad dynasty.

However, the unity of the great state was splintered by differences in economic systems, beliefs, traditions, and lastly the perpetual disputes about the government. In this fight, involving everyone, all antagonisms were concentrated on the Omayyad dynasty. Protests were especially vociferous in Persia, for there the eastern theocratic conception of authority favoured the sacred family of the Prophet, chosen by God, as candidates for the throne of the caliph. The rising wave of opposition came from the eastern borders of the state, and swept through the military camps, causing civil war, the object of which was to depose and destroy the Omayyads who were accused of harming the Prophet's family and thus of contravening God's will.

Caliph Abu'l-Abbas in 750 began the rule of the new Abbasid dynasty. It was a victory for the Persian conception of the social organism in the Arab world and this found outward expression in the transfer of the capital of Islam to Baghdad on the Tigris. When the Abbasid dynasty came to power it was not merely the replacement of one ruler by another: it had very far-reaching consequences with regard to the formation of political structure. In place of the laicist Omayyad dynasty, there now appeared rulers who were enthusiastic advocates of a religious type of state. Deriving their rights from God, they felt themselves to be at once rulers and the highest among priests. The outward sign of their divinity was the alleged cloak of the Prophet, that had been given to them and which made their reign lawful.

The constitutional programme of the Abbasids was the absolute subjection of the state to the demands of religion. The Persian conception of ecclesiastical organization was followed—and thus empty religious phrases, ceremonious ritual, and prodigal wealth became an inseparable part of life in the court of the new dynasty. The role of the priesthood was filled by those well-versed in the doctrine of Islam. In place of a system that preserved the privileged separate life of the Arabs in their conquered territories, the structure of a theocratic absolute monarchy with its developing bureaucratic apparatus was established along Persian lines. Its purpose was the uniform government of all the population in the great state. It was the Abbasids who brought the conception of the universal Muslim state into being. Persian models were swiftly and readily adopted at the caliphs' court. The caliphs, surrounded by the ceremonial reserved for God, and given a feeling of limitless power, designated their successors through the official government. Such a procedure had, in fact, been instituted in the time of the Omayyads. The hierarchical structure of the new government meant that the people were far removed from the court of the divine caliph, contrary to the ideas of the first believers of Islam. The principal management of the state lay in the hands of the vizier, who was the first man in the land after the caliph, and in his care was the administration of the law with the help of judges. A chief of police watched over the peace and internal security of the state, over markets and the religious cult; a treasurer was responsible for the financial affairs of the religious cult; a postmaster was in charge of gathering information about affairs of state, and of communications in the country. The largest state concerns were the central and local tax offices (since the system of duty, taxes and tributes was highly diversified), and the judicial apparatus which was on the look-out to keep religious and political order. The provinces had their own offices in Baghdad for the representation of their affairs, and in the tenth century these were divided into three ministries, one for the eastern provinces, another the western provinces, and still a third one for Babylonia. The central government was represented by appropriate offices in the provinces, the heads of which were emirs, nominated by the caliph. The bureaucratic centralization constantly required new offices; the rules of the Abbasids in Baghdad were a continuation of the theocratic despotism of the East

Under the Omayyad rulers, even those who had embraced Islam were not treated as the absolute equals of the Arabs. Under the Abbasid dynasty, however, a process of assimilation with the local folk began, the Arabs becoming farmers, merchants, and bankers, treated as no more than the equals of the believers in Islam of whatever tribal origin. Many factors suggested the possibility of maintaining a universal Abbasid Empire—many things united the people of this vast area: a common creed; the Arabic language, used in offices, in religion, and in science;[21] unlimited possibilities for trade, from the Atlantic Ocean to China, aided since the eighth century by reliance on the Arab monetary system; Greek culture, encountered by travellers in the conquered lands who acquired it for themselves.[22] However, the unifying tendencies proved too weak to oppose the disintegrating forces in the great state which were not only socio-economic differences, but differences of custom as well, which might be expected in the huge areas subject to Islam. The provinces made themselves remarkably independent, which led to their separation from the Baghdad capital. In the tenth century Spain also became independent of the Omayyad rule, and in North Africa, Far, Central and Near Magreb and Egypt followed suit. These last came under the rule of the Fatimid dynasty in the tenth century. In the east, Khorasan achieved independence.[23]

The tendencies towards disintegration found expression as a result of the divergence of views among the faithful on philosophy, politics, and religion, as well as of the plurality of sects and splinter groups in Islam. Then, too, the power of the caliph in Baghdad was noticeably weakening. The doctrine of Mohammed became the subject of bitter disagreements; in them the socio-political conflicts of the Arab state could be seen.

4. THE STUDY OF LAW

As a result of the policy of conquest, wars, and the assumption of power over new territories, the business of regularizing legal intercourse in occupied lands became a burning question in the Arab state. The conquerors had found evolved political and legal institutions, which in principle they supported. The local law (*adat*) neither regulated the relationship of the conquerors to the conquered, nor the internal relationships among those Arabs who found themselves in new conditions of life in foreign lands. The problem had to be solved by a decision of the Arab leaders which would be in accord with the religious doctrine of Islam. The only guides for the creation of legal norms were the sayings contained in the Koran, the decisions and solutions of the Prophet (*sunna*) and the instructions of the caliphs. In their law-making the provincial governors regulated their intercourse on the basis of their own pronouncements; taking advantage, on the one hand, of analogies, that is, seeking support for their decision in the Koran and in tradition, on the other hand, they followed precedents in the locally developed law. In those territories where Roman law had shaped society, the Arabs unconsciously fell under the influence of that law, which they were also familiar with through the Jews. Life in the new situation called for the resolution of contradictions, sometimes from the Koran or sacred tradition; even such decisions became law if they enjoyed the universal approval of the Arabs.

For the first two centuries sacred law of Islam (*sari'a*) was being formed. The most widely differing norms were borrowed, from Roman, Byzantine, and Judaic law, as well as a series of customary norms from pre-Islamic Arabia. The main pillar of the sacred law was the Koran, the principles and ideas of which became the basis for interpreting the items composing the *sari'a*. The conglomeration of principles and legal norms remained linked with the idea of Islam, which integrated elements from many sources. Those living then were not aware of the factual process of creating a law which depended on a universal all-embracing reception of foreign norms, for the great ideo-logical dynamism of Islam, a conviction of the exceptional significance of the accepted doctrine, caused the conviction that the chief source for the holy law was the Koran. Traces of foreign legal institutions were either preserved as legal constructions or used as ingredients in legal conceptions. So, for example, the principle of *consensus prudentium*, and the maxim *pater est quem nuptiae demon-strant*, were borrowed from Roman law; also the construction of the buying–selling contract, in which three, at first distinct, kinds of suitable transactions are joined, on the Roman model: *locatio-conductio rei*, *l. c. operarum*, and *l. c. operis*. Arabic terms robbery *liss*, making use of the Greek word λῃστής. Similarly the Latin *dolus* had its local equivalent in *dallas*.[24]

In the Arab State the guardians of all the rules of the holy law, in religious, public, and private matters, were the judges (*qadi*).[25] In time, only inspection of the observance of the ritual and family norms and norms dealing with inheritance came within the judges' jurisdiction while other departments of the law separated themselves from the religious elements and ceased to be the *qadi's* competence. By way of contrast to the practical legislative procedure of the Omayyad administration, speculative theories about the sacred law were rife in Medina. The learned lawyers and theologians interpreted the sayings of the Koran and sacred tradition, which led to an infinite number of commandments and duties for the faithful, utterly impossible to fulfil. Between the practical formulation of the norms of *sari'a* and the theo-logical considerations on the law arose a marked disagreement. The science of law, in its break with practice under the Omayyads, created a system of ideal norms imbued with religious spirit but far removed from daily life.

These abstract, devout considerations on the sacred law by which the fol-lowers of Mohammed were obliged to direct their lives gave rise to schools of law in Islam. Their centres were Mecca and Medina, Syria and Iraq. At first their geographical location determined the peculiarities of the schools. Gradu-ally these peculiarities became more and more marked, owing to the differing economic and cultural levels of the various areas, together with the degree to which neighbouring legal systems influenced them.

The laicist outlook of the Omayyad dynasty treated incomprehensible theologico-legal speculations with scant attention; although these were divorced from practical application, inquiries first carried out in Medina caused a great development in legal studies, which almost equalled Roman jurisprudence. It was only half-way through the eighth century, when the Abbasid dynasty assumed power in the new capital of Islam, that the legal theologians were heard, formed schools of law, and promulgated the official thesis that the caliph was the guardian of the sacred law—considered to be one of the most important elements uniting the Muslim world. From these theologico-speculative inquiries grew the jurisprudence of Islam, and were formed those legal schools which in turn developed legal ideas, precision in thinking, logical argumentation, and, finally, appropriated the principles of Roman law.[26]

These historical investigations of the sacred law were called *fiqh*—jurisprudence—and were the preserve of those learned in the doctrine (*fukaha*) who made a collection of the rules (*sari'a*) and then systematized it. Among the first collections of *sari'a* is the famous collection of Malik known as *Al Muwattā*, which still exists today; and there is the earlier, lesser-known work of ibn Zaid.[27]

In principle, norms are divided into two groups: purely religious norms, and the norms of public and private law. Besides this there were other divisions of the rules in *sari'a*: e.g. norms dealing with cult duties (*ibādāt*), norms of civil law (*mu'āmalā*), and criminal law (*uqūbāt*). According to another division of *sari'a* rules there are norms of the religious cult (*ibādāt*), rules governing contracts (*uqūd*), norms regulating a declaration of intention by one party (*ikaat*), and the remaining articles (*ahkām*).

Problems of legal sources and their relation to one another took up most of the lawyers' time and caused most of the disputes. The norms of the *sari'a* were derived from four sources:

1. The Koran: The rules of behaviour as given by the sayings of the Prophet collected in the sacred book.

2. Custom (*sunna*): Legal rules made on the basis of the sayings and decisions attributed to the Prophet, but not collected in the Koran.

3. Analogy (*qiyas*): Decisions of officials who, turning to the Koran and *sunna* for support, regulated social intercourse in a new way by making use of analogies. Norms made by pronouncements from analogies played an important role in the development of the law, for neither the Koran nor the tradition sufficed the state, now that it was a world power.

4. Agreement (*ijma*): Rules made pragmatically which by general recognition gained legal force. In time learned scholars of doctrine came to understand *ijma* as agreement.

Discussions on the priority of norms derived from these above-named sources were in principle the basis for the differences between the four leading law schools, each of which served its own well-defined territories, thus making the differences between them wider.

The oldest law school in Islam was founded by Malik in Medina. It flourished in the eighth century, especially in the Hejaz province. From the biography of the founder of the school we learn that this most eminent lawyer of Islam took up jurisprudence against his own inclination. He dreamed—so say his spiteful opponents—of being a singer, but had to give this up because he was not handsome enough. Malik's greatest service was the collection of all the articles of the *sari'a*, which he did not, however, systematize. Malik's collection was the result of a suitable choice of legal norms and this contributes to the coming uniformity of the law. It showed what great differences could arise from a free choice of analogies by officials. The title of his work, *The Smooth Road (Al Muwatta)*, was meant to signify the author's intention—to reduce the law to order and make it uniform. This does not mean that Malik forbade the support of analogies in the taking of decisions. He even permitted it when the decision went against the norms, where justice demanded it. A member of Malik's school was, above all, concerned with bringing the theory of law (*fiqh*) into touch with practice. That is why Malik takes into consideration in his collection, besides the Koran and *sunna*, the pronouncements of the government in Hejaz, which thanks to popular approval (*ijma*) received legal force.

The school in Iraq represented another direction in the law. It was founded by Abu Hanifa and two of his most famous pupils, Abu Yusuf Yakub and al Shaibani. Its centre was in the Abbasid capital, Baghdad. Abu Hanifa was born in A.D. 700 in Kufa. He was Persian by origin, a merchant by profession, and gathered a considerable number of pupils around himself, all of whom in turn directed the study of law in the east of the Islamic State. Abu Hanifa himself never wrote a legal work, although his pupils named a collection of traditions after their master: *Musnad Abu Hanifa*.

This legislator, from the school officially recognized by the Abbasids, himself came into conflict with the government. He did not receive an official position and most likely ended his life in prison. The main argument of Hanifa's school was the assertion that legal norms could be made in a rational, logical way, looking for support to the Koran as the chief basis and guide in legislation. Abu Hanifa's followers also recognized other sources of law, although they put the emphasis on the subjective decision of officials, who thus shaped social intercourse. In this way it was possible, using the principles of the Baghdad school of Abu Hanifa, to create completely new divisions of the law, and this did, in fact, take place. Thus in the tenth century the partisans of this school created the water-laws in Khorasan, where the system of irrigation canals played an important role in the economy. In comparison with other schools, the Iraqui tendency was to give as much scope as possible to suiting the law to actual needs. The guiding remarks in the Koran were not numerous, and this too provided Hanifa's school with an unlimited field for new legislation, as a certain flexibility of attitude towards traditional norms. This, perhaps, was why the school was officially recognized by the Abbasids, and later by the authorities in the Ottoman Empire.

The founder of the third new law school was ash-Shafi'i, Malik's most eminent pupil. He was active in the period directly after the death of Malik and Abu Hanifa. At first his studies were linked with Arabia, with Mecca, and especially with Medina, where he made the already extensive collections of laws made by Malik still more comprehensive. Basing himself on this material, ash-Shafi'i began theoretical investigations, becoming the father of the most profound school of jurisprudence in Islam.

His predecessors had limited themselves to making collections of norms and setting limits to governmental decision. Ash-Shafi'i, however, actually formed legal conceptions; he defined *sunna*, indicated the role of *ijma* and also systematized sources showing their natural interdependence, while giving priority to the Koran and *sunna*. His service to legal studies is an analysis of the method of application of the law, and the elaboration of the main principles of jurisprudence, which in the legal literature of Islam bears the title *usul-al-fiqh*. The school of ash-Shafi'i, in comparison with his predecessors, clearly distinguishes for the first time the subject-matter, competence, and problems of jurisprudence. Because of this, the founder of the school is known as the father of legal theory in Islam.

The chief theologian of Islam was connected with the school of ash-Shafi'i. He was Ghazali, who at the age of 31, in 1095, resigned from a series of important positions which he had occupied in the theological world, in order to work exclusively at philosophy. Criticizing the existing theology and study of law, as represented by the law schools, Ghazali required pure faith based on experience through intuition, instead of the dialectical and casuistical religious disputes. His system was a contradiction of the aims of the rationalistic thought of Islam. It tended to veer, in his works towards mysticism, Ghazali himself having ascetic and mystical inclinations to Sufiism.

The school founded in the ninth century by Ibn Hanbal (d. 855) had less significance. The reason for its limited influence was his desire to conform to the Koran and above all to the sacred customs (*sunna*). The fanatical cult of tradition among the followers of this school caused their law to be too rigid and incapable of adapting itself to the changing needs of practice. Hanbal's adherents, reducing the scope of legislation, fulfilled the principles of the Koran and the *sunna*, under the pressure of necessity, only by means of fictitious traditions allegedly forgotten.

The above-mentioned law schools influenced the whole world of Islam. Thus, east Africa and southern Arabia came under the influence of ash-Shafi'i; the school of Malik had an obvious influence on northern Africa and

Spain; the eastern territories of the Muslim State were reached by Abu Hanifa's influence, while a considerable number of Ibn Hanbal's adherents were to be met in Mesopotamia, Palestine, and Syria.

With the official recognition of the law school, in principle the process of forming the sacred law was over. For the first 200 years after the *hegira* the Islamic conquerors created the fundamentals of their sacred law from the various norms, rules and customs observed on their victorious marches, carefully adapting it to the principles of the Koran. After the second century, when the schools were recognized, the system underwent a kind of petrification. Among the manifold theories of the schools can be sensed a general tendency towards religious dogmatization of the legal system. Gradually the theory which ruled out the possibility of creative legislation by lawyers gained the upper hand. The principle of uncritical acceptance of the law (*taqlid*) was victorious. This was eventually formulated in the recognized textbooks of the law schools. Although the activity of the law schools marked the end of creative legislation, the systematic and theoretical studies of these schools demonstrate the relatively considerable independence and originality of legal thought.[28]

It was, from the start, far from the intention of the lawgivers of Islam that the lives of the faithful should be complicated with instructions. They called on the words of the Koran: "God wants to rule you mildly that you may fulfil his commandments and voice his praise . . . ." (II. 181). One of the earliest authorities of Islam in the first half of the seventh century, Abdallah ibn Masūd, taught: "The man who forbids things that are allowed ought to be treated with the same severity as the man who permits forbidden things."

A similar concern not to multiply new duties and commands is expressed by the eighth-century lawyer, Sufijan al Tauri. "Wisdom", he says, "lies in giving new authorization and permission, while relying on a trustworthy authority; for it is not difficult to restrict and forbid". There was even the proverbial saying, which became widespread: "If there are doubts as to whether something is permitted or forbidden, accept that which is permitted."

The theoretical disputes of the law schools were harmless skirmishes; the social, organic and philosophical conflicts of the Islamic state were not reflected in dogmatic speculations.

5. DISCORD IN THE DOCTRINE OF ISLAM

The doctrine of Islam was far from being uniform. On the contrary, there were all kinds of indications that many trends, schools and sects would arise. Many causes were responsible, above all the material differences among the faithful, as also the different socio-economic arrangements in the conquered lands, and the powerful infiltration of foreign philosophical and religious systems. Finally, the obscurity and variety of possible interpretations, both in the formulation of the Koran and the sayings of the Prophet, was another cause. When his contemporaries asked the Prophet about the significance and meaning of contradictory sayings, or those with double meaning in the Koran, they heard: "The Koran was not given to you that you might oppose one of its revelations with others, as was done by nations before you with the sayings of their prophets. In the Koran one revelation is confirmed by a second. What is clear to you in the Koran ought to be a guide for your behaviour, while whatever causes you to doubt, you ought to accept humbly." Despite these instructions, Mohammed must have had grave doubts whether he could succeed in maintaining unity among the faithful, as soon as he could foresee that his followers would split into seventy-three sects.

It is impossible to discuss all the disagreements in Islam, although it appears that with regard to the political aspect of the doctrine, philosophic, organic and social antagonisms have the greatest significance.

The secular outlook of the Omayyad dynasty had not indicated special interest in the dogmatic disputes of the Muslim theologians; above all, the practical activity of the state was engaged in the struggle to preserve the government. However, in one exceptional case the rulers departed from their principles, when they thoroughly investigated the religio-philosophical controversies on fatalism and indeterminism, because the Omayyads were personally interested in these discussions. The adherents of fatalism easily found in Islamic doctrine grounds for the argument that man is utterly dependent on God, that he is a thing without will, deprived of any influence on his destiny. The adherents of extreme determinism thought that man who is rejected by God, and left to himself, is afflicted with the greatest misfortune.[29] However, almost from the rise of Islam, that is from the seventh century, there had been doubts about the absolute dependence of man on God. It was especially among thinking circles in Damascus, the capital of the Omayyads, that discussions began on the blind destiny of fate (*quadar*). The opponents of believers in blind destiny put forward the view that man alone decides his future, and therefore the idea of the importance of destiny should be much restricted—hence the name of these opponents (Kadarites). The intelligent opposition of the Kadarites among Muslims is a visible result of the influence of Hellenistic philosophy. This is shown by the fact that the Kadarite movement sprang up in Syria, a country where Hellenistic and Christian influences had strongly penetrated. In so far as the orthodox believers of Islam thought that evil, sin, and disobedience have been foreordained by the will of God, the Kadarites said that the autonomous will of man is the only reason for breaking the divine laws and commandments.[30] The Omayyad rulers subscribed markedly to fatalism and belief in predestination, finding weighty arguments from the orthodox interpretation of the faith in support of their rule. Many of the faithful were convinced that the Omayyads were usurpers who had usurped power from the descendants of the Prophet in opposition to the sacred law—in a word, they had defied God's will. Against this the Omayyads resorted to the arguments of fatalism, basing their authority on predestination. Their court poets and sages affirmed that "the rule of the Omayyad was foreordained in the eternal divine plan". The conviction, among some subjects, of blind destiny made governing considerably easier. Everything that happens was explained—defeats and victories, successes and failures, achievements and adversity—by inevitable necessity, over which the rulers had no influence. In these circumstances the ruling circles disapproved of the Kadarites, the earliest critics of the Islamic doctrine.

In later ages, particularly the period between the tenth and the twelfth centuries, the Mu'tazilites represented the ideas of the Kadarites. They for their part were philosophers concentrated in Baghdad and enjoying the official support of the Abbasid rulers. The Mu'tazilites made use of the method of discussion to defend the doctrines of Islam against the ever-widening influence of Aristotle in the Arab world at that time. They saw the chief source of religious knowledge as the intellect; their defence was logical argumentation, through the help of which they hoped to explain and substantiate the sayings of the Koran. That is why they too are called the rationalists of Islam.[31] They were the first to try to formulate religious doctrine in categories of logical thought, rejecting its allegorical and fabulous side. From them came the characteristic sayings of the growing scepticism among the educated élite: "The first sign of knowledge is doubt", or "Fifty doubts have greater value than faith in one dogma."

The links between Kadarites and Mu'tazilites can be seen in their common denial of fatalism. Both advocated absolute justice which defines the limit of the divine might. In place of the fatalistic argument that man is a puppet in the hands of heaven, they said that man is free in his activities, while God, who is always above man, is the principle of absolute justice. In opposition to the orthodox believers who saw the sources of good and evil in the unrestricted will of God, the Mu'tazilites accepted the existence of absolute good and evil, while the appreciation and choice of absolute values depend on the human intellect. Unlike the Kadarites, they referred to problems of government. For the Mu'tazilites put forward their indeterminism and rationalism for the approval of the government; it was an officially supported attitude, characterized by an absolute lack of tolerance towards opposing viewpoints.

Opposition in Islam was also indicated in the slogans calling man to an ascetic life. As Mohammed's doctrine came to have a positive efficacy in real life, especially after the death of the Prophet, the thought of the damnation of the temporal world was driven away by the idea of world authority. The words of the Prophet "You desire temporal riches, and God wants to give you eternal treasures for He is mighty and wise" (VIII. 68) slipped into oblivion. The treasures of the rich towns of Ktesiphon, Damascus, and Alexandria lured the Arab warriors. Longing for wealth inspired many aggressive expeditions. The words of Mohammed, which permitted the accumulation of wealth on condition that it was used for the temporal good of poor people, and for fruitful purposes, were remembered. The Arabs easily found sayings of the Prophet which justified them in their views on profiting from temporal life. Almost everywhere asceticism and the life of monks, whom the Arabs met among Christians and Buddhists, were despised. They ascribed many sayings to the Prophet in which condemnation for the ascetic life is expressed. "There is no monastic life in Islam; the monastic life of the community is the holy war." Mohammed insisted that his followers should have physical vigour and courage. Therefore he taught: "The Arab taking care of his physical strength loves God more than a sickly invalid." The Prophet himself was no model of asceticism, he did not despise the joys of this life, as can be seen from a saying with no possible second meaning: "From the sphere of this world I like women and fragrant smells, but my consolation and solace I find in prayer." The Arabs gladly surrounded themselves with luxury and pomp, considering that it was God's will that they should show what good fortune they had received through His kindness.

However, the more the Arabs paid almost exclusive attention to temporal matters, material things taking pride of place with their leaders, the more, among the believers, the ideal of an ascetic life began to spread as a protest against the luxurious and hedonistic way of life. The ascetic movement sprang up when the conquests of Islam were already reaching their peak, i.e. in the eighth century. It is known as Sufiism, on account of the straight woollen robe, the *suf*. Sufiism was formed under the influence of the idea of Christian and Buddhist monasteries, as well as of the doctrines of Neo-platonism. The adherents of Sufiism were sunk in Neoplatonic mysticism. They taught that radiations of the divine power could be felt in the whole universe. The world of matter and real phenomena was only illusion, like images reflected in a looking-glass. They believed that man, through searching deep within himself, by subduing his material limitation, the body, may know the splendour of God, His beauty and goodness. The adherents of Sufiism declared that Mohammed had confided secret knowledge to Ali, the husband of Fatima; therefore Ali too was considered a patriarch of Islamic mysticism. Voicing their absolute negation of this world, the Sufists wanted to achieve union with God, and despised all intellectual arguments. Abu Said Kharraz said, on the intuitive knowledge of God, "The man who returns to God . . . . lives near God, loses himself and forgets all but God. In such a state, if he is asked whence he comes and what he longs for, he can give no answer but the one word: Allah."

The denial of life, organization, law, and the principles of community living, caused the decision, in Baghdad at the close of the ninth century, to punish and condemn the ascetics and even to kill their chief representatives. This was done under the pressure of the orthodox believers.

It is characteristic that the chief reason for the division into sects was the problem of state organization. After Mohammed's death, disputes arose among the Arabs as to who should be the Prophet's successor. Those who thought that the highest position in the world of Islam was most appropriate for a descendant of the Prophet, regarded the three caliphs, Abu Bekr, Omar, and Othman critically. The nearest relations were Ali, married to the Prophet's daughter, or the sons of this marriage. When caliph Othman blatantly promoted his own family (the Omayyads), it led to bitter conflicts with the followers of Ali. After Othman was murdered, Muawija was the head of the Omayyad family. Thanks to cunning policy he avoided conflict with Ali's party, which led to the summoning of an arbitration court to decide on Ali's rights to the caliphat. At that time many left Ali's party, saying that the decision on the succession to the Prophet rested only with God, who would show his will in the result of the contest. Those leaving Ali's camp were called the "leavers" (Kharidzhites). They were advocates of the most democratic principles for choosing a caliph. They said that the highest authority among the Arabs ought to be filled by the worthiest man, chosen by general election. At the same time they were against choosing the caliph from a small section of the aristocratic *élite*. In their opinion, only high moral qualities, complete subordination of self to the divine, and an assurance that he would fulfil his duties, could inspire confidence, irrespective of his social origin, in a man's worthiness to be the "prince of the faithful", the caliph, even if he were an Ethiopian slave. The Kharidzhites represent the puritan standpoint.

By the cleanliness demanded by the ceremonies they understood not merely physical cleanliness, but ethical. They were not a closed society, for their slogans of general election for a caliph, and insistence on high morality, together with their protest against inequality and injustice, made them enjoy wide popularity among the poorer classes. Their democratic slogans also met with sympathy not only among the people but among intellectuals connected with the first Abbasids,[32] and were very popular among the conquered peoples; for they advocated absolute equality of all tribes with the Arabs in the conviction that God would give divine sanction to their universalist ideals through the revelation of a new Koran to a prophet among the Persians.[33] The Kharidzhites expressed open opposition to the Omayyads, so that the movements for freedom among the Berbers in North Africa, directed against the caliphs of that dynasty, made use of their doctrines.[34]

Independent of the democratic ideas on choosing a caliph, there were two others: the Shiite theocratic conception, and the aristocratic *sunna* conception. Believers in the first thought that the leader of the Arabs ought to be an imam, combining in one person the highest secular and religious responsibilities and only the person nearest in relationship to the Prophet could fulfil this honour according to the will of God. The famous day of the battle of Kerbala was a day of catastrophe for the Shiites, and later the symbol of battle with usurpers, the grandson of the Prophet, Hussein, dying in this battle with the Omayyads in 680.[35] The Shiites formed secret unions, the aim of which was the cult of Ali and his descendants; their organization was a dangerous source of opposition to every reigning government, and also a source of unrest in the state. Their methods were conspiratorial, since they were as much in conflict with the Abbasids as they had been with the Omayyads. Constantly pursued and persecuted, they developed for their use the theory of *kitman*, also called *taqiya*, according to which prudence commanded them to keep their genuine convictions secret. According to this theory, Shiites had the duty of hiding their true views from enemies, and of allaying all suspicions; outwardly, in behaviour and speech, they had to lull the vigilance of their opponents and win their confidence. The Shiites declared the theory of the infallibility, sinlessness and sanctity of the imam. They asserted that only Ali and his descendants understood the true meaning of the Koran, since they had divine aid, vision, and the power to foresee things; thus only those descended from the Prophet, thanks to a peculiar supernatural grace, might hold the highest position among the Arabs—the honour of being imam. According to them, fanatical love of Ali and his descendants had the power to remit all sins. The name Shiite derives from *si'a*, meaning a group of people of various shades of belief, linked by their devotion to the Prophet's family.

The Shiites did not have a uniform conception of the imam. We can distinguish three large groups among them. The most moderate view on this issue was that of the Zaydites, who indeed thought that God directed the imam, but denied him divine characteristics. The Imamites, however, considered that he manifested a fusion of divine and human characteristics. They treated his death as the joyful liberation of the divine from human elements. The most extreme tendency was that of the *gulāt* group, which means "those who cross all boundaries". In their teaching, God clothed Himself in the body of the iman, giving him supernatural powers.

It is characteristic that the progressive movement of Karmats in the question of the office of imam represented an extremist position, the views of the *gulāt* group.

The Shiites formed a theocratic opposition within the framework of Islam; in their party the argument of the absolute denial of other viewpoints found its place.

The most serious opponents of the Shiites were the Sunnites, representing the official trend; they were the most numerous, and were largely composed of the aristocracy.[36] Their views on the institution of the caliphate corresponded to the actual disposition of power: they recognized the historical fact that after Mohammed's death authority was in the hands of the Koreishite tribe; they commanded obedience to any ruler who ensured that the religious cult would be carried on and order maintained in the state. Quoting the sayings of the Prophet and sacred tradition, the Sunnites required absolute obedience to the despotic rule of the caliph, and considered this to be a religious obligation. They called the caliph "God's shadow on the earth", to emphasize, by this meaning his special position in the state. The first systematic elaboration of the Sunnite conception of the caliphate is the work of *Al Akham al sultanija*, written by Māwardi. In it are the various conditions that the ruler of the Arabs must fulfil: he must descend from the Koreishite tribe, be male, mature, of noble character, free from physical or mental handicaps, learned in theology and law, clever at organization, courageous, and a self-sacrificing defender of the unity of the state. In this work Māwardi discusses the procedure of choosing the caliph, and his function.

According to Sunnite doctrine, the caliph had, above all, to assume the highest secular authority, and at the same time the duty of protecting the Islamic religion fell upon him. Chosen by human decision, and thus chosen or indicated by his predecessor, he became the head of the believers in Islam, concentrating judicial, administrative and military power in his own hands. The position of the Sunnites also corresponds to that of later orthodox theologians of the fourteenth century, from whom we learn of the functions of the caliph:

> At the head of Arab society there must, of necessity, be somebody who would see to the observance of the law, the realization of decisions, the defence of the Arab frontiers; who would see to the salaries of the army and collection of tribute, quell violence, robbery and plundering, organize communal divine services, take care of minors who were going to be married; who would look to the division of the spoils of war, and would take upon himself other similar affairs that an ordinary member of the community could perform.

The Sunnites wanted to put the government of the Arabs into the hands of educated and experienced administrators.

Within the framework of the chief currents, among the Shiites sticking to the theme of the essence of the caliph's rule and his election, there were several scores of sects, differing in their views on constitutional, social, and dogmatic matters.

Islam was the doctrine of merchants and warriors, seeking conquest in a holy war; it was very congenial to those with energy who longed for wealth, land, and slaves, while it brought bitterness and disappointment to the landless. Blatant luxury against a background of social inequality provoked a sense of injustice which those verses of the Koran that commanded compassion and help for the needy, widows, and orphans, did nothing to alleviate. Those who did not believe in their own strength and in the possibility of creating a just state organization with their own hands, instead dreamed of divine intervention in human affairs and awaited reform through such intervention— those people were living in Utopia.

The members of one Shiite sect, the Imamites, believed that the twelfth imam, descended from Ali, disappeared at the age of eight, about A.D. 874 and that he might one day return to earth to create the true kingdom of peace and justice. The awaited saviour of the world, the imam Mahdi, was to arrest the spread of evil and bring happiness to people. This idea is derived from Jewish–Christian beliefs in the Messiah, and was the hope of those who had doubts about the contemporary social order. The idea of a future happy organization, treating grim reality as an evil prelude, was a possible protest against that reality. The conception of the future imam, the Mahdi, is also found in believers who were not Shiites. All those awaited the saviour who painfully experienced injustice and inequality. The belief that God would call the imam from among the descendants of the Prophet, so that in the place of evil and perversity he might fill the world with goodness and righteousness, was the Utopia of people passively waiting for a miracle to cure social ills.

The revolutionary doctrine causing profound ferment among Muslims in the period between the ninth and the twelfth centuries was that of the Karmathians. This name is given to rebels who about 877 lifted their weapons against the Arab government in southern Mesopotamia. It appears that the name of the revolutionaries comes from the name of the leader of the rising, Hamdan Qarmat. Among the ranks of the Karmathians were masses of peasants and artisans. Their organization, despite its extensiveness, had the character of secret unions, with communal property, hierarchical membership with gradual initiation and finally the duty of absolute obedience. History tells us that in the nineties of the ninth century, the Karmathians entrenched themselves to the east of Kufa in a military camp in which there was a communal treasure house. They arranged communal meals there, to emphasize the spirit of unity.

The Karmathian ideal was widely popular in Islamic lands. Besides Mesopotamia, there were unions in Persia, Syria, and the Yemen. Characteristic of the Karmathian movement, especially in its beginnings, were the ideas of equality, justice, tolerance, and above all the cult of the intellect. They advanced a conception of a universal religion, common to all; they treated the Koran as a symbolic and allegorical book, which if individually interpreted could serve as a gospel for all peoples. The Karmathian philosophy, despite its rationalism, was strongly coloured by idealistic elements, under the influence of Greek thinkers. They treated the universe as the sum of phenomena and matter, repeating themselves with cyclic regularity, in which God manifests Himself—God being conceived as an idea void of all attributes, comprehensible only to the initiated after they are released from their earthly integument. They taught that prophets, saints, and the initiated experienced the idea of divinity intuitively, uniting themselves with God, freeing themselves simultaneously from five tyrants: from heaven, which causes night to follow day; from nature, which brings passion and frenzy; from the law, which orders and forbids; from the state, which rules and punishes, and finally from hard necessity, everyday cares. Under the influence of Hellenism, they were some of the first in Islam besides the Mu'tazilites to pay marked attention to the elements of the understanding ('*aql*) which differentiates man from other creatures. The cult of the intellect caused a lively interest in study among the Karmathians, especially in the natural sciences, mathematics and logic. The Karmathians were so charmed by the idealistic Greek philosophy that they regarded Pythagoras, Empedocles and Plato as saintly, inspired prophets. This, however, did not prevent them from studying Indian, Persian, and Jewish philosophy. Their intellectual activity caused the adoption of Greek philosophical terminology into Arabic. Their secret hierarchical organization found many imitators; it was a model for the artisan and merchant guilds and we have it finally in the structure of Masonic lodges.[37] At first the Karmathians constituted a general movement in Islam, fighting for social reform, directed by intellectuals and supported by the oppressed and unhappy. Profiting by the disputes about the government, they propagated their ideas and created secret societies in the conviction that, as in Plato, the government of Islam ought to consist of people of the highest mental and spiritual qualities, those who reached the highest degrees of initiation in the Karmathian organization. In the course of years, the Karmathian doctrine lost its genuine radicalism; ambitious pretenders to the throne made use of it, taking advantage of the ideas and organization of the progressive movement in the dynastic struggle. At the beginning of the tenth century Ubaid Allah, fighting like a demagogue with the Karmathian teaching, became ruler in Tunisia and Egypt, starting the Fatimid dynasty. The Karmathian ideas in the hands of ambitious leaders lost their real social value; they were already propaganda slogans in which most of the people had ceased to believe.

The person of Avicenna is linked with the Karmathian ideology. He was born in Bokhara in 980 in a country where a period of economic development was in progress (ninth, tenth centuries) and the ruling dynasty (the Samanids) took care of science and art. His father, a customs official, was a member of the Ishmaelite sect, and possessed considerable influence there and in Kharezma. Abu Ibn Sina (called Avicenna in Europe), a doctor and philosopher especially interested in natural sciences, represents a markedly rationalistic trend in philosophy. Avicenna's work has given him a permanent place in the history of human thought, thanks to his efforts at a rational explanation of the world. Being a pioneer in medicine, the natural sciences, and philosophy, he came into sharp conflict with the official theological teaching of Islam. However, his political views did not deviate from the traditional: he expressed the hope of maintaining a harmonious state organization. He wanted to transfer the order reigning in the cosmos to human society. He recognized the need for a hierarchical, centralized government; he approved Plato's model society divided into three estates, of which the highest was to direct the affairs of the state. Avicenna, like Aristotle, explained the existence of the state by a natural need for community life, which would give the individual an opportunity to better himself and to develop. In his remarks on state organization, attention is carefully paid to the ensuring of stability. He calls on all citizens on pain of sin to fight usurpers. For Avicenna, law is the guarantee of order, of the lawful management of the state, obedience to authority. Although he opposed religion with science, he at the same time admitted the need for religion as a weighty element indispensable for lawful governing. He wanted to see in religion a factor substantiating the right to govern, and promoting in the citizens a religious sense of obedience to the state and the law.[38] While the rationalism of Avicenna provoked an unfriendly reaction from Muslim theologians, thus conferring immortality on him, his political doctrine is striking in its desire for stability and for the maintenance of an unchanging order, based on the constitutional ideas of Plato and Aristotle. It seems that this versatile scholar expressed his personal longing for order and peace, which he could not find in his tempestuous wandering life or in his political views.

Avicenna was the last important thinker of the eastern Arab countries. Only in Spain was there a still active centre of philosophy, where Aristotle's writings were translated and commented on. From there Aristotelianism radiated beyond the Pyrenees, hastening the reception of the Stagirite in western Europe. In this centre lived and worked Averroes of Cordoba (1126–98), under whose influence the progressive school of Aristotelian European philosophers was to develop. In one man, Averroes combined the occupations of lawyer, philosopher, naturalist, mathematician, author of scientific tracts and high official of the caliph's court. But above all he was the famous commentator of Aristotle. In his writings, suppressed by the Muslims, he began the materialistic interpretation of Aristotle directed against the state.

When Europe entered into the inheritance of Arab philosophy, the victory of reaction in the Muslim world put an end to the growth of intellectual life, beginning the long period of the persecution of thinkers.

NOTES

1. Isaiah 60. 6. The Holy Bible, King James Version, American Bible Society. New York.
2. Ezekiel 27. 22–4.
3. The problem of Arab religion before Mohammed is discussed by G. Ryckmans in his *Les religions Arabes. Préislamiques*, Louvain, 1951. The author divides these beliefs into three geographical groups: Arabie Centrale (7–18), Arabie Septentrionale (19–24), Arabie Méridionale (25–49).
4. Much light has been thrown on the influence of foreign religious doctrines on Islam. The influence of the Jewish religion is discussed by A. J. Wensinck: *Mohammed en de Joden te Medina*, 1908; that of the Christian religion by C. H. Becker; *Christentum und Islam*, 1907. The influences from lands in the south of Arabia on Islam are described by H. Grimme: *Mohammed*, 1904.
5. There was a wide circle of people under whose intellectual influence Mohammed fell. During his journey to Syria he contacted the Nestorian monk Sergius. Later he met the Jew Abdalah ibn Salam; the Greek Zabbar, Qais living in Mecca, and finally his cousin Warag ibn

Asad, the first to translate into Arabic some extracts from the Old and New Testaments, had a great influence on him.

6.   The view that Islam was a complete religio-social system immediately on ist inception cannot be supported. This incorrect theory was formerly put forward by A. Kuenen: *National Religions and Universal Religions*, 1882, p. 293, where he remarks that Islam "enters the world as a rounded system".

7.   J. Goldziher: *Vorlesungen über den Islam*, 1910, in giving a remarkable analysis of the religious doctrine of Mohammed, says (on p. 12) that the original element in Mohammed's religious system is the negative aspect of his thought, for he ordered the Arabs to break with their beliefs and customs.

8.   C. H. Becker: *Islamstudien*, 1924. On p. 340 he writes: "The famous *hegira* was no flight—it was, rather, a journey undertaken absolutely of his own free will .... That happened only later under the rule of the Caliph Omar at the beginning of the era of Islam, thought to be the 16th July A.D. 622."

9.   In the year after the battle at Badr, Mohammed's adherents were defeated in a fight with the Koreishites not far from Medina, at the Uhud mountain. The victors did not follow up their success, however.

10.   The translation is not literal. The text runs, *La ilaha illallah wa Muhammadum rasulu llah.* (There is no god but God and Mohammed is his messenger.)

11.   The final text of the Koran was made in the Caliphate of Othman in A.D. 653. At the same time all other versions of the Koran were destroyed, so as to avoid different interpretations of the sacred book.

12.   L. Caetani: *Das historische Studium des Islams*, 1908. On p. 9 he shows that in the beginning the Arabs treated Christians and Jews on their occupied territories in an almost brotherly fashion, and that it was only later that new converts from Christianity introduced fanaticism and intolerance on the pattern of Byzantium.

13.   This was a burning question, the more so as Arabs in Syria, Egypt and Persia met with flourishing state and legal institutions.

14.   T. Andrae: *Die Person Muhammeds*, 1918; on p. 175 and the following pages, discussing the relation of the Koran to *sunna*, he emphasizes that some Muslims ascribe greater significance to the sacred book, others to sacred customs. On p. 190 we find this definition of the *sunna:* "The word *sunna* generally means, in Islamic theology, everything derived from the Prophet, with the exception of the Koran."

15.   C. Cahen: *The Body Politic* in the symposium *Unity and Variety in Muslim Civilization*, 1955. On pp. 156 ff., he observes: "In reality there was no political doctrine in Islam. There were only ardent but fluid aspirations . . . ." This author's viewpoint is the outcome of his narrow formulation of the term "political doctrine", by which he understands a definite organic conception. Cahen denies the character of the political doctrine in Islam, because Islam did not create a uniform pattern which all states under the influence of Mohammedanism might accept.

16.   A typically idealistic theory of the genesis of the doctrine of Islam is that of T. Andrae in his exhaustive biography of Mohammed. In a later work, *Mohammed, sein Leben und sein Glaube*, 1932, on p. 7, Andrae writes: "In all dynamic religions whose history we may discover, the stimulating force is the personality of the individual . . . the Master, the Prophet and his pupils are the primary cell, from which the new life, in the world religion, develops".

17.   C. Cahen: *op. cit.*, pp. 132 ff., puts forward a convincing theory of the different attitude of the Church to Christian and Muslim states. Islam was the single organization with a religious authority which simultaneously fulfilled a political role. A similar situation existed only in the Judaic theocracy, whereas the organization of the Christian Church had developed within the Roman State which was not dependent on any political organization. After the death of the Prophet, who was the only mediator between God and the faithful, thanks to the situation in Arabia there was nobody who could continue the theocracy as Mohammed had understood it. Cahen even observes that after the Prophet's death bankruptcy of the doctrine occurs, decay of the whole structure sets in, and thence springs the multiplicity of Muslim states. Mohammed's organic conception was not suitable for continuation, for it was only he who gave voice to Allah's revelations. In Cahen's opinion, the modern state in Europe was formed at the time of the separation of the church organization from that of the state. Such a

division did not occur in Islam, for the state authority, having developed with the religious organization, could hardly be in opposition to it.

18. E. Diez: *Glaube und Welt des Islam*, 1941. On p. 78 he advances the theory that, "a union of the Arab tribes, which had for centuries been warring against one another, would never have been realized without Islam . . . ." It appears that this theory underlies the whole of the author's reasoning; in company with C. H. Becker, he wants to show the sociological reasons for the rise of the doctrine. As I understand it, Islam only prompted the objective necessity for Arab unity.

19. C. H. Becker: *Islamstudien;* on p. 70 he tells us: "Not religion, but hunger and desire for possession are the motive forces; religion, however, gives the necessary unity and centralization . . . . Wanderings had taken place a long time before Islam gave them a slogan and organization."

20. C. H. Becker: *op. cit.*, remarks that Omar only regulated, according to the way of those days, the organization in the conquered territories, whereas the whole of the system took form in the reign of his successor. It does seem, though, that Omar had his own distinct organic conception; liberalism and tolerance for the townsfolk, together with the setting-up of compact, privileged centres for the Arabs. We know that before the capture of Jerusalem, that is before A.D. 638, Omar was still in Syria for the purpose of settling policy in the conquered territories, the government of which had delivered them to the experienced administrator.

21. B. N. Zachoder writes in *Istoria wostocznogo sriedniewiekowija*, 1944, p. 81, on the significance of the highly developed Arabic tongue. *Sbornik Biruni*, 1950, contains on p. 65 the following speech of the eminent eleventh-century scholar, Biruni, who, not being Arab by birth, wrote: "The sciences of all the countries in the world have been translated into Arabic and made more beautiful—they are become a delight to the heart, and the fine language flows through the arteries, veins and blood-vessels, although every nation thinks its own dialect is beautiful. I base my conclusions on my own analogy: my own mother-tongue is such a language that, were I to try to perpetuate any kind of knowledge in it, it would seem as strange as a camel standing beneath a rain-spout to shelter from the rain, or a giraffe amid fine Arab bloodstock."

22. The inventor of the Arab monetary system was Caliph Abdal Malik (685–705) who in the West (on the pattern of Byzantium) took a unit of gold as the basis of the system, and in the East (modelling himself on Persia) took a unit of silver.

23. A. Zajączkowski: *Awicenna i jego epoka* (Avicenna and his epoch) in the collection "Awicenna", 1953, writes on pp. 18 ff., "The cultural world of Islam exhibited symptoms also remarkable from a political standpoint in the Xth century. That great area, stretching from Fergana to Tangier, in the words of the contemporary traveller al-Masud, formed a distance of almost four thousand parasangs; that area, which could only be covered after 10 months' travelling, bore the name of the "Arab Caliphate", a name that was conventional but also incorrect. This huge tract, conquered by the Arabs with their banners of the war-like half-moon, formed a series of provincial regions, where local dynasties came to power. They looked for support to the townsfolk and to ethnic groups to whom Arabic was foreign, thus creating the embryonic nationalist movements of the Middle Ages in the Near East."

24. J. Schacht: *The Law* in the collection *Unity and Variety in Muslim Civilization*, 1955. On pp. 65 ff., he discusses the process of the formation of the sacred law, emphasizing the manifold inclusion and assimilation of foreign legal precepts by the sacred law. The author gives a series of examples which give evidence of the inclusion of foreign legal institutions and even terminology.

25. A discussion of Islamic law will be found in the article *Sharia* by J. Schacht—*Shorter Encyclopaedia of Islam*, 1953, pp. 524 ff. There is also a bibliography.

26. A. von Kremer: *Kulturgeschichte des Orients unter den Chalifen*, 1875, vol. I. p. 535. He remarks that many of the precepts of Roman law adopted by Islam can be found in the *fiqh*, through the intermediation of the Jews.

27. E. Griffini published a collection of *fiqh* under the title: *Corpus iuris di Zaid ibn Ali*, Milan, 1919, ascribed to the founder of one of the sects, Zaid ibn Ali, who died in A.D. 740. Whether the author of the collection was indeed Zaid or someone from his circle, he ought to be recognized as the absolute pioneer of his time in codifying laws in the Islamic world.

28. J. Goldziher: *op. cit.*, pp. 55 ff., characterizing all the schools in a general way, gives a

very just estimation of them, emphasizing the common tendency of all jurisprudence to manifest itself in legal liberalism, as well as to limit the law-making activity.

29.   In the Koran occur sayings in which the threat of leaving the Arabs without divine protection is contained: "Empty are their deeds, they have perished forever. Muslims! If you reject your creed, God will call upon nations . . ."! (V. 59.) "They turn away their eyes and heart from the truth, they do not believe in the first miracle, I leave them to stray in the darkness of transgression." (VI. 10.)

30.   J. Goldziher: *op. cit.*, pp. 96 ff., emphasizing the great significance of the position of the Kadarites, remarks that that movement approved indeterminism, not in the name of the freedom of the intellectually active man, but because it was a movement of devout fanatics, who wanted, by limiting fatalism, to increase the duties of the faithful to God.

31.   H. Galland, in *Essai sur les Motazélites, les rationalistes de l'Islam*, 1906, was the man who called the Motazélites the rationalists of Islam.

32.   G. Levi della Vida expresses this thought in *Kharidjites—Shorter Encyclopaedia of Islam*, p. 248.

33.   Jazid ibn Abi Anisa says that God will reveal a new Koran to a prophet from among the Persians, for whom he will create a new religion as divine as Judaism, Christianity, and Islam.

34.   J. Wellhausen: *Die religiös-politischen Oppositionsparteien im alten Islam*, 1901 p. 93. J. Goldziher, *op. cit.*, p. 206.

35.   B. Lewis: *The Ismailites and the Assassins* in the collection *A History of the Crusades*, 1955, pp. 100 ff., shows that after Mohammed's death a political opposition formed among the Arabs, which opposed the son-in-law of Mohammed, Ali, to Abu Bekr and his first successor. After a time the vanquished peoples, not content with the rule of the Arab aristocracy, supported the political opposition, whose banners were the figures of Ali and his descendants. B. Lewis emphasizes that the first skirmishes about authority contributed to the creation of a new, different philosophical and political doctrine of Islam.

36.   In European literature the erroneous belief in the liberalism of the Shiites is repeated; Carra de Vaux expresses it in *Le Mahometisme, le génie semitique et le génie aryen dans l'Islam*, 1898, p. 142. He says that "the Shiites reveal the reaction of a free wide intelligence against orthodox dullness". However, J. Goldziher (*op. cit.*, pp. 242 ff.,) carefully exposes the spirit of intolerance among the Shiites; he says that in their doctrine ". . . powerful intolerance exists against those who had changed their outlooks. The Shiite interpretation of the law did not admit of any relaxation in opposition to the orthodoxy of the *sunna*".

37.   This view is expressed by L. Massignon in the article *Karmatians, Shorter Encyclopaedia of Islam*, pp. 218 ff.

38.   A discussion of Avicenna's philosophy may be found in *Awicenna jako filozof* (Avicenna as philosopher) by L. Kotakowski in the above-mentioned collection, *Awicenna*, pp. 155–87. There the author also surveys Avicenna's political views.

3

BYZANTINE POLITICAL THOUGHT

1. THE SEPARATION OF THE BYZANTINE EMPIRE FROM ROME

From the third century onwards the barbarians had been constantly attacking and crossing the line of the Rhone and the Rhine. For many years the western parts of the Roman Empire had been a battlefield and eventually they succumbed to the invaders. Through the Danube provinces passed the Goths, the Huns, the Lombards; Gaul, Spain, Northern Africa were in turn occupied by Visigoths, Sueves, Vandals, Franks, Burgundians, Alemanni; in the end Rome was captured by Germanic tribes.

War, the helplessness of the rulers, plague, misery, lawlessness and violence, all disrupted normal life. Rome became more interested in the Eastern provinces because of their economic importance for the Empire. The necessity for the reorganization of the state became imperative. Diocletian divided the Empire into four large areas under independent rulers in order to improve the defence of the state and to strengthen public authority. He himself took up residence at Nicomedia in order to supervise the Eastern provinces. The territorial division was followed by a reorganization of the central powers; old Republican offices gave way to a more efficient administration subject to the Emperor.

The army was also transformed, divided into mobile units (*comitatenses*), easily transferred from one theatre of war to another, and into units of peasant–soldiers (*limitanei*), settled on the frontiers for defence. The attempts of Diocletian to reform economic life were, however, unsuccessful; price-edicts did not stop a wave of inflation, the Emperor could not restore confidence in the currency, so that in Egypt the old coins from the time of Ptolemy were preferred to the imperial ones.

The abandonment of the great historical town and the transfer of the capital of the Empire 1500 km to the east was neither an accident nor a whim of the Emperor—it was determined by the political situation.[1] The long distance from Rome to the Eastern provinces complicated both the transfer of armies and the supply of corn for the capital from Egypt and the Black Sea provinces. Here too, far from the Roman temples, it was easier for the emperors to proclaim Christianity the state religion. In 392 pagan offerings were forbidden, the Emperor Gratian refusing to be *Pontifex*

Maximus. The ideas proclaimed by the emperors of the divine origin of absolute power, ideas very foreign to the traditions of the Roman Republic, were more quickly understood and accepted by the Eastern people.[2] Thus Rome ceased to be the capital of the world, *caput mundi*.

The Diocletian concept of a divided Empire with an Eastern capital was continued by Constantine and his successors. During the fourth century the Western and Eastern provinces of the Empire formed one whole for only 25 years.

On 26 November 326 at Byzantium, a place long remarkable for its strategic and economic position, Constantine established a new capital, which he was to call 4 years later Constantine's New Rome. The Emperor placed the heart of the Empire in the East, close to a barrier dividing both continents and seas. Byzantium was the centre of routes leading from the Danube Valley to the banks of the Euphrates, tracks joining the European continent with the Indian Ocean.

Within reach of the Byzantine fleet lay the Black Sea and the Basin of the Mediterranean and roads led from Byzantium in all directions, to the Balkan Peninsula, the Valley of the Danube, the shores of the Adriatic, the Black Sea shores, Asia Minor, the lands behind the Caucasus, Upper Mesopotamia and northern Syria. The Empire now had a maritime capital; according to Procopius, "The sea surrounds the town like a crown so that the remaining piece of land serves only to close the crown" (*De Aedificiis* I. 5, 10). But it was safe-guarded even by land, because already in the time of Constantine, the building of fortifications was begun, and after over 100 years, during the reign of Anastasius (491–518), the town was surrounded by walls from sea to sea.

The intersection of land and sea routes made for the power of Byzantium in times of expansion but it was also a weakness. The same routes which enabled the transfer and manoeuvring of armies also led enemies easily to a rich city. Along the roads in all directions came armies, merchants, goods. They were followed by Hellenic and Eastern ideas. Here the great traditions of Rome met with Christian mysticism and formed a new culture. In contrast to the deserted Rome, Constantinople grew and expanded, vibrating with life. In the sixth century the population of a million, all calling themselves Romans, consisted of multilingual tribes. They were Armenians, Syrians, Egyptians, Jews, inhabitants of Thrace, Slavs, Germans and of course Greeks, who gave the city its essential tone. As in Rome corn had to be imported for the inhabitants, whose existence depended on regular supplies, coming mainly from Egypt. The yearly freight of corn from Egypt, called *embole*, came to 8 million artabs, or about 11 million bushels, and it cost 80,000 solids a year.[3]

The division between East and West constantly deepened; it was determined by economic, social, political and ideological differences which paralyzed all attempts at creating a uniform, universal Empire. Justinian himself saw the failure of the attempt to restore the old Empire. His troops, after heavy casualties, occupied Italy in 536–46 and in 536 Rome herself. But his attempt, as well as some others initiated later, was quite fruitless. Although the disruption of the slave economy affected both East and West, so that the old political and social structure disappeared, it nevertheless took a different shape in either part of the Empire.[4]

In the West imperial power was weakened by the constant movement of troops, by wars and defeats. On the ruins of this power the Church was beginning to found its rule. The helpless and unarmed population sought protection from the landowners, and, by becoming thus dependent, loosened the grip of the state. Already at the beginning of the fifth century the landowners were undermining the power of the state, having at their disposal their own officials, police, postal services, and even armed forces (*bucellari*), which were kept on army pay (*bucella*). They also obtained the right to impose and collect taxes. The state now collected taxes indirectly through the landowners. The great mass of the "colons" had every day less contact with the official government administration. Their dependence on the landowners was preparing the ground for the social degrees of the feudal ladder.

In the East, however, the Byzantine emperors prevented this process. Laws were enforced imposing penalties both on those who abandoned "freedom" in order to enter into dependence on a feudal lord, and on the landowners who extended help and protection. In Justinian's Codex we read, "Nobody should promise his patronage to peasants or take them under his patronage in exchange for a fixed rent or other services. Whoever breaks this prohibition will be punished . . . " (*Cod. Iust.* XI. 54).

In *Novella* XXX Justinian writes to the governor of Cappadocia as follows:

> It appears to us that in your province there are terrible happenings and you will not achieve anything on your own. I blush with shame to hear about the incredible lawlessness of the magnates, who, with incredible arrogance, move about surrounded by armed troops composed of servants and local inhabitants, plundering without shame or conscience. We wonder how our subjects can tolerate such lawlessness. We hear of numerous complaints from ecclesiastics and women about the plundering of their estates.
>
> Even our own possessions have passed into private hands, the imperial studs have been wasted, and nobody has said a word because their lips were sealed with gold.

Similarly, in *Novella* XVII, *De mandatis principum*, Justinian writes to the governor of a province: "The 'patronage' which is spreading widely in our provinces should be opposed by all means; do not allow anybody to subject the lives of people to their own power and to oppose thus the authority of the state."

The war against "patronage" went on through the whole history of Byzantium. Emperor Constantine Porphyrogenitus (913–59) still says after his predecessor Romanus Lecapenus:

> Very often it has come to my knowledge that the wealthy men of Thrace, disregarding laws proclaimed by emperors and derived from natural human rights, and disobeying

our orders, continue to infiltrate into the countryside. They expel the poor from the land which belongs to them, by tyrannizing them and by buying either gifts or wills. In consequence, having deliberated upon those cases . . . we establish a law that all those who, although forbidden by the orders of our predecessors from buying land from the poor, . . . have dared to infiltrate into the villages or to seize the land of the poor, must immediately, without any delay or explanations, vacate land obtained in such a way. They will not be entitled to claim any damages . . . .[5]

In the East the big estates, due to the action of the emperors, had constant restrictions imposed upon them. No independent, self-supporting economic organisms were formed; on the contrary, Byzantium, with its pulsating economic life, drew the big estates into the orbit of its own commercial interests.[6] The emperors were anxious to preserve communities of free peasants, which supplied good recruits as well as taxes.[7]

From the middle of the seventh century the free population in the country was growing and providing support for the imperial power.[8]

In the forties of the seventh century the Empire suffered a heavy military defeat and lost two-thirds of its territory to the Arabs in the South and to the Slavs in the East. It also lost its character as a world empire, preserving only the Eastern parts of it and ethnically and socially evolving several new characteristics. The mass settlement of Slavs and Armenians distinctly strengthened the class of small freeholders. The Slavs settled in the European provinces as well as in Asia Minor. The freeholder communities increased in number; the system of the "colonate" fell into abeyance. The free peasants formed the basis of the army and were for many years to defend the frontiers. The independent peasants, owning their own land, were the support and strength of the imperial power. Only now, after centuries, with the appearance of new tribes in the Empire, did the former abortive plan of the Gracchi to buttress the power of Rome with the support of the free peasants become a reality. Whereas in the West the free Frank peasant was unable to keep his independence, because the weakness of the imperial power forced him to seek the patronage of the local lords, the free Slavs in the Eastern Empire strengthened the imperial power, which was thus able to control the process of feudalization of the East.

Economic development was also different in the Eastern and Western towns, based either on local government of the Hellenic type or on the model of the Roman *municipium*. From the third century onwards there are more and more instances of citizens declining official posts which they were unable to shoulder. Helpless in the face of increasing disorder, they abandoned their estates and fled. In the ruined and depopulated towns in the West commercial life and crafts came to a standstill, whereas in the East, Constantinople developed commercial relations with great impetus, penetrating as far as China, India, Ceylon. Men and money flowed into the city. The privileged citizens of Constantinople looked with contempt at those from the old Greek cities. "Now", writes the Greek historian Eunapius in the fifth century, "the corn of all Asia, Syria and Phoenicia is not enough to feed the hungry mob which Constantine has herded to Byzantium from the bereaved towns of the Empire."[9] However, the jealousy of other towns could not stop the rapid development of the main market of the Empire, the world centre of exchange between East and West.

From the descriptions of the traveller Cosmas, a merchant and monk who lived in the reign of Justinian, we learn about the commercial routes to the Far East, about the value of the Byzantine currency and goods transported. The citizens of the new capital were convinced that their currency was of world importance, as we see in a boastful remark of Cosmas about the apparently high valuation of Byzantine coins by the ruler of Taprobane, i.e. Ceylon.

When a Byzantine of the name Sopater found himself in Ceylon together with some Persian merchants, the local ruler inquired about the power and influence of the kings of Persia and Byzantium. The Persians described their monarch as the most powerful master in the world, king of kings. Sopater, on the other hand, showing a Byzantine *nomisma* (coin) and a silver Persian coin, with emblems of their monarchs, apparently declared that coins are a proof of importance. Then, according to Cosmas' report, "the king examined the coins . . . compared them, and, being very impressed by the Byzantine ones, said that the Romans are powerful, marvellous and exceptionally wise. He also ordered Sopater to be treated with special respect. He was put on an elephant and taken round the town, accompanied by the music of caldrons."[10]

The merchants undertook long journeys by land, through Samarkand to the frontiers of Persia, and then through Persia to the city of Nisibis on the eastern frontier of the Empire, all in order to bring materials and spices for the court and the rich men of the Empire, who were always in need of luxuries. The maritime commercial routes converged on Ceylon and then led to the Persian Gulf or to the shores of Africa. The needs of the new capital, the volume of trade, the sumptuous life and love of luxury, all stimulated the merchants' activities and the enterprise of craftsmen even in the provincial towns of the East.

There was also a difference between the Eastern structure of power and its Roman models. There existed in Byzantium the traditional offices of consuls and praetors—there was even a senate formed from the landed aristocracy—but they were merely symbols, titles of honour, vestiges of the past which were of no consequence in the real organization of the state. Justinian, wishing to restore the universality of the Empire, declared:

"We are re-establishing all that existed in the past, although its value has been minimized . . . by respecting the name of Romans we will ensure that the past will in a greater measure come back to life in our state" (*Nov.* XVII).

The preservation of ancient titles aimed at restoring only the memory of a uniform state, because in fact, apart from the army and the emperor, a centralized bureaucracy held the reins of power. The emperor's deputy, appointed especially for the provinces, was a high official called *praefectus pretorio per orientem*. The government lay in the hands of the *quaestor sacri palatii* who was in charge of justice; the *comes sacrarum largitionum*, who was in charge of the mint and taxes, the *comes rerum privatarum*, who looked after the emperor's estates and income, and the *magister officiorum*, who had the highest power and supervised the postal services, the emperor's enormous office, internal transport and foreign missions. The highest officials formed the council of state (*sacrum consistorium*), which occasionally also included the military chiefs (*magistri militum*). To the ruling *élite* belonged the Patriarch of Constantinople and the mayor of the city (*praefectus urbi*), who also held the office of chairman of the senate.

In the entourage of the emperor were many officials for his personal service (*cubicularii*), headed by a high ranking official (*praepositus sacri cubiculi*).

Originally the official language was Latin, but later, in the sixth century Greek came into use. From the beginning of the seventh century, after heavy defeats and the loss of two-thirds of the Eastern provinces to the Arabs and Slavs, the eyes of the emperors were turned not to Rome but towards Athens. The idea of restoring the Roman Empire was abandoned; after an unsuccessful attempt to expand westwards the main interest became focused on Greek culture, the treasures of the Greek past, the discovery of Greek drama; there was a revival of Aristotle and, more especially, of Plato. The Greek language triumphantly replaced Latin. These were the first signs of an approaching renaissance in Byzantium.

The Greek language of Byzantium differed from the Hellenic models; pathos and emphasis obliterated the sharpness, simplicity and clarity of the words. It seems that an attempt was made to restore vitality to a language which had lost its quality and strength by the use of a great number of adjectives and unnecessary repetitions. However, it meant that Byzantine Greek should preserve for the world the greatness of antiquity when the splendour of Rome was waning.

During its long history (over 1000 years) the Eastern Empire did not enjoy good relations with its neighbours, for its shining luxury roused both jealousy and apprehension. Where diplomacy and money failed, Byzantine armies intervened, repelling the onslaughts of calculating Persians, fearless Slavs, fanatical Arabs, invidious Crusaders, to succumb in the end to the power of the Turks. Within the Empire confusion was increased by the struggles of pretenders to the throne, palace revolutions and interminable, barren theological disputes.

In the eighth century the marks of the slave system gradually disappeared from Byzantium, and at the same time there started strong heretical and plebeian movements led by the Paulicians. The stormy surface of actual events tends to veil the deep social conflicts which cut through the history of Byzantium. Revolutionary demonstrations of the people, armed struggles against rich and hated rulers, and the tactics of the emperors to win over by concessions or to frighten by threats are proofs of class conflicts. Not only the interests of the poor and the rich clashed but also those of various ruling cliques. The landed aristocracy quarrelled with the financial aristocracy. Big landlords, using their privileges, tried through their own bureaucracy to eliminate the state apparatus, which was on the other side supported by the moneyed merchant class, aiming at security for their own commercial enterprises.

Whereas the free peasants, who grew in number from the seventh century onwards, were the strength of the central power, they were the cause of the weakness of the landed aristocracy, because their presence checked the spread of slavery. The rulers of Byzantium exploited this lack of unity among the possessing classes by turning the financial aristocracy against the landed aristocracy. The more enterprising emperors sought the support of the populace, like the Emperor Phocas (602–10) who reached the throne with the help of the people[11] or the Emperor Andronicus Comnenus (1182–5) when the empire was on the point of disintegration. A hostile historian, Theophylact Simocatta, then wrote about Phocas

> . . . amid the shouts of the people, who demanded a complete reversal of existing conditions, a usurper was acclaimed as Caesar, and so ignominy was perpetrated, evil triumphed over good and the disasters of the Romans began . . . At the church of St. John the Baptist that villain was crowned, and then he drove into the capital in the imperial carriage, drawn by four white horses, took possession of the palace, took gold from the treasury and scattered it in the streets, like rain from a golden cloud . . . .[12]

A contemporary historian, Acominatus, wrote otherwise about the Emperor Andronicus: "without infantry or cavalry and armed only with justice he went lightly to the capital which loved him . . .". To him Acominatus also turns with delight: ". . . we have known for long that you are gentle to the poor, terrible to the greedy, that you are a defender of the weak and an enemy of the violent, that you do not turn the scales of Themis either to the left or to the right and that your hands are clean from any corruption".[13]

The thousand years' history of Byzantium, where power was held by men and women alike, was marked by splendour and glory, defeat and decline. Out of 107 rulers between 395 and 1453 only 34 died a natural death; the others fell as victims of conflicts, uprisings, wars. There were 65 palace revolutions. In the seventh century the Empire went through a difficult period, losing most of its territories to the Arabs, Slavs and Avars. The believers of Islam found themselves under the walls of Constantinople in 674–8; in the Balkans a new serious danger formed and consolidated, that is, a Bulgarian state. Inside the Empire began the disruption of the slave economy and sharp social conflicts, leading to revolutionary movements among the plebeians, directed by the Paulicians.

From the beginning of the eighth century for 100 years the rulers of the Syrian dynasty, started in 717 by Emperor Leo III, used the free peasants to try and restore the greatness of the Empire. They evolved an absolute state, successfully opposed the authority of the religious orders and regained most of the lost possessions. Under this dynasty took place the unification of the state, the reorganization of administration, and a struggle against the dominance, wealth and ignorance of the monasteries. The Syrian rulers resurrected in Byzantium Hellenic ideas, proclaimed laws making all citizens equal under law, guaranteed free court proceedings, and above all strengthened legally the position of the free peasants.

The powerful commercial situation of Byzantium, its accumulated wealth, the exertions of the military commanders together with the shrewd political tactics of the government, made possible a long period of glory. For nearly 200 years during the rule of the Macedonian dynasty (867–1056) and of the Comnenian dynasty (1081–1185) the Byzantine court successfully rivalled that of the Baghdad caliphs. However, in the internal structure the courageous and progressive measures of the Syrian dynasty were gradually disregarded. The free peasants became feudalized, reactionary clergy came to the fore, fiscal exploitation brought in dissatisfaction and revolt.[14]

From the end of the twelfth century the centre of world economy shifted to Venice and Genoa and their merchants grasped the strings of Byzantium's economic life. Their incomes surpassed the sums paid into the treasury and the profits of Byzantine citizens. Economic difficulties caused inflation; the value of the *nomisma* decreased several times; currency was no more made of gold but of an alloy of silver and copper. The Italian Republics defeated Byzantium commercially and in 1204 were to destroy it at the hands of the Crusaders. For many tens of years Christian knights left ruin and poverty in the capital of the Empire. According to the testimony of the historian Gregoras Nicephorus, even in the fourteenth century there were still traces of the Crusaders' destruction. "Imperial palaces and the residences of the aristocracy", says the historian, "lay in ruins, serving as public conveniences for passers-by, and the big and splendid houses surrounding the Church of Sophia, which were formerly the pride of ancient architecture, lay in ruins or were razed to the ground . . . ."[15]

In 1397 the Turks besieged Byzantium and finally, on 29 May 1453, when they occupied the capital, they brought the Eastern Empire to its end.

From this mass of social and economic contradictions developed political doctrines, deriving from the state concepts of both East and West, from the cross-section of religious beliefs in this borderland of Asia and Europe, from dogmatic controversies and elements of Greek philosophy. The mass of the people were opposed to the official doctrine, tainted by theocracy; misled by

their own leaders, they were not always conscious of their role. Side by side
with the imperial and popular ideas there spread scepticism and pessimism,
either steeped in Greek philosophy, or expressed in a religious doctrine.[16]

2. THE OFFICIAL DOCTRINE

During the reign of Justinian (527–65), who reigned for nearly 40 years, the
official doctrine of the Byzantine Empire received its best form. It was composed of three elements: the Christian religion, ideas from Roman law, and
belief in the divine origin of power. Already under his predecessors Christian
doctrine had enjoyed the position of the state religion, requesting from the
faithful obedience and humility towards the ruler. The Stoic concept of law,
in its Roman interpretation, attributed to the generally accepted norms of
the empire the power of bringing about natural order in the world. And the
Eastern theocratic conception of the divine power of the ruler, influenced the
formation of the official Byzantine doctrine.[17]

All possible external signs were used, both in private and in public life, to
stress the divine origin of power. The emperors themselves were convinced
that their power derived from God. Justinian believed that he himself was
chosen by God and looked after by angels with all care in all his under-
takings.[18]

Emperor Basil I (867–86), addressing his son Leo, says: "You received the
power from God . . . you will receive the crown from God through my
hands."[19] Constantine VII Porphyrogenitus (913–59), in his treatise about
the art of government (*De administrando imperio*), says to his son: "God puts
emperors on the throne and gives them power over all . . . . Your throne, like
the sun, will stand in front of Him, and His eyes will be fixed on you, and
nothing will be terrifying to you, because God has chosen you and separated
you from your mother and transferred His power to you, recognizing you as
the best of all."

During the coronation the Patriarch crowning the emperor was meant to
represent the will of the state, and, at the same time, when anointing he
underlined the divinity of imperial power. The emperors used Greek letters
to describe their dignity, with the additional word θεῖος, which corresponded to the Latin *augustus*.

Whereas the highest dignitaries of the Church had the right to use the
titles ὅσιος or ἅγιος to stress their sanctity, for the emperor only was
reserved the title θεῖος, divine. In the presence of the emperor they fell down
with outstretched arms and kissed his feet. The historian of Justinian's time,
Procopius, says that the Eastern way of paying homage, from Justinian's
reign onwards, bound also the senators, who had previously greeted the
emperor only by kissing his right breast. All that surrounded the emperor at
his court was divine, saintly, and almost an object of cult. All was in the
charge of Cubicularii, under the leadership of the *praepositus sacri cubiculi*.[20]

The form of theocratical concepts was determined by the belief of the emperors that they were called by God to regulate matters of faith and to decide the choice of the leaders of the Church. They took part in dogmatic controversies, issued directives and religious decisions, convened councils, proclaimed the validity of the rulings of the courts.

In the West, which was evading imperial control, the popes and the bishops successfully strove for independence. Conflicts took place later between the secular and the religious power. In the East the doctrine of a state Church was established; in the West an independent Church defended a dual concept of two powers, religious and secular, of which the secular was dependent on the religious. In the East the influence and direction of the Church by the emperors were particularly strong; here religion was an important element in ideas and organization, binding together the multi-lingual empire of the East.[21] "Trust in God", says Justinian, "is the only support guaranteeing the existence of the Empire; in it lies the salvation of our soul, and therefore it is necessary that all our jurisdiction derive from this principle, which ought to be the beginning, the middle and the end" (*Nov.* 109 *praef.*). Justinian considered himself to be the highest theologian, called by God to decide in matters of faith. In 533, for instance, he issued to the citizens of all towns a proclamation on questions of dogma, condemning heretics; and in 553 he arranged for a council at Constantinople, to stress the unity of Church and state. He then officially condemned any philosophy, which might contaminate the Christian religion. The Byzantine emperors, following the example of the Persians, made the Eastern Church into a state Church, and the Western Church and papacy they treated as political partners, useful in an attempt to create a universal empire.[22]

They raised Christianity to the rank of the official religion, reserving for themselves the last word in all matters of the Eastern Church. The tenth-century book of ceremony for the election of the Patriarch of Constantinople, who in fact ruled the Eastern Church, explicitly underlines the decisive role of the emperor in the election. At the command of the emperor the metro-politans gathered in the Church of St. Sophia and presented to him three candidates. If the emperor rejected all three and nominated his own candidate, the gathering of the metropolitans simply acknowledged that the candidate was worthy to be patriarch. In the presence of the senate and the clergy present, the emperor specifically declared to the newly chosen patriarch that "by the will of God and Emperor" he received that honour.[23] In turn, the candidate of the emperor had an influence on the policy and choice of personnel of the Church, and this served to strengthen the unity of the Eastern state.

Justinian quite officially favoured the Church, often having recourse to injustice, which was in his mind justified by religion.

In the Christian religion [says Procopius about Justinian] he considered himself unyielding, which meant defeat and misery for his subjects. He left the clergy complete freedom to impose methods of force on the people. If they spoiled the estates of their neighbours, without exception he gave them his approval and support, assuming that in this way he was showing his piety. He considered it a service to God if he praised ecclesiastical decisions enabling the clergy, under the pretext of the interests of the Church, to occupy by force estates not in their rightful possession, later obtaining confirmation of such lawlessness in court. The Emperor saw the ideal of justice in the victory of the clergy over their opponents. He himself took possession of estates belonging either to living or deceased landlords and then offered them to the churches and boasted about it, covering his sinful deeds by such pious behaviour, so that the appropriated estates would never return to those who suffered such violence" [*Historia arcana*, XIII, 4–6].

The openly supported Church did not remain indebted to the emperor, but offered him support in the administration of the state.

At the head of the dioceses were bishops, formally elected by the faithful, but in fact by the clergy of the diocese, with the approval of the metropolitan and of the patriarch. The bishops were subject to the metropolitans, whose jurisdiction covered the territory of an administrative province; and the metropols in turn were parts of five patriarchates—Rome, Constantinople, Antioch, Jerusalem, Alexandria.[24] In the Byzantine State the bishops exercised social and state functions, proclaimed imperial laws, kept hospitals (νοσοκομεῖα), orphanages (ὀρφανοτροφεῖα), old people's homes (γεροντοκομεῖα), hostels (πτωχοτροφεῖα). Eastern Christianity was the official doctrine of the Byzantine Empire and ecclesiastical institutions were to facilitate rule over the people by discreetly smoothing over social and tribal differences among the faithful.

Whereas the organization of the Eastern Church was of help to the emperors in the government of the state, the essence of the Christian doctrine, differently interpreted by the faithful, was a source of constant controversies. Confused and full of understatements, the Christian religion provided many opportunities for discussions and dogmatic quarrels. The subjects of the controversies changed, as well as the arguments and sympathies of the rulers; but there remained discord between the Western and Eastern parts of the Empire, reflected in never-ending religious conflicts. So long as the Byzantine emperors were trying to restore a universal empire from Spain to the Euphrates, they made every effort to resolve dogmatic controversies. Their attempts, however, to change the course of history proved futile; in practice the economic and political situation sundered the attempted unity.

The differences tearing the Empire apart were accompanied by strong religious divergences, alienating the faithful in the East and West from each other.[25] The conflict between the Western Orthodox and the Eastern Monophysites was long and unyielding. The orthodox followers of Rome defended the dualistic concept of the divine and human nature of Christ, the Monophysites advanced the doctrine that Christ was only divine. The conflicts and wars between them went on for centuries, starting with the declaration of Origen, who taught that God is pure spirit, timeless, not perceived by the senses, first cause of creation, and from him came Christ, mediating between God and the world. The teaching of Origen started a speculative discussion in the Church, to ascertain the relation of the divine to the human nature in Christ. The Emperor Constantine, in an unsuccessful attempt to end the quarrel, proclaimed "the identity of the nature of Father and Son".[26] In Syria, in the first half of the fifth century, Nestorius came out against the official Church. Starting from Aristotle's philosophy, Nestorius and his followers distinguished the divine from the human nature in Christ, and consequently denied sanctity to the Mother of God. The condemnation of the Nestorians at the Council of Ephesus in 431 did not close the controversies in the Church.

As a result of unending barren discussions a temporary agreement was reached that Christ is God and Man, but at the same time theological speculation found a new subject: whether the divine and human nature in Christ preserved their identity or whether, as the Monophysites said, the divine and human elements merged into one. The Council of Chalcedon in 451 accepted the dualistic thesis of Rome about the different natures of Christ, "true God and true man . . . with an unchanged nature both divine and human . . . ."[27] The Monophysites did not accept the decisions of the Council, and with the support of the emperors Zeno (474–91) and, later, Anastasius I (491–518), opposed Rome. The continuing dogmatic controversies did not prevent Christianity from being the official doctrine in the Empire. On the contrary, the discords in the Church offered the emperors an excellent opportunity to regulate their relations with the papacy by adopting a varying policy towards both sides. When, for instance, Justinian wanted to create unity in the Empire he officially supported the orthodox view in order to preserve good relations with Rome. At the same time he had in reserve the support of the Monophysites, backed by his wife Theodora.

Behind the speculative and dogmatic discussions about the nature of Christ there were different social interests and conflicting tendencies in East and West. In the belief of the Monophysites the dualistic concept of the orthodox faith was only a ruse on the part of the official Church to sanction the possession of wordly riches and a love of earthly life. Hence the call to asceticism proclaimed by the Monophysites was an attack on social inequalities, the possession of estates and the wealth of the Church.[28] In addition the Monophysites represented the separatist tendencies of the Eastern peoples, who opposed the superiority of both Rome and Byzantium.

The epilogue of these ecclesiastical controversies was the Eastern Schism. On 16 July 1054 in the capital of the Byzantine emperors the papal legates anathematized the Eastern Patriarch Michael Cerullarius. In return the dignitaries of the Eastern Church anathematized the papal legates, calling them "wild boars", and this disturbed the peace of the "holy city".[29]

The predecessors of Justinian had recognized the Christian religion as an official one, realizing the usefulness of Christian humility and of ecclesiastical organization for the state; but Justinian also wanted to bind the empire together by a unified system of law. In this way the multitribal population was to be unified by religion and law. Almost from the beginning of his reign Justinian started the work of codification; a unified system had to be evolved from multifarious legal norms. Until then had been in force the precepts of the XII tables, popular declarations, motions of the Senate, pretorian edicts; the last were codified by the lawyer Salvius Julianus at the request of the Emperor Hadrian. The collection of these multifarious rules, full of repetitions and contradictions, also included imperial constitutions and the cases of famous lawyers. By order of Justinian a codifying bureau was formed, directed by the minister of justice (*quaestor sacri palatii*), Tribonian, a man of wide learning and legal experience. He began codification on 15 December 530, with the help of his officials and also of professors from Berytos and the more prominent members of the Supreme Court.[30]

In a special declaration, named after its first words *Deo auctore*, there was contained the directive to prepare a codex, πανδέκται in Greek, *Digesta* in Latin. In it we find the maxim of the Stoics that Roman law realizes the natural order permeating divine and human matters.

> ... There is nothing more important for things in the world than the fact that they are subject to law; both human and divine matters are regulated by the orderly power of law, removing injustice. The origins of our law are very distinct, going back to Romulus, to the founding of Rome. Hence their ever increasing number and obscurity, so that they have ceased to be available. Our most important task is the correction and ordering of all laws in a clear way.[31]

When after 3 years there appeared the *Digesta*, Professor Dorotheos and Professor Theophilos were given the task of preparing a textbook, *Institutiones*, for student lawyers. At the same time, the Emperor, in a special letter, expressed his views about the role and importance of the idea of law for the Empire.

> ... Imperial Majesty should rest not only on arms, but should also be equipped with law in order to be a leading force in war or peace. The Roman Emperor is not only victorious over enemies in the field, but is also the highest guarantor of law, destroying those who break it; therefore he is not only the most responsible guardian of law but also the most complete victor over the defeated enemy ... for that reason, do learn law with all your strength and be so educated that you might, at the end of your studies, rule the country from your official positions.[32]

Justinian several times repeated the principle that a legal codex cannot be a rigid whole; he understood the necessity of adjusting law to the changing circumstances of life, considering himself as the only person entitled to decide about any changes. "Human problems", he says in *Novella* 49, "change and never stay the same, they are always in motion, never stable". "Nature", he says in *Novella* 85, "brings changes in all directions . . . and as long as it is like that, we will be forced to declare new legal norms."

After codification, the uncodified norms lost their legal validity. The work of Justinian became law on 30 December 533. It was forbidden to publish any commentaries; to avoid confusion it was forbidden to use any abbreviations when copying the *Digests*, in order to exclude any possible ambiguities and the necessity of interpretation. The Emperor gave permission to teach law to the professors of Rome, Constantinople and Beirut only, because in these towns his ideas found full appreciation; he forbade any teaching in Alexandria or Athens, where he met with criticism. He claimed that the professors tended to change the laws by their critical lectures—"*non leges docent sed in leges committunt*".[33] He did not wish, under any circumstances, to create a situation where it would be possible to break the law or avoid it. "If an order, even were it given by the divine power of the emperor, directed the judge to conduct the proceedings one way or another, the judge should nevertheless obey only the law. According to our wish", says Justinian (*Nov.* 82, 13) "only what is expressed in the law should be legally binding."

Justinian demanded absolute obedience to a unified and universal law, hoping thereby to avoid any possible disorder as a result to exceptional judgements passed outside the law. In *Novella* 92 and 94 the Emperor quotes the wisdom of antiquity in order to prove that judges are not to solve problems or unique situations but only occurrences of a universal character.

The codex of Justinian was supposed to give to the state a feeling of stability and security. Justinian realized that the durability of a multilingual empire could not be sufficiently preserved by administration or by a multilingual army, nor would the traditions and splendour of Rome constitute a sufficient bond. What was necessary was an officially recognized idea which would bind the population together, giving citizens a feeling of security and the rulers a guarantee of stability.

Such an idea was provided by the religious and legal doctrine of Justinian, grounded on Church and Roman law. By going back to the history of pagan Rome the emperor wanted to buttress the authority of his Christian state and law. "In the life of our state", says Justinian, "we must bring about a return to antiquity in order to maintain the glory and respect due to Roman names" (*Nov.* 24). But simultaneously he demanded a rigid observance of the principles of the new religion in its fight against the pagan past.

The political ideas of Justinian, in their form of a compact doctrine, can be found in a political treatise of the sixth century. The extant fragments of this treatise, whose authorship is ascribed to Peter the Patrician, illustrate the views of the aristocracy, who tried to combine the legal concepts of Justinian's state with their own interests.[34] Following the idea of the Platonic *utopia*, the treatise expresses the view that only the aristocracy is called upon to govern because political wisdom is an attribute of that class, and the aristocracy can assure legal order and prosperity for the whole of society.

There are four political principles in the treatise representing the programme of the aristocratic circles of the time of Justinian. The first is a recognition of the divinity of the emperor, in whose hands lies the general management of the state. Secondly, the institution of an aristocratic senate is regarded as the pillar of the state. Thirdly, it is postulated that the highest apparatus of power should belong to the aristocracy, which ought to be in charge of state affairs. Fourthly, the people should be completely separated from the affairs of state, because, being subject to changeable moods, they cannot rule, but can only be ruled and educated by aristocratic leaders. The political doctrine of the treatise expressed the desire and intention of one class, while on the contrary, political practice in Byzantium had to reckon with the people, who often intervened efficiently in the most important affairs of state.

The religio-legal doctrine based on Justinian's principles was accepted 200 years later by the Syrian dynasty, especially by Emperor Leo III (717–41), who adapted it to changed circumstances. Leo was a Syrian, speaking Greek and Arabic fluently. He used the doctrine, not for the restoration of a universal Roman Empire, as did Justinian, but to consolidate the Graeco-Byzantine Empire, leaving out the distant provinces of West and East. He realized that the defence and strength of the Eastern Empire depended both on a good army and on the strong internal unity of the state. Following the example of his predecessors, he gave the military commanders complete power in the provinces. The government of many provinces had already passed into the hands of the commanders of army corps. Administrative units were now also known as "corps" (θέμα). Leo III was concerned for the unity of the state; thus he increased the number of military districts to 35, so that provincial commanders might not constitute too strong a power within the Empire. The commanders of army corps were in turn subject to central military headquarters (στρατάρχαι). Only the judges (κριταί) and tax collectors (ἐπόπται) in the provinces were subordinated to the central offices. By issuing in 726 an extract from the existing laws ('Εκλογή) the Emperor tried to impose on the citizens a uniform legal system.

The rulers of the Syrian dynasty took from Justinian the idea of basing the state on a uniform codification but they changed the essential sense of the legal norms. The statutes of Leo III ('Εκλογή) express progressive ideas in comparison with the laws of Justinian. They proclaim the principle of the equality of all Christian citizens under law, forbid "contempt for the lowest classes and lawless toleration of the crimes of the powerful". The statutes about slavery disappeared, the enforced obligations of the peasants were reduced, as well as the sphere of paternal rights; husband and wife became equal in law, Church estates were taxed, and free and professional judicature was guaranteed and made subject to new laws. As a result of his concern for the security of the state, in the statutes of Leo III high treason did not only constitute, as in Justinian's code, an offence against the majesty of the Emperor, but an attempt against the entire state. "If anyone intends, plans or organizes an attempt against the emperor or against the Christian state he deserves to be killed as one who wants to destroy everything." [35]

The policy, introduced in the seventh century, of the settlement on imperial territories of free peasants, who were to cultivate the land and defend the state, gradually replaced the system of the "colonate". Now a new agrarian law (νόμος γεωργικός) a collection of established shepherd laws, officially sanctioned their freedom and economic liberty. The Emperor also issued a maritime statute (νόμος ναυτικός) to revive maritime trade, and a military statute (νόμος στρατιωτικός) in order to restore discipline and obedience in the army. Leo III and his successors wanted to rule by law and through a centralized apparatus of government and religious doctrine. [36] At the head of the government was the chief of the treasury (σακελλάριος) assisted by four high officials (λογοθέτες); in charge of internal transport and diplomacy was the general tax collector (τοῦ δρόμου); the general army quartermaster (τοῦ γενικοῦ) the administrator of imperial estates (τοῦ στρατιωτικοῦ); judicature was administered by the quaestor (τῶν ἀγελῶν). Like Justinian, the emperor considered himself, "I am emperor and priest". Exploiting the tendencies of iconoclasm, he opposed the reactionary monks and religious orders, who kept the people in ignorance and superstition and were themselves the most determined followers of the cult of holy pictures and relics. The emperor liquidated the monasteries, removed backwardness and ignorance. He undertook a cultural revolution to shake off the influence of uneducated monks and repaired the finances of the state by confiscating the estates of monasteries and churches. However, the acitivities of Leo III and of his successors, already full of ideas of a renaissance, penetrated religious fanaticism only with difficulty.

The rulers of the Macedonian dynasty gradually liquidated the progressive legislation of their predecessors. Justinian's concept of binding the state together by means of religion was revived for the benefit of a developing feudalism. Basil I (867–86), in his introduction to the collection of laws, ('Επαναγωγή) writes about the legislation of the iconoclasts that they were "unreasonable norms, contrary to divine law and breaking the useful codification of Justinian". About 888 Leo VI issued a collection of laws entitled *Basilica*; this is a restitution of Justinian's codex for use in Church organization. In the introduction to the *Basilica* we read:

> As society, like the human body, is composed of parts and members, its most important parts are the emperor and the patriarch. Therefore the peace and happiness of the subjects depend on the entire material and moral harmony between two powers—the empire and the archpriesthood . . . . The emperor is the legal supremacy and the common good of all subjects. His duty is to do good. He ought especially to carry out the decisions of oecumenical councils, the precepts of *Holy Scripture* and the laws of the Empire. [37]

The views of the feudal gentry are found in a heroic epic about Digenis Acritas. This national song describes the life of a provincial feudal lord, who spends his time in endless fights, hunts, love-affairs and banquets. Among the sayings of the hero of the Byzantine epic we find the provincial gentry's opinion of the emperor. "They think", says Digenis, "that it is the duty of the ruler who desires fame, to love his subjects, take care of those in misery, defend the unjustly injured, not to listen to hypocrites, not to meddle illegally with other people's property, but to fight heretics and defend the true faith." [38] In the epic can be discerned the pride of the provincial magnates, who, although recognizing the primacy of the emperor and of the Church, at the same time have contempt for the courtiers, believing that force makes law and that the sword is the ruler.

The provincial Byzantine gentry, whose ideals incorporated those of Digenis, were soon to find a common interest in the European feudal lords, who came to the Empire during the crusades.

In the middle of the eleventh century there appeared a political treatise containing official theocratic doctrine. Its author was a higher military official, Katakalon Kekaumenos. In his remarks about the divine nature of the monarch the author tries to connect the unlimited power of a divinely authorized ruler with the precepts of religious ethics, which, according to him, should be the limits of executive power. His main thought expresses the belief that a ruler reigning morally and justly is an example and a benediction to his subjects. Giving the ruler practical advice, Kekaumenos sees an efficient and wise reign as dependent on shrewd advisers, a fighting army, an efficient staff of honest officials, equal treatment of all citizens, and a uniform and just levy of taxes. Kekaumenos must have been shocked by the influence of foreigners at the Byzantine court because he often repeats the axiom "restrict them in their privileges". Kekaumenos was a man of action rather than of abstract thought, and his treatise is an attempt to translate a theoretical doctrine into the language of practical needs.[39]

3. THE PLEBEIAN MOVEMENT AND ITS IDEOLOGY

The populace of the Byzantine towns, and of the capital in particular, participated in the elections of the emperor, and both the high officials and the ruler standing for election had to reckon with their opinion. The support of the populace was an important factor in the disputes between groups of the ruling class. The favour of the town populace was sought after by both the moneyed aristocracy and by the court. Its prestige grew daily, because everywhere people were flocking to the big towns, and particularly to the capital. Justinian reflects with fear: "The provinces are continually deprived of population and our big cities are overcrowded by an influx of people from various parts of the country" (*Nov.* 80 *praef.*).

In order to stop the flow of people to the capital, various measures were taken, forbidding entry or limiting the length of stay in the capital. This only improved matters provisionally, and could not change the general tendency.

The population of the town was organized, according to the urban districts, into "demes", which until the eleventh century did not influence politics directly because the then known organization consisted of two parties in the circus, factions embracing in their organization the population of the demes. From the middle of the seventh century the activities of the circus party considerably decreased and this directly stimulated the development of the demes. The latter had no separate and compact doctrine; the enforced religious beliefs and the existing legal order excluded the possibility of another school of thought whose ideas would clash with the interests of the possessing classes. When the population of the towns was exploited in internal conflicts, the property-owning classes tried through their voiced opinion to create the impression that their own interests were the same as those of the people.[40] However, the people were conscious of their injury, and, although they had no leaders, no programme, no compact doctrine, they continued to accuse the emperor and the officials in the face of the army and armed bureaucracy, and by revolutionary deeds they confirmed the legitimacy of their demands. Gatherings in the circus served for many occasions; in every bigger town in the empire the circus was the place where the populace gathered for the parades of the professional sportsmen, and it also acted as a tribune from which judgement was passed on the current government.[41] Here people assembled for the election of the emperor, here he showed himself to the people; here the victorious generals, returning from wartime expeditions, were admired and acclaimed; here the populace had a chance to show their dissatisfaction, and here, by the staging of sumptuous spectacles, attempts were made to win the support of the people.

The people of Constantinople always assisted formally at the election of emperors, but in fact the choice was made by higher military commanders and the army.

The election took place on the military parade ground, where assembled the commanders, higher officials and the army. The people in the hippodrome showed their approval or disapproval by shouting when the names of the candidates were called out. We know that the commander of the military camp (*campiductor*) hung an imperial chain on the neck of the newly elected ruler. The people then raised the shout, "He is worthy." When the emperor appeared to the crowd they shouted the formula, "Divine emperor, you are victorious, you are pious, you are noble. God has sent you, may God protect you. If you worship Christ, victory will always be yours. He will be emperor for many years." According to the ceremonial, the emperor thanked only God and the army for his election.[42]

According to tradition there was a division of the spectators into the supporters and the opponents of those fighting in the arena. They were distin-

guished by emblems, the "greens" and the "blues", as these were the colours
of the fighters in the circus. From these initial sympathies and antipathies
towards the professional sportsmen there grew in the course of years two
compact parties, also called factions, which came to exist independently of
circus spectacles. The factions had their separate organizations and their
representatives at the imperial court; the supporters of each party occupied
special seats in the circus and even wore distinctive clothing. Although the
parties had no established political programmes, there was great hatred
between their members, a hatred sustained by the ruling classes. The financial
oligarchy, rich craftsmen and merchants, usually looked to the greens for
support; in that party prevailed the anti-papal, separatist tendencies, hence
the support of the greens for the Monophysites. The landed aristocracy, on the
other hand, were supported by the blues, who approved of the pro-Roman
policy of the Empire.[43] It was in the interests of the rulers to preserve lasting
discord among the people, and they thus created mutual antagonisms. The
emperors influenced the activities of the parties through their leaders, who,
belonging to the imperial court, occupied important posts in the state hierarchy. The rulers in turn supported personally one or another. The monarchy
approved of the divisions among the members of the demes, reflected as they
were in the animosities between the parties, because the division of the people
strengthened the position of the monarchy.

The discord in the demes, the mutual hatred of both parties, were not
properly understood by their contemporaries. Procopius said "Nobody knows
why they hate each other mortally, why they fight, why one belongs to the
greens, another to the blues. Everybody puts party above everything else, so
that for him there is no family, no friendship, no human or divine law—he is
concerned neither with state nor with country. Both women and men are
possessed by this blind madness" (*Bell. Pers.* I, 24).

However, in spite of those, as Procopius calls them, mad and incomprehensible party struggles, there was occasionally an agreement among all
the people when they joined together (above the head of the Caesar and
his subordinates) to continue the fight against violence, exploitation and
injustice.

The necessity to fight to the end the hated ruler, the officials and the
possessing classes, was a kind of programme for the united parties. At critical
moments the people were roused to the point of action, seeking the overthrow of the ruling emperor, war against foreigners, the replacement of hated
officials and the establishment of a new power which would have the confidence of the people. By the middle of the seventh century the parties of the
circus no longer had importance in the political life of Byzantium. The financial oligarchy, which used the party of the greens in its political manoeuvres,
lost its economic position in the middle of the seventh century and was no
longer interested in circus factions. The military failures of Byzantium

and the loss of the Eastern territories brought about a considerable decrease in commercial transactions and, in consequence, the economic collapse of the big merchants, financiers and bankers. The end of the political role of the factions did not weaken the importance of the demes. On the contrary, so long as the idea of going back to the Greek traditions prevailed in the Empire, the political importance of the demes increased. The revolutionary demonstrations of the demes revealed the social conflicts of the Empire; the official religious and legal doctrine could not level down the differences of wealth among the people of the Byzantine Empire.

History has recorded for us the revolution of *nika*, which took place in the time of Justinian. The Emperor obviously favoured the members of the party of the blues, called *venets*, who supported his expansionist policy and his attempts to restore the historical empire. The blues, enjoying the support of the government, terrorized their opponents, but at the same time showed their sympathy with the Emperor; in the circus they occupied seats on the right of the imperial box, thus expressing their attachment and loyalty. In spite of these mutual sympathies between the Emperor and the *venets*, the interest of the people proved stronger. In August 532, in the hippodrome, the opponents of the blues, that is, the greens (called πράσινοι) demanded the release of certain members of their party who were imprisoned; at the same time they accused the Emperor of breaking the law. To the surprise of the ruling circles, the two parties joined forces against the government.

> So long as the names of the colours divided the demes, [writes Procopius (*Bell. Pers.* I, 24)], ... the ministers could govern with impunity. But when ... the demes came to an agreement and the rising broke out, the whole city showed its hatred for them (the ministers) and demanded their death .... When one day the authorities responsible for the demes in Constantinople conducted a few of the rioters to the scene of execution, the members of both demes rose up in arms, freed the condemned, and afterwards took the prison by force and set free those who were detained for rioting, or for any other crime. They murdered without mercy all representatives of the government; the leading citizens fled to the other shore while the insurgents set the town on fire as if it had been conquered by an enemy. Hagia Sophia was burned, as were also the baths of Zeuxippe, the whole area between the imperial palace and the field of Mars, the big portico which stretched up to the square of Constantine and numerous palaces and precious possessions of the rich. Meanwhile the Emperor Justinian remained inactive in his palace, together with his wife and some of the senators. The rallying call of the insurgents were the words, 'be victorious' (νίκα), from which the whole rising took its name.

The antagonisms between the two parties disappeared; the people, united by hatred of the oppressors, with shouts of *nika* (victory) rushed to the quarters of the rich and surrounded the imperial palace. Constantinople was burning, and members of the landed aristocracy crossed the Bosphorus to seek refuge in the cities of Asia Minor. Justinian, by means of hired troops, restored order with difficulty, sending his best commanders, Belisarius and Mundus, against the revolutionary mob. With the death of some 30,000 people (*Bell. Pers.*) the hired troops quelled the revolutionary outburst of those who, in the name of victory, rose up against the rich. Although the main forces of the insurgents were broken up, for a long time fires and armed demonstrations testified to their hatred of the state.

Imperial edicts showered down and the smallest disobedience was severely punished, for example, common theft was punished by cutting off the hands. The people were deprived of weapons, Justinian decreed that no private person could manufacture arms, and the workers in the state arms-factories were forbidden to sell anything except short knives to private persons. Disturbances also took place in Alexandria, and so the Emperor ordered the local powers to take special precautions for surveillance.

The prohibition on arms was, however, not kept for long. When Byzantium was facing an invasion of Slavs and Avars the Emperor Tiberius II (578–82), having only an undisciplined army at his disposal, armed the demes for the defence of the city. When Tiberius died, transferring his power to Maurice (582–602), a man associated with the aristocratic groups, the armed people of the capital could again voice their demands. Constantinople again became the scene of popular demonstrations and Maurice was overthrown in 602. Power was transferred to Phocas (602–10), a military commander famous for his animosity towards the senate and aristocracy. At first he ruled with the support of the people and of the soldiers. Soon, however, he caused resentment among the people by his religious policy. In order to maintain good relations with the Pope, Phocas persecuted the Monophysites, refused the Patriarch of Constantinople the title *oecumenical*, and attacked the Syrian Jews, suspecting them of having contacts with unfriendly Persia. By yielding to the demands of Rome he lost the friendship of the people. Although in 608 a column dedicated to Phocas was erected in the Roman Forum, as a symbol of friendship with Byzantium and the glory of the emperor, he lost the support of the people. The Byzantine aristocracy, using armies stationed in Africa, easily overthrew him.

The revolutionary movement of the people came to the fore in the eighth century, in the time of the iconoclasts. It was especially strong among the followers of the Paulicians, who were extremists. The followers of the sect of the Paulicians, popular among the Byzantine peasantry and plebeian masses, employed diatribes against the cult of images. At the same time they spread radical social ideas directed against the wealthy classes, and especially against the organization and policy of the Church. The popular and radical social movement of the Paulicians was used to advantage by the moderate adherents of iconoclasm, who were patronized by Leo III and later by Constantine V. In the fight against the monasteries the vast estates of the religious orders aroused the greedy anxiety of the magnates and the hatred of the poor.

The disruption of the serf-economy created favourable conditions for the eruption of social movement. The Paulician opposition to the cult of images and relics came to Byzantium from Asia Minor. It appears that the iconoclastic ideas of the Paulicians were formed under the influence of the followers of Islam, who in their beliefs rejected the cult of holy images. In the Empire the chief effect of the doctrine of iconoclasm, taken up by Leo III, was to unite the military aristocracy in the provinces and the plebeian masses, who supported the Emperor in his Church policy. In the name of the fight against the cult of images and relics, Leo III and his successors increased the income of the treasury by confiscating the wealth and estates of the Church and particularly that of the monasteries.[44] The policy of the iconoclastic emperors must have enjoyed great popularity if the people, long after the death of Constantine V, could believe that he would soon be resurrected and restore order in the state. The historian Theophanes says: "Many years after the death of Constantine V the people, when hearing of military defeats, gathered at the tomb of the beloved emperor and shouted: 'Rise up and save our dying country'."[45]

In the third decade of the ninth century throughout the territories of the Byzantine Empire occurred an agrarian revolution, aimed directly against the big estate owners who were trying to curtail the liberties of the free peasants. During the constant wars against Islam the position of the military commanders was strengthened, as they became owners of vast estates and skilfully managed to combine military power with economic influence. The Armenian commanders in particular took possession of numerous landed estates, and this gave them independence in their relations with the imperial court and unlimited power over the free peasants. The new military landed aristocracy (δυνατοί) came into acute conflict with the peasant settlers, who had to fight with arms for their rights and liberty. In the spring of 821, Thomas, a Slavonic military colonist, entered the Empire with the support of Arabic troops. He attempted to obtain power by launching a popular slogan of war against the hated imperial power.

> So Thomas [writes the historian, Theophanes Continuatus], taking over the state taxes for his own use, won over people to his side by lavish gifts, and thus from a lowly station rose to the heights. Those who were nurtured by a passion for wealth and revolution, he befriended by promises and kindness, others, who were doubtful, by persuasion and force. Thus a civil war started . . . . The serfs rose against their masters, soldiers against officers, military units against commanders. The whole of Asia groaned under an immense burden of misery. The Asiatic cities, wherever they were, surrendered to Thomas in fear; those cities which tried to keep faithful to the emperor and resisted a little longer had, after surrendering, to pay for their resistance with the death of many of their inhabitants and great loss of property. In such a way the whole of Asia declared themselves for him . . . .[46]

Thomas thus became the leader of a social revolution and the masses of Macedonian and Thracian peasants gathered under his standard; the fleet chose his side, the demes of the Greek cities and slaves also stayed with him. Byzantium lived through a phase of revolution directly aimed against the feudal demands of the big estate owners. After 2 years, in 823, the insurgents were defeated, and all those who had fought for their rights were destroyed in bloody warfare.

Some of the citizens [says Theophanes] came to an agreement with the emperor and, after securing his pardon, captured Thomas, bound him and brought him to the emperor. Following an old custom of the rulers, the emperor had Thomas thrown under his feet, put his feet on Thomas' neck and ordered that his legs and arms be cut off and that the mutilated body be put on a donkey and taken round the city for everybody to see . . . . In such a way, in October, the usurper ended his life in slow tortures like a hunted animal . . . .[47]

Contemporary chronicles say that the landed aristocracy soaked the earth with the blood of the revolutionaries. The revolution of Thomas was strangled because of the armed intervention of the Bulgarian ruler, Omortag. He himself was threatened by an uprising because the masses of the Bulgarian peasants approved and supported the peasant revolution in Byzantium.

In the first half of the tenth century, weighed down by taxes and the duties of serfdom, oppressed by the arbitrary seizure of land, the peasants again rose against the feudal lords. The direct cause of the revolutionary disturbances was hunger, which descended upon Byzantium after the catastrophically bad harvest in 928. For 6 years afterwards, with some intervals, the Empire was convulsed with the struggles of a peasant revolution led by the fearless Basil Copperhand. The legends say that his hand was cut off when he rose for the first time against the magnates, and that after his escape from his enemies he used a copper-hand with a sword attached to it. After heavy fighting the revolution was squashed. Its result was a bill in 934, partially satisfying the demands of the peasants. The statute ordered the feudal lords to return all the land they had seized.[48] In 1182 another rising broke out, led by a member of the ruling Comnenan dynasty, 67-year-old Andronicus. The revolution was mainly directed against foreigners and particularly against the Venetians and Genoans who had gradually captured Byzantine trade. Andronicus, in his 3 years of rule, was originally backed by the aristocracy, who were anxious to curtail foreign influences in Byzantium. The new ruler undertook some serious reforms restricting the influence of the aristocracy and bureaucracy and tried to improve the economic and political position of the masses, who according to Eustathios of Thessalonica, loved Andronicus more than God. However, the aristocracy, joining with the foreigners, at once stopped this last attempt at reform in Byzantium.[49]

Both the revolution in 1258 at Nicaea in Asia Minor and the rising of the peasants there in 1262 ended in defeat, bringing complete victory to the aristocracy in Asia Minor. A hundred years later the Eastern Empire became again a battlefield of bloodthirsty social struggles.

In the middle of the fourteenth century, in many towns and municipal districts, arose a popular movement of Zealots; this included peasants and townspeople, but the sailors were predominant. The insurrectionists rose against the aristocracy and demanded the liquidation of private and Church estates. The revolutionary movement was at its most powerful at Thessalonica between 1342 and 1349. For 7 years the *plebs* ruled in the town, confiscating the estates of the Church and of the patricians, abolishing the privileges of the nobles and destroying long-established traditions, all for the sake of the non-possessing classes.

We know the doctrine of the Zealots only from the accounts of historians unsympathetic to them, and especially from the prosecutor's speech when the revolution was being crushed (the speech is preserved in manuscript No. 1213 at the Bibliothèque Nationale in Paris).[50]

The chief principle of the Zealots was the common good. They understood this to justify the taking over of large properties for the benefit of the democratic society of the Zealots. "The rulers", argued the insurrectionists, "can deprive the rich of their estates and use them for social purposes, even using violence for the sake of the common good."[51] They refused to acknowledge the sanctity either of custom or of written laws. They issued new revolutionary edicts reducing the taxes for the lower classes and annulling their debts. They also subjected the Church to the restrictions applied to estates, and in particular deprived the monasteries of their wealth, leaving them only a bare means of existence. They abolished the immunity of the churches, cancelled the laws allowing legacies to be made to churches or monasteries, reserving for themselves the right to appoint various dignitaries in the Church. In their fight against the abuses of the Church they often used the sign of the cross, which was their symbol. "Taking the cross from the altars", writes the historian Joannes Kantakucenos, "they took it as their symbol, proclaiming that under that sign they would conduct war against their enemies."[52] In their political programme they represented an extreme democracy; they introduced mass rallies, filled government posts with properly elected candidates, instituted equal rights for all.

The doctrine of the Zealots was formed in revolutionary fights, in the negation of the tradition of established privileges. Believing deeply in the right of their cause, they said:

> What is curious in the fact that having taken the land of the Church, we fed many poor people? . . . It will not be an injury to the monasteries, as they have enough left for their needs, and it will not be going against the will of the donator, who wanted to please God and help the poor . . . . How do we break the law if we repair the roofs and broken-down lodgings of the poor, if we take care of the fields and pastures to feed those who fight for freedom . . . ? We do not increase our personal wealth, do not decorate the houses, and when issuing orders we always have in mind the common good.[53]

Whereas the initial stimuli of the movement of the Zealots were hunger and exploitation by the rich, their political programme was in fact considerably influenced by the republican cities of Italy, whose constitutions were designed to achieve a higher standard of living.

The movement of the Zealots covered the whole Empire. From the historical sources we learn that "the rising spread through the Empire like a terrible and cruel epidemic, attacking many who formerly were quiet and moderate . . . . And so all the cities rose against the aristocracy . . . . The whole empire was in the throes of the most cruel and desperate struggle . . . . The people were ready to rise in arms under the slightest provocation and committed the most violent deeds because they hated the rich . . . ." [54]

The defeat of the rising of the Zealots destroyed all possibility of restoring the economic–political structure of the state; there was no real force in the Empire which could aim at reform. [55]

4. SCEPTICISM AMONG THE INTELLECTUALS AND IN THE CLOISTERS

The raising of the Christian religion to the status of the official doctrine, whose observance was backed by force, the fruitless dogmatic quarrels only increasing antagonism among the population, the religious policy of the emperors, all must have been objected to by critically thinking persons. Although Hellenism was officially persecuted, the leading members of the possessing classes followed its precepts for many centuries and made it the basis of their education.

During the first decades of the sixth century the work of Boethius (480–525), *De consolatione philosophiae*, enjoyed great renown and popularity. The author took up the ideas of the Greek philosophers and translated many of them into Latin, somewhat to the displeasure of the Church.

In the Hellenic traditions carried on by Byzantium two trends can be clearly distinguished, the Platonic and the Aristotelian, both veiled in mysticism. The first was based, until A.D. 529, on the Athenian Academy. Neoplatonism here has been described as a mixture of Stoicism, Epicureanism, Scepticism, and the teaching of Plato and Aristotle. [56] The followers of Neoplatonism gave the Hellenic movement its tone, formed special organizations, practised pagan cults in private houses. The followers of Aristotelianism were centred in Alexandria. In the sixth and seventh centuries the latter movement also included some enemies of Christianity. The traditions of positive scientific work, study of sources, interest in mathematics, logic and natural sciences, curbed the spread of Neoplatonic and Christian mysticism. Simplikios, expelled from Athens by Justinian, tried to combine Neoplatonism with Aristotelian philosophy against the teachings of the Church. As dangerous to Christianity was another Athenian philosopher, Damaskios, who, together with Simplikios and five professors, had to leave Athens. Although the Athenian Academy ceased to exist, the two trends of Hellenic philosophy constantly, but with varying force, influenced Christianity.

From the seventh century, when Byzantium suffered the loss of much territory and when the gradual dissolution of the serf-economy became more serious, the ruling classes fell under the spell of mysticism. The main role in spreading mysticism in the East must be attributed to Maximilian the Confessor. A hundred years later John Damascene, by his work on the sources of knowledge, laid the foundations of medieval scholasticism. He argued on the basis of Aristotle's philosophy that to prove the dogmas of faith one can use pagan philosophy, which may thus become the servant of theology.

Platonism prevailed until the eighth century, but later the followers of Christianity officially and more and more often referred to Aristotle. The Patriarch of Constantinople, Photius (c. 820–93), gave precedence to the Stagirite, Psellos (1018–96), in his quarrel with Xiphilinus, specifically quoted Plato.

At that time there were in Byzantium two schools of philosophy and literature. One, deriving from Photius, leaned towards Aristotle; its followers were under the influence of ancient historians and orators and devoted their attention to epics and elegies. There existed another school, hostile to the former, whose chief exponent was Leo Choirosfactus, a man sympathetic to Platonism and Neoplatonism. In this school the cult of Greek tragedy flourished and attempts were made to revive ancient music. The school was violently attacked by the pupils of Photius, who accused it of Hellenism and paganism. Another charge made against it implied that it rejected Christianity and accepted the philosophy of Plato and Epicurus. We have from that time a virulent pamphlet by Arethas, in very violent language, to undermine the popularity of the followers of Plato, who were, according to the author, making more adherents.[57]

Justinian, from the first days of his reign, fought against Hellenism. In his opinion any doctrine contrary to Christianity was a "madness of faithless Hellenists" (Cod. Just. I, 11), who ought to be persecuted and put to death. Imperial decrees were mostly directed against the Neoplatonists, who were the most numerous and who were forbidden to organize associations or even to discuss their views in private houses; and all people "infected with the illness of faithless Hellenists" (Cod. Just. I, 11), were deprived of the right of teaching.

In 529, after 900 years of existence, by the decree of the Emperor the Academy of Athens was closed and all the professors expelled. They found refuge at the court of the Persian king, Chosroes, who was very popular in Byzantium.

Constantinople was very well aware of the ideological conflict which Persia underwent during the reign of Kavadh and his son Chosroes. Liberal and magnanimous toward the Byzantine intellectuals, Chosroes was at the same time ruthlessly fighting all social ideas. These ideas had spread in the form of a religious doctrine with the friendly support of Kavadh, who was recognized in the capital of the Eastern Empire.

A little earlier, in the reign of Justin (518–27), the bewildered citizens of Byzantium had heard of Kavadh's proposal that the Roman Emperor should adopt the Persian prince Chosroes. The proposal was declined. It was well known that Persia was torn by an internal struggle, finding expression in the doctrine of Mazdah, who called himself a prophet. He proclaimed his socio-religious teaching during the reign of Kavadh (494–531). He asked for social reforms; he taught that the system of common property should be revived, that all men are brothers, that all derive from the same parents and so there are no grounds for inequality. He opposed violently any family ties. In a word, he considered that the source and cause of all evil is the institution of property and the family, and he insisted that to find happiness is impossible without the abolition of both institutions. Kavadh favoured the doctrine of Mazdah and thus brought people to his side in opposing the Persian aristocracy. However, the aristocractic circles, hostile to a radical social doctrine and against Mazdah, won over to their side the crown prince Chosroes. The latter had already in the lifetime of his father, Kavadh, opposed the spreading of the doctrine and after succeeding to the throne he liquidated all the followers of social reforms, all the followers of Mazdah and the passive opposition of the supporters of Mani. The ruling classes called him Chosroes the Magnificent—they found in him the defender of their endangered position.

Chosroes eliminated all tendencies towards social reform in Persia, but at the same time he treated liberally and with friendliness those refugees from Byzantium who sought asylum in his state because of the Christian fanaticism of the Emperor.[58] In 523 Chosroes signed a treaty with Justinian whereby all the expelled professors could go back to Athens and were given the freedom to express their opinions.

A special emphasis was laid by Justinian on the necessity of closing the school of law at Alexandria, where there was strong opposition to the religious policy of the emperors. That traditional centre of mathematics and the natural sciences was not easily won over to mystical philosophy. Simplikios' commentaries on Aristotle were very popular among thoughtful circles in Alexandria, who accepted the concept of religious mysticism with reluctance. Alexandria, with its lead in natural sciences, had retained a relatively widespread independence of thought, in spite of the aggressive policy of the emperors against the centres of Hellenism, where criticism and scepticism grew apace.

The religious doctrine forcibly imposed by the emperors provoked many objections from intelligent circles. The populace, reacting emotionally to legends, superstitions and miracles, was easily drawn into fanatical struggles. In this atmosphere of intolerance many educated people pretended to be Christians. Some of them held important posts; it is well known that even in Justinian's closest entourage there was no enthusiasm for religious doctrine. Tribonian, the author of the codex, a man, according to Procopius, "of such incredible knowledge, that no one among his contemporaries could surpass or even equal him" (Bell. Pers. I, 24), viewed Christianity sceptically and did not conceal his sympathy with Greek philosophy. An accusation of sympathy with Hellenism was also raised against the well-educated John of Cappadocia, who for many years took second place after the Emperor as *praefectus praetorio per orientem*. Scepticism bordering on complete pessimism is perhaps most to be noted in the activities and writings of Procopius, the historian of the age of Justinian.

In the reign of Anastasius Procopius came to Constantinople from his native Cesarea to acquire the art of rhetoric. Procopius entered the entourage of Belisarius as a simple clerk, but, thanks to his abilities, he soon became the adviser of the commander-in-chief. He accompanied the Byzantine armies in the war against Persia, took part in the battles against the Vandals, and later against the Goths. While he was in the capital, between 545 and 550, he wrote an account of Justinian's wars, at the same time outlining with admiration the Emperor's building programme. Showered with privileges at court, he took a very active part in the political life of Byzantium; he became a senator and was even nominated by the Emperor to be *praefectus urbi* of Constantinople.

In spite of such glory Procopius wrote another true history, not available to his contemporaries, a thorough accusation of the court and of the policy of Justinian. He made the accusation that Justinian, after the death of Zeno, the grandson of Anastasius, had taken possession of a vast estate and that his aim was to take over all the possessions of the aristocracy. "Without any proofs of any crime", he goes on, "Justinian tried some for belief in deities, others for heresy and faulty observance of the Christian faith, others for homosexuality or love affairs with nuns or any other relationship contrary to law. He also accused some of attempts on his life or of using forbidden words and expressions and declared himself the heir of both the dead and the living . . . ." (*Historia Arcana*, XIX, 11).

Cruelty, lawless force, false denunciation, hatred, cowardice, lies became the *personae dramatis* of the secret history of Procopius. Distrust in the regime made Procopius sceptical; he realized how the daily behaviour of the Emperor contradicted his doctrine, how practice contradicted the official concepts of the state. "Neither law", says Procopius, "nor decrees had any stability or force, everywhere lawlessness and violence prevailed. The structure of the state was like a tyranny, not like one which is consistent and firmly established, but a tyranny in which everything kept changing every day and in which everything was always starting again from the beginning" (*Hist. Arcana*, VII, 31).

Officially Procopius belonged to the church—it was an essential condition of his brilliant career—but in fact he judged events and his contemporaries very sceptically and was convinced that man is helpless and subject to blind fate. This educated sceptic could not see the sense of religious disputes, and in the quarrels about the nature of Christ he saw a communal madness. "I think all disputes about the nature of God are nonsensical madness; man cannot even know his own nature and therefore one should abandon all deliberations on the nature of God" (*Bell. Got.* I, 3). It seems that the sceptical historian is overcome by pessimism when he looks at his country, badly affected by war, beggary, inflation, ruin of roads and waterways. Helpless, he would say of his times, "Universal sadness prevails, nobody hopes for anything better, nobody finds life joyful" (*Hist. Arcana*, XXVI, 10).

A more representative example of scepticism in the ruling classes of the sixth century was Agathias (536–82), an orator and Byzantine lawyer who continued Procopius' history of the reign of Justinian. Agathias looked with complete disbelief at the dogmas proclaimed by the Church. Brought up in the tradition of Hellenic thought, he saw in the last philosophers of the Academy of Athens (those expelled by Justinian) the foremost thinkers of Byzantium. He was impressed above all by the independence and courage of those philosophers who stood out against Christianity. He himself viewed all ideas of absolute truth sceptically, was an enemy of all opinions imposed by force, and condemned the Church's fight against heretics. In his history we read: "To think and believe that one can understand the essence of things is conceit and twice as stupid as ignorance" (III, 16), "Those who have not attained truth need help rather than any insult, because they wander and stumble not intentionally but in a search for good" (I, 8).

In his political doctrine this aristocratic sceptic expressed the tendencies of those who wanted to restore the pagan splendour of historical Rome. Disliking and even hostile towards the people, he based the greatness of the state, according to Plato's teaching, on the government of perfect rulers. In their minds and character he sees the essential conditions of the restoration of past glory. Agathias discusses the deeds of Justinian with respect and admiration, but he views the activities of the people with suspicion. "The people cannot properly estimate problems and things, because they easily fall into moods and ecstasies, judging according to their advantages and desires." [59]

The intelligent scepticism of circles brought up in the spirit of Hellenic philosophy did not appeal to the people; they were influenced more by the ideas of Christian mysticism or of pessimism.

Among a wide section of the people one sign of pessimism was a strong tendency towards the hermit's life and a withdrawal from active life, together with contempt for honours and riches. The Eastern concepts of passivity and pessimism, and hermitical life, the teaching of the cynics to abandon the conventions and return to nature, coupled with Christian doctrine, brought about a revival of organized monastic life. So not only a love of God led people to adopt an ascetic life in a hermitage; more often the decision was a kind of protest against the reality crushing the helpless individual. Here came town people, escaping from their families and social obligations, military deserters unjustly condemned, sluggards or people tired of life. Masses flocked to the cloisters and were accepted without discrimination. "Whoever comes to the monastery", says John of Ephesus, "having committed a crime because of slavery or debt, a quarrel with his wife or theft, and comes to escape the court, is here received without any difficulty. They do not consider that in the hearts of such people nestle unbridled desires and worldly habits."[60]

Wars, poverty, tax exploitation, breaking of the law, government abuses, all formed a basis for the popularity of monastic ideals, which were particularly widespread in the eastern parts of the Empire, under the influence of the Buddhist monasteries and Egyptian hermits. Already in the third century there were many monasteries in the East, particularly in Egypt, where they were organized by Pachomius. In the sixth century Egypt had the greatest number of monks, followed by Syria and Palestine. Originally the monks lived far away from human habitations, but eventually monasteries were also founded in cities like Alexandria or Antioch. In Constantinople itself in the sixth century there were 76 religious houses. The life of the monks was organized either into a κοινόβιον, where they lived in a community, or into a μοναστήριον, where they lived a hermit's life. The ever increasing number of monks leading the lives of beggars seriously affected the organization of the state. The ideology of passivity absorbed in unproductive contemplation, or following ascetic practices, had to be broken down, asceticism condemned, and the monasteries incorporated into productive life; above all, the wandering hermits, who were a pest to the inhabitants and to the government, had to be controlled. The Church took the religious houses in hand, and made the monks into a fanatical army; the passivity and pessimism of monastic life was transformed into a useful weapon of the Church hierarchy.[61] Now religious life could also develop in the West, where the Eastern models were transferred; the rule of Pachomius was translated into Latin and organizational forms for the monasteries were worked out.

The founder of the monastery at Monte Cassino, Benedict of Nursia, wrote his rule in the first half of the sixth century. He divided the monks into categories, distinguishing (1) *anachorites*, who fight a lonely fight with the sins of the flesh and spirit; (2) *sarabaitai*, wandering in small groups and subject to no discipline whatsoever; (3) *girovites*, beggar-monks who wander through the state like *sarabaitai* and are as much of a nuisance; and (4) monks who live in a community, an organized army of God under the direction of superiors (*militans sub regula vel abbate*).

Recognizing only the fourth group as monks, Benedict described precisely the principles of communal life in the monasteries, the subjection of younger brethren to the elder ones, the food, the work. The rule imposed on the monks comprises: *oboedientia* (obedience), *taciturnitas* (silence), *humilitas* (humility), and the duty to work is expressed in the principle that "*otiositas inimica est animae*" (laziness is the enemy of the soul). This attempt to take over the monasteries was successful and it broke down passivity and pessimism. The monasteries now became a weapon of the Church.

In Byzantium the government for a long time supported the founding of monasteries, considering their development both laudable to God and politically sound and good. "If those clean hands and holy souls will pray for the Empire, through such love of God the army will be stronger, the prosperity of the state increased, agriculture and commerce more flourishing" (*Nov.* 138, 5).

The greatest development of the monasteries in Byzantium took place between the fifth and the seventh centuries. Later, when the position of the state became rather difficult, the emperors realized that it might be a danger to the state if the Church or the monasteries held too much property. The privileges of the Church as regards taxation and the incessant flow of men to the cloisters caused serious difficulties. The pious hopes of Justinian that the prayers of the monks would bring the Empire to its former glory and prosperity proved futile. Caesar Maurice in 593 restricted the freedom of entry into religious orders and forbade all state officials to hold any posts in the Church. Above all it was forbidden to enter a monastery before doing military service, because that was a common way of escaping one's duties towards the state. The edicts of the Caesars led to an organized reaction on the part of the Church. Pope Gregory I protested in a special letter to the Byzantine ruler:

> I cannot be silent [writes the Pope], because his law is directed against God Himself and I was given power over all people by gracious Heaven to help those who want to attain good, to prepare for men an easier way to Heaven and subordinate the secular empire to divine rule. You on the contrary decide openly that he who has entered the army can only serve Christ after finishing his service or if his health warrants an earlier release. But Christ plainly emphasizes: From a notary I made you the leader of the excubites, from the leader of the excubites I made you an emperor, from an emperor, an imperator, and even the father of an imperator. I put priests under your power and now you turn away your soldiers from my service.[62]

The constant growth of the Church estates and of the power of the monasteries brought about the movement of the iconoclasts. Under cover of the fight against the cult of pictures, the imperial power, supported by the army and part of the aristocracy and episcopate, was enabled to take over ecclesiastical and monastic riches. Constantine V (741–75) carried out a mass confiscation of monastic lands, distributed them among his forces, and forced the monks to return to a normal existence in the state. In 765 the inhabitants of Byzantium witnessed an unusual spectacle; Constantine V ordered the monks to contract marriages and organized in the hippodrome a procession of monks and nuns, who were, according to Theophanes, accompanied by the shouts of an excited populace overjoyed by the dissolution of the monasteries.

Revolutionary demonstrations of the masses, and particularly those of the supporters of the Paulicians and the rising of Thomas the Slav, brought about a compromise between the supporters and enemies of the iconoclastic movement, for the sake of the unity of the ruling classes. The confiscated lands of the monasteries remained in the hands of the military aristocracy. After taking over the monastic lands the emperors were no longer interested in struggling with the iconoclasts. In 843 the Empress Theodora arranged a reconciliation by which the iconoclasts made concessions to the worshippers of icons.

In a religious chronicle of 843 we read:

> Realizing that nothing will more favour the security of the state than the ending of ecclesiastical struggles and controversies, the Empress Theodora, after consultations with the higher state officials, called to her all the influential monks, instructing them to solve the problem of the cult of pictures . . . requested the monks to find in the holy books texts to prove the necessity of worshipping pictures . . . suggested a council and issued a manifesto to the nation . . . the opponents of the cult of pictures, changed their views and said anathema on the enemies of the holy pictures.[63]

The discontinuation of the struggle with the monasteries led to a new increase in monastic riches. However, after over 100 years, during the reign of Nicephor Phocas II (963–9), further restrictions were put upon properties, though dogmatic controversies were not involved. The Emperor tried in his "novella" to justify logically his decision to impoverish the monastic estates. At the end of the "novella" we read: "Whoever has attained the faculty of seeing through the outer illusions of things and is able to reach the root will understand that the edict issued by us will be useful to all true Christians and to the whole population."[64] Phocas forbade new monasteries to be founded, forbade the clergy to possess any real estate, and at the same time ordered the landed aristocracy to release estates previously occupied by them. This policy, however, met with no support and raised a strong reaction in the aristocracy and clergy. The edicts and laws of Nicephor were abolished by Basil II (976–1025) who considered them . . . "to be a constant cause and source of worries and of a great revolution in the state . . . . Not only was sacrilege committed against the churches and houses of God, but we also sinned against God himself . . . . Thus nothing ever succeeds now and no calamity passes us by."[65] The social legislation of Phocas is an exception in the reactionary policy of the rulers of the Macedonian dynasty.

In the eleventh century we find among the ruling circles of Byzantium a typical attitude of political opportunism bordering on ethical nihilism. The ideology of the courtiers is reflected in the political activities of Michael Psellos (1018–97). That talented adviser of the emperors possessed an all-embracing knowledge of his times. The Empress Anna Comnena wrote about him: "Psellos, thanks to his inborn talents and quickness of mind, or perhaps thanks to divine help . . . attained the summits of wisdom, mastered Hellenic and Chaldeic learning, and was at that time an intellectual celebrity."[66] Psellos possessed the rare faculty of detecting and abusing the weaknesses of the rulers, and this enabled him to keep his high position as adviser to as many as ten emperors. In his external servility toward the rulers Psellos overstepped the limits of moderation, he called the emperors immortal gods in whose hands is the fate of the world, the happiness, the life and death of men. His excessive servility and humble submission to the emperors cannot, however, veil the great importance of Psellos as a scholar. The fame of his knowledge reached beyond the frontiers of the Empire; he knew the wisdom of both East and West. When the priests accused him of glorifying the Hellenic thinkers, particularly Plato, whose system he considered as the "philosophy of all philosophy", Psellos responded, "If I belong to the Christian Church this does not imply that I have to forego the knowledge of all the wisest achievements because I do not intend to renounce the understanding of existing things . . . . In prayer I come near to God, but when I walk on earth, I occupy myself with study." [67] Although he openly based his work on the system of Plato and the Neoplatonists, Psellos had his own system of knowledge. He attributed intuitive knowledge proper to theological thinking, which is the opposite of logical, strictly scientific thinking. In the latter field he gave priority to mathematics, considering its rules as models for all branches of knowledge. Influenced by Plato, he spoke for the reign of philosophers, whose decisions stood above even the law itself. In his *Apology* he says with sorrow: "What high prestige did philosophy have in previous times; now people look at it with contempt, considering jusrisprudence as much more useful and important." He realized how feeble and weak were the rulers and asked that philosophers should take part in active political life. About himself he said: "From my youngest days I fulfilled two tasks; on the one hand I occupied myself with philosophy, and on the other with affairs of state. Thus I did not shut myself in a chamber and busy myself with wisdom only, nor did I do what is only done in the offices . . . . Holding in my hands the books of wisdom I also took part in affairs of state." [68]

Psellos declared that the highest power should be in the hands of a secular ruler and to the ecclesiastics should only be left the problems of faith. In a letter to the Patriarch Cerullarius he writes: "Let there be one ruler, one emperor . . . to the one it was given to govern, to the other (the Patriarch) to fulfil ecclesiastical duties. Lift thy hands to heaven and implore peace for men, but let the affairs of state remain in the hands of those to whom they belong. Do not order, do not rule, because the majority do not wish it." [69]

What is striking in this very wise man is an incomprehensible toleration of law-breaking. It could not be in the name of Platonic ideas that Psellos advised magistrates to disregard laws, saying that justice is an attribute of the saints only. In an opportunist manner he instructs officials: "Looking, do not see, listening, do not hear . . . if you wish to avoid an accusation of illegal behaviour." [70]

The personality, activity and views of Psellos show a combination of great talent with scepticism, opportunism and even moral nihilism, so characteristic of high courtiers in the Byzantine Empire. [71]

At the turn of the twelfth century, when the Empire was declining, ideas of complete pessimism and disbelief in the state are expressed by the official historian Nicetas Choniates (c. 1155–1213). His history is an illustration of the gradual decay of Byzantium. He lays blame for the pitiful fate of the state on the Comnenian dynasty, the organization of power, and the clergy. He considers that they are all marked by duplicity, servility, laziness, sloth, egoism and profligacy. About his contemporaries he speaks with reproach that "they have lost military courage, justice, patriotism, generosity, and, apart from their name (of Romans), they hardly differ from the barbarians." [72]

Unfriendly towards revolutionary movements, sceptical towards the ruling class, Nicetas lost all his faith in Byzantium, defeated as it was. His only consolation was the memory of the past glory of Rome, which he revived in full splendour in his history.

Gregorius Gemistus (Plethon) closes the history of Byzantine political thought. His long life, of nearly 100 years, covers the last century of the Eastern Empire. The fame he won in his lifetime arose neither from an administrative career nor from political influence; it appears that he did not hold any official post. Only a burning admiration for Platonic philosophy made Plethon a famous and widely known teacher. Gemistus spent most of his life far from the capital, in the Peloponnesus in a place called Mystra, which was at that time one of the more lively intellectual centres. There he inculcated a love of Plato's philosophy into the minds of his students.

Gemistus viewed the prospects of Byzantium sceptically, not believing in the survival of a state whose existence was closely bound up with the Christian religion and Church organization. In principle indifferent to the future of the Empire, he dreamed out his ideas of the state only with the thought of recreating in the Peloponnesus the ancient Hellas. He was convinced that a modified Platonic Utopia might restore the greatness of Greece. We know the political doctrine of Gemistus mainly from his memoranda, addressed to the Byzantine Emperor Manuel II and his son and discussing the reformation of the state in the Peloponnesus. His main work, however, Νόμοι, which he wrote towards the end of his life, has only reached us in fragments. After the death of Gemistus the only manuscript of Laws was burnt by the order of Patriarch Gennadius as a heretical work. [73]

Gemistus formed a religious and philosophical system which was at the same time an expression of his political ideas. It was a combination of Zoroastrianism with the ideas of Pythagoras and Plato. The main idea of Gemistus is a conviction that the whole universe is subject to cyclical and orderly changes. The laws of necessity and regularity reigning in the universe are thus a sign of an all-embracing divinity. Gemistus thought the counterpart of the divine order in society to be a division of the people in the state into three groups. The first is composed of peasants and shepherds, the real producers who use the common earth. They, from part of their income, are to pay taxes for the upkeep of the army and state administration. The second group consists of the merchants and the craftsmen, who fulfil a function of service towards the first group. The third group is the team ruling the state, the advisers of the king, entirely devoted to the work of the state. Gemistus, in his ideal state, did not foresee any place for priests and monks; apart from these three groups he only distinguishes the army, the guardian of the entire state. He wanted this imaginary society to live according to the rules of Platonic and Stoic morality and to conduct a self-sufficient economy.

Helpless in the face of the policy of both the Eastern and Western Church, he attempted to revive the Platonic Utopia, seeing in it a source of new strength, and above all he strove for the restoration of the Peloponnesus. Although Gemistus viewed sceptically the possibility of a united action by the Western and Eastern Churches against the Turks, in 1438 and 1439 we find him in Ferrara and Florence, where he was a member of the Byzantine delegation trying unsuccessfully to bring about the reunion of the Churches. Here, however, according to the Italian chroniclers, Gemistus showed no interest in the negotiations, devoting all his time to the propagation of Platonic philosophy.[74] At that time, under his influence, there arose in Italy the idea of recreating in Florence the Platonic Academy, soon to be established by Cosimo dei Medici.

Gemistus infused into Western Europe a spirit of revolt when he awoke an enthusiasm for Platonic philosophy, thus opposing the teaching of Aristotle, which had been officially recognized and adapted to the needs of the Church. Europe did not forget her teacher. In 1475, 25 years after his death, the ashes of the philosopher were brought back with great piety from the Peloponnesus to Italy, to be placed in a church crypt at Rimini. The inscription on the grave proclaims: *Gemistus Bizantinus philosophus suo tempore princeps*.

5. MANICHAEAN PESSIMISM

The followers of Manichaeism presented a serious threat to the regime in Byzantium. They proclaimed a universal negation of life; they detested everything serving the propagation of life; they detested everything temporal, condemned social institutions, both legal and political, seeing in them an expression of eternal evil. Whereas the Christians saw in their God the Lord and creator of all good things and treated evil as the simple negation of good, which was superior, the Manichees saw in the eternal principle of evil an absolute element, positive, creative, fighting the eternal principle of good. The material world, as they understood it, personified evil, and all contacts with reality, participation in family life or in social and economic life, were considered as a sinful consolidation of evil.

The Manichees pessimistically declared that only by a complete negation of earthly things can man keep away from eternal and indestructible evil.[75]

The doctrine was popular among the poorest people, especially from the time when Christianity became the property of the ruling classes; the religion of the non-possessing classes then became a belief in the indestructibility of evil and the necessity of an absolute negation of earthly affairs. Manichaeism became the doctrine of the poor when they could find no more hope or support in official Christianity.

For this passive protest against existing reality both emperors and Church fought the Manichees. Justinian adopted the severest legal measures to root out an idea contrary to his concept of the state. "The followers of Manichaeism", we read in the codex of Justinian, "are relentlessly pursued, because they are excluded from human society, being outside the written and customary law . . ." (*Cod. Just.* I, 5, 4). ". . . If anybody passes from the godless superstition of the Manichees to the true and real faith . . . and then in future it is discovered that he has returned to the Manichean heresy or that he has contacts with members of the sect and has not reported them to the authorities . . . he is subject to the penalty of death . . . . We also decree that the death penalty will be the punishment for anybody who possesses Manichean writings which have not been surrendered to be burnt or destroyed, or has such writings in his possession for any other reason" (*Cod. Just.* I, 5, 16).

Manichaeism was a religious system that lasted 1000 years but its popularity waned between the fourth and the eighth century, especially in the lands within reach of Byzantium.

The Manichaean doctrine was formed in the middle of the third century in Persia and was the fruit of the inter-penetration of two worlds; at that time the East came into contact with the Graeco-Roman world and each influenced the other. The Manichaean doctrine is thus composed of various elements, like the Syrio-Chaldeic myths, the natural beliefs of the peasants, the ideas of Zoroastrianism about the struggle of good and evil, the Buddhist negation of earthly life, the Judaic conception of prophets and the social ideas of early Christianity.

Secular and Church powers persecuted Manichaeism with passion; its believers were sentenced to death and their writings burned. An account of this doctrine can today be found only in the polemical works of Christian theologians, passionately opposing Manichaeism. One of the oldest documents about the doctrine is *Acta Disputationis Archelai Cascharorum in Mesopotamia episcopi cum Manete haeresiarcha*. In this fourth-century document Hegemonius presented the dispute which Mani apparently conducted, together with his disciple Turbo, against Bishop Archelaus. St. Augustine, himself a follower of the doctrine for some time, published many writings against it and fought it with the zeal of a neophyte. In the East in particular the activities of Christian theologians were lively. In the fourth century Eusebius of Cesarea wrote:

At that time also he who indeed was Mani the Mad and who impressed his name on his demoniac heresy he also intended to bring human reason to duplicity. The Devil himself who fights with God has pushed that very man to the foreground for the perdition of many men. In life, he was a barbarian in speech and manners; in his mind he was indeed possessed; and such were his intentions. He wanted to be a living image of Christ. Once, moved by pride and madness, he said that he was the Paraclete and the Holy Ghost in one person; on another occasion he chose 12 disciples to share in his new teaching, as if he were Christ. He collected his false and godless principles from innumerable heresies, also godless and forgotten a long time ago, and from Persia he poured them out on our countries like some deadly poison. Since then the godless name of the Manichees has spread among the people up to our own day (*Historia ecclesiastica* VII, 31).

In the East Basil of Cesarea, Gregory of Nyssa and Diodorus of Tarsus also spoke and wrote against the Manichees. During the reign of the Emperor Anastasius I Heraclian of Chalcedon devoted twenty volumes to polemics against the Manichees; under Justinian they were also fought by Bishop Zacharias Rhetor. Between the years 867 and 871 an unknown poet lists the errors of the Manichees in pompous verse. At that time, however, the Manichaean ideas were taken over by the Paulicians, who later passed them on to the Bogomils and Cathari, who were also fighting the doctrine of the Church.

Apart from the Graeco-Roman sources we also find information about the doctrine in two Arabic authors of the tenth century, an-Nadim and al-Biruni, who read the original writings of Mani and often refer to the words of the founder of Manichaeism.

The life and work of Mani are veiled in legend. From the Arabic sources we learn that Μάνης was born about A.D. 215–16 in a place called Mârdinû, in Babylonia.[76] His father Fâtak apparently came from the Persian town of Hamadan. He wandered through Babylonia to settle at last at Mârdinû, where Mani was born. Even before the birth of his son Fâtak had joined a sect of *mughtasilah*, which means self-cleansing, in which he is thought to have held an important priestly function. Among the members of that sect a belief prevailed that the Highest Person ruling the universe begot Christ and Satan and in consequence caused a continuous struggle between two elements, good and evil, beauty and ugliness, fire and water. The members of the sect recognized that water is a means of cleansing the elements of evil; therefore they looked on baptism as an entrance to a holy way of life, and from that moment they were committed to asceticism. From his youth Mani apparently lived among the "cleansing ones". "When he reached the age of twelve," writes an-Nadim, "Mani, according to his own testimony, received a revelation from the Lord of light, brought to him by the angel Eltaum, who said to him 'Abandon this community! You do not belong to these worshippers. Your task is to regulate manners and put a stop to voluptuousness'."[77] The legend says that Mani only left the sect of the "cleansing ones" when he was 24, to teach in Asia for 40 years. In the reign of Bahram I Mani returned to Persia, where the priests, afraid of his possible influence on the ruler and hoping to intimidate his followers, had him condemned to death. Mani apparently died a martyr's death in 276. "Mani", says an-Nadim, "died in the reign of Bahram, the son of Sapor; his body was afterwards crucified, and then cut into two and put on two gates leading to the town." [78]

Mani was the author of many writings, of which only reminiscences have remained; his works have not survived because even the possession of Manichaean writings was punished by death. According to an-Nadim, Mani wrote seven books, one of which was written in Persian and the other six in Syriac; in addition to this he was the author of many short treatises, numbering up to 76 items. [79] He illustrated his writings with beautiful drawings. He was an artist of whom it was said that he could draw circles with his hand as accurate as those drawn by a pair of compasses. According to Arabic tradition Mani executed a whole series of symbolical paintings illustrating his doctrine. He considered himself a prophet equal to Zoroaster, Buddha or Christ; he treated his doctrine as a revelation, contained in four principles—belief in God, in the light of God, in his power and wisdom. The divinity was composed of these qualities, which symbolized the kingdom of light, the elements of earth and the wisdom of the Manichaean church.

The fundamental thesis of the Manichees was a belief in the equal and eternal existence of two powers, good and evil, fighting each other. [80] The Manichaean Faustus, with whom St. Augustine argued, says: "*Duo principia doceo deum et hylem—vim omnem maleficam hyle adsignamus, et beneficam deo ut congruit*" (*Augustinus contra Faustum* XXI, 1). This artist-prophet often spoke to his disciples in symbols and in the language of images, so that it is difficult here to distinguish the contents from the form; the doctrine of the struggle of the two elements is expressed by means of a poetical allegory.

For the Manichees the purest light was the external expression of good; the essence of God was understood as the brightness of light without any material attributes. Darkness was evil, which very strongly permeated matter. In the context of Manichaeism the elements of evil had the same properties as the elements of good. Evil was eternal, indestructible, it possessed the faculty of thinking and willing. In spite of the complete equality of rank of good and evil, only good was called "god" whereas evil was called ὕλη, matter and demon. "Is there one God or two?"; this is a rhetorical question posed by the Manichaean Faustus, to which he replies, "never in our doctrines were mentioned the names of two gods. It is true that we believe in two principles (*duo principia*) but we name only one of them god, the other is matter (ὕλη), or, as we usually say, demon" (*Augustinus contra Faustum* XXI).

Everything that exists contains these two contradictory and opposing elements. The Manichees believed that the creation of the universe and its existence is conditioned by the struggle of good and evil. In this doctrine man is a part of the universe, and at the same time, its miniature. [81] Man is a microcosm in which the opposing elements of good and evil come to the surface at their highest tension. The Manichees stated that human nature reflects the conflict of the universe, that it is split by contradictions and that in it rages a struggle between good and evil, common sense and stupidity, sobriety and passion, virtue and sin, beauty and ugliness. The human body, the external cover, is the prison of the soul, as all contact with matter is a sinful bond with the elements of evil.[82]

The thesis that matter in itself is evil led the Manichees to a quite peculiar idea of sin; they considered as sin all contact of light with matter, soul with body. So sin was only the result of a physical state and not the consequence of ethically erroneous behaviour.

This radical negation of concrete reality and condemnation of material conditions prejudiced the social doctrine of the Manichees. They declared that the aim pervading the universe is the cleansing of light from material elements, and man, being a miniature of the universe, should attain the same ideal. They thought that, thanks to the revelation of Mani, man should realize the necessity of renouncing matter to come closer to the light; they looked at their Manichaean community as at the only focus of light, surrounded by the material elements of evil and darkness.

Their condemnation of the material side of life led the followers of Mani to an absolute negation of property; they imposed on the faithful a renunciation of all the goods of this world. All that had any material value or made life easier was without any importance for the Manichees. They did not recognize marriage vows or any blood relationship; they were indifferent towards existing social and political institutions tolerating sinful activities. They ordered their believers to live without property, without money, without work, so that they could avoid contact with the material world and would not be soiled by the elements of evil on their way to light. Their social doctrine was symbolized by three seals, mouth, hands and seed (*signaculum oris, manuum, sinus*). These three seals were supposed to guard the Manichees from the external world. "*Videamus tria signacula, qua in vestris moribus magna laude ac praedicatione iactatis. Quae sunt tandem ista signacula? Oris certe et manuum et sinus. Quid est hoc? Ut ore . . . et manibus et sinu castus et innocens sit homo.*"[83]

Mani was supposed to have said that the mouth symbolized all the senses, contained in the head of man, the hands all the activities, and the seed all the sensual passions.

The seal of the lips was to defend the followers of Mani from all that might soil their lips; they were forbidden to eat meat, to lie, to curse, to judge, to condemn or to make speeches.

The range of prohibitions covered by the seal of the hands was very wide. A Manichee could neither wound nor kill a man, could not take part in war, could not carry weapons, could not kill animals, cut flowers or even harm objects of inanimate nature. In consequence, the Manichees could not work, possess any articles as their own property, take part in social life or hold any honours.

Lastly, the seal of the seed was to prevent the spreading of evil, and a prohibition to bear children or have sexual relationships was to serve that end. The believers of Mani were not to be contaminated by the whirlwind of human passions.

Of course, these prohibitions embraced only a small circle of the most faithful ones—they were the chosen, the perfect (ἐκλεκτοί). A large group of disciples (κατηχούμενοι) formed the bulk of the Manichaean Community.

Whereas ἐκλεκτοί possessed the ability utterly to renounce sexual life, the κατηχούμενοι were those who could not obey these precepts; it was sufficient for them to have only the intention to be perfect Manichees. By their work and activities they made possible the existence of the perfect ones. How far the ἐκλεκτοί cut themselves off from earthly life is shown in the words of the prayer which they said when eating bread: "Oh bread! I did not cut the wheat, nor mill the flour, nor prepare the dough, nor bake the bread—someone else did it and brought it to me so I am eating you without any guilt."[84]

The Manichees recruited their followers mainly from the non-property-owning classes. Judging by their myths and cults, it appears that originally Mani had followers among the peasant population. The stories in which the doctrine of Mani was couched are connected with rural life. For instance, the passing of human souls from a lower to a higher state takes place through a wheel-mechanism such as that then in use for the irrigation of fields. Death was personified by a mower cutting the ears of human life. Melons and oil were thought to contain the greatest quantity of light. Their feasts and prayers were connected with the phenomena of nature; they observed their feasts and said their daily prayers according to the position of the sun towards the earth.[85]

Already at the beginning of the fourth century the doctrine of the Manichees had a strong hold on the poor of the towns. When Christianity ceased to be the religion of the poor and oppressed, the social ideas of Manichaeism became a popular doctrine among the non-property-owning classes.[86] From the *Acta disputationis Archelai* we learn about the complete condemnation of the rich. "Whoever is rich in this world must necessarily, after leaving the body of the rich man, enter the body of a poor man to wander and beg and endure eternal tortures" (X, 3). It is not surprising that, as the *Acta Archelai* show, the dispute of Mani with bishop Archelaus, to which the listening mob of poor people, widows, and orphans, reacted with sympathy, made the bishop very indignant. Whereas the dispute of Archelaus with Mani took place in the provinces in a rural setting, the first official document about Manichaeism talks already about the influence of that "sinister" idea on town dwellers.

Around A.D. 290 the proconsul of Africa informed the Emperor of the danger of the spread of Manichaeism in that country. In reply, the Emperor in the first years of the fourth century issued a decree, in the introduction of which he talked of the influence of Manichaeism among wicked and thought-less people; this doctrine, he said, was causing unrest among the peaceful and pious ones, and was a danger to the towns.[87]

Its negation of the social structure and passive protest against all legal and political institutions made Manichaeism a popular doctrine among the poor people, who, helpless and confused, were only capable of a pessimistic con-demnation of reality.

The attitude of the Manichees was not without interest for the ruling groups; all means were used to stop the spread of the doctrine, and to dispel this passive protest of the masses. The Byzantine emperors, especially Anastasius I and Justinian, fought Manichaeism with the sword. During the reign of the Vandals in North Africa, and particularly under Genzeric and his son Huneric, vast numbers of them were burnt at the stake. The rulers of Persia were no less cruel towards the followers of Mani. During the reign of Chosroes in the sixth century 80,000 Manichees were condemned to death. Thus the passive opponents were exterminated by fire and sword. The behaviour of the secular power was supported by that of the Christian Church. Whereas at first Christian theologians had simply polemized with the doctrine of Mani, from the second half of the fifth century the Church began to use coercion in its fight against Manichaeism. The African Manichees were the most active; their writings reached Spain, Italy and Gaul. In 431 Pope Leo I ordered a search for Manichaean writings in Rome so as to exterminate the demonic idea. The destruction of Manichaean literature on a large scale was undertaken by Popes Gelasius I (492–6), Symmachus (498–514), Hormisdas (514–23), and Gregory the Great (590–604). Even Islam was not favourably disposed towards the Manichees. In the tenth century, says an-Nadim, in the Islamic lands there were only a few small groups of the followers of Mani. The last echo of the fight with the Manichees are the articles of the Chinese Codex Ming from the end of the fourteenth century, condemning the believers of light.

The uncompromising doctrine of complete negation was destroyed by force; an idea which lacked the strength of courage and deed disappeared. For many centuries the elements of the Manichaean ideas were to be re-created in various heresies against the Church.

6. THE REVOLUTIONARY CONTINUATION
OF MANICHAEISM

We learn from the *Patrologia Graeca* that a certain Constantine of Samosata, an Armenian, "wished to restore Manichaeism, and with a really diabolical energy proposed that men cease reading anything except the Gospels and the letters of the Apostle . . . . From the Manichaean books he took as a point of departure all manner of evil thoughts and managed, with the help of Satan, to explain the wisdom of the Gospels and of the Apostle in a crooked and twisted manner. He destroyed the Manichaean books, probably because he knew that many had been killed for possessing them."[88]

It was in the reign of Constans II (641–68) in Armenia that Constantine of Samosata taught for 27 years the necessity of the simple life and of the need to return to the principles of the early Christians. His contemporaries called the supporters of Constantine Manichees; they referred to themselves as Christians, as opposed to the faithful of the official Church, whom they called Romans. Later they were referred to as Paulicians because, apart from the Gospels, they recognized only the letters of the Apostle Paul as valid for them. This admiration for St. Paul is shown in the fact that they named their communities by the names of the Churches founded by the Apostle.[89]

The movement of the Paulicians gathered strength. Its criticism of the rich ecclesiastical hierarchy, its renunciation of earthly riches, its struggle with the cult of holy images, its rejection of the saints, its idea of the equality of all peoples, its slogans urging the abolition of social distinctions, all appealed to the peasants and to the plebeian population in the cities. This took place in the middle of the seventh century, when the inhabitants of the Empire were suffering from the onslaught of the Arabs. The population was exhausted by continuous war, the slave-economy was breaking down, and the official church was the only point of stability for the helpless state.

Through the religious doctrine of the Paulicians the masses expressed their protest against the existing regime. The social and political doctrine of the Paulicians did not take shape at once. Its formation was influenced by many elements, and as the class-antagonisms increased, its revolutionary spirit developed.

The Paulicians took from the Manichees their negation of the material world, from the early Christian communities their social ideas. As Nestorians they refused to worship Our Lady; like the followers of Islam they did not recognize the cult of saints and holy images. It appears that from the latter they also took their attitude of active opposition to their enemies.

The rulers of the Syrian dynasty, in their struggle against the omnipotent position of the Church and the religious orders, sought support in the movement of the Paulicians. Already the Emperor Leo (717–41) had, in the last years of his reign, concluded an understanding with the leaders of the sect. His successor, Constantine V, in order to strengthen the camp of the iconoclasts, transferred the Paulicians to Constantinople and Thrace.

At the turn of the eighth century the Paulician movement covered the whole Empire. At that time the leader of the masses was a certain craftsman, a linen weaver, called Serge, who adopted the name of Tychikos. He led the Paulicians for 34 years, and under his leadership was formed a large revolutionary movement that fought with arms for a change in the social system. In the church chronicle of Peter Siculus we read: "That defender of Satan, Serge, learned the heresy from a fatal woman and then, taking the name of

Tychikos, he passed fearlessly through all cities and towns; he turned many away from the universal faith and drew them to Satan."[90]

During the struggle of the Syrian emperors with the defenders of the cult of images, the Paulicians represented the extreme plebeian current. Their religious programme suited the iconoclasts. But the social demands of the Paulicians foreshadowed the sharp social conflicts which were to break out in the near future. Their doctrine was fully formed by the first half of the ninth century.[91] The Paulicians proclaimed that the creator of the material world is Satan, they denied the cult of Our Lady, of the saints, of the prophets and angels; in consequence they opposed all ceremonies and fasts, the cult of holy images and symbols, and rejected hierarchical Church organization and all the decisions of the universal and provincial councils. After the death of Serge Tychikos (830) they introduced in their communities the principle of common property, of equality between men and women, an iron discipline of all the faithful bound only by social and religious ideas and irrespective of race relations; they demanded a ruthless struggle against all enemies.

Because of their radical doctrine and uncompromising loyalty to their ideas, the Paulicians often found themselves in conflict with the ruling classes. In the middle of the ninth century the iconoclasts made a compromise with the Church. Thus there disappeared the means of co-operation, through religion, between the ruling classes and the Paulicians, who actively supported the agrarian revolution of Thomas. A period of heavy fighting and of Paulician persecution began. "The Empress Theodora", according to Theophanes Continuatus, "decided either to convert the Paulicians to the true faith or to exterminate them without leaving anybody alive . . . . Up to about 100,000 of them perished, and their possessions were taken and transferred to the imperial treasury."[92] The Emperor Basil I (867–86) organized two big expeditions against the Paulicians, destroying them by fire and sword. Those who survived left their ruined strongholds and went to either Thrace or Arabia.

When in the thirties of the ninth century the period of persecution began, the Paulicians in Cappadocia founded three big military camps, the biggest of which was Tephrika.[93] They must have presented a considerable force, because their commander, Chrysocheir, demanded from Basil I that all Asia Minor should surrender to them.

The proverbial honesty, courage and generosity of the heretics and their fearless bravery could not stand up to the power of the mighty, who, thanks to the friendly indifference of the caliph, over-ran the camps of the revolutionaries. The ideas of the Paulicians persisted for a long time among the Byzantine people, and we find their ideals in Bulgaria in the anti-feudal movement of the Bogomils. The doctrine of the latter was not, however, a simple continuation of the ideology of the Paulicians, as it was formed in different times and circumstances.

In the middle of the tenth century Bulgaria, exhausted by the wars with Byzantium, went through an internal crisis; the military–aristocratic regime gave way to a feudalism which was ever increasing in strength as the peasants were gradually deprived of their lands.

The heresy of the Bogomils embodied the anti-feudal protest of the peasants and lower clergy against the pride of the upper classes.

The undoubted affiliations of this doctrine with Manichaeism and with the ideology of the Paulicians and Messalians cannot hide the specifically Bulgarian character of a heresy which enabled the Bulgarian peasants to declare war against the feudal system in the name of religious reforms. The followers of this doctrine did not restrict themselves to an attack on the social system; on the contrary, believing in the victory of good, they proclaimed positive social ideals which they wished to realize in their communities.

The first information about the Bogomils comes from a treatise of Cosmas against the heretics.[94] Who Cosmas was is hardly known. We know that he was a Bulgarian and higher clergyman and that at the turning point of the tenth century he published his treatise against the Bogomils. Through it we learn of the moral corruption of the official clergy, whom Cosmas accuses of lack of piety, ignorance, decay and bribery. The treatise of Cosmas is directed first of all against the heretics for their opposition to the Church, but at the same time it shows the danger inherent in their social ideas: "The Bogomils", says Cosmas, "call their believers not to submit to the authorities, but to hate the rich, to hate the emperors, to jeer at superiors, to insult the rulers. They believe that God dislikes those who work for the emperor and advise all servants not to work for their masters."[95] Such ideas must have awoken warm sympathy among the persecuted, together with a sharp reaction among the ruling classes. The doctrine of the Bogomils was born of the protest of the masses against inequalities of wealth tolerated by the official Church.

We do not know anything about Bogomil, the founder of the sect. Cosmas only says that Bogomil, whose name meant "a man worthy of divine mercy", was a poor clergyman living in the reign of the Emperor Peter (927–69). "Bogomilism" must have originally gained believers also among the lower clergy who often took the side of the poor in their fight against the rich. It seems that such a doctrine, protesting against the abuses of the government, urging a return to evangelical simplicity, condemning the riches of this world, and particularly profligate luxury, suited the lower clergy. Cosmas distinguishes two groups among the clergy, one the educated and independent, the other, the ignorant, poor, country clergy, unfriendly towards the rich priests. He sees an obvious relation between education and wealth. "The rich", he says, "have concentrated the books in their hands, do not let them out to the poor, and so hide truth and make education a privilege unattainable by the poor." [96]

As the doctrine of the Bogomils spread, the number of writings directed against it increased. The Church fought it through her representatives at the councils, excommunicating them wholesale and condemning their judgements. In his stubborn fight with the heretics the Tsar was helped by the property-owning classes, who discerned in the doctrine a clear danger to the social system of the Middle Ages.[97] The official hierarchy of the Greek Church had many reasons for fighting the Bogomils, who persistently taught that the privileged position of the higher clergy cannot be reconciled with the duties of the servants of God. Rejecting the ritual of the Greek Church, they did not recognize the hierarchical organization of the clergy, declaring that it did not follow the precepts of early Christianity or the examples of the Apostolic Communities. The Bogomil criticism of the higher clergy appealed to the majority of the Bulgarians, who only reluctantly submitted to the authority of the ecclesiastical class. Similarly, there was a lively response among the people to the Bogomil teaching condemning the private property and landed estates carefully accumulated by the higher clergy. Their principle was contained in the words of Christ to the young man who tried to become His disciple. "If thou hast a mind to be perfect, go home and sell all that belongs to thee; give it to the poor, and so the treasure thou hast shall be in heaven: then come back and follow me" (St. Matthew XIV. 21). The Bogomils were deeply convinced that the poorer one is the easier it is to practise virtue. In their view wealth was incompatible with any moral system, and therefore they considered poverty the greatest benefaction and an indispensable condition of perfection. As with the Manichees, the doctrine allowed only the ordinary members to possess and dispose of estates; the perfect ones had to renounce all property for the benefit of a common fund which was the financial basis of the Bogomil communities. Whoever wanted to become perfect had to take a vow of renunciation of all property for the benefit of the community. In the Bogomil communities women enjoyed equality with men. Work was the duty of all members; nobody could avoid it. Similarly, the heretics condemned begging and the distribution of alms as undignified to both God and men.

Bogomil communal life involved the sharing of all goods, a system modelled on the early Christian communities, which in turn, imitated the way of life of the Essenes, a sect preceding and influencing early Christian doctrine. The communism of the Bogomils sanctioned the missionary work of the perfect ones and simultaneously assured an existence to those who had no wealth or who because of illness had to stop working. The Evangelical precept of mutual aid had become a fundamental moral duty for the Bogomil communes.

Whereas in the religious and social doctrine the Bogomils through centuries were incredibly consistent, on the other hand, their idea of the state kept changing, depending on their relation with actual governments. They had no fixed theory of state or power. They wanted to remove injustice by preaching the need for moral perfection, by spreading the teaching of mutual help, and by the renunciation of earthly goods. They thought that a good ruler by his virtues could put an end to all evil. This varying attitude towards the government showed itself in their estimate of the Tsar Peter, whose reign they originally condemned passionately in their sermons. They did not miss any opportunity of accusing all who collaborated with the Tsar or helped to consolidate his power. But when in 1014 Bulgaria lost her independence, the Bogomils rebelled against the Byzantine yoke, and their opinion of Tsar Peter changed; he became for them symbol of a happy and just reign. In their chronicles we read: ". . . and he (Tsar Peter) reigned on Bulgarian soil twelve years without any sin, not knowing a wife, and blessed was his rule. In those years and days of the reign of the Holy Tsar Peter the Bulgarians had an abundance of wheat, butter, honey, milk and wine; innumerable were the gifts of God and in nothing did they suffer poverty."[98]

Previously condemned, Tsar Peter now, during the struggle of the Bogomils with the Byzantine rule, won an aura of sanctity, and his reign was as a dream come true.

The religious and social doctrine of the Bogomils expressed the views of the oppressed masses, who in the atmosphere of the Middle Ages could only use heretical ideas in order to fight with those main supporters of feudalism, the Church and the state.

The history of the political thought of Byzantium as outlined here presents only a fragmentary picture of the doctrines of the Eastern Empire. Expressed as they are in religious creeds, in dogmatic quarrels and heresies, they are difficult to decipher. Hence their unjustified neglect in the traditional history of doctrines, although Byzantine political thought was not without influence on the shape of medieval Europe. Under its influence the universalist concept of the Western Empire was formed, as well as the social movements of the heretics, who in their beliefs touched on the ideals of Manichaeism.

NOTES

1. One cannot agree with F. Lot (*La fin du monde antique et le début du moyen âge*, Paris, 1927, pp. 43–4) who calls the transfer of the capital to Byzantium a "caprice of the despot" born of religious exaltation.

2. R. Guerdan (*Vie, grandeurs et misères de Byzance*, Paris, 1954) goes even as far as to defend the thesis that the Gospels were the basis of the Byzantine state (pp. 17 ff). The author expresses the view that the Eastern emperors considered themselves to be the vicars of Christ, which, on the one hand, implied a special ceremonial, and, on the other hand, a belief in the emperors that they were a bodily personification of the Spirit of Christ. According to the author the theatrical and unnatural behaviour of the Emperors was a result of that belief (p. 4).

3. The dates of the dispatch of corn were strictly observed; each year before the 10th of September the corn had to be brought to Alexandria, from where it was shipped to Byzantium. The cargo went to Byzantium from Alexandria two or three times a year.

4. "The most important reason for the continuity of Byzantium in comparison with the

Western Empire", writes З. В. Удальцова: Византийский временник, II (27) 1949, pp. 342–3, "was its highly developed economics. At a time when in the West economic decay was increasing and a civil war was raging which led to the fall of the Western Empire, in Byzantium production and commerce developed apace. The existence of rich cities put in the hands of the emperors the material means to strengthen the central power and to increase the military might of the Empire, and thus made it possible to quell the revolution of the slaves and to preserve the Empire before the onslaught of the barbarians. The stability of the Empire was furthered by the fact that feudalism grew very slowly in Byzantium, because of the peculiarities of the serf-system in the East."

5. *Konstantinos Porphyrogennetos*, col. III, nov. 6, *Ius Graeco-Romanum*. Ed. J. and P. Zepos, I, Athens, 1931, p. 215.

6. М. В. Левченко: Материалы для внутренней истории Восточно-Римской империи V–VI вв., Византийский сборник, Leningrad, 1945, pp. 76 ff. The author states that in the Eastern Empire, as in the West, there were big properties whose owners claimed the functions and rights of government. As in the West the free peasants were subordinated and oppressed by the large property owners. But in spite of many common features the ownership of big property in the East can be differentiated from that in the West. Large property in the East was not economically independent as in the West. In the East large property was not transformed into a self-sufficient economic unit, as the owners were interested only in luxury articles and had no contact with either the towns or the larger markets. In Byzantium large property was more intensively incorporated into the commerce of the Empire, likewise the big cities, with their hundreds of thousands of inhabitants which used agricultural products in large quantities.

7. The importance of the free peasants is pointed out by Е. Э. Липшиц: Византийское крестьянство и славянская колонизация, Византийский сборник, Moscow–Leningrad, 1945, pp. 142–3. ". . . . In Byzantium, the free peasants were one of the main sources of income tax and also an inexhaustible source of military manpower, being thus the essential basis of a centralized Byzantine state."

8. "Soviet historians of Byzantium presume," writes М. Б. Левченко (Византийский временник, II, 1949, p. 325) "that in the 7th century the majority of the Byzantine peasants became free; they won their freedom from their oppressors in a bitter struggle, largely owing to the military defeat of the Empire in the war against the Arabs and Slavs, and particularly by the invasion of the Slavs and the Slavonic colonization of the Empire. Hence, if slavery lost its predominant position in the Byzantine Empire, the credit must largely go to the Slavs. They did not destroy the Empire as the Germanic tribes and other barbarians did in the West, but, on the contrary, the Slavs contributed in a great measure to the change in the social system, and by their barbarism 'rejuvenated' Eastern Europe."

9. *Eunapios*. Ed. Boissonade, Paris, 1849, p. 462.

10. *Kosmas XI*. Ed. E. O. Winstedt, Cambridge, 1909, p. 323.

11. L. Bréhier: *Vie et mort de Byzance*, Paris, 1947, pp. 47 ff., shows that Phocas, in his struggle with the Emperor Mauritius, was supported by the lowest classes of the population and army and was opposed by the aristocracy, state officials, and the higher military commanders.

12. *Theophylakt Simocattes VIII*, 10, 5 (p. 303 de Boor).

13. *Michael Akominatus*. Ed. Lampros, I, Athens, 1879, pp. 163, 145.

14. The problem of agrarian reforms in Byzantium is treated in G. Ostrogorskij's work: *Agrarian conditions in the Byzantine Empire in the Middle Ages. The Cambridge Economic History of Europe*, vol. I, Cambridge, 1942, pp. 194–223, 579–83). The author stresses the role of tax-pressure in the transformation of the structure of the big landed properties through a gradual extinction of small peasant holdings.

15. *Historia Bizantina XI*, 2. Bonnae, 1829.

16. In the literature on Byzantium there prevails an opinion that Byzantium had no interesting or worthwhile political doctrines. This attitude was lately adopted by Sir Ernest Barker, who brought together several texts relating to social and political questions. The author published his work under the title: *Social and political thought in Byzantium from Justinian I to the last Palaeologus* (*Passages from Byzantine writers and documents*), Oxford, 1957. In the introduction he stresses the absence of originality in Byzantine political thought. According to Barker (pp. 2–10) Byzantium could not produce a more original political doctrine because

the strong traditions of Greek philosophy put a brake on any more original thought. In addition, says Barker, the absence of political struggles and controversies between the parties, as well as between the Church and state, restrained any development in political thinking. The present writer takes the opposite view. The value of political doctrines does not depend on the degree of their originality but on the social function they fulfilled or fulfil. The strength and importance of a given political idea is decided first of all by the degree in which it expresses class interests and by its effect on social relations and political and legal institutions. From that standpoint the history of political thought in Byzantium is here treated.

17.   F. Dölger: *Byzanz*, Berne, 1952. In the chapter, "Die politische Gedankenwelt", p. 93, Dölger states that Constantine the Great had already tried to justify the divinity of the Byzantine ruler and his right to rule the world and the Church in the name of Christ.

18.   C. Diehl: *Justinien et la civilization byzantine au VIe siècle*, Paris, 1901, pp. 27 ff. The author draws attention to the theocratic elements in the official doctrine of Justinian.

19.   *Basilleios*, Migne, *P.G.* 107, XXV, XXXII.

20.   We read in a minute account of court etiquette, "*De cerimoniis aulae byzantinae*", that when all are in their places, ". . . the ostiarius with a golden rod . . . brings in the foreign envoy . . . . The envoy falls on his face in front of the emperor and at the same moment the music of flutes is heard. The envoy gets up and goes nearer, remaining, however, at a certain distance from the throne. As the envoy approaches the throne there enter carefully chosen members of his suite, and after submission to the emperor these halt. When the logothetes puts the usual questions to the envoy, lions begin to roar and the golden birds on the throne and on the golden trees begin to sing melodiously. The wild animals sitting on the steps of the throne lift themselves up and stand on their hind legs. While this is happening the proto-notary τοῦ δρομόυ of the court brings in the presents of the envoy who offers them to the emperor on behalf of his master. Soon after there resounds the sound of drums, the lions stop roaring, the birds cease singing and the wild animals go back to their lairs. After giving the presents the envoy, at the sign of the logothetes, pays his respects to the ruler and backs away. When he turns to the door . . . he is accompanied by the music of flutes, the roar of lions, the singing of birds and the wild animals again rise on their legs. The moment the envoy disappears the drums are heard, the birds become silent and the animals return to their lairs".

21.   "Frightened by the risings of the slaves and colons in the West of Europe, the ruling circles of the Eastern Roman Empire tried to form a permanent state unified by one religion. They expected that the Church would assure the moral and political unity of the exploited and of the exploiting. Many efforts were undertaken to make the Church completely dependent on the state and the population of the Empire completely dependent on the state Church" (М. В. Левченко: Византийский временник II, 1949, p. 13).

22.   The rulers of the Sassanide dynasty reigned in Persia from A.D. 226 to the middle of the seventh century, that is to say from the Arab conquest. During their rule Zoroastrianism became the state religion and the magi—priests collaborated closely with the state.

23.   *De cerimoniis aulae byzantinae*, II, 14. Bonn, pp. 564 ff.

24.   As equals to the foremost landowners, the Episcopate took part in the election of the municipal officials, controlled the municipal accounts, supervised through special commissions the upkeep of the public baths, store-rooms, water bridges, weights and measures (*Cod. Iust.* 1, 4, 46). The Bishop defended the interests of the city and in his capacity as a city representative he could submit petitions direct to the emperor. The practice of mediation gradually gave the bishops the right of supervision over the civil provincial officials . . . . In addition to the civil court there also functioned an ecclesiastical court. The Bishop himself was a judge and the formalities of his court were reduced to the minimum (М. В. Левченко: Византийский временник, II, 1949, p. 14).

25.   W. Schubart: *Justinian und Theodora*, München, 1943, gives a very detailed and well-documented picture of the reign of the Emperor, but his view that the division between West and East derived from spiritual differences (pp. 260 ff.) is a completely idealistic concept, because in fact economic, social and political differences conditioned the ideological disagreements.

25.   *Concilium Niceanum I 325.* H. Denzinger, No. 54, ed. 18–20.

27.   *Concilium Chalcedonense 451.* H. Denzinger, No. 148, ed. 18–20.

28. М. В. Левченко (История Византии, Moscow–Leningrad, 1940, p. 38) refers to the social aspect of the doctrine of the Monophysites.

29. А. П. Лебедева (История разделения церквей в IX, X и XI веках, St. Petersburg, 1905, p. 347) gives a translation of the Greek text of the excommunication, the MS of which was in one of the episcopal libraries in Moscow. It is not known where it is now.

30. C. Diehl (*op. cit.*, pp. 259 ff.) says that to do Justinian's codification they had to look through 2000 books containing about 3 million lines. From that material they built, as Justinian put it, "the most sacred temple of Roman justice" (*Corpus Iuris Civilis*, I. Ed. Krueger–Mommsen, p. XIII), which had 150,000 lines. Thus, to quote the Emperor, they closed "as if in a fortress the whole of the ancient law (*vetus ius*) which had not been codified for 1400 years" (*Corpus Iuris Civilis*, I, pp. XIII, XXV).

31. *Corpus Iuris Civilis*, I, p. XIII.

32. *Corpus Iuris Civilis*, I, p. II.

33. *Corpus Iuris Civilis*, I, p. XVI.

34. V. Valdenberg: Les idées politiques dans les fragments attribués à Pierre le Patrice, *Byzantion*, II, 1925, pp. 55–76.

35. *Ekloge*, XVII, 3. *Jus Graeco-Romanum*. Ed. J. and P. Zepos, II, Athens, 1931, p. 53.

36. An extensive discussion of the legislation of the Syrian dynasty is to be found in В. Г. Василевский: Труды IV, часть 3. Законодательство иконоборцев, Leningrad, 1930. However, L. Bréhier: *op. cit.*, p. 77 denies to Leo III any original legislative activity.

37. *Epanagoga* 2, 1 and 38. *Jus Graeco-Romanum*, op. cit., pp. 240–2.

38. *Basilios Digenis Akritas*, 6, 1526–9. Ed. K. Sathas and E. Legrand, *Coll. de mon. N. S.* Paris, 1875.

39. *Cecaumeni strategicon et incerti scriptoris de officiis regiis libellus* was first published in 1881 by В. Г. Василевский: Советы и рассказы византийского боярина XI в. Журнал М.Н.П. 1881, No. 6, pp. 242–99, No. 7, pp. 102–71, No. 8, pp. 316–57. It is again discussed by М. В. Вальденберг: История византийской политической литературы в связи с историей философии и государственного устройства. The manuscript of Valdenberg's work is in Leningrad in the Archives of the Academy of Sciences USSR Fond. 346, op. 1, No. 1. The description of the treatise is in the 4th chapter.

40. А. П. Дьяконов: Византийские демы и факции в V–VII вв. Византийский сборник, Moscow–Leningrad, 1945, p. 171 refers to the position of the demes in the politics of Byzantium as "the constitutional force", which, in his view, gave the exploited masses a basis on which to face the ruling classes. On the other hand, says Diakonow, the comparative weakness of the ruling class made them seek the support of the demes organizing them into factions, of course with great benefit to themselves. The author points out that the political structure of Byzantium was a peculiar combination of three constitutional elements: the monarchy, the aristocracy of which the senate was composed, and the meetings of the demes, plus the influence of the army.

41. In Upper Egypt, in the town of Oxyrhynchos, during the circus spectacles the followers of one party cheered the horses called *plebeians*, while their opponents put their bets on the horses called *patricians*. Quoted after W. Schubart: *op. cit.*, p. 85.

42. *De cerimoniis aulae byzantinae*, I, 91. J. B. Bury rightly points out the influence of the army during the election and revocation of the emperors. (*The Constitution of the Later Roman Empire*, Cambridge, 1910, pp. 8 ff.) "It was a principle . . . in the earlier period of the Empire, that the people who elected the emperor could also overthrow him . . . . There was not any formal procedure for deposition but the population of the capital, when too much afflicted by the rule of the emperor, put forward a new one . . . and if he found sufficient support in the army and senate and amongst the people, the old emperor was forced to vacate the throne and retire to a monastery with his eyes plucked out, or else he was murdered, depending on the wishes and temperament of his successor. The new emperor was recognised as the legal ruler from the day he was proclaimed . . . . If, however, he had an insufficient number of allies to make the proclamation a reality, he was treated as a rebel. However, during the fight, until the day of defeat, the fact that he had been proclaimed by the army gave him a conjectural constitutional right, which could be proved or annulled by the result of the fight."

I think, however, that Diakonow, in his very well-documented work, overestimates the influence of the demes on the politics of Byzantium. We read in Diakonow (*op. cit.*, pp. 714–15):

"The emperors themselves admitted that the sources of their power lay in the demes. During the rising in 512 Anastasius presented himself in front of the demes in the circus without the crown, to give them to understand that he did not consider himself an emperor any more, because the people had turned their backs on him. He put his crown on only when the demes asked him to do so in appreciation of his statement."

"Justinian, during the rising 'Nika', admitted his own mistakes to the demes in the circus and made some sort of oath on the Gospel in front of the people . . . . Often the Emperors themselves called the demes to the circus (sometimes to the battle-field or to the Church of St. Sophia) to give approval to the domestic and foreign policy during political crises or in times of war. Even more often, in critical moments, the demes appeared in the circus on their own initiative or gathered in other public places to put forward their views and demands, previously arranged among the demes, organised in factions."

43.   Diakonow (*op. cit.*, pp. 195 ff.), discussing the social composition of the headquarters of the two parties, assumes that among the greens (πρασινοι) the commercial and industrial elements prevailed. On the other hand, in the party of the blues (βένετοι), in addition to the aristocracy and landowners, there was also a minority of merchants and craftsmen. Diakonow rightly points out that the masses of both parties were socially similar and that the difference between the two was in their leadership. The masses of the two parties could not have had conflicting interests, but deep class differences separated them from their leaders.

44.   М. Я. Сюзюмов: Проблемы иконоборчества в Византии, Ученые записки Свердловского государственного педагогического института, 1948. 4, pp. 101 ff. puts forward the thesis that the iconoclasts took away only the ecclesiastical and monastic treasures and not the estates.

45.   *Theophanes*, p. 501, 10. Ed. de Boor.

46.   *Theophanes Continuatus* II, 11 (p. 53, Bonn).

47.   *Theophanes Continuatus* II, 19 (p. 69, Bonn).

48.   The peasant rising of 928–34 is discussed in the following monograph: A. П. Каждан: "Великое восстание" Василия Медной руки, Византийский временник, IV, 1951, pp. 73–83. The author draws attention to the very scanty sources that exist for this rising.

49.   *Eustathii metropolitae Thessalonicensis opuscula*. Ed. Th. L. F. Tafel. Frankfurt a/M 1832, p. 273.

50.   The movement of Zealots is discussed by O. Tafrali in *Thessalonique au quatorzième siècle*, Paris, 1912 pp. 265 ff. (we find here the above-mentioned prosecution speech against the Zealots) and by C. Diehl in Journées révolutionnaires bizantines, *La Revue de Paris* 35, 1928 No. 21 pp. 151- 72. The movement of the Zealots appears to have been a continuation of a plebeian current whose beginnings go back to the meetings of the two circus parties. The continuity of the revolutionary tradition is also pointed out by P. Charanis in Internal strife in Byzantium during the 14th cent., *Byzantion*, vol. XV, 1940–41, pp. 208–30.

51.   O. Tafrali; *op. cit.*, pp. 265, 266.

52.   *Ioannes Kantakucenos* III, 38 (II. p. 234, Bonn).

53.   C. Diehl: *op. cit.*, p. 170.

54.   *Ioannes Kantakucenos* III, 28 (II p. 177, Bonn).

55.   А. Бергер: Демократическая революция в Византии XIV века, Архив К. Маркса и Ф. Энгельса, Книга V, 1930, pp. 455 ff., giving an account of the movement of the Zealots compares them to the extreme left wing of the French Revolution. It would seem that this is an unjust view, because the Zealots did not form part of a wide social current, but were rather a compact and self-sufficient revolutionary movement.

56.   К. Маркс и Ф. Энгельс: Соч. 1932, p. 122.

57.   The MSS of Archbishop Arethas (who lived at the turn of the ninth century) is preserved in the Museum of History in Moscow (MSS No. 315). We find the Greek text with a Russian translation and notes in the following work: М. А. Шангин: Византийские политические деятели первой половины X в., Византийский сборник, Moscow–Leningrad, 1945, pp. 228–48.

58.   The doctrine of Ahura Mazdah is discussed by Н. В. Пигулевская: Идея равенства в учении маздакитов in a collective work, Из истории социально-

политических идей, Moscow, 1955. pp. 97–101, and also by A. Christensen in: *L'Iran sous les Sassanides*, 3rd ed., Copenhagen, 1944, pp. 345 ff.

59. *Agathias* II, 11 (*Historici Graeci minores*. Ed. L. Dindorf, II, Leipzig, 1871, p. 198. Social and political opinions are discussed by М. В. Левченко: Византийский историк Агафий Миринейский и его мировоззрение, Византийский временник, 1950, III, pp. 62–84. М. В. Левченко published in 1953 a translation of the history of Agathias: Агафий, О царствовании Юстиниана, Moscow–Leningrad, 1953.

60. *AnecdotaSyriaca*. Ed. J. P. N. Land; II, Leiden, 1868, 154. John of Ephesus was a missionary and a chronicler of the Church in the times of Justinian. His work is discussed in the book by А. Дьяконов: Иоанн Эфесский и его церковно-исторические труды, St. Petersburg, 1908, p. 3. We find references to the monasteries of John of Ephesus on pages 16 and 394.

61. In one church alone, that of St. Sophia in Constantinople, in 563 there were 60 presbyters, 100 deacons, 40 deaconesses, 90 hypodeacons, 40 lectors and 25 cantors—altogether 425 ecclesiastics. To these have to be added 100 doorkeepers. Under Heraclius in 612 the number of clerics at St. Sophia's was increased to 80 presbyters, 150 deacons, 40 deaconesses, 70 hypodeacons, 160 lectors, 25 cantors .... Not less numerous were the clergy in secondary provincial cities like Edessa, which had 200 clergymen, or even more, because even its bishop at the Council of Chalcedon could not give the exact number of the clergy in his town .... There was a large number of monasteries in the Eastern Empire .... In Constantinople in 518 there were 56 monasteries and in 536 as many as 76 .... According to a chronicler at Oxyrhynchos the clergy equalled in number the lay population .... Under Justinian, as a result of the mission of John of Ephesus, 70,000 pagans were baptized by force in Asia Minor. For them in 542–71 12 monasteries and 99 churches were built .... М. В. Левченко: Церковные имущества V–VII вв. в Восточно-Римской империи, Византийский временник, II, 1949, pp. 19 ff.

62. *Greg. Epist.* III, 61. Ed. P. Ewald and L. M. Hartmann M.G.H.I., Berlin, 1891.

63. *Acta Sanctorum* VII, *Martii.* II, Paris–Rome, 1865, pp. 314 ff.

64. *Nikephoros Phokas* coll. III, nov. 19. (*Jus Graeco-Romanum.* Ed. J. and P. Zepos, I, Athens, 1931, p. 252).

65. Coll. III, nov. 26.

66. *Annae Comnenae "Alexiad".* Ed. Reifferacheid, Leipzig, 1884, I, 179.

67. *Michael Psellos, epist.* 175 *Bibliotheca graeca medii aevii.* Ed. V, Sathas, Venice–Paris, 1876, p. 450.

68. *Michael Psellos, apol.* Ed. cit., pp. 175 ff.

69. *Michael Psellos, epist.* 207, Ed. cit., p. 512.

70. *Michael Psellos, epist.* 252, Migne, *P.G.* 136, 1329–30.

71. A monograph by П. В. Безобразов: Византийский писатель и государственный деятель Михаил Пселл, 1899, is devoted to the writings of Psellos. The author in his extensive work puts forward the thesis, questioned today, that the system of Psellos was only a compilation of ancient philosophy (pp. 192–4). Ch. Zervos also discusses Psellos in: *Un philosophe néo-platonicien du XIe siècle, Michel Psellos, sa vie, son oeuvre, ses lettres philosophiques, son influence*, Paris, 1920, as does В. Вальденберг: Философские взгляды Михаила Пселла, Византийский сборник, Moscow–Leningrad, 1945, pp. 250 ff.

The works of Psellos were edited in *Bibliotheca graeca medii aevi*, IV Athens–Paris, 1874 and V, Venice–Paris, 1876.

72. С. Ф. Успенский: Византийский писатель Никита Акоминат из Хон, St. Petersburg, 1874, p. 47.

73. The political views of Gemistus can be found in Παλαιολόγεια καὶ Πελοποννησιακά. Ed. Lampros, vol. III, Athens, 1926, pp. 246–65 and vol. IV, Athens, 1930, pp. 113–35.

Fragments of Νόμοι were edited by C. Alexandre in *Pléthon, Traité des lois*, Paris, 1858. Transl. A. Pellisier.

74. C. Oudinus writes about Gemistus and the propagation of his philosophical concepts at Florence in *Commentarius de scriptoribus ecclesiae antiquis*, Part III, Lipsiae, 1722, 2358 and J. Corsius: *Vita Marsilii Ficini*, IV in: *Philippi Villani Liber de Civitatis Florentiae famosis civibus*, Florence, 1847, pp. 187 ff.

75. We find a discussion of the ideology of the Manichees as found in their writings in P. Alfaric: *Les Écritures Manichéennes*, Paris, 1918, 32–53.

76.   There is another version of the life of Mani, quoted by Hegemonius (from Graeco-Roman sources), according to which the founder of the doctrine was Scythianus ex genere Saracenorum, who lived in the first century; he was initiated into the secret science in Egypt. Scythianus' disciple, Terebinthus, put the doctrine into writing. After the death of Terebinthus a certain Corbicius studied his writings and adopted the name of Mani.

77.   *Ibn Abi Ja'kub an-Nadim.* Transl. G. Flügel: *Mani, seine Lehre und seine Schriften.* Leipzig, 1862, p. 84.

78.   Ibn Abi Ja'kub an-Nadim: *op. cit.,* p. 99.

79.   The books composed by Mani had the following titles: (1) *Mysteries,* (2) *The book of giants,* (3) *The book of precepts,* (4) *The book devoted to king Shapur,* (5) *The book of life,* (6) *The book of actions,* (7) *The Gospels specially illustrated.* About Mani's artistic talent writes Mirchônd, a Persian historian. Ed. K. Kessler: *Mani, Forschungen über die manichäische Religion,* I, Berlin, 1889, p. 380.

80.   In bourgeois literature, ever since the publication of F. Ch. Baur's: *Das manichäische Religionssystem,* Tübingen, 1831, there prevails the opinion that the source of Manichaean dualism is the dualism as received from Zoroastrianism (p. 89). Baur points out strong affiliations with Zoroastrianism and underlines the fact that Mani took over from that religion both the dualism and the conflict-idea. А. Л. Кац argues against this standpoint of bourgeois literature in Манихейство в Римской Империи — по данным. *Acta Archelai,* Вестник древней истории, 1955, 3. pp. 168 ff. He states that one ought to look for the sources of dualism in the objective contradictions which Mani detected in the surrounding world, and he then concludes that there is a universal principle of dualism. Кац quotes Epiphanios, whose statements seem to prove the hypothesis.

81.   *Acta Disputationis S. Archelai,* IX, 4.

82.   A. A. Bevan (*Encyclopaedia of Religion and Ethics,* VIII, Edinburgh, 1915, pp. 394–402) states on the basis of Arabic sources that the antithesis of good and evil is not, according to Mani, an antithesis of matter and spirit; evil can spread in the sphere of spirit as well as in the sphere of matter. Bevan says that in Manichaeism "the soul is not completely good and the body is not completely bad". He convincingly tries to prove that the idea attributed to the Manichaeans, that the spirit is good and that matter is bad comes from St. Augustine, who wrongly interpreted Manichaeism.

83.   S. Aurelius Augustinus: *De Moribus Ecclesiae catholicae et de moribus Manicheorum.* 10, Migne, *P.L.* 32, 1353.

84.   *Acta Disputationis S. Archelai,* X, 6.

85.   А. Л. Кац (*op. cit.*) underlines the agrarian character of the Manichaean beliefs and places it in the early stages of the doctrine. See K. Kessler: *op. cit.,* pp. 243 ff. about the forms of the cult and prayers and their affinities with Babylonian prayers.

86.   The reasons for the popularity of Manichaeism have been differently interpreted. A. Harnack (*Lehrbuch der Dogmengeschichte* II, Tübingen, 1931, pp. 524 ff.) thinks that Manichaeism gained followers by combining mythological elements with materialistic dualism and also because of the simplicity of its worship and rigour of its moral precepts. F. C. Burkitt (*The Religion of the Manichees,* Cambridge, 1925, p. 71) attributes the popularity of the doctrine to the personality of the founder and to the pessimism permeating the doctrine. H. Ch. Puech (*Le manichéisme, son fondateur, sa doctrine,* Paris, 1949 p. 35) sceptically declares that in present conditions it is impossible to find the sources and understand the popularity of the doctrine.

87.   *Mosaicarum et Romanarum legum collatio cura.* F. Blume: *Corpus Iuris Romani Anteiustiniani,* Bonn, 1841, p. 375 (Tit. XV, 3, 4–7).

88.   Petros Sikeliotes: *Historia utilis et refutatio atque eversio haereseos manichaeorum qui et Pauliciani dicuntur.* Migne, *P.G.* 104, 1377 B.

89.   Ф. И. Успенский: История Византийской империи, ч. II, 1. Leningrad, 1927, pp. 340 ff.) thinks that the Paulicians fought in the name of rationalism against Church ceremonial and the cult of holy images. The author underlines the strong connection of the sect with the teaching of Paul the Apostle.

90.   Migne, *P.G.* 104, 1288.

91.   Е. Э. Липшиц (Павликианское движение в Византии в VIII и первой

половине IX вв., Византийский временник, V, 1952, pp. 66 ff.) presents the process of the formation of the doctrine in the first decades of the ninth century.

92.   *Theophanes Continuatus*, IV. 16 (Bonn. p. 165).

93.   This fact is stressed by Ch. Diehl (*Cambridge Medieval History*, vol. IV, *The Eastern Roman Empire*, Cambridge, 1923, p. 42).

94.   H. Ch. Puech, A. Vaillant: *Le traité contre les Bogomiles de Cosmas le Prêtre*, Paris, 1945. Travaux publiées par l'Institut d'études slaves 21. In discussing the treatise the authors remark: "The heresy of the Bogomils has a deeply peasant character. It would be a mistake to connect this so rigorously Christian doctrine with the paganism still latent in Bulgaria; it is a simplified Christianity" (p. 32). It seems that this theory is open to discussion, because the struggle of the Bogomils against ecclesiastical hierarchy was rooted in the pagan tradition of the Bulgarians, as the Bulgarian historians point out.

95.   М. Г. Попруженко: Козма Пресвитер, болгарский писатель X века. "Болгарские старини" 12, 35. Sofia, 1936, s. 11–14.

96.   М. Г. Попруженко: *op. cit.*, p. 72.

97.   A comprehensive monograph about the Bogomils was written in Bulgarian and from a Marxist point of view by Д. Ангелов: Богомилството в България. It was translated in 1954 into Russian. Ангелов analyses the doctrine as a mass-movement, national and heretical, and undergoing changes caused by transformations in the social, economic and political life of Bulgaria in the Middle Ages.

98.   Български апокрифен летопис published in the work by И. Иванов: Бъгомилски книги и легенди. Sofia, 1925, p. 284.

4

THE POLITICAL DOCTRINE
OF THE MONGOLS

THE end of the tenth century is marked by a period of great expansion of
Western Christianity. From that time on the borders of the Latin world are
constantly being shifted toward the north, south and east.

Though in the times of the Emperor Otto I the risings of the pagan
Slavonic tribes caused the destruction of Hamburg and the removal of
Germanic settlers from the districts of Havelburg and Brandenburg, the
rivers Elbe and Saale marking the temporary border line between the
Christian and the pagan worlds, already toward the end of the tenth
and the beginning of the eleventh centuries a renewed expansion of
the Latin world started. New dukedoms and kingdoms, remaining in
religious, and not infrequently in political dependence on Rome, were
established on the north-eastern frontiers. These were Norway, Sweden
and Denmark in the north, and Poland, Hungary and Bohemia in the
east.

The southern frontiers undergo no slighter changes. Towards the end of
the tenth century the Pyrenees still separated the Christian world from that
of the Arabs, who were rulers over the western territories of the Mediterranean, embracing also Majorca, Corsica, Sardinia, Malta and Sicily.
However, the adherents of the Western Church were to become masters
over two-thirds of Spain and to win full control over the Mediterranean
as a result of fights with the Moslem world. The Westerners created their
feudal states in Greece and Macedonia, and eventually they mastered
Byzantium. All the losses and the painful failures of the crusaders, even the
fall of Jerusalem which in 1187, after 88 years, was again in the hands of
the Moslems, did not soften the deluded optimistic belief of the Westerners
in their supreme power. The expansion of Western Christianity brought
the majority of European knights into contact with the Moslem and the
Byzantine world. The West, while bringing destruction to their cultivated
neighbours, started to assimilate their culture, particularly the comforts and
luxuries of the East. The ruling classes of medieval Europe started to form
their way of life, their ideas and views, under the ever increasing influence
of Byzantine, and especially Arabic culture.[1]

The attitude of Western Christianity towards the Byzantines remained
unchanged for a period of two centuries. The generally accepted view was

146

that of Liutprand, bishop of Cremona and ambassador of the Emperor Otto I, who visited Byzantium twice, in 949 and 968, and who used to stress in his reports that the Byzantines were proud and boastful and disdainful of the heroic adherents of Western Christianity.[2]

The elaborate ceremoniousness, the forced courteousness and the lofty erudition of the Byzantine court must have been much against the taste of the primitive people of the West. How long-lasting was the attitude of the West towards the Byzantines may be illustrated by the fact that the chronicler of the second crusade,[3] 200 years after Liutprand, accuses the people of the Eastern Empire of being false, perverse, heretical and arrogant, and contrasts "the meanness of the Byzantines with the magnanimity of the western knights".

The Westerners regarded the Byzantines as sinful heretics who had betrayed the teaching of Christ, hence Eastern and Western Christianity was divided in, so to say, a passionate family quarrel. The imagination of the Westerners was stimulated by the legends about the inexhaustible treasures allegedly possessed by the court and the people of the Byzantine capital. They were excited too by the news of a multitude of holy relics; the Eastern Church boasted and created legends about their possession of the holy rood, the crown of thorns, Christ's blood, and relics of saints and martyrs. While the lustre of Byzantine gold evoked a maddening greed, the desire to deprive the heretical Byzantium of the holy relics and to bring them to orthodox Christian churches gave a justification of robbery.

The attitude of Europe to the Moslem world, however, was different. At first the followers of Islam were looked upon with hostile indifference, and incredible stories concerning their religion were current among the Christians. However, with time, in spite of bloody wars, Europe tended to see Mohammedanism in a more objective light. This change was, to a large extent, the result of the influence of Giraldus Cambrensis, a sober thinker of the twelfth century who, while discussing some features of Islam, discloses the influence of Judaism on Arabic doctrine.[4]

In fact, the Arabic world was to become a teacher for medieval Europe; the influence of Byzantium remaining slight. Though the sending of the Ptolomean *Almagest* to the king of Sicily in about the year 1160 marked a great step forward on the part of the Eastern Empire, the translation of the Greek texts accomplished almost immediately afterwards soon disappeared, and a Latin translation from Arabic took its place.[5]

Bloody battles fought by the crusaders did not interfere with a strong infiltration of Arabic learning into primitive Europe, the more so since intellectual and commercial contacts had started in earlier times. It is known that Gerbert, the future pope Sylvester II, had studied mathematics and astronomy near Barcelona, wanting to investigate the wisdom of the Arabs, whose renown in these fields was widespread. The commercial route from eastern Europe led through Verdun beyond the Pyrenees, and along it merchants drove the pitiful crowds of slaves to be sold in Arabic Spain. This must also have been the route for the Arabic thought which penetrated into Christian Europe toward the end of the tenth century. Contrary to expectation, the intellectual influence of the Arabs was constantly growing with their gradual retirement from south-western Europe and the islands of the Mediterranean. In the former Arabic territories there remained centres of learning and learned people speaking Arabic, especially Jewish scholars, who were the transmitters of Moslem wisdom to medieval Europe. It is due to them that the West came to know the works of ancient thinkers, not in the best translations thinkable, but in editions enlarged by the queries and comments of Arabic scholars.

This was the dawn of the development of science in the darkness of magic thinking. Under the influence of Arabic translations science started a new course, with changes affecting natural sciences in the first place. In the twelfth century serious mathematical and geometrical studies started with Euclid, astronomical studies with Ptolomy, while in medicine translations of Galen and Hippocrates were used. The Latin world became acquainted with the achievements of Arabic medicine, thanks to the most diligent work of Gerard of Cremona in the years 1175–87. The translation of Arabic and Greek works, and especially the cognizance of Aristotle's works on nature, led to an enrichment of European learning in the twelfth century, with new branches like physics, optics, mechanics, biology. A picture of the state of learning in the Western world is contained in the work of Bartholomew Anglicus.[6] In the year 1230 the provincial of the Franciscans in Saxony asked the provincial in France to send him the Franciscan brother Bartholomew Anglicus to lend a hand in the work of organizing a new province. We do not know whether Bartholomew did go to Saxony, but his reputation must have been great and widespread, since it was he who was asked to lecture at the University of Paris and to write a handbook of contemporary lore for the use of priests and monks. The author, in his attempt to deal with all topics and problems, writes on questions concerning God and the angels, and after discussing problems referring to fire, water and air passes to terrestrial matters and social relations. Bartholomew's work, translated into English, French and Spanish, constituted for a number of generations a reference book embracing all the learning accepted by Western Christianity. Bartholomew bases his work on Albert the Great who, in the thirteenth century, assimilated Aristotle's works on nature. In addition, the Franciscan friar quotes a number of Arabic and Jewish scholars. After him all Europe echoed the strange-sounding names of Eastern scientists and philosophers: Albumazar, Al-Farghani, Al-Farabi, Avicenna, Averroes, Al-Ghazali. Europe learned about the medical works of a number of Jews, like Ibn Gabirol in *Fons Vitae*, and Haly. The latter's work, *Complementum Medicinae*, was translated by the Benedictan monk, Constantine the African.

For the time being learning was only accumulated, but it was to bear fruit two centuries later. Meanwhile, however, the results of the crusades were directly painful for the medieval society in all its strata and classes. The period of great hopes was followed by one of great disappointments. Absorbed as they were in the holy wars, contemporaries did not notice far-reaching changes, namely, an increase in economic activity which was to determine the future course of the crusades as well as the fate of Western Christianity.

In the tenth century and at the beginning of the eleventh Europe had not many goods to offer to her neighbours. For luxuries, like spices, silk, perfumery, ivory, brought from the East, the Westerners had to pay in gold, as they were unable to balance the cost of imported goods from overseas by selling weapons and people.

Gold coins, spent on luxuries imported from the East, ceased to be current and silver coins took their place. While in Byzantium and the Moslem world gold coins were in use, the economically weak Europe had to use silver coins in her small-scale internal commercial transactions. The economic situation, however, changed in the thirteenth century as a result of an increase in western production. The area of cultivated land had become larger and cultivation itself was intensified. Because of the development of sheepbreeding, Flanders and England became the centres of the textile industry. Textiles and woollen clothing were, side by side with timber, weapons and furs, the chief items of European export to the East. The amount of export was greatly increased as compared with that of the preceeding period. In the lowlands of Lombardy, and especially in Pavia, various goods from eastern and northern Europe were being sold to Genoese and Venetian merchants, who, competing with each other, monopolized between them the trade with Byzantium and the Arabs. This brought about a change in the situation: the East paid in gold currencies for imported goods from the West, hence the amount of gold coins in Europe constantly increased and soon there was more gold than silver.[7]

While the fanatic preacher Peter the Hermit was the hero of the first crusade, the same position was occupied in the time of the fourth by the clever doge of Venice, Enrico Dandolo, who managed to "make the naive crusade a profitable commercial undertaking".[8]

The western world took the initiative. It reached the frontiers of the world mentioned by Pope Urban II, who initiated the crusade of 1095. In Clermont the pope spoke of three continents, the Christian Europe, and Africa and Asia, both in the hands of heathens.[9]

In the eyes of the Europeans the limits of the world were set by the vastness of the Atlantic Ocean in the West, the vertical line connecting the

Dnieper with the Nile in the East, while the Mediterranean, dividing Europe from North Africa, was considered the axis of the world.[10] The eastern boundary, that is the Dnieper–Nile line, used to be crossed by merchants attempting to penetrate into the country of the Volga, or trying to establish closer commercial contacts with Arabic caravans on their way from Persia and Khorezm. The eastern peripheries of the world were of special interest to Western Christianity, since for many centuries all kinds of stories had been repeated about various communities, even Christian states, allegedly existing there. The belief that Christians lived amid the flood of heathenism, far beyond the Dnieper–Nile line, led to a desire to help them to become unified with the Church. The stories were to some degree founded on fact, at least in so far as it was still remembered that the Nestorians, because they refused to recognize the divine attributes of Christ's mother, had been excluded from the Eastern Church in the fifth century and dispersed all over Asia.

In the year 1122 all Rome was stirred by the appearance in the eternal city of a mysterious person who caused amazement even in the court of the pope. He presented himself as the ruler of a Christian kingdom situated in distant eastern territories. Two years after this event a false letter, allegedly sent from the unknown Christian country, was circulated among the courts of Europe. In it the ruler of the country, generally called Father John, presents a magnificent description of his powerful state and demands from all a recognition of his supremacy over the Christian world. In the year 1177 Pope Alexander III, under the influence of this mysterious report, sent his personal physician on a special mission to the mysterious Father John in order to make clear to him the claims of the Holy See.[11]

There must have been in Europe a convinced belief in the existence of the mysterious Father John; indeed, almost 100 years later the Franciscan friar, William of Rubrouck, while giving an account of his mission to the Great Khan, also mentions the legendary father. William of Rubrouck identifies him with Toghrul, the Nestorian ruler of the Keraites, who, having been the friend of Jenghiz Khan, the founder of the Mongolian power, changed into his enemy. Following William's account, Marco Polo, in his *Description of the World*, repeats the story of the friendship and fight of the mysterious Father John and Jenghiz Khan. Knowledge of the Far East, however, was not limited to the more or less fantastic stories of Father John, of the communities of Christians lost in the Islam world, or of the immeasurable wealth of Asia. The two worlds were to meet in the thirteenth century, when the people inhabiting the eastern frontiers of Europe experienced the brutal invasion of the Mongols who came from the steppes of Asia.

"This was an event", to quote the Arabs of the thirteenth century, "whose sparks dispersed over all and the evil of which affected everybody; it ran through the settlements like a cloud driven by a gust of wind."[12]

In the first half of the thirteenth century it seemed that no power would be able to resist the destructive impetus of the Tartar cavalry. The Venetians entered into trade and other negotiations with them, the Church dreamt of their conversion, and only the Slavs attempted to hold back their aggressive impetus.

In the year 1222 the best sections of the Mongolian army, after having plundered and destroyed Georgia, (Gruziya), passed through the territory between the Black and the Caspian Seas, and arrived at the South Russian steppes covering the vast spaces east of the Dnieper line and reaching far beyond the Volga. On these steppes, called the "Land of the Kipchaks", the Mongols encountered the nomadic tribes of the Polovtsi, whose level of cultural development almost equalled that of the Mongols themselves. The leaders of the Mongolian army, as it approached the frontiers of Europe, were two fierce men, Chepé and Subutai. They were two of Jenghiz Khan's four most faithful and most cruel leaders, whose reputation in the East was well established as "the four dogs of Jenghiz Khan, fed with human flesh; he held them on chains; these dogs have brows of brass, hewn teeth, tongues sharp as awls, hearts of iron. . . . They drink the dew, ride with the wind, and in battles eat human flesh. . . . The four dogs are Chepé, Kublai, Chelme and Subutai."[13]

Fire, destruction and death marked the track of the Mongols. Commerce, so far quite animated in the region of the Dnieper and Volga, was declining. It was there, along the Volga, that the commercial track from the country of the Bulgarians led through the Caucasus towards Central Asia, or to the Far East, or through the steppes to the Crimea. The use of the commercial tracks was in the hands of the Arabs, whose wares reached the West by means of the Genoese merchants settled in the Crimea. This commerce suffered severely from the invasions of the Mongols, who mercilessly destroyed the storehouses of the Genoese merchants in the Crimea, but at the same time saved those of the rival Venetians and Armenians in order to obtain information about Europe.

The Russian dukedoms, which lay close to the pasture lands of the nomadic Polovtsi, were also involved in eastern trade, since from them corn and flax were exported to Central Asia. Relations between the nomadic Polovtsi and the settled Russians were changeable: forays and wars mingled with periods of peaceful, even friendly coexistence. The Mongolian invasion, however, made the Polovtsi ask the Russian dukes for help, and this help was granted. The epilogue of the first Mongolian invasion in Europe is generally known: on 16 June 1223 the Russian and Polovtsi forces suffered a bloody defeat at the river Kalka. The unified and disciplined Mongolian army proved triumphant over the divided, disunited regional dukes. A chronicler of these times made the following note: "A great multitude of people fell, and there was lamentation and weeping and sadness in the towns and villages. . . . The Tartars, however, turned back away from the Dnieper. And we do not know whence they came, or whither they went."[14]

After this fierce attack the army of Chepé and Subutai retired beyond the Dnieper far into the steppe. Thirteen years later, in 1236, an army of several thousand Mongols attacked Europe again. The expedition was headed by Batu, accompanied by the bloody victor of the battle at the Kalka, Subutai, who provided the necessary inspiration and advice. This was not an unprepared, spontaneous foray; the situation was quite the contrary. For many years before the actual attack numerous commercial caravans of the Venetians and Armenians had been passing through Russia, Poland and Hungary, effectively uniting their own profitable commercial transactions with collecting information about Europe to be passed over to the Mongols. That is why Subutai was well acquainted with everything concerning the forces of his enemies, while Europe had only a vague idea of the dangerous storm approaching from the East. After over-running the steppe of the Kipchaks and destroying the Russian dukedoms, the Mongolian cavalry began to devastate Poland, Hungary and Dalmatia. In 1242–3 the Mongolians took their route back through Wallachia and Moldavia to the Kipchak steppe, in order to found there, in these vast territories, their huge state, called Golden Horde.

The destructive invasion of the Mongols was felt very painfully on the eastern frontiers of Europe, and their cruelty and fierceness could paralyse even the boldest men. The disunited Christian world was unable to take any measures of united action against the Asiatic invaders. While Louis IX of France was involved in struggles with his vassals, and the quarrel between Gregory IX and Frederick II was reaching its peak, the Slavonic world was left to itself in the fight with the Mongol invaders.

The Mongolian highlands, bordering on Siberia in the north, China in the south and Manchuria and Dzungaria in the east and west respectively, are divided into the mountainous north-western part and the flat land of the south-east, the latter constituting the central part of the Gobi desert. The nomadic population of the vast highlands led the lives of shepherds and hunters and moved from place to place on the steppe in search of new pasture land and suitable hunting ground. The migrations of the Mongols were to a large extent dependent on climatic conditions, which determined their nomadic existence. During the winter, when the north-western territories lay under a thick layer of snow, the Mongols moved toward the south-eastern regions, where there was much less snow and it was easier to find food for the animals. In the late spring, however, they abandoned the dried-out steppes for the north-western territories which abounded in both water and grass. The Mongols lived close to the pastures in tents made of felt. Life on the steppes determined their primitive religious beliefs. They worshipped as divinities natural powers and phenomena; the highest position in the hierarchy was attributed to the "Heavens" (*tengri*), which they regarded as the source of life and all justice. The cult of the gods was concentrated in the hands of the *shamans*, who were both priests and seers, officiating at religious services as well as disclosing the decrees of the heavens.

In the course of many centuries the patriarchal system of the Mongols underwent only slight changes, and it was shortly before the time of Jenghiz Khan's empire that the feudal system developed. Out of the mass of nomadic Mongols certain rich families (*ajil*) pushed themselves into the foreground. These families ran large, independent households, including not only relatives but also a number of dependants, and thus an aristocracy was formed, subjugating the poorer nomads. This nobility of the steppes, distinguished by wealth and influence, was given the name of "white bone", in contrast to that of "black bone" used in reference to the poorer Mongols.

Towards the end of the twelfth century the aristocracy of the steppes constituted a considerable part of the Mongolian society, which was composed of a number of nomadic tribes. In this period Mongolia was the scene of incessant fights between the leaders of different tribes in order to win new pastures, flocks and herds, and power. Hosts of Mongolian warriors took part in the fights on the steppes, and upon their united bravery depended the prestige of their leaders.[15] By the aid of warrior-bands the economic position of the aristocrats was strengthened, since they were able, by means of military power, to master the rest of the population and the slaves taken during the numerous domestic fights.

The chaos of inter-tribal conflicts must have brought to the minds of the more ambitious leaders the idea of organizing a uniform state. The unification of the nomadic tribes into one organism reflected the interests of the aristocracy. They desired to preserve their position, as well as that of the shamanistic priests who, aware of the growing infiltration of Nestorianism, Buddhism and Islam, expected support from a powerful state organization. The priests sustained the belief among the Mongols that the "Heavens" would send them a supernatural being (*dżajagatu*) who, endowed with miraculous power, would create a mighty state among the nomads.

Sometimes, in periods of impending danger for all, the nomads gave up domestic fights. The particular tribes were then united and temporary unions formed, and the rule over them was put into the hands of one of the leaders. Controversial matters were, at such times, solved at meetings (*kurultai*) of the leaders and the aristocracy, and these meetings also decided about the tasks of the leaders of the tribal union.[16]

One of the tribal leaders who wanted to unify the nomads was Yesukai, the father of Temuchin, the future founder of the Mongolian empire, Jenghiz Khan. The latter was born in the year 1155. But even before his birth people said about his mother, Yulun, that "the son born of her will be a hero". At the age of 10 Temuchin lost his father, whose death impoverished the family and brought about the loss of the position it had so far held in the tribe. After Yesukai's death his band of warriors was also destroyed, and Yulun had to bring up her son by herself. She awakened in Temuchin a belief in his heavenly mission to rule over all the Mongolian tribes.

His unusual personality enabled him to organize his own host of warriors. His abilities as a leader and politician put him into an advantageous position in his relations with the other tribal leaders, who eventually acknowledged him as their superior and frequently turned from enemies into the most faithful fighters for his cause. One of the people closest to the leader of the Mongols was Mukhuli, the future conqueror of China, who, like Yulun, spread among the nomads a belief in Temuchin's divine mission. Dzirguadai, of the tribe of the Isuts, compensated for his former hostility with absolute faithfulness to Temuchin, who entrusted him with the highest military functions and, for his exceptional fierceness in battle, called him Chepé (Arrow), a name of distinction for warriors of the steppe.

The support of the *shamans*, who showed their approval of Temuchin's actions by attributing religious authority to them, was of especially great importance for the beginning of the leader's career. Temuchin's step-brother Kekcze, the chief *shaman*, called the "Spirit of the Heavens" (*Tebtengri*) and generally recognized as an intercessor between heaven and the people, made an official statement about the mission to be fulfilled by the new leader of the tribes of the steppes.

Temuchin knew how to make good use not only of military power and negotiations but also of the belief of the Mongols, spread and sustained by the people close to him, that it was he who was the creator of the Mongolian power, sent by the heavens and long waited for by the people. At the same time he took great care that booty was distributed among the warriors, which ensured his popularity with them. In the eyes of the aristocrats and the *shamans* he represented a power able to unify the tribes so far divided by strife.

After his victory over the Nestorian ruler of the Keraites, and after defeating the Naimans, Temuchin became the incontestable ruler of all Mongolia. During the *kurultai* at the river Onon in the year 1206 the aristocratic representatives of the Mongolian tribes proclaimed Temuchin khan of khans of all Mongolia (great khan over khans), and gave him the title of Jenghiz Khan. A horse's tail with nine white bones symbolized the power over the new steppe empire, the capital of which was Karakorum, located at the spring of the river Orchon. Thus a huge state was brought into existence, one that stretched as far as the Altai Mountains and the Argun river, the Siberian Taiga and the Great Wall.

Once Jenghiz Khan succeeded in his task of unifying all the tribes inhabiting the Mongolian highlands, he turned towards China and proceeded to attack it. The result of this undertaking was a quick subjugation of the Tangut Empire. This accomplished he turned towards the northern parts of China and, after a long series of fights, conquered the Kin Empire, to which he had so far been in allegiance. In the course of the invasion of China the Mongols made use of all the fierce cruelty they were capable of and they terrorized the population, depriving them of all their property. In conquering the fortified towns they made use of the inhabitants. It was here that Jenghiz Khan learnt the method of besieging and conquering towns, a knowledge of great importance for his future wars in the West. A seemingly negligible event which took place during the Chinese war proved of great importance later. After the conquest of Peking Jenghiz Khan discovered the great Chinese thinker, Yeliu-Chutsai, a descendant of a princely house, who enjoyed the reputation of being the most perfect of all men. This man became one of Jenghiz Khan's most influential counsellors and helped him in the task of creating a world empire. Educated Chinese people who came over to the side of the victorious Mongols lent a hand in working out the proper structure for the steppe empire. The wise Chinese thinker tried to oppose the idea of absolute terror by suggesting that the subjugated peoples should be governed by means of a well organized administration, one that would be guided by law. The Chinese repeatedly told the warlike Mongolian leaders that "it was possible to conquer the whole world on horseback, but it was not possible to govern the world on horseback".

However, Jenghiz Khan never stopped fighting, being convinced that Heaven had commanded the nomads of the steppes to conquer the whole world.

After the conquest of China the Mongols turned westward. In the year 1216 Subutai passed the Altai Mountains, all covered with snow, and in the lowlands of the upper Irtish defeated the Merkits army. A year later Jenghiz Khan's son, Juji, attacked the Khirghiz tribes, and Chepé invaded the vast Karakitai territory. The latter undertaking was preceded by the activity of Mongolian emissaries who organized riots and revolts against the ruler of the country, Kushlek Khan. Kushlek Khan, while supporting Buddhism, persecuted the adherents of all other religions, and this caused dissatisfaction among the people. As soon as Chepé found himself within the boundary of the Karakitai country, he made public the proclamation of Jenghiz Khan in which it was announced that all people would have religious freedom and that priests and people who had anything to do with religious service, whatever the religion, would not be taxed. Thanks to religious tolerance Chepé managed to master the vast spaces of the Karakitai country in a short period of time and made them part of the Mongolian Empire. The domains of the Mongols now bordered on Khorezm, which included almost the whole of the Turan lowlands and the Iranian highlands. At this time the ruler of Khorezm was consolidating his country by force, and in the first decade of the thirteenth century his army occupied Bukhara, Samarkand and Ferghana. Thus the warriors of Khorezm became the masters of Pamir and, marching through the Iranian provinces, reached the borders of India.

Jenghis Khan's great success encouraged him to claim, in the year 1218, allegiance from Khorezm in order that he might be the sole master of the commercial routes passing through Central Asia. He did this because he was aware that, after the defeat of China, Mongolia had become the chief transmitter of Chinese goods exported to the West, and also of the imported western corn which the East needed so badly after the great desolation in the northern provinces of China.

The inhabitants of Khorezm reacted to the provocative proposal of Jenghiz Khan by massacring a caravan of 450 merchants, whom they treated as Mongolian spies. This happened in the wealthy commercial town of Otrar, located on the eastern frontier of Khorezm, which the caravan had reached together with Jenghiz Khan's diplomatic emissaries. In consequence the army of the steppes rushed like a hurricane towards Central Asia, leaving desolation behind them and bringing destruction to the highly civilized towns of Khorezm. In spite of desperate attempts at defence, the invaders soon conquered Bukhara, Samarkand, Merv and Urgench, and in the course of less than 3 years (1219–21) the complete conquest of Central Asia was achieved. The unprecedented cruelty of their treatment of the inhabitants evoked general abhorrence and fear. After the flood of the Mongols over Khorezm, life in the country stopped for a number of years. The barbarians of the steppe saved only those merchants, priests and craftsmen who declared themselves ready to co-operate. Thousands of craftsmen were sent far into Mongolia, or else had to perform various tasks at the time of besiegement. From Samarkand alone Jenghiz Khan sent 30,000 craftsmen to the East.

The invasion of Khorezm in the year 1223 gave Chepé and Subutai an opportunity of over-running Iran and devastating its northern parts, after which they passed the Caucasus and attacked the Polovtsi and the Russians.

In the year 1222 Jenghis Khan led his chief army to the lowlands of the Indus, whence, however, he soon withdrew, probably after receiving the news about the rising in China. Thus the invincible nomads returned to their home country from far-off lands. In 1225 Jenghiz Khan was again in his capital, Karakorum, and 2 years later the cruel tyrant of the empire of the steppes, who called himself "God's scourge on earth", was no longer alive.

According to Jenghiz Khan's will, his third son, Ogotai (1229–41), became khagan. Following the imperialistic policy of his father, he continued to organize the great empire. The huge Mongolian State could not do without an effective administration. The system of communication, the monetary system, taxes, administration of the conquered territories, military supply, judicial activities, all called for a well thought-out organization and precision in execution. With the help of the wise Jeliu-Chutsai, Ogotai laid the foundations of his state of the nomads, and in this he made use of the Uigurs, the Moslems, and above all the Chinese. In the first period the Uigurian alphabet was used for official purposes in the state, modifications to suit the requirements of the Mongolian language having been introduced. With time, however, administration came more and more into the hands of the Chinese, whose diligence and precision in action brought about the more and more frequent use of the Chinese language side by side with Mongolian.

During the *kurultai* of 1235 the Mongolian leaders decided that an invasion of Europe was the most important task for them. The leadership of the army was given to Jenghiz Khan's grandson, Batu, who was accompanied by the bloody Subutai, well remembered from the first invasion of Europe. Seven years later the Mongolian army was seen in Hungary, where, at the beginning of the year 1242, Batu received the ominous horsetail, indicating the death of Ogotai.

The Mongols gave up the idea of any further conquest of Europe and retired to the vast territory of the Kipchak steppe, where Batu founded his own, independent state, *Ulus* of Juji, Golden Horde.

The Christian world was horrified at the desolation the Mongols made in Russia, Poland, and Hungary. Europe was stricken with fear by the unknown power of the steppe empire. Christianity was endangered by the eastern military state, organized according to the pattern of a dynastic monarchy governed by the whole family of the ruler. Each of the members of the dynasty was master over his own district, over which, however, the khagan had supreme authority. In spite of the fact that the whole family of the ruler governed the country, the powerful individuality of Jenghiz Khan was a guarantee of unity. He himself was the absolute ruler, and the khans only represented his power in the particular *uluses* and acted on his behalf. He also managed to impose his will on the *kurultai*, reducing its sphere of activity to the acceptance of the suggestions made by the khagan.

The State of the Mongols, created by and for the conquests, had to adapt its inner organization to the needs of the huge army of the nomads. The skeleton of the state organization, in principle, consisted of the tribal–patriarchal system. The nomadic society, however, was not a disorganized crowd. Each tribe fell into larger and smaller organizational units, each embracing a definite number of tents. They were headed by appointed chieftains, who were hierarchically dependent on their superiors. The army, however, was the backbone and the essential feature of the state of the nomads. From the age of 15 up to 60 each Mongol had to serve in the army, the organization of which reflected the decimal system. The smallest organizational group of the army consisted of ten warriors. That which embraced 100 people was the next unit; a still larger one, called a *hezareh*, amounted to 1000 warriors; the largest unit equalled 10 *hezarehs*, that is, it consisted of 10,000 warriors and was called a *touman*. The army of the warriors of the steppe consisted first of all of cavalry. The fierceness and perseverance of the Mongolian warriors was well known everywhere. From an early age they were used to horses, their inseparable companions in the migrations on the steppe. They became a part of the vast Asiatic steppe on which they grew up. The severe climate hardened them and their nomadic way of life made them physically strong. Marco Polo says of them: "In all the world there is no such army that would be more persevering in toils and hardships, none that would be cheaper, or better qualified for the conquest of countries and kingdoms.... And take it from me, they are able to ride for 10 days without stopping, if necessary, without eating or burning a fire, living only on the blood of their horses."[17]

With the territorial expansion of the invasions into countries whose inhabitants led a settled life, the Mongols adopted the Chinese methods of besieging and conquering towns, hence, side by side with the cavalry, there appeared in the army squadrons specially trained in this field.

The personal division of the khagan, his guard (*keshichan*), constituted a school for military leaders and was at the same time the heart of the Mongolian army. Simple warriors in this division had the respect of commanders of *hezarehs*. "My simple, ordinary warrior", Jenghiz Khan used to say, "is of higher rank than any of the commanders of a *hezareh*."[18]

The characteristic feature of the army of the nomads, apart from the extremely rigorous discipline, the breaking of which was punished by death, was the collective responsibility of a division for the appointed task, and thus there was little chance for individual heroism. The Mongolian cavalry was extremely mobile; its divisions often managed to cover as many as 60 km a day, and this repeatedly so for a number of weeks without stopping. In the course of covering thousands of kilometres, the army was victorious again and again.

The successes can be accounted for by the warriors' speed in attack, their blind obedience, physical strength and knowledge of the enemy. In order to lead the enemy astray the Mongols invaded a country from various angles. Information about the location of the enemy forces, received from merchants, who penetrated the given land before the attack, allowed the Mongols to move about even more boldly.

Jenghiz Khan made war the regular job of the Mongols, conquest their vocation, plundering their source of income. The desolation which marked the routes of the Mongols brought them new power and new wealth. The occupied country had to provide food and maintenance for the nomads; the devastated fields were changed into pasture land for the nomads, and the subjugated population had to serve in the army of the invaders.

In the subdued countries the Mongols introduced methods of unprecedented and most cruel terror in order to prevent even the slightest opposition. News of their cruelty spread through various countries even before an actual invasion, rousing unnecessary panic, and this frequently enabled even small divisions of the warriors of the steppe to be victorious over a more numerous enemy.

When towards the end of March 1242 the army of the nomads suddenly withdrew from the banks of the Danube into the steppe, Europe was overwhelmed by fear and uncertainty. Nobody knew whence the Mongols came, whither they went, or when they would be back again. In the year 1245 Pope Innocent IV sent two missions to the East, to the unknown ruler of the Mongols, asking him to discontinue the wars with the adherents of the religion of Christ, at the same time threatening him with God's revenge for wrong done to the Christians. One of the Pope's emissaries was the Franciscan friar Giovanni de Plano Carpini, the same who first informed Europe about the military state of the Mongols. Together with the archbishop of Antivara and Benedict of Poland, in the year 1246, he reached the capital of the Mongols, Karakorum, where, 5 years after Ogotai's death, his son Kuyuk (1246–8) had just become khagan.

Fra Carpini brought from Karakorum the news that the Mongols were planning an invasion of Europe. He also brought Kuyuk's letter in which the Great Khan demanded absolute obedience from the pope, since such was the Decree of the Heavens.

The controversies between Kuyuk and Batu, the khan of the Golden Horde, prevented the Mongols from organizing a new invasion of the West. It had become increasingly difficult to preserve the unity of the nomadic empire. In these attempts an important role was played by Siurkukteni, the influential and wise widow of Tule, Jenghiz Khan's youngest son. After the death of Kuyuk her sons held, one after the other, supreme rule over the Mongolian Empire. These were the times of Mangu (1251–9) and of Kublai (1260–94), a period during which the victorious invaders were absorbing the culture of the conquered tribes.

In the West the follower of Batu Khan of the Golden Horde, Bereke, accepted Islam. The Arabic historian wrote the following words about him: "Bereke ... made a renewed vow of faithfulness to Islam, and the *sheikh* obliged him to proclaim (Islam) officially. He (Bereke) spread (Islam) among all his subjects, started to build mosques and schools in all the countries under his rule, was himself surrounded by learned men and lawyers, and was in friendly relations with them."[19]

In the East an analogous increase of interest in the culture of settled societies can be observed. Mangu was surrounded by learned men; in Karakorum he built an observatory for the famous mathematician, Nasir ed-din, whom he brought to Mongolia after the conquest of Iran, bestowing great honours on him. Kublai was brought up in the Chinese tradition and remained from an early age under the influence of his wise teacher, Lao-shi. The latter inculcated into his pupil the idea of the superiority of Chinese culture and at the same time taught him a new attitude to life, one that was foreign to the Mongols. He dedicated to Kublai a dissertation containing eight chapters: on the necessity of perfecting one's personality, on eagerness for learning, on respect for learned men, on love of relatives, on obedience to the decrees of Heaven, on compassion for one's neighbours, on good conduct, and, finally, on condemning flatterers. This work must have been much at variance with the ideas and ways of the warriors of the steppe.

The toil of the wise Chinese bore fruit; the cultivated Chinese became victorious over the barbaric Mongols. Jenghiz Khan's grandson, Kublai, moved his capital from Karakorum to Peking. The ruler of the Mongols became the heir of the Chinese emperors.

The shift of the axis of the Mongolian Empire towards the East caused a complete break in the former unity. The Great Khan of Peking had no longer any influence on the policy of the *uluses*, which grew increasingly independent. The ruler of the Golden Horde, Bereke Khan, was involved in a war in the defence of Islam, one that he had undertaken, together with the Egyptian Seljuks, against the Mongolian ruler of Iran, Hulagu. On the battlefield after the defeat of Hulagu's army the victorious Bereke Khan is said to have uttered words which illustrate the tragedy of Jenghiz Khan's empire: "May Allah send ignominy on this Hulagu, who caused Mongols to be killed with the swords of Mongols. Had we acted together we would have conquered the whole world."[20]

The East, too, was not spared from barbaric wars. Here Kublai fought against his brother Arikbugha, the ruler of Mongolia proper. This was a struggle between two ideas: Arikbugha represented the idea of war and the steppe tradition, the centre of which was Mongolia and Karakorum, while Kublai defended settled life and the idea of peaceful government, which he tried to put into practice in Peking, the new capital of the Mongols.

In spite of the warnings of Jenghiz Khan, an end was put to the unity of the ruling family, which he had regarded as the essential condition of the power and greatness of the Mongols. The military empire of the Mongols became a thing of the past. On its ruins the independent states, *uluses*, were built, but these were unable to continue the idea of mastering the whole world.

The views of the steppe aristocracy, supported by the priests of shamanism, constituted the political doctrine of the Mongols in the period of their great expansion. Its content was a primitive kind of Messianism which justified their deeds by the belief that according to the decree of heaven the ruler of the nomadic Mongolian tribes ought to conquer all the world. With every new military success the Mongols made a clearer formulation of their ideas, which reflected the desires and the ways of the warriors of the steppe.

The first words of Jenghiz Khan uttered about his exceptional role were rather reticent. At the beginning of his career, when his hair was just beginning to go grey, Jenghiz Khan said to his people:

"The Almighty Lord has made me leader of divisions of a thousand and ten thousand warriors and has raised my horsetail, the symbol of my power; that is also why He marked me with grey hair, which indicates my seniority."[21]

Priests and divinators had first to proclaim the person of the ruler as divine and as fulfilling a divine mission before all this could become a truth for everybody. The authoritative pronouncement of Kekcze (*Tebtengri*), the chief *shaman*, gave religious sanction to the attempts to unify all the tribes. This priest charged Jenghiz Khan, in the name of God, with the duty of ruling over all the world. "I speak with God, and I visit heaven", *Tebtengri* said, "God has decided that you should be the ruler of the world. It is His will that you should be called Jenghiz Khan."[22]

The great victories of the Mongols, such as that over China, the conquest of the huge Karakitai country and that of Khorezm, led to radical changes in the formulations of the doctrine. It expresses the desire to completely exterminate settled peoples, a tendency seen as early as the period of the conquest of China, when the aristocracy of the steppe demanded a massacre of all the settled population and wanted to turn all the fields into pasture land.[23]

An even more radical variety of Messianism was being propagated at the time of the wars conducted in Central Asia. Jenghiz Khan raised cruelty to the dignity of the highest virtue, which endowed the warriors of the steppe with everlasting fame. The Persian historian of the times of Jenghiz Khan, Juzjani, says that the Mongolian ruler was boastful of his cruelty. In Central Asia he said to his people that the numerous massacres in the conquered countries would bring him everlasting fame and would fill all countries of the world with awe of his name.[24]

Jenghiz Khan demanded absolute obedience from subjugated people, and regarded any discussion or negotiation as a sin against himself and against heaven, not to speak of any attempt at opposition or defence. In a speech delivered to the citizens of Bukhara, after the town was taken, Jenghiz Khan said:

". . . And I am telling you, be afraid of me, for I am the punishment sent by God on you. If you had not committed great sins, the Almighty God would not have punished you by sending me."[25]

During this campaign all the towns of Khorezm received decrees (*yarlighs*) in which the Mongols repeatedly expounded their doctrine very clearly.

"Let it be known to all emirs, aristocrats and to the people", the *yarlighs* said, "that the Almighty gave us (Mongols) all the world from the East to the West. Those who show obedience to us will be saved, and so will their wives, children and relatives; but those who act otherwise will die, and so will their wives, children and relatives."[26]

The messianic idea, which unified the nomadic tribes in their attempt to conquer the world, at the same time promised concrete advantages and profits for the life of the Mongols on the steppe. Jenghiz Khan speaks of the definite tasks awaiting him, and in future to be carried on by every ruler of the Mongols.

"It is my desire", Jenghiz Khan declares, "that my shooters and my guards . . . as well as their wives, their betrothed and their daughters should, thanks to my generosity, eat only the most exquisite food; that they be dressed, from head to heel, in robes with gold inwoven; that they ride the best horses properly broken in; that they have clean and fresh-tasting water and good pasture land for their flocks and herds; that they move about in the country along tracks that are free from all obstacles and dangers. . . ."[27]

The doctrine of the Mongolian Messianism, so cruel in its essence, had certain unique features resulting from the primitive social relations of the nomadic system. The fanaticism of religious strife was incomprehensible to them, the inequality of women was a thing unknown, and divergence between doctrine and practical life was alien to them.

Completely adapted to the life of the vast, wild steppe, they worshipped the powers of nature, and showed no understanding of the theology of the other beliefs which they encountered in their country. Here they met the Christian Nestorians, the Chinese Buddhists, and the adherents of Islam, but these different religions, rites and ceremonies must only have deepened the scepticism of the nomads. Those who, by the decree of the heavens, were destined to rule over all humanity, could not accept any of these beliefs, so hostile to each other. Their God spoke to them in a simple and clear language when He commanded them to fight for rule over all the world.

The Mongols, while demanding absolute obedience from their subjects, left them complete religious freedom. At the same time they freed the priests of all religions from tax duties, because they were aware that the priests and their prayers for the success of the invaders might prove helpful in the task of fully mastering the subdued territories. Thus the most cruel leader did not neglect religious tolerance.

"Chepé, accompanied by his personal division of warriors, made special messengers announce that everybody was to stick to his belief and be faithful to the religion of his forefathers."[28]

The Persian historian of the latter half of the thirteenth century, Juwayni, mentions a typical example which illustrates the complete religious indifference of the Mongols. He says about Batu Khan, the ruler of the Golden Horde, that "he (Batu) did not belong to any religion or sect, neither did he feel any desire to know God".[29]

As well as their religious tolerance, the position of the Mongolian woman deserves to be stressed. Women had an almost equal share with men in economic duties, and among aristocratic families, in ruling also. The Mongolian warriors, frequently away from their home-tents (*yurts*) by hundreds or even thousands of kilometres, during hunting or in war-time, left to their women the leadership in economic and political life. The women of the ruling dynasty were present at *kurultais* and took an active part in them.

It is possible to multiply examples to show that Mongolian women took decisions even in the most crucial affairs. Rashid al-Din says that the mother of Jenghiz Khan "was a very talented and wise woman, who took care of her son as well as she could, and at the same time was in charge of her husband's possessions, service, soldiers and supporters, everything that Yesukai left her".[30]

Particularly memorable in the history of the steppe empire is the prudent wife of Jenghiz Khan's youngest son, who managed to prevent a fratricidal fight between Kuyuk and Batu Khan. Her *ulus*, which included Mongolia proper, the heart of the empire, constituted a model of good administration. Her judicious assignment of pasture land and the alertness of her warriors, always equipped for quick action, made Siurkukteni a respected and influential woman at the court of the Khan. The mother of Mangu and Kublai, the two future khagans, formed the views of her sons by choosing their teachers properly, and she could to a large extent foresee their future policy. The common law of the nomads said that ". . . a wife, whose husband had to leave for hunting or for war, should be so efficient in running everything, that any guest or wanderer who chances to arrive, cannot but praise her. Only such a wife brings her husband good fame and raises the glory of his name among members of the tribe."[31]

The position of women in the nomadic society evoked an understandable surprise among the strangers who encountered them. At the beginning of the fourteenth century the Arabic traveller, Ibn Batuta, wrote: "I saw miracles in this country (Mongolia), resulting from the high respect the people have for women. Women are more respected than men."[32]

A similar report is given by the Arabic historian, Al-Omari, who says that the Mongolian aristocratic women "take part in ruling on equal terms with their husbands, the decisions taken being common". In his surprise the historian adds: "Indeed, I have not seen any women in our times that would have as much power as they have there."[33]

The Messianism of the steppes is also characterized by a surprising correspondence between the idea and practical life. The simple aims of the imperialistic doctrine were amplified by rules which guaranteed their execution.

Shortly before his death the founder of the Empire ordered the common law (*Yassa*), in which the doctrine as well as the measures for its realization are expressed, to be engraved on iron plates. *Yassa* has not survived to our times, but we know its content from the reports of chroniclers; it is a collection of principles referring chiefly to the technique of ruling over the nomadic society, which undertook to fight for rule over all the world. The chief idea of *Yassa* may be reduced to the thought that the victory of the Mongols depends on unity of action, proper choice of leaders, and bravery in the army of the steppes.

It seems that the greatest worry of Jenghiz Khan was the preservation of unity among the members of the dynasty. It was in connection with this problem that he approached his sons in his testament: "For you, my sons, I have won and mastered, with the help of God and the Heavens, a large and vast state from the centre of which it takes a whole year to reach any of the frontiers. Now I am passing to you my last wish: be of one mind and one thought both in fighting enemies and in winning friends—this will bring you a rich and happy life and joy in ruling. . . ."[34]

Similarly, he starts the *Yassa* with the reminder that inwardly divided societies were soon overpowered by the Mongols, because they were too weak to resist.

Jenghiz Khan thought that the best guarantee of unity was an absolutely consistent adherence to the steppe traditions which the *Yassa* included. Thus we read in it: "If members of the dynasty occupying the khagan's throne in the future do not change the customs of Jenghiz Khan, which regulate all the affairs of society, but keep them, they will rule in happiness and joy, with the help of Heaven, . . . for ever."[35] *Yassa* expected from the Mongolian leaders a constant perfecting of oneself, ability in leadership, discipline, sobriety and courage.

"Only such a person", *Yassa* says, "who is able to remove his personal faults is able to remove the malice that is around him. . . . Only he who can manage his tent (*yurt*) will be able to manage a district. Only he who effectively leads ten warriors into battle may be given a larger unit. . . .

If a chieftain is unable to lead ten warriors, he will be punished and in his place another warrior from among the unit will be nominated. The same procedure will be adopted in relation to bad leaders of larger units. . . ."[36]

War was to be the aim of life and the sum of happiness for all Mongols.

"The greatest happiness for a man", Jenghiz Khan taught his people, "and the greatest joy is to defeat and exterminate the enemy, to destroy him in his very roots, to take all he possesses, to force his wives to weep, to ride his best and beloved horses, and to have the joy of possessing his beautiful women."[37]

Yassa includes a number of rules concerning courage, mutual help, sobriety, discipline, the same perseverance in all situations, all of which were binding for the nomadic army. And the Mongols acted as *Yassa* told them to, for it was 20 years after Jenghiz Khan's death when Fra Carpini, having reached the capital of the Mongolian Empire, informed Europe that the Mongols

> were more obedient to their leaders than any other people in the world. . . . Quarrels, brawls or fights are not known among them. They are extremely perseverent. They may be hungry for a day or two, having nothing at all to eat, but will not show discontent; just the contrary, they will sing and dance as if they had just finished a feast. . . . They are extraordinarily haughty and proud towards other people, whom they despise and treat as nothing. . . . Their emperor has a most surprising power over his subjects. . . . whatever decision he takes, at any time or place, be it in war, or their lives or deaths, this they accept without any hesitation. . . . It should be remembered that they do not negotiate with any state, but only demand absolute surrender. . . . This is so because Jenghis Khan commanded them to subdue all people and make them obey them.[38]

Fra Carpini came to the court of khagan Kuyuk, who was an eager adherent to Jenghiz Khan's doctrine and the idea of the steppe Messianism was also apparent in his policy. It is also found in a letter from the khagan to the pope, in which he haughtily says that by heaven's decree he is the lord of all the world and demands the complete surrender of the Christians and homage to be paid to him by the head of the Church.[39]

The title which Kuyuk used also stresses his divine right to rule all the world; it ran, "God rules in heaven—Kuyuk Khan, God's power on earth —the emperor of all peoples."[40]

However, Kuyuk was the last khagan to represent radical political Messianism. In the Mongolian Empire more and more clearly and more and more often the idea of peaceful rule over the subjugated peoples gained prominence, and during the time of the second generation after Jenghiz Khan it eventually became victorious. While the founder of the empire was still alive, the ideas of radical Messianism were opposed at the khagan's court. His eldest son, Juji, was against the mass extermination of the native population, a view opposed by the steppe aristocracy, who persistently objected to the rebuilding of towns and to any concession towards the defeated people.[41]

Juji's policy was continued by his sons, Batu and Bereke, in the Golden Horde. The latter even went as far as accepting Islam.[42]

During the reign of khagan Ogotai, and especially of Mangu, the doctrine of peaceful rule is the dominant one in the policy of the Mongols. The idea of the military Messianism of the nomads was opposed by that of peaceful rule under the centralized and strong authority of the khagan. The adherents of the peaceful doctrine had to oppose the steppe aristocracy by seeking support from the wealthy classes of the subjugated people. They gave up radical Messianism and supported the native aristocracy and the system of settled life, towns, commerce, trade, and agriculture.[43]

The traditions of the steppe lasted longest, in fact until the beginning of the fourteenth century, in the former *uluses* of Jagatai, which included Turkestan; in the country of the Hulagids in Asia Minor they were liquidated slightly earlier, during the reign of Ghazan Khan (1295–1304).

The idea of peaceful rule, developed by association with the economy and culture of the subjugated peoples, led to an eventual discarding of primitive Shamanism. The Mongols accepted the religious beliefs of the subdued peoples and, contrary to the principle of tolerance, became involved in religious quarrels, a phenomenon which was particularly striking in Iran, especially during the reign of Ghazan Khan, who associated the idea of peaceful rule with privileges for Islam. Rashid al-Din says of him:

"All the rules of *shari'ah* and *tarikah* had been, with time, forgotten. . . . , He (Ghazan Khan) revived them and made them binding, and at the same time completely removed all wrong beliefs and customs, thus making the bases of Islam stronger."[44]

Ghazan Khan also tried to improve the economic situation of his country, lowered the taxes of the peasants, improved the irrigation system, introduced stability into the value of money. His programme of peaceful rule was in obvious contradiction to the idea of destructive Messianism.

"Order," Ghazan Khan said, "the financial situation, the prosperity of the country, and all our affairs depend on the conscientious work of the peasants, on the level of agriculture and the development of commerce. If we rob the peasants, who will provide our necessities? Just think! If we take the cattle and the seeds away from the peasants, they will leave the soil. And then what will you do, when they give up their work"[45]

While the steppe Messianism left only millions of slaughtered people, ruins and devastation, the system of peaceful rule led to the development of contact between the distant West and the Far East. The last decades of the thirteenth century brought peace to all the territories occupied by the Mongols. This was the victory of a new policy. During the reign of Kublai *pax tartarica* existed in Asia, and a period began in which the two cultures came into contact with each other.

On the one hand, European craftsmen, at one time deported to the unknown eastern countries, became teachers in the art of the goldsmith, the production of weapons, mining and weaving. The young Venetian, Marco Polo, while at the court of Peking, managed through his narrative ability to evoke the interest of the Great Khan, Kublai, in the life and culture of the Italian towns.

On the other hand, distant China had much more to offer to Europe. The West came to know not only things of luxury, like costly silk textiles, but also the achievements of the inventive Chinese mind, as for instance the counter, so far not in use. It seems more than coincidence that the Franciscan friar, Schwartz, the discoverer of gunpowder, was a member of the order whose brothers were the first emissaries to the Far East, where gunpowder had been used for military purposes long before that time. In the fourteenth century the Chinese printing technique is found in Europe; this consisted in printing only one side of the pages, which then were glued together. Before the invention of Gutenberg letters of clay or metal were used in China and Korea for printing purposes. European painting is influenced by Chinese art, as seen in the appearance of the landscape background, a greater mobility in the human figure and in an asymmetry in composition which had so far been unknown. The East penetrated unnoticed into Europe.

NOTES

1. My presentation of the relationship of western Christianity to the Moslem world is based on the book, *The Making of the Middle Ages*, by R. W. Southern, London, 1956.

2. *Liudprandi episcopi Cremonensis Opera.* Ed. J. Becker, *M.G.H., Scriptores rerum Germanicorum in usum scholarum*, 1915.

3. *De Profectione Ludovici VII in Orientem.* Ed. V. G. Berry, Columbia, 1948, pp. 27, 41, 55 ff.

4. Giraldus Cambrensis: *De Principas Instructione.* Distinctio I. Cap. XVII; and U. Monneret de Villard: *Lo studio dell'Islam in Europa nel XIIe nel XIII secolo*, 1944.

5. C. H. Haskins: *Studies in the History of Medieval Science.* 1924, pp. 157 ff.

6. *Medieval Lore*, from Bartholomew Anglicus, texts chosen by R. Stell, London, 1905.

7. M. Bloch: *Le problème de l'or au Moyen Age.* Annales d'histoire économique et sociale, V, 1933, pp. 1–33.

8. The Marx and Engels Archive, Russ. ed., vol. V, p. 194.

9. William of Malmesbury: *Gesta Regum.* Ed. W. Stubbs, vol. 2, p. 395.

10. R. W. Southern: *op. cit.*, pp. 68 ff.

11. R. Zarncke: *Der Priester Johannes.* Abhandlungen der Königl. Sächsischen Gesell. der Wissen., VII, Göttingen, 1879. K. F. Helleiner: Prester John's letter: a mediaeval Utopia, *The Phoenix*, XIII, 2, Toronto, 1959, pp. 47–58.

12. Ibn al-Asir, according to В. Г. Тизенгаузен: Сборник материалов, относящихся к истории Золотой Орды, I, p. 2.

13. Б. Я. Владимирцов: Общественный строй Монголов. Moscow, 1934.

14. Новгородская летопись, pp. 219–20.

15. Б. Я. Владимирцов: *op. cit.*, pp. 91 ff.

16. R. Grousset: *Histoire de l'Extrême Orient.* Paris, 1929; H. H. Howorth: *History of the Mongols.* London, 1880–88; J. Curtin: *The Mongols*, Boston, 1908.

17. Marco Polo: *Opisanie świata.* Polish ed., 1954, pp. 194–5.

18. *Secret History*, a work of the thirteenth century, which in the form of an epic saga describes the events connected with the rise of the Mongolian Empire, quoted after Б. Я. Владимирцов: *op. cit.*, translated by С. А. Козин.

19.　Ibn Khaldun: *Arab historian of the fourteenth century,* quoted after В. Г. Тизенгаузен: Сборник материалов, относящихся к истории Золотой Орды, 1884, p. 379.

20.　В. Г. Тизенгаузен: *op. cit.,* p. 75.

21.　Rashid al-Din, Persian chronicler of the thirteenth–fourteenth centuries, Сборник летописей, Moscow, 1952, I, book 2, p. 265.

22.　Rashid al-Din: *op. cit.,* book 1, p. 167.

23.　И. Бичурин: Записки о Монголии, История первых четлрех ханов из дома Чингизова. Russ. transl., St. Petersburg, 1829, p. 153.

24.　Juzjani: *The Tabaqat-i Nasiri.* Ed. W. Nassau Lees. Calcutta, 1863–4, p. 352.

25.　Rashid al-Din: *op. cit.,* I, book 2, p. 205.

26.　Rashid al-Din: *op. cit.,* I, book 2, p. 211.

27.　Rashid al-Din: *op. cit.,* I, book 2, p. 263.

28.　Rashid al-Din: *op. cit.,* I, book 2, p. 183.

29.　Juwayni: *The Tarikh-i Jahán gushá of Ala ud-Din Atá Malik-i Juwayni.* GMS, XVI, part I.

30.　Rashid al-Din: *op. cit.,* I, book 2, p. 265.

31.　Rashid al-Din: *op. cit.,* I, book 2, p. 261.

32.　В. Г. Тизенгаузен: *op. cit.,* I, pp. 208, 288.

33.　В. Г. Тизенгаузен: *op. cit.,* I, pp. 208, 288.

34.　Rashid al-Din: *op. cit.,* I, book 2, p. 234.

35.　Rashid al-Din: *op. cit.,* I, book 2, p. 260.

36.　Rashid al-Din: *op. cit.,* I, book 2, pp. 260 ff.

37.　Rashid al-Din: *op. cit.,* I, book 2, p. 265.

38.　Plano Carpini, Russ. transl., St. Petersburg, 1911, pp. 12, 13, 23, 32; see also Johann de Plano Carpini: *Geschichte der Mongolen und Reisebericht 1245–1247.* Übersetzt u. erklärt von F. Risch, Leipzig, 1930.

39.　The original text of the letter is preserved in the Vatican Archive. The text is quoted by M. Prawdin: *Das Erbe Tschingis-Chans,* 1935, pp. 56 ff.

40.　Plano Carpini, *op. cit.,* p. 37.

41.　The fight of the two tendencies in the policy of the Mongols is dealt with by И. П. Петрушевский, introduction to Rashid al-Din, *op. cit.,* pp. 12 ff.

42.　B. Grekow, A. Jakubowski: *Złota Orda i jej upadek.* Warsaw, 1953, pp. 70 ff.

43.　E. Blochet: *Introduction à l'histoire des Mongols de Rashid al-Din.* Leiden–London, 1910, pp. 308–14.

44.　Rashid al-Din, *op. cit.,* I, book 2, p. 13.

45.　Rashid al-Din: Сборник летописей, Moscow, 1946, III, p. 262.

5

POLITICAL THOUGHT IN THE
PERIOD OF TRANSITION (1350–1450)

1. THE HUNDRED YEARS' WAR

FOR Western Europe the years between the middle of the fourteenth and
the middle of the fifteenth centuries were a period of restless fermentation.
It was a time of great tension, sharp conflict, glaring oppositions—a time
of feverish disquietude. At every step contrasts and oppositions were dis-
played. Extremes were wrecking the established order. Dichotomy pervaded
the whole reality disrupting traditional unities.

It was a period when the Church had at the same time two legally
elected Popes, and when there coexisted two mutually opposed conceptions
of governing the faithful—the idea of the absolute power of the Pope and
the doctrine of the supremacy of the General Council.

In England and France the established monarchies were opposed by the
newly formed institution of the representation of the Estates.

In the Germanic Empire the thought of the Roman Empire ran counter
to the dynastic ambitions of the rulers. This divided policy seems to be
reflected in the two-headed eagle placed on the Emperor's coat of arms
from the time of Sigismund of Luxemburg.

While Latin remained the language of the Church, the Bible began to
be studied in national tongues.

The feudal idea of honour and loyalty was at odds with the brigandage
and hired soldiering of the knights. We see, on the one hand, a cruelly
severe attitude towards the subjects, and on the other—a sense of imaginary
perfection of chivalry. Discrepancies between tradition and reality became
evident in the battlefield, where armoured riders were more and more
effectively opposed by mercenaries on foot, increasingly assisted by the
artillery.

Unities were split almost in every branch of life. Counterpoint came into
use in music, double-entry book-keeping in trade accounts. Even love
seemed to reveal two different aspects: universal love was a different aspect
of sensuous love, and earthly love was a condition of attaining heavenly
love.[1]

The medieval image of the universe was going to pieces. The graded
hierarchy of the spheres rising upwards through the spheres of the moon,

the sun, the stars, towards heaven and going down to the very depths of hell was disappearing. The well-ordered system of worldly matters in which every object and value had its fixed position now began to totter. Those were years when the rule of the old had not yet passed away, and when the new had not yet acquired enough strength.

Europe was going through a period of becoming, a period when feelings of pessimism and depression were contrasted with nervous excitement.

People thought in those days that evil powers had disturbed the order of the world. Indeed, the period of general disquietude began with a series of elemental disasters. The Black Death raging in Europe from 1347 carried off one-third of the population. People were alarmed both by dearths recurring in France (1351, 1359, 1418) and by earthquakes which destroyed Villach and scores of parishes in Corinth in 1347–8. The flooding of considerable areas in the Netherlands in 1377 and 1421 caused widespread anxiety.

Uncertainty besetting man everywhere in this fearful world filled him with nervous excitement. A belief in evil forces and a struggle against the powers of hell absorbed pious feelings. The myth of the devil's power assumed the form of religious ecstasy. Sobriety in everyday life alternated with the most fervent outbursts of passionate piety.

Strong emotional tension did not wholly eliminate common sense. People capable of practical activity provided a contrast to exaltation and a mood of excitement. Their effort initiated the technical changes that imperceptibly determined the direction of the development.

Itinerant mechanics spread the use of wind power and water power by building windmills and watermills. The practical man harnessed the horse to plough the fields when it left the battlefield or the courtyards in which tournaments were held. Rivers were made navigable and roads, provided with rock surfacing, began to be used regularly for transportation. Sailors used the compass in their voyages. The hands of the mechanical clock divided the day into 24 hours supplanting the older custom of indicating time by reference to prayers said in churches and monasteries. People learned how to distil spirits that came to be regarded as the best protection against the plague. In the near future two inventions were destined to play an important part: gunpowder which began to be used in military operations bringing about an essential change in the methods of warfare, and the spread of the printed word—an efficient means of influencing wide circles of people. Ever after the printed word was to mould social opinions and to inspire deeds. Owing to print ideas gained broad powers of forming thinking. Side by side with inspired orators the printed word, with its durability and wide range, was destined to fashion social relations in a decisive manner.[2]

Those who were then alive understood neither the causes of the changes that were happening nor the consequences of the events that were taking place. They did not know the way. Their aims were not clear. They were standing at the crossroads, as it were in twilight dividing darkness from light, plagued by elemental and political disasters.

The years of the ruinous Hundred Years' War coincided almost exactly with the period of European ferment. It was a typical dynastic war, lasting for several generations, conducted without any deeper purpose and bringing along with it only poverty and ruin. In the first period of the war Flanders was the object of interest of both sides. For economical reasons the country remained closely connected with England, as the Flemish clothiers were largely dependent on the English wool of which the islanders were sending to Europe every year 30,000 bales, each weighing 364 lb.

The immediate cause of the war was the claim of the English King Edward III to the French throne on grounds of blood relationship with the house of Capet. But there were other forces and aspirations behind this Anglo-French dynastic conflict. The initial successes of the English were the result of the skilful policy of Edward III, who managed to give his claims the appearance of a national enterprise. For the English it was primarily a war against the immoderate revenues of the Church, several times as high as the king's own, and against the Pope's interference in matters of state.

Unlike England, France suffered defeat as long as her defence depended only on the feudal nobles and her support came from an alliance with the Pope residing in Avignon. As soon as the expulsion of the English invaders became the task of the whole nation, when the peasant Saint Joan of Arc expressed the desire of her people, the fortunes of the war began to look different.

Feudalism suffered losses under the pressure of the national forces but also because of the traditional methods of warfare. In three successive battles: at Crécy-en-Ponthieu in 1346, at Poitiers in 1356 and at Agincourt in 1415, the French feudal knights were defeated by the pedestrian English bowmen. It was also then that the knights heard the roar of cannons for the first time.

With the war dragging on for years the maintenance of an army and the building of a fleet required considerable financial means, usually acquired by imposing taxes. It became clear that states could not carry on any normal activity, much less wage wars, merely on the royal revenues or on loans. To cover the state's expenses it was necessary to introduce a definite system of taxation. That, however, was an excellent opportunity for those on whom taxes were to be imposed to present their political demands. Granting financial supplies they at the same time wanted to have a share in decisions about how to spend the money thus acquired, or at least to have a right of controlling the expenses. Demands were formulated for the representation of the Estates, which were effectively trying to share in the government of the state. Such was the development of the States General in France, which expressed their political demands in the Great March Ordinance of 1357. Fifty-six years later the demands of the States General were repeated by the representatives of Paris University, who in 1413 drafted a project of reform for the insurgents of the French capital. The English Parliament, which from the time of Edward III included two chambers, was also advancing in the same direction.

The Hundred Years' War did not essentially change the balance of power but it caused a lot of destruction. In 1360 Petrarch called France "a heap of ruin". Towards the end of the war one-third of all the land in France lay uncultivated. After the struggle that had lasted 100 years the English held only Calais, and their rulers boasted the title of the kings of France, which they used until the nineteenth century. But the war made it clear to those who were then alive that the Christian world contained neither forces nor authorities above the contenders and that the Pope, who took the side of the French, ceased to be an arbitrator of conflicts.

The disintegration of the unity of the Christian world precipitated the process of the formation of new ties. New organisms came into existence and new associations were formed to fill the void left by the decaying universalism. Side by side with political bodies there appeared associations that had economic objectives or else were the result of dynastic policy.

Economic considerations led to the formation of leagues of towns in the Germanic Empire. In the middle of the fourteenth century about eighty towns in northern Germany formed the Hanseatic League. The other two leagues came into existence somewhat later. The cities on the upper Danube formed the Swabian league with Augsburg and Nuremberg in the lead. In western Germany cities lying on the Rhine made another league.

The power and fortuity of dynastic aspirations are illustrated by the brief history of the State of Burgundy, which turned the scale of victory in favour of England during the Hundred Years' War. Owing to its dynastic policy the house of Luxemburg extended its influence to Bohemia and Hungary. Poland and Lithuania formed a union under the Jagiellos. In 1397 the Kalmar Union bound together Denmark, Norway and Sweden. Lastly, in the second half of the fifteenth century dynastic marriages joined the kingdoms of Aragon and Castile forming a framework for united Spain.[3]

But the most durable ties were those in the states where national feelings were aroused. For while dynastic policy was of interest only to the reigning houses and the feudal magnates, and while the leagues of cities represented the interests of the *bourgeoisie*, the national ties were cherished by the broadest circles of society. Societies were consolidating their interests behind their monarchs, who opposed the feudal anarchy for the sake of safety and stable market. National states were additionally cemented by their mother tongues which were successfully replacing Latin in literature and on the pages of the Bible. The process of national integration within every country was precipitated by dangers from without. In England the feeling of national unity grew stronger in the struggle against papal intervention. In France it was the hatred of the English invaders that united the people. The Czech opposition against the German invasion resulted in an awakening of the national consciousness. In Poland the struggle against the aggression of the Teutonic Order inspired national feelings.

The national ties were durable because they were significant for all social classes. They were in keeping with the logic of history, while the other bonds could not last because they were of more temporary character.

The distintegration of Christian unity set in from the top and from the bottom. The top of the hierarchy broke down, as both the Papacy and the Empire lost authority and position. The bottom of the hierarchy was going to ruin under the blows of the revolutionary movements.

The decline of the highest authority was symbolized by Rome, an abandoned, neglected city. The papal court, residing in Avignon since 1314, was outside the city's walls. Nor was the old capital any longer interesting for the Germanic emperors, who were now busy increasing their hereditary holdings in the East.

Petrarch deplored the cruel fate of the capital of Christendom that made the impression of a provincial town. And yet he had a great admiration for the glorious past of Rome. He sang its greatness in his poems, and was crowned for it with laurel on the Capitol in 1341, receiving at the same time the citizenship of Rome—an honour once so desirable—and the title of master of poetry.

In 1347 on the same Capitol Cola di Rienzo declared himself a "Tribune of the People" and assumed his rule over the city. Petrarch offered his pen and he—his deeds to revive the past glory of Rome. On his banner he had the proud inscription *Roma caput mundi*. At first he was supported by the people and warmly encouraged by Petrarch. But when his attempts threatened the interests of the Roman magnates, the latter turned their power against him, and the embittered and disappointed tribune had to flee from Rome after several months. Seven years later, thanks to the help of Pope Innocent VI, Cola di Rienzo returned to Rome to continue his work. But, fascinated by the past, he did not understand the present; appearance and theatricality kept him from recognizing real values. Lonely and misunderstood he was finally put to death by the Romans, who were more inclined to listen to the flattery of the magnates than make the sacrifices demanded from them by the luckless tribune.[4]

Meanwhile at the Avignonese court the thought of moving the Apostolic See back to Rome was clearly maturing. The Church, accused before of simony and luxurious living, had another charge directed against it: that the head of the Church became dependent on the French monarchy. In the years 1314–77, when Avignon was the capital of Christendom, the number of Frenchmen in the College of Cardinals increased alarmingly. The long-lasting succession of French Popes was also causing justified anxiety. Favouring France the Papacy came under criticism for its partiality and thus its return to Rome was precipitated. In 1378 the cardinals met in Rome, for the first time in 75 years, to elect the head of the Church. The new Pope, Urban VI, was an Italian, formerly Archbishop of Bari. At the same time the faction of the French cardinals elected another Pope to reside in Avignon. The Church had now two heads, two Apostolic Sees, two centres conferring Church dignities. In this situation it was hard to sustain the authority of St. Peter's successor. Passed was the time when monarchs tried to obtain papal recognition; now two Popes were competing with each other for the favours of secular rulers. The dual leadership caused a split which affected the whole of Christianity. There were two separate spheres of influence: the Avignonese and the Roman. The first included France, the kingdom of Naples, Scotland, Castile, Aragon; the second— England, Germany, Bohemia, Poland and Hungary. This grouping was determined not by religious sympathies or considerations, but by the current political situation, which in itself was largely the consequence of the Anglo-French conflict.

To put an end to the growing confusion within the Church the cardinals took an unprecedented step: they convoked the General Council at Pisa in 1409 without the approval of the Popes. The election of a new Pope was to put an end to the Great Schism. But as the formerly elected Popes did not resign, the result of it was a situation in which the Church had as many as three heads. Only in 1417 at the Council of Constance did it become possible to end the dissension and restore a single rule in the Church.

However, the authority that the head of the Church had lost was not easily regained. The Pope was criticized by the representatives of the religio-national opposition, which was initiated in England by Wyclif and in Bohemia by Hus. And inside the Church the adherents of the conciliar movement expounded the doctrine that the council is superior to the Pope. Nor was the prestige of the papacy increased by the Union of the Western and Eastern Churches solemnly promulgated at the Council of Florence in 1439, as it was rejected by the Eastern Church.

The decrease of papal authority was accompanied by a decline of the imperial power in the Christian world. The title of the Emperor, which the German rulers coveted, did not in any degree increase the scanty monarchic prerogatives. Germany consisted of several scores of independent duchies and principalities, ruled by lay and ecclesiastic lords, and of a considerable number of free cities. It was a highly differentiated fabric, without a uniform legal or financial system, and, above all, without strong political leadership. The seven Electors who after 1356 had the constitutional right to nominate and depose the monarch made the accession to the German throne a matter of bargain and intrigue. No wonder that the Luxemburgs, whose rule in divided Germany lasted from 1347 to 1437, directed all their efforts towards strengthening their dynastic position in the East. Charles IV (1347–78) formed efficient administration in Bohemia and made that country the core of the Luxemburg rule. His son Sigismund, who became the King of Hungary in 1387 and was elected Emperor in 1411, marched into Prague in 1434 after suppressing the national opposition, and continued the dynastic policy of his father. With his death in 1437 the line of Luxemburg became extinct and was replaced by the Habsburgs who were to continue with better results the policy of their predecessors.

The weakness of the popes and the emperors was not the only one apparent in the Christian world. The social system with which the Christian Church was linked up was convulsed. The symptoms of the disease of feudalism were becoming manifest.[5] The system of monetary payment for goods was successfully replacing natural economy, but at the same time increase in the production of goods was checked, as there were not enough consumers. The feudal system did not provide sufficient market for the new kind of economy.[6] Trying to get more money the feudal lords commuted villein services into cash payments. They introduced various dues, took part in aggressive wars, and when these sources were not sufficient, they turned again to the exploitation of their villeins, and were even ready to pillage their own country. The oppression of the peasants increased as there was a general shortage of labour following ruinous wars and mortality from the Black Death.

What made the economic situation worse was the constant fluctuation of prices resulting from depreciation of money. How frequent the changes of currency were can be seen from the example of John the Good, King of France (1350–64), who changed the value of the silver coin eighty-six times during his reign. Devaluing money was such a common device that the contemporaries came to regard it as something "worse than the Black Death or an invasion of the enemy", and wished for money of fixed value—*denarius perpetuus*. The content of precious metals in money was decreased as a rule, Venetian ducats and florins being the only exceptions.[7]

Against the background of general confusion and hardship that became the lot of the whole Christian world only the towns situated on foreign trade routes were flourishing. This was true especially about the cities in north Italy, which controlled the world commerce in those days. Through their stores and trading stations along the coast of the Black Sea and in Egypt the cities kept connections between northern Europe and the Russian lands, Turkistan, Persia, India, and China. The economic prosperity of northern Italy was so exceptional that it provided a sharp contrast for the generally stagnant life in European cities. After the middle of the fourteenth century cities closed their walls before new population flowing in from the country, and the gilds became lifeless organizations destined only to linger on in their self-destructive egoism.

The difficulties which Europe was facing were increased by a wave of peasant revolts and riots in cities that threatened the established social structure. The age of ferment that coincided with the Hundred Years' War was filled with a series of class conflicts.[8]

In Salonica sailors and craftsmen managed to impose their rule on the proprietary classes for 10 years, from 1342 to 1352.

In 1358 the Parisian burgesses seized the control of the capital and supported the demands of the States General formulated in the Great March Ordinance. Townsmen were given arms to fight mercenaries prowling about the country. The king received sixty-seven articles, which demanded control of the royal officers and the participation of the States General in granting financial supplies as well as in collecting and spending the taxes. Though the *bourgeoisie* of Paris suffered defeat, it won for a long time indisputable leadership in the French anti-feudal movements.

A little later there occurred clashes between the poor and the rich in centres of the textile industry.

In the south of Europe Florence no longer manufactured cloth within the gild organization, but owing to the development of the textile industry employed about 30,000 workers at the end of the fourteenth and the beginning of the fifteenth century. Those poorly paid labourers—the *Ciompi*—succeeded in their struggle for a separate gild, a share in the administration of the commune, the right to appear in courts of justice independently of their employers and finally—division of their debts into parts to be paid in the course of 12 years. When the *Ciompi* passed from participating in the administration to the full exercising of their authority in 1378, their rule was overthrown after several weeks and followed by a despotic rule of the principate.

Some longer-lasting uprisings that were also spread over a wider area occurred in the north European centre of cloth manufacture—in Flanders. In 1379 the weavers and fullers of Ghent seized the rule of the city. Their example was soon followed by two other cities, Bruges and Ypres, where the city proletariat also rose against the rich. Yet Ghent retained the leadership in the long civil war remaining a symbol of the undaunted will of the insurgents.

The Flemish revolution was applauded by the people of Paris and Rouen; cries of "*vive Gand*" resounded in the streets of these cities. A feeling of sympathy for city insurgents clearly increased when in 1382 the inhabitants of the French capital, armed with hatchets and leaden mallets seized from the store in the town-hall, became the masters of the city. From the weapons used by the rebels the uprising got its name—*la sédition des Maillotins*. Fearing connections between the Flemish and Parisian revolts the regents of the young King Charles VI decided to attack first the insurgent cities regarding them as the inspiration of the French riots. The French forces defeated the troops of the Flemish insurgents at Roosebecque to strike next at the Parisian Maillotins.

In 1413 Paris again became the theatre of war. An alliance between the intellectuals and the craftsmen triumphed briefly over feudalism. People from the University of Paris expanded in their programs the ideas of the Great March Ordinance issued 56 years earlier, while the city was ruled by the Gild of the Butchers.

Though uprisings in cities affected the feudal fabric considerably, yet the peasant revolts turned out to be a more serious threat to it. A wave of revolts was going over Europe; suppressed in one place they would revive in another with increased force. A sense of oppression and injustice drove the peasants to a desperate struggle. They fought against feudalism in Italy, Denmark, Sweden, Spain, but the widest repercussions were produced by the peasant revolts in France, England and Bohemia.

In the spring of 1358 100,000 armed peasants, contemptuously called the *Jaques*, wreaked their wrath on the nobles. They charged the knights with exploitation and made them responsible for the defeats suffered in the war with England. In the peasants' view the French knights could no longer claim a privileged position, because their cowardice in the war with the English invaders had disgraced them. At Meaux and Clermont the feudal nobles succeeded in breaking the opposition of the French peasants. The latter were crushed not so much owing to the power of the feudatories, as because they let themselves be fascinated by the idea of the noble monarch, who is able to restore just government when he is separated from his mean and greedy advisers.

The same conviction betrayed the English peasants in 1381, when they believed the deceitful promises of the king that in opposition to the ruling classes he would fulfil the desires of the peasants, i.e. abolish bondage, make all the Estates equal and divide Church lands.

While the hatred of the French peasantry was directed chiefly against the knights and nobles, the English peasants were fighting first of all against the rich ecclesiastical hierarchy.

The situation changed basically during the Hussite Wars. By then the peasants were already aware of the common interests of feudalism and papacy, because their grasp of the situation had been developed during the struggle that had lasted for over 10 years—from 1420 to 1431—when they had to repel crusades sent to Bohemia by Rome and by the Germanic Emperor. They had lost all illusions about the good and just ruler, and wanted to destroy entirely the state and the Church to build on earth the

Kingdom of God from the foundations, and to bring up people according to the principles of the scriptures.

But feudalism was destined to be victorious, because it had its roots in the economic life, while the forces that were attacking it were neither strong enough nor consolidated. The revolutionary movements in cities viewed peasant revolts with hostility or at least with indifference. Class differences turned out to be stronger than the newly formed national ties, and a desire for better living conditions—more real and familiar than a vague vision of power.

The decay of the internal unity of Christendom was specially alarming because there was a steadily increasing danger of Turkish invasions. Preoccupied with internal affairs Europe turned a deaf ear to voices calling to arms against the Turks. Though at the time of the victorious march of the Mongols in the middle of the thirteenth century the Turks withdrew to the mountains of Armenia, after less than 100 years they again undertook the invasion of Asia Minor, to strike at Europe next. In 1352 the Turks settled on the first strip of European land seizing the fortress Tzympe on the Gallipoli Peninsula. From that moment they were moving steadily up the Balkans. Their victory over the Serbs at Kossovo (the Field of Blackbirds) in 1389 and the blow dealt at the crusade of European knighthood at Nikopolis in 1396 opened the way for them to Constantinople. As the fourteenth century was coming to its close the Turks were already ruling in the Balkans having reached the line of the Danube. Christian temples were open there only in the mountains of Albania, in Salonica and in Constantinople. When the fall of Constantinople seemed certain, the aggressive march of the Turks was temporarily stopped by the approach of the Mongol army of Tamerlane coming from Central Aisa.

If the advance of the Mongols was as rapid as it was unexpected, the collapse of their power after the death of Tamerlane was equally sudden and surprising. Nothing could any longer keep the Turks from continuing their conquest of Europe. In 1453 they entered Constantinople, which they were to call the city of Islam—Istanbul. The city that had for centuries inspired admiration and envy—two inseparable feelings—now fell victim of the Turks.

A military power that threatened Christianity was thus established at the point where Europe and Asia met. The Turks began to control the routes of commerce leading beyond the Black Sea into the Far and Near East.

Fear swept over Europe. It was not wrath hurled down from the heights of imperial or papal throne, but a mortal fear that Christianity would be ruined. This is how Dlugosz wrote of Constantinople: "one of the two eyes of Christianity was torn out, and one of her hands cut off".

The lethargy that followed the Turkish victories initiated in Europe a comparatively peaceful period which lasted several decades.

In a way the fall of Constantinople closed the age of ferment, the age of fluidity during which everything was only germinating, not yet clear or ready, not yet born. The age that had witnessed the great tension and nervous activity was passing away, but it had also been the age of active attitude, the age which had no desire for contemplative wisdom.

University auditoria were places promoting the development of the programs of two main political currents in that unquiet epoch: religio-national opposition and the Conciliar Movement. The former was struggling against the feudal Church, the latter aimed at its reform. Both doctrines, however, derived from the continued decay and weakness of the Christian universalism.

At the same time in the Islamic world Ibn Khaldun was evolving a theory of state and society on the wreckage of the broken Arab universalism, the decay of which had preceded by several centuries the decline of Christian universalism.

While the two European doctrines found their expression in action and became an essential factor in the changes, the Arab doctrine resembles the situation observable in modern political thought where theories are more often worked out by thinkers.

2. RELIGIO-NATIONAL OPPOSITION

Names given to political doctrines characterize them as a rule only in a general way: they indicate the dominant tendency of the given current. The same qualification applies to the term "religio-national opposition", which denotes the process of emancipation of states from papacy, the hard and slow breaking away from the conception of unity of the Christian world. This process went on gradually as states and nations became increasingly aware of their distinctness. Their aspirations found ideological expression in Wyclifism in England and Hussitism in Bohemia.

The 50-year-long reign of Edward III (1327–77) was a period of an awakening of national consciousness of the English.[9] The causes of the process, however, did not remain the same throughout the period. Until the sixties of the fourteenth century national ambitions of the English were stirred up by the victories in France. The military successes shared alike by the knights and free yeomen who formed the ranks of the bowmen were the principal factor that inspired strong patriotic feelings. The last 25 years of Edward's reign, on the other hand, made a full realization of national distinctness harder to attain, because it was a period of serious financial difficulties. While England was short of money, needed continually for maintaining an army and building a fleet, and as a consequence could not keep sufficient control over the conquered districts of France, the great wealth of the Church contributed nothing to state expenses paying revenues only to the Apostolic See. Understandably voices of protest against papal intervention in English affairs and criticism of clerical privileges were listened to with approval. People began to question the traditionally accepted view that the Church should play the most important part in the Christian world. The clash between Church interests and state interests resulted in a conflict between universalist idea and the idea of nation and state.

Rome's interference in English affairs was considerable. The Pope gave England cardinals of his own nomination, generally foreigners, confirmed appointments to vacant bishoprics, imposed taxes on Church estates and collected them scrupulously through his collectors; finally, he had at his disposal a vast army of clerics. The threat of excommunication, used both in religious and in political matters, assured effectiveness to apostolical enactments.

Papal influence strengthened the privileged position of the clerics, who already had exceptional status in the country in economic, legal, political, and social matters. They enjoyed special advantages in spite of the differences between the prelates and poor country parsons, and in spite of the antagonism between secular clergy and the orders who owed obedience only to the Pope.

The growing estates of the Church, many times as large as the king's own lands, were subject only to papal taxation. An attempt made by the House of Commons in 1371 to get a single payment of tax from Church estates for the Crown produced little result. In 1377 it was discovered that money exported to Rome was used to provide aid for the enemy of England.[10]

Economic independence of the Church was only one aspect of the exceptional status of the clerics. Owing to their education they managed the affairs of state being almost exclusive holders of government offices. In addition to that they enjoyed legal advantages. If the clergy committed any offence against the law, they were tried only in ecclesiastical courts, while those courts had the whole population under their jurisdiction in matters of matrimony and inheritance, and, what is more, they tried people to whom committing a sin had been proved.

Yet what most distinguished the ecclesiastics in society was their sacral character. In the opinion of the people the right to administer sacraments, and even more—to grant absolution, also the miraculous power to change bread and wine into Christ's flesh and blood during Mass, gave the clerics heavenly attributes. Other things increased their distinction: their exclusive right to the study and exegesis of the Holy Scriptures, their knowledge of Latin and of the complicated ritual increased further the distance between themselves and the faithful.

The Pope's interference in the affairs of state and the independence of the clergy brought about understandable protests in the period of financial difficulties through which England was going. In 1371 the lay Estates petitioned in the House of Commons that churchmen should be deprived of all higher offices in the government and that Church property should be taken over by the Crown. The English poetry of the period is permeated by the atmosphere of criticism. Geoffrey Chaucer in his *Canterbury Tales* and even more William Langland in his allegorical poem *Piers Plowman* denounced the corruption of the upper classes without sparing the clergy.[11]

While the men managing the affairs of state regarded with disfavour ecclesiastical estates which brought England no revenues, the faithful found the materialism of the clergy and the Church especially offensive. In the fourteenth century penance, indulgences, pilgrimages were commercialized to such an extent that each could be replaced by a definite sum of money.

After 1370 Oxford University became a flourishing centre from which criticism was directed against the Church. The university enjoyed both papal and royal privileges, and had thus favourable conditions for the clash of two conceptions, two opposed points of view—lay and ecclesiastic, one with the state at its centre, the other—with the papal authority uppermost. At first the learned controversy remained within the walls of the university where it engaged the attention of only a narrow circle of men, also, where it was conducted according to the rules of medieval disputes, and besides— in Latin.

For years differences of opinion arose whenever the problem of dominion was discussed there. Though the initial assumption that dominion comes from God was undisputed, the conclusions drawn from this differed. For papists only dominion received through the Church was justified; for their opponents the agency by which it was received did not matter much; they shifted the centre of gravity to the person of the ruler and were convinced that committing a grave sin makes him unfit to exercise power. In the middle of the fourteenth century an eminent Oxford theologian Richard Fitzralph applied this view to clergy asserting that mortal sin makes a priest unfit to perform sacerdotal functions. This thesis was to become the principal argument in the struggle against the churchmen, who, driven by desire for temporal gain, lived in the state of sin. After 1370 the Oxford discussions passed outside the university and the Oxonian masters became intellectual leaders of the opposition. Rallying round the person of John Wyclif (1325– 84) they criticized the abuses of the clergy not only from their professorial chairs but also from the pulpit, addressing the faithful in English—the tongue they all understood. The speakers were Lollards—poor priests. The name was applied even before Wyclif to those whose religious views differed from orthodox teaching. Later the Lollards were identified with Wyclifism. Following the example of their master they denounced the Church, whose organization was far removed from the examples shown in the Book. Their only authority was the Bible, which they translated into English thanks to the efforts of Wyclif and to his direct help. Removing the bar of the Latin tongue they made of the Bible a living book for all believers.

In 1371 Wyclif entered for the first time the arena of politics declaring that ecclesiastical property should be secularized and clerics removed from the government of state. By then he had become a distinguished Oxford scholar; the boldness and courage with which he defended national interests gained him recognition and disciples. He had the ability to link together the wisdom of a scholar and a sense of reality, theological learning and clarity of judgement, religion and the needs of his own country. "Two virtues", he wrote, "be in mannes soule by which a man should be ruled: holynesse in mannes wille, and good cunning in his witt. Holynesse should put out sin, and good cunning should put out folly."[12]

In 1374 he was a member of the royal commission sent to discuss with papal representatives the bestowal of ecclesiastical benefices. He soon sacrificed diplomatic career for political activity. The course of his life followed from the university through social agitation to heresy. His popularity can be measured by the defence offered him in 1377 by the people during the trial conducted against him at St. Paul's by the London episcopate. It was in that year that Pope Gregory XI sent to Oxford University a bull urging the arrest of Wyclif and handing him over to the Bishop of London. In the schedule of Wyclif's errors it was mentioned that he attacked private property and was thus undermining the established order of Church and state.

The Great Schism, which began in 1378, weakened the authority of the Apostolic See so much in England that Gregory's bull was disregarded; what is more, Wyclif became a national hero who defended England against Rome, defended the state against the Church. A few years before his death he withdrew from political life, remained incumbent of Lutterworth and worked at his doctrine, which he expounded most succinctly and systematically in the *Trialogus*—an allegorical discussion between Truth, Falsehood, and Wisdom.

Wyclif's conception of state organization was gradually changing and becoming more radical, but criticism of the papacy and of the unjustified privileges of the clergy were always at its core. These two problems were the main theme of his numerous works and the object of his political activity.

As Wyclif went on writing works his attitude to papacy was becoming increasingly uncompromising. At first he opposed Rome's interference in state affairs and criticized the papal collectors who were raising taxes in England for the Apostolic See. At the end of his life he already wanted a state-controlled Church, without Pope or hierarchy. He rejected the doctrine that England is a part of the Christian commonwealth governed by the Pope, and advocated the opposite conception—that of the full independence of the state. When the King's Council asked him whether England could, in the interest of the state, forbid payments to Rome, his reply was uncompromising: he said that the law of Christ contained in the Gospels as well as conscience and common sense indicate decisions in keeping with the interest of England.

He realized that the threat of papal anathema increased the political influence of the Church and argued that in worldly matters it was meaningless. He considered such anathema unjust and therefore invalid, and though he admitted that it could sometimes inspire fear and even cause some damage, he maintained that it had no real significance.[13]

Another blow was dealt at excommunication by his theory of predestination, according to which people are either born in the state of grace and are predestined for salvation, or in the state of sin and are foreknown for damnation.[14] Deeds and not acceptance of dogmas distinguish the elect from the damned, hence an anathema imposed by a sinful Pope is of dubious value.

On the one hand, the theory of predestination undermined the established system of the remission of sins, which became doubtful in view of the decrees of Providence; on the other hand—the theory provided ground for a new conception of Church without a Pope or hierarchy.[15] The elect, i.e. those predestined for salvation, compose the Church whose head is Christ himself. "If you say that Christ's Church must have a head here in earth," Wyclif wrote, "sooth it is, for Christ is head, that must be here with his Church unto the day of doom."[16] In order to be saved the Church must get rid of the Pope and the over-developed hierarchy and retain only the priests who have under their immediate care communities of the faithful. The institutional character of Church hierarchy, foreign to the spirit of the Holy Writ, and the introduction of sacraments together with elaborate ritual separated man from God. Wyclif found his ideal in poor humble priests who were teaching the truths of the Gospels in simple language. He argued that the Holy Writ does not in any way justify the exceptional position of the clergy, whether financial, political, legal or social.

Wyclif's demand of the full disendowment of Church property was preceded by a general discussion on possession. Since everything belongs to God, then only the righteous can hold goods, while the sinful have no right to possession. For practical purposes, however, both the possession of the sinful and their lordship have to be tolerated.[17] It is not unlikely that the conclusions of the Oxonian master influenced the formulation of communist ideas propagated during the Peasant Revolt, though Wyclif himself rejected this interpretation.

Arguments for secularization of Church property were found in the Gospels and in the political situation. Wyclif realized that the great wealth of the Church could result in a complete subjection of the state to the clergy.[18] In order to protect independence of the state he postulated dissolution of monasteries, which were autonomous organizations controlled only by the Pope. "Merchants and warriors", he wrote, "sometimes cause great loss to the commonwealth, but they are also a source of great gain, whereas monks are a continual loss."[19] He wanted ecclesiastical and monastic estates to be taken over by the poorer knights to diminish in this way the burdens of the peasants. Also, the knights enriched by former ecclesiastical property were to pay higher taxes that would be spent on the maintenance of additional military forces.[20]

Finally, Wyclif rejected the medieval idea of the superiority of contemplative life over active life and made this another argument for the dissolution of monasteries. He regarded a life of contemplation as false piety, while active life was for him a measure of man's true worth.[21]

But when he came to deal with the political and legal privileges of churchmen, he did not need many arguments, because to papal doctrine he opposed the idea of a national Church, controlled by the state. The problem is discussed in his treatise *De officio regis*, where he argued that the Church, incapable of self-improvement, must be protected and supervised by the state. The monarch was to be given legal superintendence of clerical education and jurisdiction over the clergy; he was also to give cures as well as to recall priests. To keep a clear division between religious and secular matters Wyclif declared that no man had a right to hold a temporal and an ecclesiastical office simultaneously. When in 1381 the rebels beheaded the English Primate, Simon of Sudbury, who had also been the Chancellor, Wyclif took the opportunity to remark that the prelate had sinned by holding an ecclesiastical and a temporal office.

While the unique place of the clergy in economic, political and legal life was the result of the social balance of power, their social privileges were the consequence of the generally accepted Christian dogmas and liturgy. Sacraments and rites created in the Church an aura of holiness around the clerics; this referred specially to the remitting of sins by the priest during confession and to transubstantiation performed during Mass. Wyclif advocated, first of all, a public confession; he regarded the remission of sins as unfounded, since nobody can be certain that God forgave him his sins. Further, he asked the disturbing question, which he himself did not answer: can the change of attributes happening during Mass, when the priest announces transubstantiation of bread and wine into Christ's flesh and blood, really take place without the corresponding change in substance?

Wyclif wanted his priests to lead simple, exemplary lives and to teach and propagate unceasingly the principles of the Holy Scriptures. He entirely rejected ceremony, recommending to all the study of the Bible which was translated into English by his closest disciples.[22] He argued that "An unlearned man with God's grace does more for the Church than many graduates."[23]

For Wyclif's doctrine the moment of crisis came in 1381 when armed peasants rose against fiscal oppression and villein services were re-established by the famous *Statutes of Labourers* of 1349. The feudal lords were convinced that they had a hereditary right to claim field services from their villeins and that this right was confirmed by history. The peasants, on the other hand, believed their poor priests who taught that the past contained the proof of their—the peasants'—freedom, since "When Adam delved and Evé span who was then a gentleman?"

A desire for freedom and independence, and even more—unconditional condemnation of bondage dominated among the slogans of the rebels. Radical peasants went even further and demanded equality of property. They readily understood the words of John Ball who said: "My good friends, things cannot go well in England, nor ever will, until everything shall be in common; when there shall be neither vassal nor lord and all distinctions levelled. . . . And for what reason do they thus hold us in bondage? Are we not all descended from the same parents, Adam and Eve? . . . It is from our labour they have wherewith to support their pomp. We are called slaves, and if we do not perform our services we are beaten."[24]

In June of 1381 John Ball, released by the rebels from the king's prison, made a speech at Blackheath; he postulated in that speech not only economical equality but also the overthrowing of English monarchy and establishing instead a heptarchy—i.e. seven kingdoms.[25]

In face of such danger the antagonism between Church and state disappeared, and the alliance of the two resulted in a bloody suppression of the revolt. Wyclif's doctrine came to be regarded as dangerous heresy, and henceforward its adherents were to be persecuted both by Church and state. In 1382 came the official condemnation of the Lollards. Oxford University got under the control of the Church; lecturing on Wyclif's doctrine was forbidden, even the possession of his works was a punishable offence. A statute of 1401 *De Heretico Comburendo* made it a duty of the civil authority to burn obstinate Lollards on whom a sentence had been passed in ecclesiastical courts.

The epilogue of the religio-national opposition in England came in 1417 with the martyrdom of John Oldcastle, who at the head of several thousand armed Lollards had attempted to overthrow the monarchy.

In the spring of 1428 Church authorities ordered the bones of Wyclif to be cast out of his grave in Lutterworth and burnt, and the ashes to be scattered.

But the condemnation of this doctrine did not bring its history to an end; it was destined to have a splendid renaissance among Bohemian *bourgeoisie*. Wyclif's ideas were reaching Bohemia through different channels. In 1382 King of England, Richard III, married Anne, sister of the Bohemian King Wenceslas IV. The marriage, concluded for the sake of strengthening the anti-French alliance, had an unintended result, it brought about the penetration of Wyclifism into the queen's country. In 1388 a scholarship was established for Czechs studying in Oxford. At the end of the fourteenth and the beginning of the fifteenth centuries the circle of Oxford heretics included for 2 years Master Jerome of Prague, one of the most devoted friends of Hus. In those days heretics exiled from England were arriving in Bohemia and young Hus was studying and copying diligently the works of Wyclif. Again in the first decade of the fifteenth century ideological contacts with the English heretics became more animated as a result of fervent discussions on the English heresy conducted at Prague University. Masters were sent then to Oxford and Braybrooke to copy Wyclif's writings. In 1406 a young Oxford master, Peter Payne, sent Hus a letter under the university seal to express enthusiasm for the activity of the Czech reformer. Seven years later the same Peter Payne was to leave Oxford driven out by persecution, and was to offer his knowledge, strength and life in the cause of his Czech friends. In September 1410 John Oldcastle and Richard Wyche, leaders of the persecuted English Wyclifists, wrote to express their esteem for the Czechs struggling against the Church of Rome; this came as a kind of reply to the vehement attack made by Dietrich of Niem in his tract *Contra damnatos Viclifistas Pragae*.[26]

Wyclif's ideas were reaching Prague at a time when social conflicts accumulating there signalled an approaching storm. At the end of the fourteenth and early in the fifteenth century feudal Bohemia felt the consequences of the rapid spread of pecuniary economy. Considerable profits were derived from mediating in the commerce between west and east Europe; other sources of gain were: well-developed cloth manufacture, rich silver mines, expanding mining of tin and iron. Yet it was only a small section of the population that grew rich, increasing at the same time the exploitation of a vast majority of society.[27]

In addition to it there was serious trouble with nationalities in Bohemia. The long-lasting influx of Germans into Bohemia brought about a split in the ethnical unity of the country. Alongside the original population there settled down Germans who soon had a privileged place in the country. They held higher offices in Church administration; they advocated feudal exploitation of the peasants, and managed the wealth of the Church; they gathered in their hands half the landed property of the country; they composed the ranks of city patriciate that took small account of the Czech craftsmen and tradesmen; they drove the native nobles out of offices and posts at the king's court; finally, they managed Prague University established in 1348.

On account of this predominance of the Germans in economic, political and cultural life the social struggle in Bohemia had to be conducted under the banner of religio-national opposition. Czech opposition, however, was not a monolithic movement. The national principle made possible the formation of a broad front—one that included various classes of Czech society—often with conflicting interests.

Two separate camps, each with a different political doctrine, were dominant in the Czech movement; they acted together as long as national feelings were able to suppress their conflicts.

The Czech nobility and *bourgeoisie* sympathized with Wyclif's ideas and accepted the conception of tripartite society, including priests, whose care would be the salvation of souls, knights—to govern and defend the country, finally—the working people. Their demands amounted to a change of proportions and privileges among social groups. They wanted above all a "cheap" Church. This camp found in Wyclif's doctrine excellent arguments against all privileges of the clergy. His doctrine was expressed in a general way by the "Four Articles of Prague" of 1420.

The first two articles contained these demands: the Word of God to be preached in Czech without hindrance and Communion to be administered in two kinds to laymen and priests alike. The demand to administer to all believers Communion in two kinds—"*sub utraque specie*" prompted a name for the camp of the nobility and *bourgeoisie*—the Utraquists. They were also called the Calixtins, as they made of the cup—*calix*—in which wine was served during Mass, a symbol of their struggle against the Catholic hierarchy.

The third article postulated secularization of ecclesiastical estates and life of genuine poverty for priests in agreement with the teaching of the Gospels.

Finally, the fourth article demanded mortal sins to be punished without regard for the sinner's state. This article was directed chiefly against ecclesiastics, because both simony and receiving money for religious services were regarded as mortal sins.[28]

The "Four Articles of Prague" were variously interpreted. In reactionary conception they even opened the way to negotiations with Rome, when the faction of the nobility and the *bourgeoisie* were betraying the Hussite Movement.

In contrast to the nobles and burghers the camp of the peasants and the proletariat in which artisans played a decisive role remained virtually indifferent to the arguments of the Oxford master and his Czech followers. What appealed to them was the vision of the happy society which was to come after the defeat of the devil's rule in the Church. They considered themselves to be God's elect, called by Him to cleanse the earth with the sword of all evil; they were convinced that ascetic strictness of living, rejection of compromise in the fight, and unshaken belief would make the chiliastic prophecies come true and would soon open the way to the rule of Christ on earth.

The radical leaders of the opposition wanted to break with the existing social order; they aimed at overthrowing all politico-legal institutions and in their religious ecstasy gave biblical names to mountains and rivers. An example of it was the centre of the popular Hussite Movement, Mount

Tabor in south Bohemia, which soon became famous. The chiliastic beliefs of the Taborites were akin to the prophecies of Joachim of Floris and the predictions of Cola di Rienzo, who, during his stay in Prague before his arrest in 1350, foretold that there would surely come an age of justice and universal peace. In the second decade there appeared in Flanders and Bohemia Beghards, who ardently desired the establishment of the millennial Kingdom of Christ on earth. In Bohemia there were also beliefs in a perfect political and social organization. Three hundred years earlier Cosmas of Prague had described political organization of old Bohemia when "arable fields and meadows and even spouses were common property like the rays of sunshine or the wetness of water."[29] Memories of this happy period appear in *Maiestas Carolina*, the code of laws compiled under Charles IV (1346–78), King of Bohemia and the Germanic Emperor.[30] In the second half of the fourteenth century a fiery preacher from Prague, John Milič, exhorted priests to live in poverty and self-sacrifice in face of the approaching struggle against Antichrist.

The Czech people were thus in sympathy with the radical conception of the Taborites. What they wanted was political organization from the time before the original sin, free from inequality and physical suffering. The demand of absolute equality was followed by a rejection of all authority, differences of state, property and the dues and dependence that went together with it.

The radical doctrine of the Taborites could not stand the test of life. The hard fight of the Czechs against papal invaders required a disciplined army and good organization behind the lines. Tabor, at first ruled by extreme radicals, soon turned into a medieval town of craftsmen and its army into a compact and efficient body obeying the iron will of its great military commander, Jan Žižka. Equalitarianism in legal matters was replaced by the principle of absolute equality and discipline took the place of anarchic communism.

After the death of Jan Žižka in 1424, when the leadership was taken over by Prokop Holy (Prokop the Bald), commander, intellectual and diplomat, the doctrine of the Taborites underwent further transformation and came to resemble more the Four Articles of Prague. From the past the Taborites retained only the duty of unconditional fight for the divine cause, which assumed messianic features. It was a period of splendid expeditions when the Taborites attempted to rouse nations outside Bohemia to fight against the feudal Church. In the course of 8 years—from 1425 to 1433—columns of Taborite waggons were crossing the countries of central Europe bringing along announcements of the victory of new truth.

The national doctrine of the Czechs could not yet cut itself off from religious thinking so characteristic of the men of those days. Hence all the politico-social problems of this doctrine revolved around faith and Church.

Those who spoke publicly in defence of the Czech tongue linked that cause with the fight against the privileged position of the churchmen, their luxurious living and their incomprehensible Latin. Such was the aim of Bethlehem Chapel, established in Prague in 1391. The chapel was the place where John Hus first appeared publicly to fight for the divine law, on behalf of which he demanded a just government both in the state and in the Church. Merciless to the magnates who acted against the interests of their own nation he said: "The Czechs are meaner than dogs and snakes, for a dog will defend the couch on which it sleeps, and a snake will do likewise; but we are oppressed by the Germans and endure it in silence."[31]

Though Hus himself followed, in effect, the principle of Christian humility, yet those who were calling the people to arms found justification in his saying: "I know that, as Moses bids in the Old Testament to anybody who wants to defend the divine law to gird on a sword and be ready, so should we likewise gird on swords and wield them in defence of God's law."[32]

Similarly, the struggle between the Czechs and the Germans for influence at Prague University had the character of a religious conflict. The Germans favoured the orthodox views of Rome, while the Czechs were inclined to follow Wyclif. The year 1409 brought the Czechs an undivided rule at Prague University and John Hus—the office of the Rector.

The maturing of the national consciousness was not uninfluenced by the wavering—and sometimes even friendly—attitude of King Wenceslas IV (1378–1419) towards the Czechs. Deprived by the Electors of the imperial crown in 1400 he looked for support to Bohemia and if he did not openly favour, he at any rate tolerated, the national aspirations of his subjects.

The martyrdom of John Hus in Constance and—a year later—that of Jerome of Prague shocked Bohemia profoundly. The burning national feelings and an unshaken belief in the rightness of the cause, coupled with the brilliant strategy of the Taborite forces helped the Czechs to crush five successive crusades sent against them by the Catholic Europe.

In view of the failure of the imperial and papal expeditions the only hope of defeating the Czechs was an internal division.

In 1433 the famous agreement was reached, known as the Compacts of Prague, between Rome and the Hussite burghers and nobility.

In 1434 class differences triumphed over national unity at Lipany, where the Czech *bourgeoisie* and nobility dealt a mortal blow at the Taborites.

In 1452 Tabor fell.

The Taborite ideas were echoed faintly in the doctrine of Peter Chelčický (1390–1460), theorist of the Unity of the Brotherhood. Proclaiming egalitarian principles he rejected property, state, law, thus negating theoretically the feudal doctrine of tripartite society. However, he simultaneously taught that an ideal society ought to be established without violence, through humility and self-perfection within the framework of the existing order. Such teaching was no longer a menace to the existing political organization. Those who had defeated the Taborites knew well enough that passive perfectionism would not revive revolutionary action.

3. CONCILIAR MOVEMENT

After staying on French soil for 75 years the cardinals again convened in Rome, where after the death of Gregory XI they elected the new Pope— an Italian—Urban VI (1378–88).

Yet too long had the papal Curia stayed in France, too close were its connections with the Capetians, too numerous were the Frenchmen in the College of Cardinals to make the return to Rome an easy matter. Indeed, soon after the election of Urban VI a group of cardinals left Rome, declared the election null and gave the highest ecclesiastical dignity to Clement VII (1378–94).

Such was the beginning of the Great Schism, which lasted for almost 40 years and was the period of double line in the papacy: the Roman and the Avignonese. There began bitter contention between the two rivals who were fighting for the papal tiara and questioning each other's right to supreme lordship. Christian Europe became divided into two obediences; by the side of the Church of Rome there existed the Avignonese Church. Mutual hostility of the Popes and their hurling anathemas against each other undermined the authority of both among believers and aroused understandable doubts concerning the very institution of papacy and its role in the Church.

The Hundred Years' War increased antagonism between nations and further promoted the split within the Church. An opinion was even advanced that the political division of Europe was the real cause of the Great Schism —"*Occasio schismatis et fomentum erat discordia inter regna.*"[33] It was feared that the division of all believers into the adherents of Rome and those of Avignon might grow to the dimensions of the Eastern Schism. The desire for the restoration of unity in Christendom was universal; it was felt by the believers, by the hierarchy and—most keenly of all—by the people from the University of Paris.

It was there that the idea of convoking a General Council without papal consent was first put forward by Conrad of Gelnhausen and Henry of Langenstein, both of whom modelled themselves on the conciliar conceptions of Ockham. However, the conciliar ideas did not obtain theoretical grounding or wider recognition until they were expounded in the works of two successive Chancellors of the Sorbonne: Pierre d'Ailly and John Gerson.

The convocation of the council was not the only means devised to restore unity within the Church. Three different ways of bringing the Church out of its impasse were considered: the summoning of the General Council, the joint resignation of both Popes (*via cessionis*), or the settlement of the conflict by negotiations between Rome and Avignon (*via compromissi*). When negotiations proved a failure, both Sacred Colleges decided to assemble the General Council at Pisa early in the spring of 1409. That decision was unprecedented and surprising both by its novelty and boldness. University circles found arguments for the convoking of the Council by interpreting canon law flexibly; the cardinals, on the other hand, found justification for this step in their unanimity, which they regarded as a sign of divine inspiration. Both groups were convinced that the General Council had the power to judge the Pope—"*habet iudicare papam*".

In Pisa both rivalling Popes—the Avignonese Benedict XIII and the Roman Gregory XII—were solemnly deposed and a new Pope, Alexander V, was elected; when the latter died soon after, he was succeeded by John XXIII. The dethroned Popes repudiated the decisions of the Council and thus the Church remained divided with three Popes henceforth: one in Rome, another in Avignon and the third in Pisa.

Another Council was needed to restore unity within the Church and owing to the efforts of the Western Emperor, Sigismund of Luxemburg, it was convoked by John XXIII in Constance in 1414.

The Council of Constance left inglorious memory of itself owing to its brutal trial of John Hus and Jerome of Prague, both of whom were burnt at the stake. Another memorable event of the Council was the conflict of the cardinals with John XXIII, who was accused of simony, tried and then deposed. Its last claim to fame is connected with its decree about the superiority of the Council over the Pope.

The Council had no precedent in the history of the Church; it was larger in size and longer in duration than any that had hitherto assembled. This was by no means surprising, because when the attempt made in Pisa to save the unity of the Church had failed, the new assembly seemed to be the last chance and every European country was interested in the proceedings of the Council. The Council deliberated for $3\frac{1}{2}$ years, and when at its largest it included 3 patriarchs, 29 cardinals, some 200 bishops and archbishops, more than 100 abbots and 300 doctors representing the universities. For a short period Constance became the capital of the world. The number of strangers staying in the city in connection with conciliar affairs was over 50,000, and the city had to provide food and lodgings for all of them.[34]

The presence of John XXIII at the Council did not give him predominance; the Council remained under the pressure of university groups, which forced their conceptions on the Pope. Contrary to the intention of John XXIII the Council conducted negotiations with the other two Popes, thus treating as equals all the three men aspiring to the highest dignity in the Church.

The Pope was also defeated on the question of new procedure to be adopted for the sessions of the Council. Hitherto voting had been done traditionally, by counting the individual votes of the Fathers of the Council; while in the new procedure each national group—the German, the English, the French and the Italian—was to constitute a voting unit. Somewhat later the fifth "nation"—Spanish—was added.[35] The old procedure gave the greatest advantage to the Pope, who was supported by the large Italian representation at the Council, while voting by "nations" strengthened the position of his opponents. Thus the centre of gravity of the deliberations at Constance was shifted to the "nations", composed not only of bishops but also of representatives of the reigning houses and doctors representing universities—the two latter groups also having decisive votes. When all the "nations" had agreed on an issue, it was laid before the Council for approbation, which, however, was merely a formality.

To save his position John XXIII decided to desert the Council believing that he would thus break it up and that the Council, in accordance with canon law, would lose its validity if the Pope or his representative did not preside over its sessions, and if the decrees of the Council did not obtain papal approbation.

If the convocation of the Council at Pisa might be regarded as an exceptional measure devised to reunite Christendom, then the assembly had to find theoretical grounds for the principle declaring the supremacy of the Council over the Pope, the principle opposing the doctrine of the Caesarian power of Christ's successor. The Pope's desertion precipitated the solution of this problem of organization in favour of the Council.

University representatives, Pierre d'Ailly and John Gerson, as well as the Cardinal of Florence, Francesco Zabarella, substantially assisted by Sigismund of Luxemburg, achieved a full victory of the conciliar principles at Constance. Gerson's ideas, especially, met with general approbation; in his view "*epikeia*"—flexible interpretation of canon law—was admissible if dictated by necessity, common sense and serious considerations. Gerson taught that "well comprehended rightness bids us to consider special circumstances which the legislator could not foresee".[36]

The adherents of the conciliar principles came to regard *epikeia* as a magic word before which the immovable order of the Church receded.

Even before coming to Constance Gerson wrote a tract *De modis uniendi ac reformandi Ecclesiam in Concilio Generali*[37] in which he pointed out the dimorphism of the Church. One of the two forms, the Church Universal—*ecclesia universalis*—is under Christ's leadership and is composed equally of all believers. The Son of God governing that Church gives it perpetually full and living power as well as infallibility. It seems that in this matter Gerson was close to the views of his teacher, Pierre d'Ailly, who thought that the Council should supervise the rule of the priests, because he admitted their fallibility regarding only the Church Universal as unerring. He wrote: *"Generale Concilium potest errare, non solum in facto, sed etiam in iure, et quo magio est, in fide."*[38] Gerson, likewise, ascribed infallibility only to the Church Universal. The other form of Church, which Gerson called the Church Apostolic, was, according to him, composed of all the priests with the Pope at their head. This other Church being a human and fallible institution is only an instrument of the Church Universal. Gerson thought that the Church Apostolic should be under the control of all believers, both spiritual and secular, composing the Church Universal. In case of sinful and heretical activity of the Church Apostolic all believers ought not only to demand its reform but also to deprive it of power.[39]

After the desertion of John XXIII Gerson became the principal advocate and theorist of the conciliar doctrine which acquired the form of legal decree in the spring of 1415. This innovatory act was anticipated by the promulgation of the twelve theses formulated by the Chancellor of the Sorbonne at the request of the Council and Sigismund of Luxemburg. The theses state that Christ holds the highest office in the Church and is inseparably bound to it, which assures the Church supernatural power. The Pope, on the other hand, has secondary powers and the connection between him and the Church can be severed. Then the theses deal with the General Council which being the representative of the Church possesses the Church's rights. Hence the decisions of the Council are final and binding for all believers including the Pope. The twelfth and last thesis contains the statement that the General Council and the Provincial Councils are the only efficient instruments of Church reform.[40]

Gerson's theses provided the basis for the famous decree *"Sacrosancta"* passed in 1415. That decree laid down formally that the sovereignty of the Council of Constance came directly from God, that the Council represented the entire Church, that all the believers, including the Pope, owed it obedience and that its dissolution could only be decided by itself.[41]

In a speech delivered on the occasion of the departure of Sigismund of Luxemburg from Constance Gerson postulated the extension of the Council's competence to international affairs recognizing this institution as the supreme political organization able to make decisions and settle all international conflicts. On that occasion he also announced his view that ecclesiastical organization should be modelled after the political doctrine of Aristotle, that is, should combine in itself monarchy, aristocracy and timocracy; by timocracy he meant rightly understood democracy *"in qua populus bene dominatur"*.[42]

Beside *Sacrosancta* the Council of Constance passed another significant decree, *Frequens*, which laid down that General Councils were to assemble periodically: the first after 5 years, the second 7 years after the first, and the following at intervals of 10 years.[43]

Meanwhile time was becoming ripe for ending the Great Schism. The runaway Pope, John XXIII, fell into the hands of the Council and was deposed after a trial. Of the remaining two rivals to the tiara one— Gregory XII — abdicated, and the other—Benedict XIII—was abandoned by his protectors and thus lost virtually all influence, so that his person no longer blocked the way to Church unity.

In 1417 the College of Cardinals, increased by representatives of the "nations", elected the new Pope, Martin V (1417–31) thus terminating the schism. The new Pope refused to carry out reform of the Church—a duty imposed on him at election—because he identified reform with the conciliar principles to which he was hostile. In 1418 he even expressed his dislike in public speaking against appeals from his decisions to the General Council and retracted only under pressure of the general opinion. He was also forced to conclude with several countries a new concordate in which he made small fiscal concessions, increased the share of secular authority in the conferring of ecclesiastical dignities, restricted the influence of the Church over secular courts of the countries. Further, the Pope was forced to fix the date of the next General Council in accordance with the decree passed at Constance. After the failure of two councils—of Pavia and of Siena—Martin V convoked the Council of Basle (1431–49) which did not open its session till after his death. It was the most innovatory Council in the history of the Church, most consistent in realizing conciliar principles and most determined in its struggle against papal absolutism. It occasioned the clash of two doctrines, one of which was represented by the Fathers of the Council, the other—by Pope Eugenius IV (1431–47), a fanatical advocate of ecclesiastical absolutism.

While the Council of Constance had achieved single leadership after years of schism, the Council of Basle launched a new kind of schism again bringing about a split in the Church. For beside the Pope exercising full power there was active the Council, whose decrees were meant to change the whole ecclesiastical organization in such a way as to assure itself predominance. It was a period when the conciliar principles, though interpreted in different ways, had ceased to be merely a subject of theoretical discussions and provided a practical conception of ecclesiastical organization already in the process of realization.

With the conflict between Eugenius IV and the Council growing more inflamed, firm and unequivocal decisions were needed. It was not merely a struggle for power; the conflict revolved around the basic principles of ecclesiastical organization, for the very grounds and goals of time-honoured institutions were called in question.

One of the first acts of the new Pope was the issue of a bull dissolving the Council of Basle. But the Fathers of the Council did not break their deliberations, and taking the advantage of the friendly protection of secular rulers renewed the decrees of the Council of Constance asserting that the Council is superior to the Pope. The attempts of Eugenius IV at conciliation remained fruitless, the more so that in the autumn of 1433 he published widely the bull *"Deus novit"* asserting the uncompromising attitude of the Curia towards the Council. The bull denounced as heretical the statement that the Council is above the Pope and expressly demanded papal approbation for all the decrees of the Council. There, too, the Pope summoned secular rulers to resist the Conciliar Movement.

The negotiations conducted between the Council and the Hussites mitigated for a time the antagonism between Basle and the Roman Curia, the more so that the Czech heretics were a serious threat to the Church. Ecclesiastical dignitaries were more impressed by the military successes of the Taborites than they had formerly been at Constance by the wisdom and sanctity of John Hus and Jerome of Prague.

In the autumn of 1431 the representatives of the Hussites were invited to the Council; the possibility of reconciliation with the heretics was to be examined. After 2 days fifteen Czech delegates arrived under the leadership of Prokop Holy. All Europe was then watching the Council where discussions with the Hussites were conducted in an atmosphere of unaccustomed tolerance. A compromise was reached when two conciliar deputations sent to Bohemia reported that the Hussite camp was torn asunder by internal quarrels and disputes. An agreement known as *The Compacts of Prague* was concluded. The epilogue of the compromise is well known: the Church rejoiced in the restoration of unity, and Bohemia was bleeding in a fratricidal war.

Independently of dealing with Hussitism the Council undertook to reform the Church *"in capite et in membris"*. A number of measures were proposed to transform the structure of the Church in which sovereignty was given to the General Council.[44] It was laid down that if the papacy fell vacant when the Council was in session, the new Pope must be elected wherever it was sitting. The same rule was to apply to the nomination of cardinals. The Council declared itself the supreme authority in ecclesiastical state. Papal decisions dissolving the Council or changing the place of its meeting had to be validated by the Council. Decrees were passed against clerical concubinage, also against the abuse of excommunication and interdict; free elections of bishops and abbots were restored with the exclusion of intervention from the Apostolic See; the payments of taxes and dues to the Curia were restricted, and annates as well as fees for the bulls, confirmations, provisions, consecrations, etc.—abolished. Moreover, the Council claimed full control over papal finances summoning all collectors of the Apostolic Chamber to write periodical reports.

In 1438 the Fathers decreed the suspension of the Pope and henceforward treated him as a heretic for rejecting the thesis of the superiority of the

Council over the Pope, which had meanwhile been raised to the dignity of dogma. All these decrees were to fortify the conciliar idea and bury for ever papal absolutism. Meanwhile Eugenius IV had become the leading supporter of the projected union of the Greek Church with Rome and thus improved his position. Alarmed by the advance of the Turks the Eastern Church sought association with Rome hoping vainly for help from the West. In 1439 after long negotiations the decree *Laetentur Coeli* appeared; it promulgated the Union of the Eastern Church with the Latin Church and the primacy of the Pope. The Greek people repudiated the reconciliation of the two ecclesiastical hierarchies, nevertheless the conclusion of the union was regarded as a success of the Curialists and the Pope. Moreover, through diplomatic manoeuvres, concessions and promises the Pope managed to win over to his side the secular rulers, while the Council, transferred before its termination from Basle to Lausanne, was losing influence.

The principle of papal absolutism came to triumph in the Church. The Curialists who gained victory over the adherents of the conciliar doctrine now had indisputable predominance. They had the advantage of the long experience of papal rule assisted by the wisdom of generations of canonists. The adherents of the conciliar idea, on the other hand, had only one advantage: they were unanimous in their refusal to accept absolute monarchy claimed by the Pope. In the matter of positive programme, however, they differed considerably. The Fathers of the Council of Basle held divergent views on the problem of ecclesiastical leadership. Some thought that the Pope was the head of the Church by divine right and could only be supervised by the Council. To others he was merely "*caput ministeriale*", i.e. he was to execute functions appointed by the Council. In the opinion of still another group sovereignty rested with the bishops, who allotted functions to the Pope; this was a kind of federal conception. Lastly, not a few thought that the papacy was a human invention and concluded hence that the Church could entrust its executive power to a Council, a special committee or the College of Cardinals.[45]

The leaders of the Council of Basle were already the second generation of the upholders of conciliar principles. They were familiar with the opinions and arguments put forward in Constance, but at that time the conciliar idea had been regarded as an effective measure against the schism, while in Basle it was to be an instrument of ecclesiastical reform. There the Fathers were attempting to reverse the set of values hitherto regarded as unchangeable.

If the Council of Constance found its principal theorist in John Gerson, in Basle the same role was played by Nicholas of Cusa, who best expressed the ideals of that Council in his tract *De concordantia catholica*. He assumed as the basis of his argument the thesis of the universal "coincidence of opposites—*coincidentia oppositorum*"; he saw the source and essence of all existence in this coincidence of opposites. According to him God unites contraries in Himself being at the same time the absolute maximum and the absolute minimum, and the world is a combination of the elements of singleness and the elements of multiplicity, both of which, in turn, are reflected in man who is "*parvus mundus*". Nicholas of Cusa also discerned coincidence of opposites in social matters convinced that there, too, "*Omnia enim concordantia differentiarum est*". Lastly, his own life and work were the best instances of contradictions and he himself was in some way a symbol of the period of transition. He was a mystic and a forerunner of the mathematical and scientific outlook on life at the same time, a traditionalist and an innovator, a heretic and a cardinal, a determined leader and theorist of the conciliarists and later, when he went over to the curialists, its passionate enemy. And to him fell the writing of *De concordantia catholica*—a tract which is the most classical item of conciliar literature. Nicholas of Cusa defended there his view that the unity of the Church expresses itself in the manifestation of differences and that dogmatism hinders all necessary and desirable change. For different views—he argued—can be reconciled with the idea of ecclesiastic unity, if they are expressed without dogmatic obstinacy.[46] Differences in rites do not threaten the unity either. Tolerance, so alien to the Church, is according to the author of *De concordantia* the best means to, and guarantee of, the unity of Christendom. Advocating tolerance he also wanted to see realization of the idea of representation in the structure of the Church and so he insisted that all offices in the ecclesiastical hierarchy should be filled by election. He was also aware that the narrower the circle of persons the better the elected represent the electors, and was consequently convinced that the Pope represents the Church Universal only symbolically. To complement or explain his emphasis on tolerance and representation he asserted that common consent is necessary to justify the activity of the authorities. Natural law provides arguments for the need of such consent, without which, according to Nicholas of Cusa, neither government nor law can be just or right.[47]

The history of the conciliar doctrine covers the time of the three Councils —of Pisa, Constance and Basle. Yet it would be misleading to restrict the doctrine to those three religious assemblies, to theological deliberations or to academic disputes, even though universities played an important part in its formation.[48]

More than anything the conciliar doctrine inspired an unusually wide discussion of ecclesiastical organization, which spread over the entire Christian Europe. Discussions went on in dioceses, parishes, university auditoria, at royal courts, in monasteries and in cities. As usual public opinion was more effectively moulded by news of current events than by learned treatises. The simultaneous reign of two or even three Popes released forces which transformed the conciliar doctrine into a social movement.

The organization of higher ecclesiastical administration might appear remote from everyday life, but in reality it directly affected all believers through the heavy and ever-increasing papal taxation. The Conciliar Movement provided an opportunity for those who did not want to break away from the Church to evaluate its functioning critically. For a brief period dogmatism grew less rigid and the danger of regarding all doubt as heresy also diminished.

For a number of years the Christian society had watched the rivalry for power between Church administration and state administration. Marsilio of Padua and Wyclif were condemned by the Church because they had advocated transference of all power to the state both in secular and in spiritual matters. Now people grouped in the conciliar camp strove to change ecclesiastical administration and to revise the principles of Church organization. In a general way it can be said that the conflict centred on the problem of sovereignty in the Church. The curialists thought that as Christ had given the keys to St. Peter, it was a sufficient justification of the monarchic conception of papacy. The same conception was advocated by the canonists who produced numerous arguments for the papal *plenitudo potestatis*.

The conciliarists, on the other hand, referred to the words of St. Paul who wrote in a letter to Corinthians: "Know ye not that ye are the temple of God, and that the Spirit of God dwelleth in you? If any man defile the temple of God, him shall God destroy; for the temple of God is holy, which temple ye are."[49] In the opinion of the adherents of the conciliar idea the interest of the Christian commonwealth was a criterion of the evaluation of ecclesiastical sovereignty. They upheld the principle "*Quod omnes tangit ab omnibus approbatur.*"

Conversely, the curialists believed in the sanctity and infallibility of the Pope and hence were not far from the thesis "*Quod principi placuit legis habet vigorem.*"

In search for arguments that would support the change of ecclesiastical organization the theorists of the Conciliar Movement turned to patterns from secular administration. Owing to them problems of ecclesiastical organization came to be discussed in politico-legal categories. They wanted the structure of the new Church to rest on the principles of common consent and harmonious co-operation at the top of the hierarchy. Also, their thinking was affected in some measure by the national tendencies then coming to the surface.

The principle of common consent was a consequence—as was demonstrated by Nicholas of Cusa—of the validity of natural order, which was to protect people born free and equal from arbitrary rule and arbitrary legislation. Only the consent of the whole society or of its considerable majority (*valentior pars*) can guarantee justice of politico-legal institutions. Thus just rule differs from tyranny because the former is concerned about public welfare and seeks the approbation of society expressed as a rule by current customs.

The concept of common consent is also found in the work of Gerson who says in his *Sermo ad Regem Franciae nomine universitatis Parisiensis* that monarchy exists only owing to general acceptance ("*per communen hominum consensum*") and that it is erroneous to assume that the monarch has unlimited rights. Gerson's postulate of common consent is not far removed from the feudal contract which formulated mutual rights and obligations of the subjects and the lords.[50]

Similarly Zabarella expressed the opinion that society, or else its considerable majority is the source of power. Analysing the origins of authority Zabarella mentions three ways in which power can be acquired: through divine revelation, through the consent of the subjects, and through violence or usurpation. He adds, however, that social approbation is the basic and normal way of entrusting power.[51]

As it has been mentioned, of all the theorists of conciliarism Nicholas of Cusa expounded most thoroughly the principle of common consent in Book III of *De concordantia catholica*, arguing that government and law derive their power and authority from the consent of the whole society.

The medieval idea of common consent required virtually no more than passive approbation for the ruler and the law. It was an expression of the passive attitude of society that was seeking means of opposing tyranny and wilfulness. Later the principle of common consent was to give way to the principle of collective will, which was to mark the active attitude of a society demanding active participation in nominating rulers and determining policy. The former attitude looked back to the past and to tradition; the latter was to reflect the convictions of the *bourgeoisie* orientated towards the future.

The postulate of common consent was not the only weapon with which the theorists of the conciliar doctrine were fighting papal absolutism; the other was the principle of harmonious co-operation of the supreme ecclesiastical organs. The starting point of their reasoning was the current assumption that full sovereignty lies with the Church Universal, which, in turn, can entrust it to the General Council, the Pope or the College of Cardinals. All these three organs ought to act together in harmony in order to exercise power in the interest of all believers. But the conciliarists assumed at the same time that when the supreme organs do not co-operate—when *concordantia* disappears—the General Council represents best the attitude of the Church Universal.

If one disregards extremists, most adherents of the conciliar doctrine were convinced that harmonious co-operation among supreme ecclesiastical organs is necessary. This principle was further recommended by the authority of Aristotle and his model government combining monarchy, aristocracy and elements of popular rule.

When the conciliar idea of harmonious co-operation of the supreme ecclesiastical organs was directed against papal absolutism, it anticipated mildly the future doctrine of division, balance and mutual control of authorities.

If politico-legal principles were applied by the theorists of conciliarism to ecclesiastical affairs quite consciously, the national tendencies were breaking into the Church without their intention determining all decrees and measures. In Constance the "nations" were accepted committees of the Council; in fact, they settled all problems, so that the plenary sessions remained merely solemn, official gatherings.

In Basle the division into "nations" was not formally adopted; instead members were grouped into four committees, each to deal with a different problem, but the "nations" still had a decisive voice both in the committees and in plenary sessions.

The Fathers of both Councils agreed to conclude concordats with those governments which guaranteed states some independence in ecclesiastical matters. The adherents of the conciliar doctrine concluded in fact that *Respublica Christiana* could not disregard national interests, which often clashed with narrowly understood religio-political unity of the universal Church. In France centrifugal tendencies even gave rise to Gallicanism, a movement advocating considerable restriction of papal influence in internal policy. Gallicanism obtained legal formulation in 1438 in the so-called Pragmatic Sanction, which included the decrees of the Council of Basle into the constitutional principles of France.

Yet the victories of the curialists over the adherents of the conciliar doctrine put an end to the process of reform already afoot. A period of extreme centralism began. Soon the Church was to make an oracular announcement of the infallibility of its rulers and papal absolutism was to become a model of organization for European states.

4. CREATOR OF POLITICAL REALISM

Both the religio-social doctrine and the conciliar principles grew out of social movements which found their justification in complete decline of European universalism. Striving against the traditional institutions of the Church both currents were formulating their doctrines and giving them precision. The polemical character of both doctrines determined their range and power.

At the same time we find in Arabian countries a realistic theory of society evolved by Ibn Khaldun. The lapse of several centuries between the fall of the Arabian universalism and the work of Ibn Khaldun made it possible for him to view from a distance the changing fortunes of states and dynasties that arose and then crumbled on the wreckage of the Islamic Empire.

While the European political thought of the period of transition is an immediate consequence of the declining universalism, the doctrine of Ibn Khaldun derives, in a way, from reflecting on the consequences of the shattered unity of the Arab world.

Already in the second half of the tenth century the Caliph of Baghdad had only illusory power over the Arab Empire stretching between Central Asia and the Atlantic. Gradually the provinces freed themselves from the control of the metropolis and formed a number of independent states ruled by ambitious dynasties. The disintegration of the Empire brought along with it, on the one hand, interstate conflicts and wars, but on the other it favoured the growth of many cultural and trade centres in the provinces. The Arabian universalism was rapidly breaking up owing to the decentralizing powers of the new states that aspired to become independent of the caliphate, and also owing to the invasions of the nomadic tribes breaking in through the eastern and western borders of the Empire.

The first danger that came to threaten the Islamites was the Turkish invasions, but those—on the whole—caused little damage to the development of economic and cultural life. The Arabs managed even to form a loyal and fearless military force of properly brought up and trained Mamluks who were originally Turkish slaves. Only the Mongol invasions that came in the thirteenth and fourteenth centuries crushed the cultural centres and trade centres in the eastern territories of Islam stretching between Turkistan and the Mediterranean Sea.

In the west disturbances were caused by the nomadic tribes of the Berbers. After a brief period of harmony when the Berbers invaded Spain together with the Arabs, from allies they became enemies of Islam. Their attacks drained the strength of the Arabs and led to political instability in North Africa which helped to push the Arabs gradually out of the Pyrenean Peninsula. Owing to the belligerence of the Berbers new states were forming and disappearing again in North Africa between the eleventh and the fifteenth centuries; the dynasties that ruled those states were changing but most of them sought to justify their power by religious considerations.[52]

Both the dynasty of Almoravides (1038–1145) and that of Almohades (1130–1269) came to power in this way. The history of these two dynasties provided material for Ibn Khaldun's theoretical conclusions.

After the fall of the State of Almohades three new dynasties began to share power over North Africa: the Hafsids ruled over Tunisia (1228–1554), the Abd-el-Wahids in Tlemcen (1239–1554) and the Marinids in Morocco. Lastly, in Spain, where the Arabs managed to keep possession of only a small strip of land, ruled the Nasrid dynasty, which survived until 1492 owing to their resilient policy and the superior geographical situation of Grenada.

Ibn Khaldun played an active and important role in the political life of these four states. In his career holding highest offices alternated with dire failure; he kept on entering the service of a new ruler after falling out of favour with the former one; he even knew life in prison. It is indeed hard to believe that the wide knowledge and scholarly activities of this man were for him something incidental, a kind of margin of his energetic political activity. Ibn Khaldun must have suffered from inner dichotomy, for his political ambitions were conflicting with his passion for scholarly investigation.[53] He seems to have been the reverse of Plato's ideal of politician–philosopher, as he expressed, in one of his letters his readiness to give up active life for the life of contemplation. "May God help me", he wrote, "to free myself from the fetters of hope and of political success. . . . I would much rather devote my life to knowledge, if I were only left in peace."[54]

However, his temperament, education and family traditions predisposed him to a political career. His ancestors had played an important part in the political life of Seville as long as the town was under Arab rule. After the victory of the Christians in Spain they settled in Tunis where Ibn Khaldun was born in 1332. It was there that he received a very good theological and philosophical education, and it was also there that he began his political career at the court of the Hafsids. Soon he offered his services to the Marinids ruling in Morocco, where he became involved in court intrigues and found himself in prison. The years 1362–5 were of special importance in his life; serving at the court in Grenada he became acquainted for the first time with the Christian world when he was sent on diplomatic missions to the lost Seville. His extensive knowledge and a talent for mediation gained him fame and envy, friends and enemies, but above all they made him lead a very troubled life. After leaving Grenada he was successively in the service of the rulers of Bougie, Fez, Tlemcen. It was in this period, lasting several years, that he withdrew from political life. Staying in a lonely Berber fortress he made the first draft of his philosophy of history, designed as an introduction to a History of the World. It seems very probable that he wanted to discuss or else expound his conceptions in a renowned centre of scholarship and that this desire made him undertake a journey eastward. In 1383 he reached Cairo. He was dazzled by the wealth of the town and by its intellectual life. But in this new place he still acted in accordance with his nature and soon exchanged his professorship for the office of the supreme judge. An account has been preserved, written by Ibn Khaldun's own hand, of his meeting with Tamerlane in 1400 during the siege of Damascus. The grey-headed sage managed to gain the confidence of the untamed barbarian for whom he even prepared a description of Maghreb, but he did not succeed in saving the town.[55] After the fall of Damascus he returned to Cairo, where he died in 1406. Europe was not to hear of him until 400 years later.

Ibn Khaldun's interests were very broad. We know from the titles on record—his preserved works are few—that he wrote treatises about theology, philosophy, law, arithmetic, logic. He gained fame and distinction chiefly as the author of an extant seven-volume history, *Kitab al-Ibar*,[56] of which he spoke to Tamerlane as of his *magnum opus*. Ibn Khaldun divided his history into three large parts. The first—*Muqāddima* (Introduction, *Prolegomena*)— is an exposition of the author's philosophy and methodology; the second, including volumes II to V, contains his universal history of the world; finally, the third, including the last two volumes, presents the history of the Berbers. *Muqāddima*, an introduction to the history of the world, is also a systematic statement of an entirely new theory of society.

For centuries the great work of Ibn Khaldun was unknown outside the Islamic world, but there it was treated with respect due to writings that contain profound political wisdom.

Europe discovered Ibn Khaldun in 1806 when Silvestre de Sacy published several fragments of his work.[57] Those who read him soon became aware of the true stature of the Arab thinker.[58] Ibn Khaldun's ideas began to arouse increasing interest, for few minds in social science had been as penetrating as his and few had had as keen a desire for knowledge. In 1858 E. Quatremére published *Muqāddima* in Arabic,[59] and soon the text was translated into French by W. McGucken de Slane.[60]

Owing to the studies by F. E. Schulz, R. Flint, A. v. Kremer, L. Gumplowicz, nineteenth-century scholarship recognized Ibn Khaldun as a thoroughly modern thinker, historian, philosopher and sociologist.[61] In this century he has been advanced to the rank of the greatest thinkers of the world. A. J. Toynbee considers Ibn Khaldun the creator of "the greatest work of its kind".[62] R. Nicholson writes of him: "His intellectual descendants are the great medieval and modern historians. . . ."[63] G. Sarton calls his work "one of the noblest and most impressive monuments of medieval thought".[64]

Ibn Khaldun's road to "new science", as he termed his theory of society, must have been neither straight nor easy. In a world where everything that occurs is related to God and his plan, to grant priority to sensuous cognition, to postulate comparison of statements with reality, to explain everything that happens by causal relationship and objective regularity, is to develop an idea of the world opposing the accepted tradition. It seems that Ibn Khaldun's mediating nature and his avoidance of drastic decisions in life may to some extent explain his concessions to traditionalism. In any case, he was too sensible to cut himself off from tradition; he was rather trying to absorb it critically.

Starting with the established opinions of the past he admitted that theocracy (*siyasa diniya*) gave a full guarantee of attaining temporal and eternal happiness, and that the sacred law of Islam (*sari'a*) had a superior position.[65] At the same time, however, to clear the way for true knowledge, he made a sharp distinction between sensuous cognition and contemplative or intuitive cognition. The former, according to Ibn Khaldun, belongs to ordinary people, the latter marks saints and prophets. Here, too, can be drawn a line of demarcation between science and religion.[66] Sense perceptions are the basis of cognition; they supply the mind with material for general ideas, but those ideas must be constantly controlled, constantly compared with reality and experience.[67] For the human mind has an obvious tendency, observable especially in the field of social sciences, to make hasty generalizations, which misrepresent the investigated facts and phenomena. Certainly, whatever is wrong in science comes from trying to reach eternal truths by pure abstraction, merely on the basis of dogma and with the exclusion of empiricism.[68] The variety and multiplicity of things in the world around us may be understood only through scientific cognition, which seeks support for its reasoning in sense perceptions and in empiricism, and which thus discovers the law that governs the world—the law of cause and effect. "Whatever happens in the world of reality," Ibn Khaldun wrote, "whether it be a thing or an action, must have a cause, i.e. it must have been preceded by such occurrences from which it normally originates and which determine its existence."[69] Necessity and universality of causal relationship bring about the regularity governing the world of things and phenomena, which, in turn, helps the human mind to understand the process of their changes. "If we observe this world and everything in it," Ibn Khaldun wrote, "we perceive the whole to be a closely knit system, in which everything is bound to everything else by the law of causality and in which there is a perfect order."[70]

Among phenomena and things the highest rank is given to man, or—more precisely—to human community. This Ibn Khaldun also tries to discuss in terms of cause and effect, to understand the origin, change and waning of definite human relations. In short, he wants to establish the regularity that determines those relations which he calls culture (*cumrān*). This constitutes the main object of "new science", and its aim is to acquire "knowledge of the formation of human society, or, what is the same, of culture in its various conditions . . . like savagery, organized acting, sense of community, next understanding various kinds of superiority among human beings, which is the beginning of government, further still, knowledge of human activities and occupations, which are the source of crafts, sciences and arts; finally, knowledge of all changes that can affect the character of this culture."[71]

Ibn Khaldun was convinced that the studies of history written before him were naive, sterile and full of mistakes, that they were haphazard collections of unrelated bits of information of no scientific value. The time-honoured custom of writing chronicles of the deeds of successive rulers had similarly very little value.[72] In order to discover the real forces that govern human society, one ought to get rid of every bias and prejudice, overcome the subjectivity of historians, their naiveté and credulity and, above all, free oneself from the habit of taking appearances for reality.[73] The only remedy for the shortcomings of the science of society may be the "new science"—a study of culture. Hence the study of the varying form and meaning of human relationship in the past and the present is a worthy task for a statesman and a historian.

This was indeed an uncommon widening of the field of investigation. But only this approach, Ibn Khaldun wrote, would let "the reader see clearly how States were established", and then "he will understand fully the conditions in the past generations and centuries and will even be able to form his judgement about the future."[74] One ought to look beyond the vast and manifold material of history to perceive the principal forces which determine the regularity of events. In this way Ibn Khaldun arrived at conclusions concerning the essential factors that determine the form and meaning of human relationship, that is—in his view—the culture of society. One group of those factors should be considered separately; it is the group that includes factors affecting man independently of his will: the geophysical environment, in which human beings live. Ibn Khaldun divided the parts of the globe between the pole and the equator into seven zones and concluded that only the three middle zones offer suitable conditions for the development of culture. Within the boundaries of these areas the climate and the fertility of the soil influence considerably the biophysical constitution of man.[75]

The second group of factors determining the character of culture comprises economic elements. They stand on the borderline between subjective and objective determinants of history, because the conditions of the environment determine the means of support, while work is the result of subjective motivation. Ibn Khaldun was fully aware that the manner in which means of sustenance are obtained determines the meaning and the form of social relations to a considerable extent.[76]

The third group of factors determining culture includes mental characteristics of a society, above all the sense of unity ('asabiya), for "with the help of this people protect and defend themselves, secure respect for their rights and carry out common resolutions".[77] At first, the need to struggle for means of sustenance and the need of defence against dangers make association necessary. The bond of blood is then the basic factor that keeps the members of a community together.[78] As time passes other ties become important and then asabiya grows out of them. A sense of community ensues then from social relations, common experience, common suffering, work or education.[79] Though the sense of unity varies in intensity, yet it determines the political strength of a society and the energy of its development.

Sense of unity is an element of order and inherent in it is respect for authority, which prevents any activity that would threaten the integrity of the society.

Ibn Khaldun's discussion of the dynamics and structure of society is closely connected with his realistic socio-political doctrine. The reader finds in his work neither speculation on man's social nature, nor an analysis of state institutions, nor evaluation of various kinds of government. He reveals the patience of a naturalist when he describes the social processes and changes which—like everything else in the world—are subject to specific laws of origin, growth and decline. The cycle of life and death—the universal necessity which sends death to everything that has come to existence, applies also to society. The processes of growth and decline bring about essential changes and make possible a division of the history of societies into periods.

Ibn Khaldun distinguished two great periods through which every society passes. The first is nomadic life, the second—settled life.[80] All relations between human beings are radically different in these two periods.

In the first period members of a society are kept together by blood bonds. Living close to nature people become rugged physically and morally. Solidarity in action is their rule, as is also mutual help.[81] The authority that is accepted by the whole society is paramount; it derives its strength from the general support of the people. Economic life is restricted to the satisfaction of basic needs. Religion is an experience and not a study of dogma.

Transition to settled life marks the beginning of the phase or urban life (*hadāra*). The natural bonds between people are superseded by artificial ties such as the community of occupation, education, work, etc.[82] Authority, separated from society seeks to strengthen itself by the use of force and to gain support from hired soldiers and an army of paid officials.[83] While in the phase of nomadic life spontaneous obedience was the basis of the ruler's authority, in the phase of settled life the ruler "enslaves the subjects, that is makes them obedient by force, imposes taxes, sends envoys, who can defend the frontiers and acknowledges no power over himself".[84]

It is a period when desire for luxury motivates economic life and superfluity of goods creates conditions favourable to the development of crafts, arts and sciences. Religion ceases to be an experience and becomes an object of speculation and study. But above all the phase of settled life brings with it organization of the state which becomes a factor that brings order to mutual relations between people. The state is—as Ibn Khaldun puts it— a form in which a developed culture becomes manifest.[85] However, in this new stage of social life there are visible signs of future decadence. Luxury is accompanied by the exploitation of the poor and by the decrease of the moral strength of the population. Seeking larger income the ruler increases the dues of the citizens. Increased taxation makes the citizens less interested in their work and consequently brings about migrations out of the country Increasing economic difficulties cause anxiety among hired soldiers; crafts, arts and sciences begin to decline. The provinces loosen their ties with the metropolis which stands helpless in face of invasions.

Ibn Khaldun's division of history into two periods: one of nomadic and one of settled life, led to his establishing a contrast between state and society. According to him in the first period social organization results from the principle of spontaneous unity and free acceptance of recognized authorities. In the second period the state functions with the help of the machinery of organized government, that has force at its disposal.

Against the background of the ancient and medieval doctrine this was an entirely new idea. In the conception of Plato and Aristotle the *polis*, or city-state, contained in it both the element of compulsion and of freedom— state and society. The medieval doctrine, again, understood social ties better than state ties, which were only just taking shape under the influence of national movements. At that time religion provided the dominant ties holding the faithful together; besides, members of the same estate also felt the common bond.[86] In contrast to this Ibn Khaldun's conception of two historical phases and of the accompanying two kinds of organization, social organization and state organization is the basis of his cyclic theory.

Within the period of urban culture the state passes through five phases which mark the way from its rise until its disintegration.[87]

The first phase is one of conquest and consolidation of power. The ruler gains the support of all the people who still regard unity and solidarity of action as their sacred duty.

In the second phase power becomes autocratic. The ruler strives to become the sole master of the state; he hires officials and tries to turn his family into a dynasty.

The third phase is the time of peace and acquisition of wealth. The luxurious living of the court, imitated by the subjects, supersedes the simplicity characteristic of the conquerors of the earlier period.

In the fourth phase the first sign of weakness can be discerned against the general background of self-satisfaction. The ruler, who seeks to strengthen his authority by the honourable tradition of his predecessors, pursues a policy of conciliation and compromise.

The fifth phase brings along with it the final collapse. The selfishness and pusillanimity of the ruler antagonize all his subjects. Exorbitant dues claimed by the state from the citizens injure economic enterprise. Growing economic difficulties increase political weakness.

The five phases cover the whole existence of a state from the rise of a dynasty until its fall. This period, which lasts about 120 years, covers the lives of three generations. Each of those generations has a different character in accordance with the changes in the way of living. "The differences between the cultural conditions of generations", wrote Ibn Khaldun, "can be reduced to differences in the way of living."[88]

Political and economic decadence is a signal of the approaching end of the state. The fifth phase closes the historical cycle, making room for a new one. The fate of one society is fulfilled.

Ibn Khaldun had not access to a very wide range of historical facts. His theoretical conclusions were made on the basis of the history of the nomadic Berber tribes and the Arab states of North Africa, and those usually existed for a period shorter than a century and a half.[89] But in spite of the limitations of his material he managed to make many shrewd observations which were a part of his realistic thinking.

The doctrine of the Arab thinker has inspired a number of comparisons. Students of Ibn Khaldun's thought were looking there for analogies with the realism of Machiavelli. The idea of historical cycles suggests a similarity to the conceptions of Vico. The emphasis on geophysical elements brings him near Montesquieu. Finally, his stressing of the connections between the economic life and politics seems to anticipate Marxism.

Such comparisons certainly make this deep and many-sided mind the more admirable, but on no account do they provide a basis for conjectures about possible relations between European political thought and the Arab doctrine which had long remained unknown in Europe.

The respect that the teaching of Ibn Khaldun inspires is due to its realism, correlation of everything to reality, use of concretes, dislike of speculation or dogmatic argument.

Presenting his conception of the state he excluded from consideration theocracy (*siyasa diniya*) that guaranteed eternal salvation to its citizens. Similarly, he left out ideal state (*siyasa madaniya*), which was an imaginary product of ancient philosophy. His interests revolve exclusively around the state created by man (*siyasa aqliya*), and the purpose of this state is to sustain order, to assure welfare to its citizens, to promote the development of crafts, and sciences. Rejecting visions of an ideal organization he sought models for his state neither in an idealized past nor in an imaginary future. He did not want from history a lesson in living but merely tried to explain reality with its help.

Ibn Khaldun knew that the laws determining social processes leave little room for the enterprise of eminent individuals. These laws so circumscribe divine omnipotence that even prophets cannot transcend them.[90] They diminish the state's power to mould the character of its citizens, who are already determined by environment. However, Ibn Khaldun did not regard with indifference the attitude of the subjects towards their ruler, the more so that in his view the essence of power resides in the relationship between the subjects and the ruler.[91] He knew that rule supported by force breeds in the subjects distrust, hostility and a desire for a change of government. Hence the welfare of the state requires from the ruler patience, leniency, generosity and magnanimity in his dealings with his subjects.[92]

In Ibn Khaldun's view governing is made easier when the subjects wish to imitate their rulers, to whom outstanding virtues are ascribed. He regarded this desire to follow the example set by people standing higher in the social hierarchy as a universal tendency; he noticed it in children's attitude towards their parents, in the pupils' attitude towards their teachers, and in the attitude of the subjects towards the ruling classes, of whom he said, quoting an old Arab proverb, "People profess the religion of their kings."[93]

Evaluating the ties between politics and economic life Ibn Khaldun revealed as much realism as in the other aspects of his thought. In his view the ruler, while performing political functions at the same time controls the market through his influence on the circulation of money, production of goods and determining taxes and dues. Similarly, the position of every social group within the framework of the state depends on the amount of its income, which, in turn, is the result of bringing under its own control other groups of society.[94]

Ibn Khaldun perceived clearly that political position depends on the economic potential and that these two mutually affected forces are ultimately determined by the course of history. He knew that "unless the manner of government corresponds to the state of culture, the political activity is wrong".[95]

Realism, which Ibn Khaldun moulded into a scientific theory, was his philosophy of life and a faithful companion in his ups and downs. To his contemporaries it seemed to indicate a great political talent, and in the eyes of his posterity it is a sufficient title to glory.

NOTES

1. J. Huizinga: *Herfsttij der Middeleeuwen*, Polish transl., Warsaw, 1961.

2. J. D. Bernal: *Science in History*, Polish transl., Warsaw, 1957, and A. C. Crombie: *Medieval and Early Modern Science*, Polish transl., Warsaw, 1960.

3. H. Pirenne: *A History of Europe from the Invasions to the 19th Century*, Book Eight: *European Crisis*, London, 1955.

4. I. Origo: *Tribune of Rome. A Biography of Cola di Rienzo*, London, 1938; V. Fleischer: *Rienzo. The Rise and Fall of Dictator*, London, 1948.

5. M. Malowist: Zagadnienie kryzysu feudalizmu w XIV i XV wieku w świetle najnowszych badań, *Kwartalnik Historyczny*, R. LX, 1953, no. 1, and E. Maleczyńska: *Ruch husycki i w Czechach i w Polsce*, Warsaw, 1959, Chapter I "Zagadnienie kryzysu feudalizmu w Europie w XIV i XV w".

6. M. Malowist: *Studia z dziejów rzemiosła w okresie kryzysu feudalizmu w zachodniej Europie w XIV i XV wieku*, Warsaw, 1954, p. 452.

7. J. Kuliszer: *Powszechna historia gospodarcza Sredniowiecza i czasów nowożytnych*, vol. I, Warsaw, 1961, pp. 326–60.

8. P. Boissonade: *Life and Work in Medieval Europe (Fifth to Fifteenth Centuries)*, Book III, London, 1949, pp. 279–336.

9. G. M. Trevelyan: *English Social History. A Survey of Six Centuries, Chaucer to Victoria*, London, 1946, Introduction, pp. XI–XII.

10. *Rotuli Parlamentorum*, Ed. J. Strachey *et al.*, London, 1767, III, 19, 22, 23, pet. XXVII.

11. M. Schlauch: *English Medieval Literature and Its Social Foundations*, Warsaw, 1956, pp. 201 ff.

12. *The English Works of Wyclif hitherto Unprinted. On Confession*, Ed. F. D. Matthew, Early English Text Society, 1880, p. 327.

13. J. Wyclif: *De civili dominio:* vol. I, Ed. R. L. Poole, Wyclif Society Publications, 1885, p. 277–8.

14. J. Wyclif: *De ecclesia*, Ed. J. Loserth, Wyclif Society Publications, 1886, I, V, VI.

15. For the consequences of predestination in Wyclif's doctrine see K. B. McFarlane: *John Wycliffe and the Beginnings of English Non-conformity*, 1952, pp. 91 ff.

16. *Selected English Works of Wyclif*, Ed. T. Arnold, Oxford, 1871, III, 342.

17. J. Wyclif: *De civili dominio, op. cit.*, 42, 96, 101, 199, 201.

19. J. Wyclif: *De blasphemia*, Ed. M. Dziewicki, Wyclif Society Publications, 1894, pp. 188 ff.

20. J. Wyclif: *Trialogus*, Ed. Lechler, Oxford 1869, IV, XIX.

21. *The English Works of Wyclif hitherto Unprinted. De officio pastorali, op. cit.*, p. 429.

22. M. Deanesly: *The Lollard Bible and other Mediaeval Biblical Versions*, Cambridge, 1920.

23. *The English Works of Wyclif hitherto Unprinted. De officio pastorali, op. cit.*, p. 428.

24. J. Froissart: *Chronicle*, English transl. by Johnes, 1804, II, 135.

25. G. M. Trevelyan: (*England in the Age of Wycliffe*, London, 1948, pp. 224, 239) thinks that as the rebels were negotiating with the king, they could not possibly attempt to overthrow the monarchy.

26. For the connections between the Czechs and the English heretics see: F. M. Bartoš: *Husitství a cizina*, Prague 1931, pp. 30 ff.; K. B. McFarlane: *op. cit.*, pp. 156–62; E. Maleczyńska: *Ruch husycki w Czechach i w Polsce*, Warsaw, 1959, Chapter VI.

27. J. Macek: *Husitské rewoluční hnutí*, Prague, 1952, pp. 30 ff.

28. E. Maleczyńska: *op. cit.*, pp. 388 ff., 412; *Archiv český čili staré písemné památky české a moravské*, Ed. F. Palacký, Prague, 1844, vol. III, pp. 213 ff. and *Ruch husycki w Polsce. Wybór tekstów źródłowych (do r. 1454)*, Ed. R. Heck and E. Maleczyńska, Wrocław, 1953, pp. 59–60.

29. Cosmas of Prague: *Chronica Boemorum*, lib. I, cap. III, *Monumenta Germaniae Historica*, vol. II.

30. *Majestas Carolina*, Archiv český, III, 68.

31. Quoted after E. Maleczyńska: *Ruch husycki w Czechach . . .*, p. 276.

32. Quoted after J. Macek: *op. cit.*, p. 45.

33. Quoted after E. F. Jacob: *Essays in the Conciliar Epoch*, Manchester, 1953, p. 8.

34. See O. H. Brandt: *Ulrich von Richentals Chronik des Konzils zu Konstanz 1414–1418*, Voigtländers Quellen Bücher, Band 48, Leipzig, n. d.

35. Polish delegation was a part of the German "nation".

36. J. Gerson: *Opera omnia*, II, Ed. E. Du Pin, Antwerp, 1706, p. 120.

37. J. Gerson: *op. cit.*, II, pp. 161–201.

38. J. D. Mansi: *Sacrorum conciliorum et decretorum nova et amplissima collectio*, XXVII, Florence–Venice, 1759–98, p. 547

39. L. Tosti: *Geschichte des Konzilium's von Konstanz*, Schaffhausen, 1860, pp. 209 ff.

40. J. Gerson: *op. cit.*, II, pp. 201–6.

41. J. D. Mansi: *op. cit.*, XXVII, p. 590.

42. J. Gerson: *op. cit.*, II, pp. 273 ff.

43. J. D. Mansi: *op. cit.*, XXVII, pp. 1159 ff.

44. For the decrees of the Council of Basle, see C. J. von Hefele: *Conciliengeschichte*, vol. VII, Freiburg im Breisgau, 1874, pp. 426–649.

45. For differences of opinion among the delegates to the Council of Basle see W. T. Waugh: The Councils of Constance and Basle, [in:] *The Cambridge Medieval History*, vol. VIII, Cambridge, 1936, pp. 25 ff.

46. Nicholas of Cusa: *De concordantia catholica*, Ed. G. Kallen, Heidelberg, 1939, p. 49.

47. For the influence of Marsilio of Padua on the doctrine expressed in *De concordantia*

catholica see P. E. Sigmund: The Influence of Marsilius of Padua on 15th Century Conciliarism, *Journal of the History of Ideas*, vol. XXIII, No. 3, 1962, pp. 392 ff.

48. The academic character of the conciliar ideas is specially emphasized by J. N. Figgis: *Political Thought from Gerson to Grotius: 1414–1625*, New York, 1960, pp. 41–70.

49. Holy Bible (King James Version), New York, n. d., Corinthians III, 16, 17, New Testament, p. 171.

50. R. W. Carlyle, A. J. Carlyle: *A History of Mediaeval Political Theory in the West*, vol. VI, Edinburgh–London, 1950, pp. 159 ff.

51. R. W. Carlyle, A. J. Carlyle: *op. cit.*, col. VI, pp. 166 ff.

52. A. Müller: *Der Islam im Morgen und Abendland*, II, Berlin, 1885–7, pp. 667 ff.

53. For the personality of Ibn Khaldun see the study by M. Syrier: Ibn Khaldun and Islamic Mysticism, *Islamic Culture*, XXI, Hyderabad, 1947, pp. 264–302.

54. Quoted after M. K. Ayad: *Die Geschichts- und Gessellschaftslehre Ibn Halduns*, Forschungen zur Geschichts- und Gesellschaftslehre, H. 2, Stuttgart and Berlin, 1930, p. 13.

55. W. J. Fischel: *Ibn Khaldūn and Tamerlane*, Berkeley and Los Angeles, 1952, pp. 29–48.

56. The full title of Ibn Khaldun's History in the translation of S. de Sacy is: *Le livre des exemples instructifs et le recueil des événements anciens et de ceux dont le souvenir s'est conservé concernant l'histoire des Arabes, des Persans, des Berbers et des nations contemporaines les plus puissantes* (Biographie Universelle, v. XXI, Paris, 1818). Ibn Khaldun's work was published in Arabic in seven volumes by Sheikh Naṣr al-Hūrīnī, Bulǎq, 1867–8.

57. S. de Sacy: *Chrestomathie arabe*, II, Paris, 1806, pp. 401–573.

58. N. Schmidt: *Ibn Khaldun, Historian, Sociologist and Philospher*, New York, 1930, pp. 1–8.

59. *Les Prolégomènes d'Ibn Khaldoun*, Notices et Extraits, XVI, XVII, XVIII, Paris, 1858.

60. *Les Prolégomènes d'Ibn Khaldoun*, Notices et Extraits, XIX, XX, XXI, Paris, 1863–8. This edition was reprinted 1934–8.

61. F. E. Schulz: Ibn Khaldoun, *Journal Asiatique*, VII, Paris, 1825, pp. 213–26, 279–300; R. Flint: *History of the Philosophy of History*, Edinburgh, 1893, pp. 157–71; A. v. Kremer: *Ibn Chaldun und seine Kulturgeschichte der islamischen Reiche*, Wien, 1879; L. Gumplowicz: Ibn Chaldun socjolog arabski XIV wieki, *Przeglad Filozoficzny*, No. IV, Warsaw, 1898, pp. 45–62.

62. A. J. Toynbee: *A Study of History*, III, London, 1934, p. 322.

63. R. Nicholson: *A Literary History of the Arabs*, London, 1923, p. 438.

64. G. Sarton: *Introduction to the History of Science*, Baltimore, 1948, p. 1775.

65. E. I. J. Rosenthal: *Political Thought in Medieval Islam*, Cambridge, 1958, pp. 84–6.

66. *Muqǎddima* (French translation, quoted further as *Proleg.*) I, p. 200.

67. *Proleg.*, II, p. 427; III, p. 232.

68. *Proleg.*, III, pp. 237, 279, 294.

69. *Proleg.*, III, p. 40.

70. *Proleg.*, I, p. 196.

71. *Proleg.*, I, p. 71.

72. *Proleg.*, I, pp. 7, 65.

73. *Proleg.*, I, p. 77.

74. *Proleg.*, I, p. 9.

75. *Proleg.*, I, pp. 105, 168, 169.

76. *Proleg.*, I, p. 254.

77. *Proleg.*, I, p. 291.

78. *Proleg.*, I, pp. 270–3.

79. *Proleg.*, I, p. 374.

80. These distinctions are treated by Levine (J. Levine: *Ibn Khaldun, arabskiy sotsiolog XIV veka*, Novy Vostok, book 12, 1926, p. 244) as a basic and universal principle of the development of society, a principle that pervades the whole doctrine of Ibn Khaldun.

81. *Proleg.*, I, p. 269.

82. *Proleg.*, I, p. 374.

83. For a full exposition of Ibn Khaldun's doctrine of state together with a selection of sources see E. Rosentahl: *Ibn Khaldun's Gedanken über den Staat*, München, 1932.

84. *Proleg.*, I, p. 381.

85. *Proleg.*, II, pp. 299, 310.

86. E. Barker: *Principles of Social and Political Theory*, Oxford, 1961, pp. 5, 13.
87. *Proleg.*, I, pp. 350, 356 ff.
88. *Proleg.*, I, p. 254.
89. M. K. Aayad: *op. cit.*, p. 149.
90. *Proleg.*, I, p. 328.
91. *Proleg.*, I, p. 382.
92. *Proleg.*, I, p. 298.
93. *Proleg.*, I, pp. 59, 306, 307.
94. *Proleg.*, II, pp. 340, 341.
95. *Proleg.*, I, p. 454.

6

THE MUSCOVITE AUTOCRACY
(Written in collaboration with Ryszard Mitaszko)

ABSOLUTE rulers usually seek justification for their authority, as if they wanted to find grounds for their rule in some ideological argumentation. Referring to the supernatural as the source of their power did not always suffice and so attempts were made to find arguments for the absolute rule now in the need for a new and better social order, now in the necessity of defending the state against threats from without. However, apart from the form and the content of the arguments for absolutism, and apart from its ideological justification, there always existed certain political practice not necessarily reflected in the doctrine. The edge of the absolute rule was directed either against the reactionary or against the progressive elements, hence this rule must be measured by its political function.

Yet neither the doctrine nor the practice can wholly explain the essence of the absolute rule, since the growth of unlimited power must be preceded by a proper atmosphere made up of objective factors which provide an enterprising individual with an opportunity for seizing power.

Such objective conditions for the development of a strong centralized power appeared sufficiently clear by the second half of the fifteenth century in the Grand Principality of Moscow which had, until then, been a cluster of independent duchies ruled by hereditary aristocracy—the boyars. The consolidation of the state had been precipitated by the constant threat to its boundaries from the Tartars and by the struggle to throw off their control. Centralized power was also strengthening the sense of security of the feudal nobility which at that time increased its income by imposing additional burdens on the serfs. Further, a strong rule was an important factor in the protection of a unified market which was emerging just then.

These tendencies towards the consolidation of the Russian provinces round Moscow were opposed by the separatism of the great feudal lords— the boyars, and the brothers of the grand prince, who wanted to see in the ruler merely first feudal lord reigning together with them. They derived inspiration and something like confirmation of their notions from the political organization of the neighbouring Poland where the nobiliary democracy effectively circumscribed the authority of their ruler. In these circumstances only conscious rulers, consistent and firm in their conduct of political affairs, could make use of the tendencies to unity and achieve the formation of a strong and consolidated state by limiting the importance of the feudal lords even by abolishing the class altogether. Those who distinguished themselves in this respect were the rulers of the Grand Principality of Moscow, later called the State of Muscovy. Their rule covered in succession the reign of a grandfather, father and son: Ivan III (1462–1505), his son Vasily III (1505–53) and finally Ivan IV called the Terrible (1547–84).

Throughout a period of over 120 years there was going on a process of gradual formation of autocratic rule, a process which was accompanied by a steady territorial expansion.

Ivan III succeeded in uniting all the Russian lands within one state which he raised to sovereignty by throwing off the yoke of the Golden Horde. After a number of well-conducted military campaigns his grandson, Ivan the Terrible, created a multinational, centralized empire. If Ivan III laid the foundations of an autocratic rule limiting the rights and privileges of the boyars, Ivan the Terrible was already able to develop a refined system of terror which practically put an end to the influence of the hereditary aristocracy.[1]

Ivan III set out, first of all, to control the boyars' right of departure (ot'ezd) which allowed them to choose the prince whom they served and in practice meant transference to the service of the grand prince of Lithuania. While put under the obligation to remain loyal to their ruler, the feudal lords also suffered restriction of the arbitrary privileges that they had as governors of provinces and towns, since the grand prince introduced in 1497 a uniform judicature, admitted representatives of local people to provincial courts, issued for many territories statutes regularizing the amount of taxes, revenues and legal dues. What is more, towards the end of the fifteenth century, on the prince's initiative, the first organs of central administration (prikazy) were formed, which developed during the next century into a competent and efficient instrument of government. Lastly, Ivan III diminished the importance of the boyars in the state by relying on the service gentry whom he often granted pomestya—conditionally-held estates to which was attached the duty of serving at the court or in the army. The land thus granted remained in the ownership of the ruler and its holder could not dispose of it freely. For these grants Ivan III used the newly conquered lands of Novgorod and Vyatka, from which he deported large numbers of feudal lords and rich merchants.

Ivan III felt that he was an absolute ruler in a united state; he controlled the boyars, restricted the freedom of his brothers and nephews and was even convinced that the choice of a successor was a matter to be decided freely by the grand prince himself.[2] He regarded his eldest son Vasily as holding a special right to the grand principality and left to him two-thirds of the country dividing the remainder among his four other male descendants. To Vasily he also granted the right of minting coins.

In his policy Ivan III relied on the clergy, giving in turn his support to the Church hierarchy, as the latter recognized his superiority over them and preached the doctrine of the divine origin of the power of grand prince.[3]

The Orthodox Church even originated the idea of treating Ivan III as the successor of the Byzantine Emperor and defender of the Eastern Church. The view found its partial justification in the marriage of Ivan III to Sofia Palaeologa. The marriage marks the adoption of the Byzantine ceremonial at the court of Moscow as well as the placing of the two-headed imperial eagle beside the figure of St. George on the prince's coat-of-arms. So convinced was Ivan III of his divine right to the throne that he refused to accept the title of king offered him by the German Emperor. About 15 years later his son Vasily was to act similarly when the Pope, Leo X, offered him the royal crown through his special legate.

Towards the close of the fifteenth century Moscow became an important partner in international politics. As Marx wrote: "Europe, which at the beginning of the reign of Ivan III barely noticed the existence of Moscow, sandwiched between the Tartars and the Lithuanians, was amazed at the unexpected emergency of a vast state on its eastern borders."

In international relations the Muscovite rulers revealed great prudence and caution. They used their friendly contacts with the West chiefly to draw to Russia scholars, architects, engineers, miners and physicians. At the same time they did not neglect good relations with Turkey. On the occasion of Sultan Selim's succession to the throne Vasily III sent to Turkey a special messenger with his greetings. His courtesy was returned and the Muscovite court was visited by the first Turkish envoy who caused a great sensation.

At the time of Vasily's death his son and successor, Ivan, was 3 years old.[4] The process of unification of the territories of Great Russia had been completed but the boyars still constituted an important political force which hindered the consolidation of the central rule.

The minority of the successor provided the feudal lords with an opportunity for seizing power. Russia came to be ruled by changing coteries of the boyars. Intrigues, plots and political murders gave rise to anarchy and insecurity in the country. In view of the ever-deepening chaos the Orthodox Church saw that the state could be saved by a strong central power. On 16 January 1547 the metropolitan of Moscow, Makary, crowned the 17-year-old Ivan as the tsar of Russia. The government of the state was *de facto* taken over by the "Chosen Council" which included many men who truly desired to improve the internal relations and to strengthen the central power through reform and compromise.[5]

The main figures in the "Chosen Council" were Silvester and Alexiey Adashev; the former, a priest of high moral standing who regarded the education of the people as the principal condition of the restoration of state, exercised a considerable influence on the sensitive personality of the young tsar; the latter, a statesman of high stature, had in his hands the main strings of internal and external policy of the country.

The way in which the young monarch thought and reacted can be gathered from his letter to Adashev.

> You are neither rich nor of high descent, Alexiey, [wrote Ivan], but you are virtuous. I am entrusting to you this high position not at your request but out of the need of my soul, which is drawn to such as yourself, who can satisfy my anxiety about those miserable ones whose fate God has left in my care. Fear not the rich or the mighty when they disdain honour and break the law. Be not deceived by the false tears of the poor, when they slander the rich out of envy. Examine all things fully and tell me the truth fearing only God's judgment.[6]

The "Chosen Council" succeeded in carrying through a number of essential reforms. The boyars were removed from territorial administration and were replaced by locally elected officials; criminal justice and the collection of taxes passed into the hands of elected "distinct elders". The codification, started under Ivan III, was enlarged and grew into a collection of ordinances of material law. Military service was reformed and came to be defined according to the size of the *pomestye*, i.e. land held by a man. At the same time the lands of the boyars were used to enlarge the holdings of those who had too little to have the obligation of military service. An important improvement came when army commanders began to be nominated. The Church, on its side, on the initiative of metropolitan Makary, introduced uniform rites and listed the saints for worship in the whole state.

After several years differences arose between the "Chosen Council" and the tsar; they became apparent first when the members of the Council were unwilling to swear allegiance to the minor son of Ivan the Terrible during the latter's illness. The conflict deepened when the tsar—against the advice of the "Chosen Council"—conducted a war against Livonia in the hope of binding Russia to Europe through the Baltic Sea. The defeats suffered in this war, the criticism of the tsar's policy expressed by the boyars and the Church, lastly—the desertion to Lithuania of Prince Andrey Kurbsky filled the cup of the tsar's bitterness. In 1565, in highly dramatic circumstances, after a threat of abdication the tsar received unlimited power and the rule of terror started.[7] He introduced truly revolutionary measures to create an efficient and blindly obedient instrument of government in the country. He marked out a number of districts (*oprichnina*) from which to deport the boyars and the princes together with their families and servants. In their place he settled 1000 men (*oprichniki*) unreservedly loyal to him and representing different strata of society. The *oprichnina* became a camp ruled by military methods, while the remaining parts of the country retained the traditional administration. The number of the *oprichniki* soon grew to 6000 and the territory covered by the *oprichnina* included rich industrial and commercial towns, important routes and, above all, roads leading to the shores of the Baltic Sea. Riders clad in black, with bundles of twigs and dogs' heads fastened to the saddles as symbols of loyalty and zeal in the struggle against internal enemies, rode across the lands of the *oprichnina* bringing terror and destruction. With the aid of terror they broke down the political power of the boyars but at the same time they brought about depopulation and economic ruin of Russia's richest lands.[8] However, two different systems of administration could not exist side by side within one state for long. Russia needed a single system of government and a single administration. In 1572 the tsar abolished the *oprichnina* and the *oprichniki*. Even the use of these names came to be forbidden and they became only expressions of contempt.

Yet the *oprichnina* played an important role in transforming the Russian state organization. The English ambassador who visited Moscow in 1558, i.e. already after the death of Ivan the Terrible, called the *oprichnina*—for all the evil that it had caused—a truly political enterprise, undertaken to end the social leadership of the nobility and to create the foundations of a new state organization.

While during the reign of Ivan III and his son Vasily III the official political doctrine was formulated by ecclesiastical circles, which coloured it strongly with religion, under Ivan the Terrible the ideology of absolute power and of struggle against the boyars was developed by the tsar and by the enterprising condottiere Ivan Peresvetov.

Thus uniform, centralized power was being formed on the basis of two sets of political views: ecclesiastic and secular.[9] The former originated in the controversy which went on at the end of the fifteenth century on the subject of the moral regeneration of the clergy through the secularization of Church estates. Nil Sorsky, who was more a philosopher and thinker than a saint and miracle-maker, for which his contemporaries took him, began to criticize the external splendour of the eastern rite. He wanted to understand while believing and to believe while thinking. He taught that the most ecstatic worship, prayers, fast and asceticism cannot change a man unless they are accompanied by inner perfection of human personality. Tolerant towards outward piety he yet asserted ironically that "it is better to drink wine reasonably than water unreasonably". His strongest attack, however, was directed against the enormous ecclesiastic estates which, in his opinion, were the source of the Church's weakness because they were depraving the clergy. For the clergy, he taught, direct all their effort towards the acquisition, maintainance and administration of the estates while, if they were to live the life of poverty and were to support themselves by the work of their hands, they would regain moral strength and would win back the authority of the Church.

The criticism of Nil Sorsky brought a response from Joseph of Volokolamsk, the founder and abbot of a rich monastery near the place which gave him his name. He expressed the views of the Church hierarchy demanding that ecclesiastic estates be retained, but at the same time he was aware that without help from the state the Church could not stop the drive towards reform. In exchange for a strong support of the power of the grand prince Ivan III took the side of the ecclesiastic hierarchy. In this situation Joseph of Volokolamsk became a spokesman of the theocratic absolutism of Muscovite rulers. In his monumental work *Prosvetitel* (*Illuminator*), directed against the heretics, he presented the tsar as a god who resembles people only in his appearance while in essence he has the authority of God and thus his conduct must remain outside earthly categories. According to him obeying the tsar was a religious duty of every person not excluding the priests. Joseph of Volokolamsk also argued that the tsar ought to be the protector and defender of the Eastern Church.

Already in the lifetime of Ivan III and even more so during the reign of Vasily III Moscow was styled in ecclesiastic circles "the third Rome" and its monarch—the new Emperor Constantine.[10] The view was also spread that the Union of Florence had been a betrayal of the Orthodox Church and the fall of the Byzantine Empire came as a punishment, while the Byzantine heritage passed to Moscow and its ruler.

Lastly, in the group of Church doctrines belongs the conception of state organization worked out by Silvester Adashev, the main figure of the "Church Council". He undoubtedly drew inspiration for his views from the ideas of Nil Sorsky. Silvester advocated a single state with centralized power rooted not in force or terror but in a high moral standard of the citizens. He postulated absolute ethical puritanism achieved through the perfection of human personality, through inner discipline and self-control, which were, above all, to develop in the fathers of families respect for human dignity, decency, honesty and sober judgement. He started with an assumption that morality cannot be divided into private and public. The state was in his view a collection of families governed by exemplary fathers.

Silvester composed for his son an everyday guidebook for a good householder and father of family—*Domostroy*. We learn from it that he himself freed all his serfs and gave them land. He also bought serfs from other men and gave them freedom. In accordance with his own conduct he bid his son be modest, absolutely faithful to his wife and restrain the passions generating evil. Silvester believed that personal example is the best educational method; he himself had among his contemporaries the reputation of a highly moral man and for a number of years exercised a strong influence on the mind of the young tsar.

However, it was not Silvester's conception of state that was significant for the reign of Ivan the Terrible, but the secular doctrine developed outside Church circles. This second group of doctrines reveals the main conflict of the period—the struggle between the boyars and the service gentry, which, unlike the same class in Poland, depended directly on the favour of the tsar on whose decision hung the ownership of their estates and their careers.

While the boyars aimed at limiting the tsar's authority through their delegates to the Duma and at preserving their feudal privileges, those representing the ideology of the gentry called for abolishing the power of the magnates and for strengthening the government of the state which would be left in the hands of an autocratic tsar.

The camp of the boyars found its leader and theorist in the person of Prince Andrey Kurbsky who polemized with Ivan the Terrible in his letters to the tsar written after his desertion to Lithuania.[11]

Kurbsky did not try to turn history back, he did not demand the reestablishment of the former division of state into provinces, nor did he advocate feudal partition; he simply wanted the aristocracy to share power with the tsar, realizing that under the pressure of reality the boyars could at best achieve a compromise between the old order and the new.

The tsar, on the other hand, firmly rejected in his writings the doctrine of the political compromise. He appears in those writings not only as a man reorganizing his state by means of terror, but also as a talented publicist. For Ivan the Terrible his pen was one of the means of reforming the organization of the Russian State. He expounded his views on the limitless nature of the tsar's power in his correspondence with Prince Kurbsky, in his letter to one of the most important *oprichniki*—Vasily Gryazny and in a message to Kirillo-Belozersky monastery.[12]

In his letters he presented—in the manner of describing a prophetic vision—his idea of divinity and illimitability of the tsar's authority, inherited from his ancestors. Convinced that he had an indisputable right to dispose of the property and the lives of his subjects he wrote to Kurbsky:

> We are free both to reward our servants and to punish them with death. [. . .] The tsar ought to be wise: sometimes soft, sometimes severe; towards the good he ought to be kind and merciful, towards the evil—severe and cruel. And if such is not his conduct, then he is no ruler, for a ruler arouses fear not in those who do good, but in those who do evil. . . . You want not to fear the ruler? Then do good, and if you do evil, live in fear, for a tsar carries his sword not in vain but to punish evil-doers and to reward the just.[13]

Nor did Ivan the Terrible have any doubt that he had power over the Church and that interference of ecclesiastics in secular matters was sinful and deserved punishment.[14]

For all the merits of Ivan's writings the finest political writer of his reign was Ivan Semyonovitch Peresvetov, whose views reflected clearly the interests of the gentry struggling together with the tsar against the aristocratic boyars.[15]

Peresvetov himself descended from humble Lithuanian gentry. At first warring was his favourite occupation; he served at the court of voivode Tęczyński, then went to Hungary to fight under the banner of John Zápolyai against the Habsburgs. While staying there he became acquainted with the Turkish army and the Turkish State organization; traces of this are found in his writings. After 3 years in Hungary he went to the court of the hospodar of Wallachia, probably with some political mission. He again joined the troops of Tęczyński to fight, this time on the side of the Habsburgs against John Zápolyai, Finally, in 1538, he went to Moscow for good. There he presented at the court his project of manufacturing hussars' shields, specially good for use in warfare against Tartars. At first the project was favourably received and Peresvetov was even given an estate and craftsmen for his workshop. However, after a time—probably as a result of wider use of fire-arms—the production of shields ceased to arouse interest. Peresvetov got into financial difficulties and even lost the fortune that he had brought from Poland. He wrote with bitterness about this period of his life ascribing his ill luck to the intrigues of the boyars who just then seized the opportunity of the tsar's minority to rob the country and the people.

As a publicist Peresvetov entered the arena of political writing about 1548, after the tsar had already attained his majority. At that time, after long years of the boyars' rule, the government passed into the hands of the "Chosen Council", whose members agreed on one point: that the central power in the country needed consolidation, but advocated different ways and methods of this consolidation, having in view the interests of certain social groups. Peresvetov was the only man who managed to present in his writings a full project of reform which made them one of the most important documents of the socio-political situation in Russia in the middle of the sixteenth century.[16]

In his writings Peresvetov dealt principally with two main problems: the criticism of the abuses committed by the boyars during the minority of Ivan the Terrible; and the project of specific socio-political reforms.[17] In his treatment these problems are inseparable, since the projected reforms were meant to make up for the harm done by the rule of the boyars.

Peresvetov openly criticized the rule of the boyars only in his *Supplications*, while in all the other works he expressed his criticism of the conditions in Russia in the form of an accusation of the Byzantine aristocracy from the time of Emperor Constantine's minority. The placing of action in Byzantium was meant as a disguise which permitted the author to treat historical events freely and to depict in the reign of Constantine—contrary to evidence

—a situation and circumstances clearly derived from the time of Ivan the Terrible in Russia.[18]

In his *A Tale of Sultan Mahmet* he declares that the Greeks were punished for violating "God's will", because, during the minority of Emperor Constantine, who was a wise and just ruler, the magnates used superstition and intrigue to bring him under their control, and then they put his wisdom to sleep and made his sword hang still by their "devilish tricks and intrigues". For this the Lord, who dislikes "deceit, pride and idleness" punished them in his merciless wrath. Peresvetov gave a lurid picture of the abuses of aristrocracy who had seized the opportunity of the tsar's minority "to draw dishonest wealth out of the blood and tears of mankind".[19] The nobles, suffering from the ruthless conduct of the magnates, were no longer willing to defend their country, and the lords themselves lost their fighting spirit in pursuit of riches.

The criticism of Byzantine society was put into the mouth of the Sultan of Turkey who simultaneously suggested a number of reforms. Towards the end of the book the critic assumed a moralizing tone, when the Latin scholars tell the Greeks that the Lord was angry with them for their "pride and lies" and gave them away to the sultan as slaves.

The charges made against the aristocracy in *A Tale of Sultan Mahmet* must have seemed to the author too mild, because he accused the magnates directly and much more violently in *A Tale of Emperor Constantine*.[20]

In *The Great Supplication*—the last of all the works that are known to have been written by Peresvetov—the author asserted openly that abuses similar to those committed at Constantinople were perpetrated by the Russian boyars during the minority of Ivan the Terrible. Here Peresvetov gave up allegory and similar literary devices and openly made references to the situation in Russia. He put into the mouth of the Wallachian Hospodar Peter the warning that history could repeat itself and Moscow could share the fate of Byzantium if the tsar did not bring the boyars under control and did not reform the government of the state thoroughly. In his view any means were justified so long as they restrained the power of the boyars; the boyars could even be punished without a court trial, because they were a threat to the state. But Peresvetov did not confine himself to a mere branding of the abuses of the boyars; he criticized the whole feudal system and argued that the Muscovite Empire could be saved by the "truth", by which he meant a system of government in which strong, centralized power, resting on a competent and courageous army, would protect the interests of the masses of nobility.

The criticism of the government of Russia in the middle of the sixteenth century was only one aspect of Peresvetov's doctrine; it is a kind of background against which he presented his conception of the ideal state of "truth".

In the part containing his positive views the most important problems are those of the ruler and the army. They form the backbone of the centralized, nobiliary monarchy advocated by Peresvetov. He was convinced that the strength of the state depended on the role of a "wise and fear-inspiring tsar". The fear of the power wielded by the ruler arouses respect for the state and its laws being thus a guarantee of order and harmony. "The tsar cannot reign without terror", wrote Peresvetov, for "a State without terror is like unto a horse that the tsar would ride without a bridle".[21] Force, however, cannot serve the whims of the ruler, for "terror" is only a way realizing "truth", which the tsar recognizes through his "wisdom". Thus the confines of absolutism are marked by two concepts: that of wisdom and that of truth, which jointly signify an absolute power protecting the interests of the nobility. In Peresvetov's conception the range of power of the autocratic ruler covers four fields: legislation, finance, administration of justice and military affairs. His ideal ruler, Sultan Mahmet, himself issues laws and regulations, himself defines the salaries of his knights and dignitaries, appoints judges and supervises their work, nominates officers to manage his finances, and, lastly, he himself is the chief commander of his army. In executing his wide power the sultan may listen to the opinion of his Privy Council without an obligation of following it. Peresvetov spoke of a "wise council" or a "wise man" and repeatedly emphasized the advisory nature of these organs which were to remain in the shade of the all-powerful tsar.

Peresvetov realized that the power of the tsar depended on a disciplined and valiant army. "The tsar is strong and famous for his knights."[22] Hence the problem of the army has in his doctrine an importance almost equal to the problem of the ruler. He thought that a regular army should be formed, composed of free men who would receive payment and whose advancement and rank would depend only on their personal courage, prudence and merit. Thus organized the army should be divided into troops defending the boundaries of the State and the tsar's bodyguard.[23]

While discussing the reorganization of the army, Peresvetov touched on the problem of freedom which in his view is an indispensable condition of valour, ambition and courage. "In a State where people live in servitude", he wrote, "none are valiant in the fight against the enemy, for a slave fears not dishonour, nor does he care for his good name."[24] When, on the other hand, the ruler frees the people who were in the power of the aristocrats, then in his service they will be brave. "Only the free are valiant; they play with death and fight the enemy fiercely."[25]

In Peresvetov's conception we often sense the coolness of Machiavellian judgement, especially when we read that the state of "truth" is above all other values, for, as the author asserts, "where truth is not, nothing else is, for God loves not belief but truth."

NOTES

1. The forming of the foundations of autocracy and with it the modern State organization in Russia has been one of the most controversial problems in the Russian historiography since the time of Karamzin. There are two opposite ways of viewing the problem: one justifying everything done by the tsars—even the most cruel murders—on account of the political successes thus achieved; the other—evaluating the conduct of the ruler on ethical grounds and from the point of view of social interest. For the former view see, e.g. Р. И. Виппэр: Иван Грозный, Moscow, 1944; for the latter see, e.g. Н. М. Карамзин, С. М. Соловъев, С. В. Веселовский, А. А. Зимин.

The different evaluations of the policy of Ivan the Terrible depend largely on a specific political situation. It seems that, to some extent, these factors underlie the discussion and diametrically opposed evaluations of the reign of Ivan the Terrible which are found in the contemporary historiography in the Soviet Union.

2. J. L. I. Fennel: *Ivan the Great of Moscow*, London, 1961, pp. 287 ff.

3. А. А. Зимин: О политической доктрине Иосифа Волоцкого, "Труды ОДРЛ", vol. IX, Moscow, 1953, pp. 174 ff.

4. С. Ф. Платонов: Иван Грозный, Petrograd 1923; А. Е. Пресняков: Эпоха Грозного в общем историческом освещении, "Анналы", Petrograd, 1922; И. И. Смирнов: Иван Грозный, Leningrad, 1944.

5. С. В. Бахрушин: "Избранная Рада" Ивана Грозного, "Исторические записки", vol. 15, 1945, pp. 49 ff.

6. Quoted after Н. М. Карамзин: История государства российского, vol. 8, St. Petersburg, 1834, p. 99.

7. A review of the Russian literature on the reign of Ivan the Terrible can be found in the work by G. H. Bolsover: *Ivan the Terrible in Russian Historiography*, included in a collected work: *Transactions of the Royal Historical Society*, vol. 7, London, 1957, pp. 71–89.

8. П. А. Садиков: Царь и опричник, "Исторический сборник", I, Petrograd 1924; Щ. А. Садиков: Очерки по истории опричнины, publication of the Soviet Academy of Sciences, series of History and Philosophy, vol. VII, No. 5, pp. 448 ff. Г. Штаден: О Москве Ивана Грозного. Записки немца-опричника, Moscow, 1925; С. Б. Веселовский: Синодик опальных царя Ивана как исторический источник, "Проблемы источниковедения", Сборник третий, publication of the Soviet Academy of Sciences, Moscow–Leningrad, 1940; С. Б. Веселовский: Исследования по истории опричнины, Moscow, 1963; А. А. Зимин: Опричнина Ивана Грозного, Изд. "Мысль", Moscow, 1964.

9. М. В. Довнар-Запольский: Политические партии первой половины XVI века и власть Московского царя [in:] Русская история в очерках и статьях, vol. II, Moscow, 1910, pp. 152 ff.

10. "Moscow is the third Rome and there will not be another." See А. А. Зимин: И. С. Пересветов и его современники, publication of the Soviet Academy of Sciences, Moscow, 1958, pp. 409 ff.

11. А. М. Курбский Сочинения, St. Petersburg, 1914.

12. Послания Ивана Грозного, publication of the Soviet Academy of Sciences, Moscow–Leningrad, 1951.

13. *Op. cit.*, pp. 30, 20.

14. М. Н. Коваленский: Из истории государственной власти в России, Moscow, 1905; Г. Н. Плеханов: История русской общественной мысли, vol. I, Moscow, 1914.

15. А. А. Зимин: И. С. Пересветов и русские вольнодумцы XVI века, "Вопросы истории религии и атеизма", Сборник III, Moscow, 1955; А. Л. Саккетти: Политическая программа И. С. Пересветова, "Вестник Моск. университета", серия общественных наук, вып. I, 1955, pp. 107–17.

16. The works of Peresvetov include 1. *The Founding and the Conquest of Tsarogrod*, 2. *A Tale of Books*, 3. *A Tale of Sultan Mahmet*, 4. *The First Prediction of the Doctors and Philosophers*, 5. *The Small Supplication*, 6. *The Second Prediction of the Philosophers*, 7. *A Tale of Tsar Constantine*, 8. *Conclusion*, 9. *The Great Supplication*.

17.   O. W. Trachtenberg: *Myśl społeczno-polityczna w Rosji w XV–XVII wieku* [in:] *Z dziejów filozofii rosyjskiej* (Polish translation), Warsaw, 1953, p. 93. Trachtenberg thinks that the practical part of Peresvetov's projects is connected with the policy of Ivan the Terrible after 1564 and especially with the organization of the *oprichnina*.

18.   А. А. Зимин: И. С. Пересветов и его современники, *op. cit.*

19.   Сочинения И. С. Пересветова, Moscow–Leningrad, 1956, p. 152—*A Tale of Sultan Mahmet.*

20.   В. Ф. Ржига: И. С. Пересветов, публицист XVI века, Moscow, 1908.

21.   Сочинения Пересветова, p. 153.

22.   *Op. cit.*, p. 156.

23.   A good evaluation of the military problems in the doctrine of Peresvetov can be found in A. Podraza: *Iwan Pereswietow, rosyjski pisarz polityczny XVI w.* [in:] *Odrodzenie i Reformacja w Polsce*, vol. VI, Warsaw, 1961, p. 224.

24.   Сочинения Пересветова, p. 157.

25.   *Op. cit.*, p. 176.

7

THE JAGIELLONIAN DYNASTY

(Written in collaboration with Jan Malarczyk)

THE aim of this Chapter is to provide a synthetic presentation of Polish political doctrines under Jagiellonian rule. In the history of this country it was a time of radical changes which can be compared—apart from their direction—to those which occurred after World War II.

To begin with, the geographic location of Poland was changing. Gradually, under the pressure of the Germans the Poles were leaving the lands in the basin of the upper Oder retaining only the areas over the Warta river. At the same time there was a marked shifting of the eastern border which, at the time of the Jagiellonian monarchy, reached as far as the Dniester, the Dnieper, the Dvina and the Niemen, while the basin of the river Vistula became the centre of the country.

Owing to these vital territorial shifts the ethnic and religious composition of Poland was also changing. Until then Poland had been homogenous as far as nationality was concerned and almost wholly bound to the Roman Church, but as a result of the expansion eastward the country became multinational and nearly half of its population belonged to the Orthodox Church. The domes of Orthodox churches standing side by side with the spires of the Catholic churches symbolized the eastward expansion and consequent religious conflicts. Towards the end of the sixteenth century Poland covered an area of about 800,000 km² and had over $7\frac{1}{2}$ million population, out of which less than 3 million were living in the truly Polish lands, that is in Greater Poland, Lesser Poland and Mazovia.

However, geographical, ethnic and religious changes were not the only ones that occurred at the time of the Jagiellonian monarchy. During this period, too, Poland acquired important economic status and became the granary of Europe as the consumption of grain increased rapidly. From the end of the fifteenth century and throughout the sixteenth the population in Western Europe was increasing steadily; about 1500 the population of the Empire was approximately twice the number that it had been in the eleventh century, i.e. it probably reached 12 million people, while towards the sixteenth century it went up to 20 million. The demand for agricultural products was increasing as were also the prices of those products, the more so because there was emigration from the country to towns. During the sixteenth century the prices of agricultural products, particularly of grain, went up in different European countries 150–200%. No small role was played in this process by the influx of precious metals which were brought from America in such quantities that their amount trebled during the sixteenth century compared with the preceding century.

Owing to this high demand for agricultural products the Polish gentry were abandoning their military craft in order to cultivate the land. Manors, whose economy was based on the unpaid labour of the serfs treated like slaves, grew in size by legal means and illegal. The expansion eastward together with the exploitation of the peasants made it possible for the gentry to produce more grain and to export it. While towards the end of the fifteenth century (1492) 25,795 tons of grain were sent annually through Gdansk, in the middle of the next century (1563) the quantity of grain exported by the same route went up to 171,366 tons annually.[1]

Seeking still greater gain the gentry were imposing economic and political restrictions on the Polish townspeople. They imposed price lists on towns and selfishly obtained for themselves exemption from duties on exported grain as well as a free import of luxury articles from abroad, thus undermining the economic position of the Polish towns. Political discrimination against townspeople took various forms: they were forbidden to buy land, barred from higher offices—both secular and ecclesiastical, they had no representatives in the Diet; finally, whole municipal districts were deprived of local government. Half a million of the gentry—for such was their number in the middle of the sixteenth century—dominated the other estates making Poland their own country.

The conflicts between the gentry of the middle level and the aristocracy determined the political line until the time when the magnates seized the whole power. For, notwithstanding the oft repeated declaration of equality among members of the gentry, the economic differences within the class increased steadily. The accumulating of more and more land in the hands of the aristocracy went on at the expense of crown property and also as a consequence of the expansion into the Ukraine; it resulted in the rise of immense fortunes. Already towards the end of the sixteenth century the lands of the magnates were transformed more and more into independent economic and political districts. A great feudal lord had absolute power over the people living on his land; he established private towns, built fortresses, had his own administration and his own army, he sometimes even regulated his politics independently of the country's interests. This increasing independence of some powerful nobles was to transform Poland in the future into a sort of federation of magnate's states, each with absolute rule within and with a weak rule of the king at the top.

But before this aristocratic rule came to prevail, the gentry-dominated Poland had a golden age under the reign of the last Jagiellonians.

The gentry were at that time changing their whole way of living, their

manners, costume, houses and feeding habits, but above all they began to
educate themselves, both in the country and abroad. This trend towards
education is particularly observable in the first six decades of the sixteenth
century. That time was also one of great national creativity; masterpieces
of literature came to be written in the vernacular; Polish political thought
aroused respect throughout Europe, and the social ideas of the Polish
Brethren (the Arians) were admired for decades by the finest minds.

Every greatness, however, has its own petty elements. In the case of
Polish history they were to prove fatal. The exclusiveness of the gentry,
their isolation from the rest of society depraved their character and led to
negative results in economic and political life. Polish trade and commerce
were paralysed by the privileges of the gentry and could not provide a basis
for the growth of a strong middle class. Thus the king had no ally except
the gentry, and when he was not able to make use of the antagonism
between the gentry and the nobility, he had to give in wholly to the oligarchy of the feudal lords.

The feeling of superiority that prevailed among the gentry made them
scorn the other estates and hold all work in contempt; they were vain and
convinced—without any grounds—that their system of government was ideal
and this attitude resulted in a complete loss of the sense of reality.

The Jagiellonian monarchy has been the subject of many studies, monographic or dealing with particular aspects of the times. The present outline
will not bring to light any new facts, nor will it attempt to throw new
light on the facts already known; its aim is to focus attention on some of
the problems that shaped the politics of the period and were the source
of political ideas. Since a certain simplification is unavoidable in any
synthesis and classification, the epoch has been divided here into three
periods according to the basic problems which were different in different
periods.

The first of the periods covers the times of Władysław Jagiello (1386–
1434); its characteristic feature is the shifting of Polish political interest
eastward. The essential problem of the time was determining the attitude
of the Polish Catholic Church to the members of the Greek Orthodox
Church, the heathens and the Teutonic Knights.

The reign of the second generation of the Jagiellonians and particularly
the time of Casimir IV (1445–92) is the second period—and the one during
which, as a result of the dynastic expansion, the main problem is the
sovereignty of the state and the central rule.

Finally, the third period is that of the reign of the grandsons and of the
great-grandson of Władysław Jagiello, in particular the reign of Sigismund I
(1506–48) and the reign of the last Jagiellonian on the Polish throne,
Sigismund Augustus (1548–72). At that time both political theory and
political practice were preoccupied with three key problems: the reform

of the state, the reform of the Church in connection with the Reformation in Poland, and finally, the social affairs raised by the Polish Brethren.

The nobles of Lesser Poland who were *de facto* rulers of the country after the death of Casimir the Great wanted by the conversion of the heathen Lithuania to form a united front against the Teutonic Knights. To achieve this they arranged the marriage of the 11-year-old Jadwiga, daughter of King Louis of Hungary and already the Queen of Poland, to Władysław Jagiello, Grand-Duke of Lithuania. For by remaining heathen Lithuania gave justification to the exterminating crusades undertaken by the Teutonic Knights. The step taken by the magnates of Lesser Poland is so described in Dlugosz's *Chronicle*: "The majority of wiser and more prudent men, in an attempt to spread wide the Christian faith as well as to safeguard the Polish Kingdom and to secure other profits which Lithuania could offer, counselled to call Jagiello to the Polish throne. . . ."[2]

When the converted Lithuanian ruler received the Polish crown, he faced two opposing political conceptions manifesting themselves in religious form characteristic of the doctrines of those times. Lithuania, of which Władysław Jagiello was the Grand-Duke, had ever since the thirteenth century experienced the pressure of two German orders: the Knights of the Sword and the Teutonic Knights; and under this pressure it developed into a compact political organization to become one of the stronger countries in Eastern Europe.

When Władysław Jagiello received the Catholic faith in one part of the heathen Lithuania, he was departing from the political conceptions of his father and his brothers who had endeavoured to create a united Lithuanian and Ruthenian State, within whose boundaries there would be the Holy See of the Orthodox Church. Władysław's father, Olgierd, had married a Ruthenian princess and had accepted the Eastern faith. Similarly, the new king's brothers, Skirgiello, Korybut and Lingwen, were of the same religion. The Ruthenian culture was boldly penetrating into Lithuania. Similarly, the influence of the Orthodox Church was growing there, and the influence of the Ruthenian language was likewise increasing, as this was the official language at the court of the Grand-Duke. It was vital for Lithuania to make their part of Ruthenia independent in religious matters of the authority of the Orthodox Church in Moscow. The knights of the Teutonic Order, on their part, maintained that the Lithuanians treated their patriarch as the Pope of the Orthodox Church. The acceptance of Catholicism by Lithuania drew the country into the Polish sphere of influence and led to closing its territory against the missionary efforts of the Teutonic Order which thus lost justification for its activity. But at the same time the very idea of a united Ruthenian and Lithuanian State with the Eastern rite in it, began to lose ground, if it was not altogether abandoned. The Union of Horodło, signed in 1413, extended the privileges of the Polish gentry to the Lithuanians newly converted to Catholicism creating thus a new *élite*, while an overwhelming majority of the Lithuanian gentry professing the Eastern rite was excluded from political influence, even though complete tolerance prevailed in religious matters.

Jagiello abandoned the idea of a Ruthenian and Lithuanian federation in order to form a united front of the Poles and the Lithuanians against the Teutonic Order which was an advocate of the German idea of imperial universalism.

When, in 1386, Jagiello came to the Polish throne, 150 years had already elapsed from the time when the Teutonic Order had been brought to the land of Chełmo. From that time onward the Knights of the Order had been gradually extending their domain in order to convert with the sword the recalcitrant Prussians; whenever it was necessary they quoted the privileges conferred on them by the Popes—Clement IV and Alexander IV—as well as those conferred by Emperor Frederick II and giving the Order all the lands won from the enemies of the Church; this last category included as a rule the pagans, the heretics and those following the Eastern rite. In this atmosphere of crusades and with considerable help from European knighthood the Knights of the Order were building their state in the estuary of the Vistula, thus seizing control of the main artery and trading route that Poland had. In 1309 the residence of the Grand-Master of the Order was moved to Malborg which also became the capital of this strange creation—the state ruled by the Order. The organization of this state was somewhat like ancient Sparta projected into the conditions of the Middle Ages. At the dawn of the fifteenth century the Teutonic Knights ruled a wide, belt-like territory stretching along the Baltic coast from Leba to Klaipeda and cutting like a wedge over 150 km into Poland. These lands were under the absolute rule of the Order whose members were divided into knights, priests and serving brothers. Affairs of government were in the hands of the knights. The head of the state, the Grand-Master (*Hochmeister*), was elected and stayed in office till his death; he had five ministers (*oberste Gebietiger*) to assist him. Responsible to the Grand-Master were the provincial masters, each of whom was the head of a province and under them were the district chiefs. Monastic discipline coupled with religious fanaticism enabled the Knights simultaneously to keep in obedience the inhabitants of the lands held by the Order and to conduct wars of conquest. Twice a year did the Knights undertake regular expeditions against infidels: on 2 February, the feast of the Purification of Our Lady, and on 15 August, the feast of the Assumption, thus making the expeditions their religious duty. For the Order was professing and spreading the doctrine of Henry de Segusio, the principal canonist of the thirteenth century, justifying religious wars. The Knights found support for their practice in the statements of the canonist that no laws, human or divine, apply to infidels and that, in view of this, war against the pagans is always allowed and always just. Hence the spreading of the Catholic faith by military means was a religious duty and the conquest of pagan land as well as subjugation of infidels were justified.

Jagiello met the German expansion with a Polish–Lithuanian alliance bringing about in this way a war within the Christian world. This step had to be explained on the grounds of religio-political doctrine, the more so as the Teutonic Knights presented to Europe the defeat that they suffered at Grunwald in 1410 as a victory of barbarity and paganism over the Church. Now, Poland, defending her policy before the whole Christian world, had to formulate clearly and exactly her conceptions opposing the assertions of the Order which accused Jagiello and tried to have Poland condemned at the Council of Constance in 1414. At that very moment the Poles succeeded in producing an independent and original political conception which became a significant contribution to the European political thought of the time.

The Polish doctrine was shaped under the influence of the struggle against the Teutonic Order and owed its inspiration to the views of the Czech preachers who combined ecclesiastical reform with anti-German movements. Under the standard of the Hussite movement the Czech people were victoriously opposing the German element that had long been suppressing them. Common enmity towards the Germans united the two nations whose languages were so like each other that the Polish people easily understood the Czech preachers. Having no dynasty of their own the Czechs offered their crown to the victor of Grunwald in order to unite the two nations within one state.

Ten years before his death, Władysław Jagiello broke with the Hussite Czechs, adopting the political ideas of Rome. What followed was a policy of conciliation towards the Order; the Polish doctrine opposed to the German conceptions was in a way discarded. In 1424 Jagiello formally condemned the Hussites. Inquisitors were then appointed for the persecution of heretics, persons returning from Bohemia were examined by priests, those sympathizing with the Hussite movement were threatened with confiscation of property and forfeiting the privileges of nobility. In order to break all ties between Poland and Bohemia even commerce between the two countries was stopped. The political conception of the Roman Curia triumphed in Poland and its epilogue was the tragic Polish–Hungarian crusade against the Turks ending with the defeat at Varna in 1444.

Among the political conceptions of the times of Władysław Jagiello the Polish doctrine, developed in polemic with the views of the Teutonic Knights, had a truly lasting value owing to its novel and progressive treatment of the problem of war and the attitude of Christianity towards infidels.

The creators of the doctrine were: Stanisław of Skarbimierz and a man a few years his junior—Paweł Włodkowic. Both had studied in Prague, both were professors of the Jagiellonian University and both held at different times the office of the rector of that university.

The battle of Grunwald separates the activity of Stanisław of Skarbimierz from the creative years of Paweł Włodkowic. When Władysław Jagiello, together with the nobles of Lesser Poland, was successfully organizing a wide military front against the Teutonic Knights, he found conceptual justification of his efforts in the sermons of Stanisław of Skarbimierz.

As a professor of law and the Rector of the Jagiellonian University, Stanisław of Skarbimierz confirmed the royal policy by his sermon *De bellis iustis* (*Of just wars*), which offered the king theoretical justification for this policy. He formulated a bold, new doctrine, directed against the policy of the Teutonic Knights even though specific conflicts are not mentioned there.[3] It was a matter of no small importance for Jagiello to hear it asserted from the point of view of Christianity and the Canon law that his efforts were leading to a just war.

The sermon starts with a definition of a just war which comes close to the views of a thirteenth-century Dominican Raymund of Penjafort, included in his manual for confessors. On the basis of quotations from the Bible and the norms of Canon law, Stanisław presented his idea of just wars, which are—according to him—only defensive wars. This kind of war fully justifies contracting alliances with, and using the assistance of, the infidels. The situation in which the attacked party finds itself (state of unavoidable necessity) permits it to make use of every means in the struggle against the enemy.

A just war is one caused by objective factors, such as defence of the native country, a struggle for the return of lands seized by the enemy, finally—attempts to restore peace. Further, the party conducting a just war must be motivated exclusively by a desire to defend itself, as any other motivation will make the war unjust.

The right of self-defence, which justifies wars, is a natural law binding equally and invariably both for Christians and infidels; hence infidels conduct just wars against Christians, if the latter invade them and their habitations. Thus it is inadmissible to wage wars against infidels with the intention of spreading the Christian faith. On the other hand, a war against Christians is just if they break peace; what is more, in such a war against wicked Christians one should use the help of infidels.

In the final portion of his sermon Stanisław of Skarbimierz spoke about the commendable death suffered in a just war. Exhorting people to obey a monarch engaged in a just war he supplied the king with arguments against those who were questioning his anti-German policy and were in doubt about the rightness of using the help of infidels and heretics in a struggle against the Teutonic Order. Thus the sermon propounds a bold and novel political doctrine about wars; it shows courage in breaking with the thesis—traditionally maintained in the Catholic world—about the obligation of an unending war against infidels.

Polish political doctrine, however, was to be developed a few years later by another law professor of the Jagiellonian University, Paweł Włodkowic.

After their defeat at Grunwald the Teutonic Knights charged that the Poles were maintaining an impious alliance with the heretics and the infidels, thanks to whom they had won the war, and also that they did not respect the privileges, received by the Order from the Popes and the Emperors, and giving it possession of the lands seized from pagans. The Poles, on the other hand, demanded the return of the lands illegally seized by the Knights.

The affairs of Poland and the Teutonic Order were discussed at the Council of Constance which convened in the autumn of 1414. The delegation to the Council had no easy task there, as the Teutonic Knights were assiduously courting general approval asserting that they were the defenders of Christianity against the invasion of barbarism. The Order met at Constance with the sympathy of European Knighthood which frequently participated in the looting campaigns undertaken by the Teutonic Knights under the pretense of converting infidels. Among the Polish delegates was Paweł Włodkowic, and the difficult task of conducting a theoretical polemic with the Order fell to him.[4] He had to develop and explain a doctrine—now no longer for his own country as did Stanisław of Skarbimierz—but in order to win for Polish views the most eminent representatives of the intellectual world of his time.

The writings of Włodkowic reveal an outline of the Polish political thought of his time.[5] Its principles are to be found first of all in a detailed study written by him in 1415 for the Fathers of the Council concerning the respective powers of the Pope and the Emperor over the heathens. The Rector of the Jagiellonian Alma Mater returned to his ideas 17 years later, almost towards the end of his life, in a letter to Bishop Zbigniew Olesnicki who was successfully placing Poland in the line of Rome's policy.[6] In order to disprove the assertions of the Teutonic Knights Włodkowic formulated, and in a sense even codified, the laws of nature in whose light the claims of the enemies of Poland became groundless. Although it was not his intention to write a systematic treatise, his polemic concerning the principles provided an opportunity for outlining a new Polish political doctrine. For Włodkowic developed a gift for combining academic knowledge with practical politics.

Viewing the Polish political conceptions with some simplification we see that it made several assumptions. Firstly, it posed the existence of laws obeyed by all nature. Among them is the law of universal struggle for the preservation of one's being. This law of self-defence, according to Stanisław of Skarbimierz, "could be observed in the behaviour of creatures without reason, which protect themselves as well as they can, and defend themselves and often rise and turn against one that strikes them".[7] From the law of self-defence issues another rule universally valid in nature; desire to maintain peace. For "not only reasonable creatures but also animals seek peace, as they avoid death and cessation in all manner, and likewise do plants, such as trees, which bud better if they are not shaken by winds. For this reason the branches of trees oppose those who want to break them off or sever them, and it would not be so if they did not wish for peace".[8]

Secondly, there are natural laws common to all people independently of their religion. Among such laws is ownership of which no one can wilfully be deprived. Similarly, freedom of religious convictions is a natural law obeyed by all reasonable creatures. Hence imposing religious beliefs by force is a breach of natural order.

In the group of natural laws one also finds the institution of power without which no human society can exist. However, only two kinds of power are justifiable on the ground of natural law; the one that is given by God and the one which the subjects accept. Power imposed by force and violence, on the other hand, is contrary to the laws of nature.

Thirdly, there are natural laws regulating the coexistence within a human society. The mutual relations of people have their foundation in the virtue of love which is "above all other virtues in importance", while "the cruelty of hypocrites is worse than any other crime or sin".[9] The injunction that should be generally obeyed in human interrelations is: "thou shalt not do to another what thou dost not want done to thee".[10] Hence it is necessary to maintain friendly relations not only among the countries of Christianity but also with the pagans. The same applies to the conclusion of treaties and agreements which "are observed even among barbarian nations on the strength of the natural law".[11]

Fourthly, Włodkowic endorsed fully the conception of just wars worked out by his academic colleague, Stanisław of Skarbimierz—a conception which affected the Polish doctrine of the time of the Council of Constance. Making the principles of the natural law his starting point Włodkowic argued that those principles were binding for the Pope and even more so for the Emperor. In view of this all privileges and all theories that are contrary to the law of nature are worthless, a statement which—when applied to the conflict between Poland and the Teutonic order—amounted to a total denial of any justification for the Order's existence and activity.

Apart from the problems related to the conflict with the Teutonic Knights the Polish doctrine put forward a novel theoretical concept: that the heathen and Christian state authority considered in terms of the natural law may stand in opposition to the idea of universalism both papal and imperial.

In the second half of the year 1416 there appeared in Constance a libel on Poland penned by a Dominican, John Falkenberg, who was calling, on behalf of the defence of religion, to an uncompromising fight against, and the destruction of, the Poles and their King who together—according to the author—had gone back to paganism and were working for the ruin of Christianity. In spite of energetic protests from the Polish delegation neither the Council nor the Pope condemned Falkenberg's libel. The affair dragged on for several years after the closing of the Council, because Polish relations with the Hussite Bohemia aroused considerable fears and objections both on the part of Pope Martin V and on the part of Emperor Sigismund of Luxemburg. Only in 1424, when Jagiello changed his attitude towards the Hussites, did the Pope issue a bull condemning Falkenberg's libel. The Poles were referred to in the bull as "true Catholics and eager confessors of true religion", while Poland was called "an eminent part of the Church militant".

Those were already the times when the policy of the Roman Curia triumphed in Poland.

The defeat at Varna meant, if not a defeat, at any rate a considerable weakening of the policy of Rome whose spokesmen in Poland were the great feudal lords both ecclesiastic and secular. The ill-starred crusade against Turkey impoverished the royal treasury; Długosz wrote about it: "throughout his stay in Hungary King Władysław contracted heavy loans offering as securities almost all towns, castles, lands, villages and even the customs and the royal income. . . ."[12]

The gentry took the opportunity provided by the defeat at Varna to oppose to the policy of the magnates their own idea of Poland fully independent both of the papacy and the empire. They found a champion of their designs in the person of King Casimir IV Jagiello (1444–92), whose reign covered most of the second half of the fifteenth century and who became the leader of the new political camp.

Soon the time of great economic, territorial and political expansion was to begin for Poland. Having a devoted ally in the gentry the King began to revoke the privileges of the Church, imposed taxes on priests and himself nominated bishops; in his policy towards the Teutonic Order he likewise took little notice of Rome.

More than half a century had to elapse before the battle of Grunwald bore fruit. The peace of Toruń brought to an end in 1466 the long-lasting wars with the Order. Poland returned to the Baltic coast and made the Order her dependent. The Baltic ports were now open to the ever-increasing Polish export of grain, wood and meat. The Polish gentry were growing wealthy, the towns great, the country was becoming increasingly stronger and could provide a good basis for the dynastic expansion of the Jagiellonians who now reached for the crowns of Bohemia, Hungary, and Moldavia.

The measures of Casimir IV found zealous supporters not only among the gentry but also among the humanists gathered round the King. As they were warm admirers of Roman law, they advocated a strong rule for the state. The views that were held in these circles were: that the good of the state justifies the revoking of class privileges, that for the safety of the country taxes must be imposed and that—in exceptional cases—private as well as ecclesiastic estates may be confiscated.

Owing to his alliance with the gentry Casimir IV succeeded in constructing a solid system of state administration, but at the same time he had to yield now and then under the pressure of the selfishness of the gentry. For he needed their approval to change the laws, to impose taxes, to declare wars. By their one-sided decisions the gentry were restricting the rights of the towns in spite of considerable burdens imposed by the state on the latter. The King gave in to the demand of the gentry to increase the control of the state over trade and commerce. Simultaneously, acting under the pressure of the gentry, he excluded the burgesses from all political influence. The towns did not obtain a right to send their representatives to the lower house—just then being formed—which became an exclusive domain of the gentry. Nor could the towns receive protection from the all-powerful royal council, called the Senate at that time, and the King, involved in the conflict between the nobility and the gentry, was likewise indifferent to their needs.

An increasingly arbitrary attitude of the gentry towards the burgesses and the peasants did not arrest the deep processes of state organization that were taking place under the reign of Casimir IV. In consequence of the weakening of class ties, also of religious and vocational bonds, the unity of the state was growing at the cost of those traditional social bonds. Many factors affected this process with varying intensity at different times. The sense of nationality was deepening in the struggle against the Teutonic Order which impersonated the German drive to conquer. The growth of economic energy created the need of a strong central rule and of the unification of laws, weights, and measures. Increasingly consolidated in its opposition against Rome, the whole society came to understand the importance of state independence. Finally, the reception of the Roman law helped not a little the process of organizational changes within the state.

Against the background of changes in state organization the political doctrines of the time appear with greater clarity and distinctness; this applies particularly to *Monumentum pro Reipublicae Ordinatione (Proposal for the Organization of the Republic)*[13] which appeared in 1475, and the *Consilia*

Callimachi (*Callimachus' Counsels*) which was written almost 20 years later.[14] These two are political programmes, or rather practical guides, written by two lay thinkers, each of whom was thoroughly versed in practical politics.

The author of the *Proposal*, Jan Ostroróg—doctor of law, senator and Wojewoda of Poznan—was an advocate of Poland's unlimited sovereignty. On the other hand, the author of the *Counsels*, Philip de Teodalio Buonaccorsi, called Callimachus, composed a concise handbook of the art of ruling at the time when the gentry were beginning to doubt whether the dynastic policy of the Jagiellonians was right. Both writers were realistic in their practical postulates, with the one difference that while Ostroróg concentrated on the interest of the state, Callimachus was concerned with the good of the dynasty.

Ostroróg formulated his programme with a passion never previously encountered in Polish literature.

> You, worthy gentlemen [he wrote in his *Preface*], are the foundation and the pillars, the axle and the support of the mother country. Strive as you always did to prove by your counsel and your deeds that your attachment to the Commonwealth is above your love for yourselves, for your private wealth, for your children, brothers, and all your success. When the common good suffers, in such a way your own well-being is affected and must break down suddenly.[15]

Within the sixty-seven chapters of the *Proposal* we can distinguish broadly two groups of problems: the first comprises questions pertaining to the national sovereignty of the state; the second deals with the conditions indispensable for a smooth functioning of the state machinery. Ostroróg sees the idea of sovereignty as related to the person of the monarch and considers the king the sole representative of the state.[16]

The *Proposal* begins with the declaration of its main principle which is that "the King of Poland does not recognize anybody as his superior and has none but God above himself".[17] Thus he must not be dependent on the papacy either financially or juridically. Payments and legal appeals to Rome are degrading. The interest of the state requires that bishops be nominated by the king.

> A painful and inhuman ailment afflicts the entire free Kingdom of Poland also in this that we let the constant cunning of the Italians so deceive and delude us as to make us pay, under the pretense of piety, which is rather superstition and counterfeit of learning, such large sums of money annually to the so-called Roman Court.[18]
>
> Is this not hypocrisy [asks Ostroróg bitterly], that whenever the Pope pleases, even when such is not the will of the king and the nobles, he sends to Poland whatsoever jubilee bulls he wishes for the sake of obtaining money under the pretense of the absolution of sins.... Ah, how we Poles let ourselves be deluded.... A sufficient absolution is granted to any that labour and gather harvest....[19]

The author of the *Proposal* is convinced that "through the slyness of the courtiers and the stubbornness of the litigants not only appeals but also special summons go to the Apostolic Curia".[20] And so he exclaims in the same chapter: "Gentlemen of Poland! Do not let the cunning Italians delude you any longer. We have bishops in our kingdom as well as an archbishop who is also the primate; let the former examine the cases and let the latter pass his final judgement, if this be necessary."[21]

Ostroróg was demanding consistently an independent ecclesiastic hierarchy for Poland. Thus he wrote: "It seems better that the king should nominate bishops to ensure their being not only learned but also well-regarded, lest their quarrelsome conduct and unpleasant personalities arouse hatred constantly . . . ."[22]

However, dependence on Rome does not alone contradict the sovereignty of the state; likewise the judiciary relations of the towns with Germany encroach upon Poland's independence. Ostroróg firmly opposed the sending of court appeals to Magdeburg: "What negligence, what shame, what ignominy, need, or rather blindness caused that this famous and free kingdom should seek justice in Magdeburg."[23]

It was the consideration of national dignity that prompted Ostroróg of the need to use the Polish language in court records (Chapter XXXIX), in monasteries and in sermons. "It is an undignified and disgusting thing," he wrote, "that Poles in many places and many churches in this country should listen to sermons in German."[24]

Besides problems related to the sovereignty of the Polish nation there is in the *Proposal* a group of problems dealing with the unity and the efficient functioning of state machinery. Now, the strength and consolidation of the state is, according to the *Proposal*, determined by the following factors:

1. Uniform law which, despite temporary maintainance of estate differences, excludes arbitrary decisions (Chapters XXXII, XXXVII).

2. Unconditional obeying of the law and of royal orders by all the citizens (Chapter III).

3. Efficient machinery of administration achieved through royal nominations of qualified salaried officials (Chapter XLVII).

4. General taxation including both laymen and clerics (Chapters X, VI).

5. General obligation of military service of length varying according to estate (Chapters XLI–XLV).

6. Guaranteed supremacy of state over Church which should serve national interests. Hence the obligation of the clerics to pay taxes and the state's right to regulate the number of priests and their education (Chapters XVI, XVII, XVIII, XIX).

7. Uniform weights and measures, stability of currency, care of the proper state and the safety of roads, control of prices, finally—suppression of vagrancy and drunkenness (Chapters LII, LXII, LIX, LIV, LXI, LXII).

In such a manner did Ostroróg draw the first Polish image of a modern state.

The other political programme of the time, Callimachus' *Counsels*, is a short outline that has never ceased to arouse interest on account of its contents and the extraordinary person of its author.

In 1470 came to Poland 33-year-old Philip Buonaccorsi, called Callimachus, emigrating from Rome where he had taken part in an uncovered conspiracy, was later accused and pursued as the chief leader of an unsuccessful republican and anti-papal *coup d'état*.

As a learned humanist he was welcome in Poland, the more so as the relations between Cracow and Rome were not of the best at the time. He remained in his adopted country till the end of his life, and for more than a quarter of a century exercised considerable influence on Polish political and cultural life. Callimachus soon joined the king's entourage and became the principal advocate and exponent of the Jagiellonian dynastic expansion. He devoted his pen and his diplomatic skill to the task of proclaiming at the courts of Europe the *laus immortalis* of the Jagiellonians, who—in his view—when strengthened by the absolute rule in Poland were the principal power in Christianity.[25]

The *Counsels*, though they are no more than a small part of the varied heritage that he left, are an important document of Polish political thought.[26] They were probably written in the last year of King Casimir's reign for the private use of the future king of Poland, Jan Olbracht; hence they have a simplified, almost telegraphic form. This brief compendium of the methods of governing offers practical suggestions for ensuring success to the dynastic policy of the Jagiellonians. Justification for the contents of the compendium can only be found in the aims and interests of the dynasty and so, in spite of some contrary attempts already made, the work cannot be evaluated on any other ground.

Callimachus' remarks, contained in thirty-five short passages, have been summarized by Estreicher[27] in the following thirteen items:

1. Privy Council ought to be formed for exclusive consideration of secret affairs.

2. Clerics and laymen within the Council ought to be involved in a quarrel. Excesses should be punished. Bishops should be excluded from the Senate.

3. The Diet should not acquire too much influence; a royal faction should exist there likewise; the gentry should not be allowed to assemble.

4. New laws directed against the sovereign should not be let either into the Senate or into the Diet.

5. The gentry should be threatened with a war and thus forced to pay taxes half of which should go into the royal treasury.

6. Officials should pay for nominations; abbots should make annual payments for holding their abbeys. Offices at court should be few and modest. Royal annuities (*jurgielt*) should not be granted. District chiefs (*starostowie*) should be supervised and should obey the king.

7. Chancellors should have as little to occupy them as possible.

8. The canonical election of the bishops should be abolished.

9. Bishops and priests should not be allowed to take part in politics. Their estates should be seized and they should live on tithes.

10. Plebeians, that is burgesses, should be favoured and given secular and ecclesiastic offices. Restrictions ought to be discontinued.

11. The privileges of the gentry (*Loisa*) should be repealed.

12. Wallachia should be invaded and brother Sigismund offered the throne. Frederick ought to be given Prussia. The principality of Mazovia should be joined to the Polish crown.

13. An attempt ought to be made to have most of the gentry killed off in the campaign against Wallachia. The rest ought to be poisoned (*venenum propinato*).

The failure of Jan Olbracht's campaign against Wallachia in 1497 put an end to the dynastic policy of the Jagiellonians. The time of expansion was over and Callimachus' *Counsels* met with general condemnation. Later on they were to be used as a weapon in defence of anarchy in state organization, until they became the main argument that the gentry had against any attempt to strengthen the central rule.[28]

The depth of the changes that the sixteenth century brought along can best be judged by considering the traits of the national character that emerged in those years. So strong was the impress of the times on society and so long was the road travelled by the Polish culture between the end of the fifteenth century and the reign of the three last Jagiellonians: Alexander (1501–6), Sigismund the Old (1506–48) and his son Sigismund Augustus (1548–72) that Poland became one of the leading countries of Europe. Erasmus of Rotterdam wrote admiringly about the Polish nation: "I congratulate the nation which, though at one time regarded as barbaric, has now thriving scholarship, law, morals, religion, and is in everything so contrary to all crudeness that it can compete with those nations of the world that are most advanced in culture."[29]

In this period of energetic intellectual activity political literature occupied no mean place, for, as usual, epochs of radical changes have a need of great politicians and ideologues.

The principal nerve of those changes was the stream of gold that was flowing into Poland in exchange for the ever-increasing export of agricultural products unrestricted by any tariffs. But it was only the gentry that were amassing wealth. At the time when their private estates were growing, the treasury stayed empty, the townspeople were prey of economic restrictions and the peasants were at the mercy of the owners of manors. Likewise, only the gentry, free from everyday cares, began to have ambitions and cultural aspirations. They took care to educate their sons, they travelled abroad and maintained contacts with the leading European intellectuals. They also built stately mansions into which a worldly style of living soon penetrated, for they were promptly spending the money obtained from exported grain on articles of luxury imported from abroad. The gentry were regarding themselves as the only citizens with full rights, being convinced that their duty of defending the country left them free from any other obligation towards the state whose course they were attempting to control. They even imbibed the ideas of ancient literature in order to make use of them. In liberty they sought justification both for religious freedom and for their own lack of respect for any authority. The notion of equality was turned by them into a weapon to be used against the magnates, while at the same time discrimination against the peasants and the burgesses was maintained. The burgesses were plebeians for the gentry and the peasants —slaves. The system of government in Poland was compared to that of Athens, Sparta, and most of all—to that of the Roman republic. Hence, while exercising absolute power in their own estates, they repeated empty phrases about the disastrous results of tyranny to attack the imaginary *absolutum dominium* of their own king. Their selfishness put an end to the municipal self-government by giving the wojewodas control over trade and commerce. Finally, when exclusive right to all foreign commerce was legally guaranteed to the gentry, the economic routes of the Polish towns were severed.

Even more ruthlessly did the gentry deal with the peasants seizing for themselves the right to decide about the lives and the death of their serfs. They passed legislation forbidding the serfs to leave their villages and then gradually increased the amount of services due to the master of the manor. As the knight was turning into the gentleman of the manor, so the enterprising merchant was turning into the pedlar and the free peasant into the serf.

The selfish policy of the gentry did not bear fruit at once, because their own wealth to some extent helped to preserve the prosperity of the towns. As to peasants, there again the wide territories in the east helped the runaway serfs to find better working conditions. At that time the Jagiellonians' interest in the eastern borders increased so much that they abandoned their dynastic policy to defend Lithuania's eastern frontier and thus got involved in a never-ending war against Moscow. The time was not remote when the magnates from the eastern territories were to decide about Poland's destinies.

Meanwhile, during the reign of the last Jagiellonians, the middle gentry were still clearly opposing the magnates. In 1504 a bill was passed to the effect that only the king could, with the Diet's consent, grant or mortgage royal estates with which previously he could freely reward his aristocratic counsellors. Another bill, passed in the same year and likewise directed against the magnates, forbade holding several high offices by the same person. An act called *Nihil novi*, passed a year later, decreed that only common decisions of the king, the senate and the lower house were the will of the state.

In the fourth decade of the sixteenth century the advocates and supporters of the Reformation among the gentry undertook the reform of Church and state. Well-educated followers of Luther and Calvin became the leaders of the Catholic gentry. Their programme aroused the gentry and soon political life and political writings began to reveal vitality hitherto unobserved.

The programme of reform did not provide a uniform and systematic political platform; it rather consisted of various postulates which were meant to combat corruption in religion and in state organization, and that chiefly through return to and improvement of forgotten laws that were no longer observed. At the Diet and local assemblies there were loud demands for "putting the laws in execution" and in this very term the gentry unwittingly combined a medieval respect for the common law with the Renaissance ideas about the role of Church and that of state.

The demands for church reforms were accompanied by demand for reform of state organization. Independence was claimed for the Polish church in which supreme authority was to be held by the synod headed by the king. Demands were also voiced that the priests pay taxes and that ecclesiastical jurisdiction over laymen be wholly and irrevocably abolished. There were attempts to diminish religious differences between the Eastern and the Western rite; this was to be achieved by the abolition of the celibacy of priests, Holy Communion in two forms and the introduction of Polish into liturgy. Some demanded that crown estates, granted by the king to his prospective supporters contrary to the bill of 1504, should be retrieved. It was hoped that this measure would permit financial and military reorganization, because the gentry were not inclined to take on themselves the burden of taxation. In the last period of the reform movement its Protestant leaders wished to strengthen the royal power regarding it as a safeguard against the attacks of the Catholic clergy.

When the general Council of Trent closed its sessions in 1563 and the Church was consolidating her strength before a counter-attack, the forces of reform in Poland had already realized their programme in part. But that was their last victory. The Jesuits, brought to Poland in 1565, at once launched a well-planned campaign that led gradually to a complete control over the political and cultural life of the country.

In the history of Polish political thought the reform movement occupies a special position, because its relatively abundant literature reflects, on the one hand—the great passions of those times, and on the other—an original conception of state organization, a conception developed through grafting the *bourgeois* ideas of the Renaissance and the Reformation upon the stock formed by the mentality of the gentry.

The first kings from the Jagiellonian dynasty introduced into Poland numerous elements of the Eastern culture: these were later multiplied in the course of frequent contacts—friendly or hostile—with Russia, the Tartars, Moldavia and Turkey. From the end of the fifteenth century onward Italy exercised a powerful influence on the culture and mentality of the Polish gentry, and in the fourth decade of the sixteenth century a wave of Protestantism coming from Germany and Switzerland swept over Poland.

Both the Renaissance and the Reformation were the products of town culture; they were the outcome of the energy of new forces which were seeking an ally and supporter in a strong rule. In Poland these ideas were absorbed by the gentry which was, as a class, indifferent, if not hostile, towards the *bourgeoisie*. For the gentry accepted the criticism of traditional institutions and of established authorities but at the same time their ideal remained the manor house dominating the surrounding countryside economically, politically and culturally. Polish gentry had little understanding either of the social dynamics of the towns or of the role of state authority as the factor that directs and regulates social life. The distinctive character of the Polish Renaissance resulted from the fusion of the elements of town culture, brought from outside, and the egocentric attitude of the gentry; and this distinctiveness is also characteristic of our political thought.

Out of the fairly large political literature that was written under the last Jagiellonians and appeared in the form of booklets, letter-proposals, scholarly studies, we have selected only a few items and have grouped them according to their authors' attitude towards the religious, political and legal institutions then in existence. On the one side are those who associate the reform of state organization with the change of traditional institutions. On the other—those who defend the traditional order together with the privileged position of the Church.

The leading position in the first group is occupied by Andrzej Frycz Modrzewski (1503–72) and Jakub Przyłuski who was almost exactly his contemporary. With them can be grouped the Polish Brethren who were indifferent, if not hostile, towards the established institutions.

The defenders of the old order are represented by Stanisław Zaborowski, the author of a short tract, and by the principal theorist of the group— Stanisław Orzechowski (1515–66).

Frycz Modrzewski made himself known to the Polish society in the forties of the sixteenth century with his small pamphlets: *De poena homicidii* and *Oratio Philaletis Peripatetici*, and with his dissertation *De Legatis ad Concilium mittendis*. He expressed in these writings his thoroughly modern view on the need of one law which should be respected by the whole community. Modrzewski opposed "the inequality of law and punishment", making reference to the current law concerning homicide for which a peasant or a burgess was threatened with the death penalty while the gentry were only fined. The idea of the same laws for all the inhabitants is connected with the writer's criticism of the regulations directed against the burgesses whom the gentry legally denied the right of possessing land.

> I have often admired the wisdom of our ancestors [he wrote], and its reflection in many laws that were formerly passed; but when it comes to this particular law, which was decreed under the influence of hatred of plebeians, I deplore it and consider it a shame. For our ancestors refused thereby credibility to the testimony of the plebeians, as if anybody who is not a gentleman were of necessity a villain, or as if a plebeian could not hold any opinion about the affairs of the knights.[30]

The idea of the same laws for all must have been strikingly bold at the time, the more so as it clashed with the established notion about the gentry as the core of the nation, and stretched the notion of the nation to cover all the social classes.

In the pamphlet discussing the sending of delegates to the general council Modrzewski expressed his conviction that the weakness of the Church could be overcome through a broad participation of the faithful in religious matters and that is why reorganization of the Church should be undertaken. Diocesan councils, provincial councils and then a national council should appoint delegates to the general council by intermediate elections. In Modrzewski's writings the problems of ecclesiastical reform received abundant attention, because he was under the illusion that he would succeed in solving a number of controversial matters which were at that time disrupting the unity of the Christian world. Meanwhile the Church rejected the idea of the Reformation in order to undertake soon a counter-attack. If religious matters in Modrzewski's writings have only historical interest for us, his principal concept of state organization is invariably stimulating and thought-provoking. For Modrzewski devised as original a model of state organization as did the great Florentine, although representing the other extreme. While for Macchiavelli the proof of the state's power is the efficient functioning of the government which finds complete justification of all its measures in the achieved end, for Modrzewski the value and the strength of a state can be measured by the moral sense of its citizens. According to Modrzewski political and legal institutions merely organize society and maintain order within it, and it is the social morality that is of real importance for the state. Is it not an aimless play of appearances when institutions change and people remain the same?

In 1551 Modrzewski published his larger work, *Commentatiorum de Republica emendanda libri quinque*; contrary to its title it contained only three books: *Morals* (*De moribus*), *Laws* (*De legibus*) and *War* (*De bello*). The remaining two books: the *Church* (*De ecclesia*) and the *School* (*De schola*) appeared only in the second edition dated 1554. One can thus say without risking any great inexactness that the *Amendment of the Commonwealth* consists of two treatises; the first three books present a model of new state organization while the remaining two—and particularly the book discussing the Church —contain a project of ecclesiastic reform.

In its general outline Modrzewski's concept of state organization corresponds with the titles of the first three books. The morals of society, being the foundation of the state, are protected from within by legal institutions and from without—by a well-organized army. The invariable weaknesses of any society arise from the pettiness of human nature which causes an unceasing drama, from that uncontrolled play of passions which reveal themselves in envy, pride, selfishness and greed. Only through self-discipline, accompanied by a strong sense of moral responsibility, can human weaknesses be overcome. External factors may also work indirectly and may be supplementary in maintaining morals. Modrzewski was aware of the role played by the law in the moral transformation of people and devoted his second book to this problem. But beside the law there are other external factors precipitating the formation of the moral sense; these are: education, the moral attitude of the rulers and the supervision of social decency. Education and knowledge mould the character and develop the habit of reflective thinking which checks the impulsive reactions of passion. The moral attitude of the rulers is of greater importance in strengthening social morals than the structure of government institutions. The confidence of the citizens in the wisdom and morality of their rulers, the real and not merely institutional authority of the latter, uphold public morality. For this reason Modrzewski demands that the sovereign, the senators, the deputies and government officers be near-perfect in character and in mind, for only men of such attributes ought to be allowed to hold public offices. The author of *The Amendment of the Commonwealth* is not a utopian prophet; he does not neglect the institutions that organize society and maintain public morals which, in Modrzewski's notion, cover family life, mutual relations among people, social welfare, public safety, honesty in trade and commerce, building, hygiene, roads, public transport—in short, everything that affects the standard of living and the culture of everyday life.

Naturally, the best guarantee of the preservation of public morality is the same law for everybody consistently enforced; with this the author of *The Amendment* deals in his second book. He invariably presents his ideas in the context of a critical analysis of the conditions in Poland. He shows that the privileged position of the gentry must give rise to their high-handed treatment of the other estates and to their indifference towards state affairs.

> Thus, there is nothing more dangerous to the Commonwealth, [he wrote], than different laws and different penalties according to the person of the offender. For one law should speak to all, and in one voice; it should have the same power over all, and when it forbids something, it should justify and explain in one and only one manner the profit of all, the displeasure of all, the harm of all.[31]

However, the law must be efficacious and that means in practice that it must rest on an efficient apparatus of administration of justice, independence and impartiality of judges, quickness and simplicity of legal procedure, finally, on a regular court of appeals. While within the boundaries of a country public morality is guarded and upheld by the existing law, social order should be defended against external dangers by a well-drilled military force to which Modrzewski devoted his third book. He included there a number of suggestions concerning the establishment of a regular treasury and taxes, the organization and drilling of an army, strategy, finally—administration of conquered lands. From the mass of critical remarks and apparently detailed suggestions concerning the reform of the state and contained in the three books of *The Amendment of the Commonwealth* there emerges a modern conception of state organization, a conception still appealing by its ethical values and its practical solutions.

After the first edition of *The Amendment* had appeared the leader of the Catholic party, Hosius, wrote indignantly: "Not only does this book sin against religion but also, whenever it discusses law and public morals, it insults our mother country and particularly the gentry, so its publication is shameful to our nation whose laws and customs it criticizes violently."[32]

The principle of the same laws for the whole society was repeated after Modrzewski by Jakub Przyłuski, the author of a collection of laws[33] which was at the same time an exposition of political doctrine contained in his detailed commentaries. Przyłuski declared openly that it is the aim of the law "to preserve equality among citizens, for which it is essential that in relation to justice all should be levelled, so that a gentleman would be no more highly regarded than a servant, nor a wealthy man be any higher than a poor one".[34]

Przyluski, one of the leaders of the executive party, saw an escape for his country in the establishment of a national church with the sovereign as its head. This project was often suggested by dissidents "who wished in general that Poland might be like England where the king is the head and where no tithes are paid".[35]

In Przyłuski's conception the king becomes the main power unifying the state politically, culturally, administratively and religiously. It seems that in order to win over the ruling circles to the idea of strengthening the rule of the king and making him the head of a national church Przyłuski abandoned criticism of existing social relations. His attacks are made—both in their content and in their tone—within the limits set by the pronouncements of the Protestant reformers, who were annoyed above all by the rule of Rome in the Church.

A special kind of opposition against the existing organization was raised by the Arians also called the Polish Brethren. Though they neither opposed nor attempted to change politico-legal institutions, yet forming their own communities as if on the margin of official life, they expressed their protest against the prevailing conditions through their highly ethical conduct. They were such a force—ethically and intellectually—that though they were few in number, they played an important role in the mental activities of the country and their writings, though forbidden, were sought for in the West, especially in Germany, France, Holland and England.

In the years 1562-5 there was a split among the Polish Calvinists and a separate Arian church was established. It was a reaction against the contradictions existing between the cant of the gentry absorbed by politics and their public and private lives. The new sect formed separate communities whose religious teaching was considerably influenced by the social ideas of the Moravian Anabaptists and by the rationalism of the Italian Anti-Trinitarians.

The Polish Brethren preached an uncompromising adherence to the principles of Christian ethics in everyday life; they were convinced that the essence of religion is to be found not in obscure dogmas but in moral conduct, and consequently not the belief in dogmas but the way of living was for them a criterion of man's worth. They demanded the right of free, rational interpretation of the Scriptures and made the freedom of religion and of professing one's religious convictions the keystone of their teaching.

Against the background of the blind and fanatical religious struggles of those times the intellectualism of the Polish Brethren, their religious tolerance and their shift of emphasis from dogmatic clashes to ethical matters guaranteed to their teaching a special position in the history of political thought. Bearing in mind Christ's *Sermon on the Mount* they were thinking not of the happy life after death, but of a reform of temporal conditions. The *Sermon on the Mount* was the foundation of their campaign and a sacred commandment that they should work for social justice and constantly perfect their own personalities. Their radical leaders: Piotr of Goniądz, Grzegorz Paweł, Paweł of Wizna, Marcin Czechowic, taught by word and by their writings that a true Christian must not hold any offices or go to war, that it is even unseemly if he reaches for a sword in his own defence, that he should have no property, let alone bondsmen and slaves.

The provost of Wilno, Rotundus, so described the Polish Brethren in a letter to Cardinal Hosius written in September 1567:

> I myself saw and read a little booklet printed at Grodno in Polish and containing such blasphemous statements about Jesus Christ which are impossible to surpass either in word or in thought. In the booklet they deny power to any institution, extol Christian liberty and establish community to all property; they likewise abolish all distinctions of estate both in Church and in State, so that there might be no difference between the king and the people, between the sovereign and his subjects, between the gentry and the plebeians.[36]

1572 offered a special opportunity for the coming forward of the radical section of the brotherhood; it was the year when the last of the Jagiellonians,

Sigismund Augustus, died and the Senate fearing foreign intervention ordered all the gentry under arms. The Arian communities were at once roused to heated discussions of "the sword and the office". Some of the Brethren advocated a compromise and were inclined to consider permissible participation in a defensive war, as well as holding such government offices which would not lead to ethical conflict. The radical Arians, however, professed the view that a true Christian must have no share in institutions that make use of force or violence, and thus insisted on the prohibition of participation in wars and a ban on holding offices. They declared that life in a true Christian community rests on the principles of evangelical ethics and hence the state must be regarded as a necessary evil. Grzegorz Paweł taught unequivocally:

> The Christians were told to obey authority and to fear it, but not to exercise authority or carry out its orders when it sends someone to death or executes criminals. Such actions do not benefit a Christian who ought to be charitable and forgive seventy-seven times, while those that are in power cannot be charitable, nor once forgive anyone, but must punish him according to his offense, for otherwise they would do injustice to the other party and not perform their duty properly.[37]

The heart of the radical movement was at Raków (Racovia), the Arians' ideal city established in 1569 in the land of Sandomierz (Sandomir); this was to remain for several decades one of the liveliest centres of progressive thought in Europe.

The situation of the Polish Brethren was far from easy; their teaching constantly aroused opposition and repressions. At first they came under the attacks of the Calvinists to the satisfaction of the Catholics whose motto was then: *Bellum haereticorum pax est Ecclesiae*. The task of suppressing them was completed by the Polish Counter-Reformation with the destruction of Raków and then, 25 years later, with the expulsion of the Polish Brethren from the country.

Much less original are the doctrines that have their roots in the established order, although they also reveal the polemical spirit which stems from topical and controversial character of the problems discussed. These doctrines adapted the medieval notions to new conditions in order to justify the thesis that stability of government and of social relations is connected with the privileged position of the Church in the state, and that the Catholic religion guarantees the gentry their rights and liberties. This thesis was to become in future the main principle of the Counter-Reformation which identified the destiny of Poland with the position of the Church.

This particular point of view is expressed in a short treatise written by Stanisław Zaborowski and published in 1507 under the title *Tractatus de natura iurium et bonorum regis....*[38] The writing of the treatise was prompted by the policy of King Alexander who favoured the gentry. The author presents his arguments as if against the background of two bills recently passed: one concerning the necessity of the Diet's consent to the donation, sale or offering as security the royal estates, and the other—to its approval of new bills. Zaborowski justifies the gentry's share in government by their exclusive duty to defend the country. Only the gentry are the society, and the opinions of the gentry must be taken into account by the sovereign who manages the kingdom but is not its owner.

Going back to Cicero's idea the treatise advocates the subordination of individual interests and group interests to public good. The sovereign may justly confiscate a private estate and not be accused of robbery if public good requires it, or if by remaining in the hands of their owner they would do harm to the Commonwealth.[39] The bold declaration of the supremacy of public good was used by Zaborowski to justify the need for retrieving crown estates which were to fill the treasury without burdening the gentry with taxes.

Simultaneously he firmly declared that ecclesiastic estates were intangible. Cicero's idea did not apply to them, because Zaborowski professed the view that secular power should be subordinated to the Church and thus thought it inadmissible that ecclesiastical estates, destined for religious goals, should be used for temporal purposes.

The author argues that the internal purpose of the state is the suppression of heretics who are the greatest threat to society as a whole, while in foreign policy its aim is the undertaking of a national crusade against the Turks. Zaborowski finished his treatise with an appeal for such a crusade.[40]

Another spokesman of traditional institutions and ecclesiastic rule in Poland was a man two generations younger than Zaborowski—Stanisław Orzechowski. A demagogic priest speaking in a pathetic manner, he came to be the principal ideologue of the gentry whose favour he could win by assuring them that they were the only free nation in the world, also the most chivalrous, and that their state was ideally organized.

The 30-year-old Orzechowski became very popular after he started his career with two pamphlets: *The Loyal Subject* and *A Speech against the Turks*. In the former he branded the lawlessness of the rule of Queen Bona, the bribery of officials, the garrulity of the Diet and the oppression of the peasants. In the latter he appealed to the gentry to make a war against Turkey, a war that was prompted by Rome in order to divert attention from difficulties caused by the Reformation.

In Orzechowski's late writings there is a mixture of personal grievances, disappointments, and political matters. This was the result of his involvement in a conflict with Church hierarchy through a luckless marriage that he made despite his being an ordained priest.

Finally, in the last period of his life, when Orzechowski was already reconciled to Church hierarchy, he developed a theocratic conception of state organization in Poland and presented it in his three works: *Chimera*, *Quincunx* and *Dialogues*.

Orzechowski argues there that the State of Poland came into existence for the defence and glory of Catholicism, and that is why the highest rank in it is due to the clergy. The sovereign receives his power from the hands of a priest in order to defend the Church, religion and the country. A sovereign who fails in the performance of his duty may always be deprived of his power by the Church. Orzechowski distinguished two notions: a broader one—the kingdom, i.e. the country and Catholicism; and a narrower one—the Commonwealth by which he understood the society composed of the gentry and the king. The supreme power in the kingdom rests with the priest, while the king has supreme power in the Commonwealth. As the king reigns in the Commonwealth, so a gentleman reigns in his village and over his bondsmen.

In Orzechowski's conception of state organization Poland appeared as a federation of small estates belonging to the gentry and ruled despotically in contrast to the rights of the king who was merely to keep order and unity in the federation of the gentry. But the basic power integrating the state in Orzechowski's system is the Catholic Church.

> If someone asked me now [wrote Orzechowski], what is the kingdom of Poland? thus would I answer: the kingdom of Poland is the single state in Sarmatia, submitted by the priest to its own king, by God's grace freely elected, gifted with the altar of the Holy Cross, illumined divinely by the Christian faith and in one common apostolic Church contained and enclosed.[41]

Orzechowski's teaching is in its essence an adaptation of the medieval theocracy to the situation in Poland. His theories were to mould generations of the gentry educated by the Jesuits who made the Catholic orthodoxy and the gentry's liberty a political dogma.

In July 1572 Sigismund Augustus died and his death ended the rule of the Jagiellonian dynasty which had held the Polish throne for two centuries.

Feeling responsible for the destiny of the state the nation-gentry took up arms to repulse a possible intervention of foreign powers; at the same time they remained convinced that on the strength of a law from 1538 they should elect a new monarch. Thus came to nought the efforts of the reform party to replace a general election by the Diet's election of the king. Their only achievement was an assurance of tolerance during the 1573 session of the Diet; a resolution was then adopted to guarantee political rights to all religious denominations and to let each profess and teach its own religion.

The Catholic party, whose influence had clearly increased, meant to hand in the Polish throne to the uneducated but orthodox masses of the gentry which regarded the viritim election as an evidence of their rights and liberties.

The ideas sown by Orzechowski began to bear fruit. Under their influence the gentry began to lose their sense of reality; steeped in vanity they admired their model of state which to them represented the ideal. And thus did Jan Zamojski, the political leader of the gentry during the first election, speak to them:

> None among us recognizes any authority if he had not earlier submitted to it voluntarily or if he did not at least vote while the majority chose another king . . . so free are we that neither the king nor any official has any power over us, save that which we ourselves gave them in agreement with public laws. According to our laws a commoner can have no office, neither can he hold any dignity. A well-born gentleman can aspire to all dignities, as he is also properly reared and has not in himself that foolish indiscretion and base humility that the common folk reveal. . . .[42]

When the European countries were growing in power as a result of a strong central rule, Poland was—owing to her political situation—advancing in the opposite direction.

NOTES

1. A. Żabko-Potopowicz: Handel zbożem w Polsce w XVI wieku, *Ekonomista*, Autumn 1952, p. 138.

2. *Joannis Długossii seu Longini Canonici Cracoviensis Historiae Polonicae*, Libri XII, Tomus III, Libri IX, X, Cracow, 1876, lib. X, A.D. 1385, p. 453: "Verum maior et sanior pars, christianae fidei favore et dilatatione principaliter et quiete Regni Poloniae, aliisque conditionibus, que a Lithuano offerebantur, permota, Jagellonem pro Rege assumendum. . . ."

3. L. Ehrlich: *Paweł Włodkowic i Stanisław ze Skarbimierza*, Warsaw, 1954, pp. 23–40; and L. Ehrlich: Polski wykład prawa wojny XV wieku, *Kazanie Stanisława ze Skarbimierza De bellis iustis*, Warsaw, 1955.

4. Paweł Włodkowic defended Polish affairs against the accusations of the Teutonic Knights on four occasions: in Buda in 1413, in Wrocław in 1420, at the General Council in the years 1415–18 and before the Pope in 1420. Długosz wrote about him in his chronicle: ". . . Vir probitate et raro patriam zelo atque amore insignis, cuilibet viro illustri coaequandus. . . ." *Joannis Długossii seu Longini Canonici Cracoviensis Historiae Polonicae*, Libri XII, Tomus IV, lib. XII, *op. cit.*, A.D. 1435, p. 567.

5. Starodawne prawa polskiego pomniki, *Rerum Publicarum Scientiae quae saeculo XV in Polonia riguit Monumenta Litteraria*, Ed. M. Bobrzyński, vol. V, part I, Cracow, 1878, pp. 147–194, and 234–316; L. Ehrlich: *Paweł Włodkowic i Stanisław ze Skarbimierza*, pp. 58–172; and L. Ehrlich: *Rektor Paweł Włodkowic rzecznik obrony przeciw Krzyżakom*, Cracow, 1963.

6. K. Górski: *Z dziejów walki o pokój i sprawiedliwość międzynarodową*, Toruń, 1964, pp. 27–43.

7. Ehrlich: Polski wykład prawa wojny XV wieku, *Kazanie Stanisława ze Skarbimierza De bellis iustis*, pp. 114–15, § 19: ". . . Hoc enim est cernere in creaturis irracionabilibus, que se prout possunt tuenter et deffendunt, et interdum in se ferientem remordendo consurgunt."

8. *Ibid.*, pp. 128–9, § 29.1: ". . . Et nedum racionalia ymmo bruta pacem querunt, quia mortem et perniciem quantum possunt declinant, et vegetabilia velud arbores, que melius germinant si ventorum concussionibus carent. Unde rami arborum dum quis frangere vel incidere ipsos velit resistunt, quod non esset nisi pacem habere velint."

9. K. Górski: "Ostatnie słowo" Pawła Włodkowica o zakonie krzyżackim z roku 1432, *Zapiski Historyczne*, vol. XXIX, No. 2, Toruń, 1964, p. 160: ". . . Et de quanto caritas maior noscitur esse omnibus aliis virtutibus, tanto ipocritarum crudelitas sibi opposita deterior omnibus aliis sceleribus vel peccatis."

10. Conclusiones, datae per Magistrum Paulum de Cracovia contra Ordinem Theutonicorum sanctae Mariae Virginis in sacro Constantiensi Consilio [in:] Starodawne prawa polskiego pomniki, *op. cit.*, vol. V, part I, p. 188: " 'Quod tibi, non vis fieri, alteri non facias', et lege divina: 'Ne transgrediaris limites proximi tui'," etc.

11. Paweł Włodkowic's letter to Zbigniew Oleśnicki [in:] Górski: Ostatnie słowo Pawła Włodowica . . ., *op. cit.*, p. 161: ". . . ruptis federibus et pacis pactis sole(m)pnibus violatis, Que eciam aput barbaras naciones iure gencium naturali firmiter observantur . . ."

12. *Joannis Długossii seu Longini Canonici Cracoviensis Historiae Polonicae*, Libri XII, Tomus IV, Libri XI, XII, *op. cit.*, lib. XII, A.D. 1442, p. 683: "Unde et accidit, quod Wladislaus Rex per eos omnes annos, quibus in Regno Hungariae commoratus est, fere omnes civitates, castra, terras, oppida, villas, thelonea et intritus regales, in pluribus milibus et amplissimis summis inscriberet et obligaret. . . ."

13. Clarissimi baronis Joannis Ostrorog, iuris utriusque doctoris, Monumentum pro comitiis generalibus regni sub rege Casimiro, Reipublicae ordinatione, published in: Starodawne prawa polskiego pomniki, *op. cit.*, vol. V, part I, pp. 115–39.

14. I. Chrzanowski i S. Kot: *Humanizm i Reformacja w Polsce*, Lwów, 1927, pp. 132 ff.

15. Monumentum pro comitiis generalibus regni . . . [in:] Starodawne prawa polskiego pomniki, *op. cit.*, vol. V, part I, p. 115: "Vos Illustres Domini! columnae et bases, cardines ac vectes patriae, ita ut semper soliti estis, facite, ut consiliis et factis vestris plus patriam quam se ipsos ametis, plus rempublicam quam privatam, quam liberos, quam fratres, quam denique fortunas omnes; sic in publico singularia crescent, et fundata quaeque stabilientur solide. Sin autem commune bonum semel casum dederit, et singularia quoque privatorum labi ac pessum iri necesse est, ruinamque comitari praecipitem."

16. W. Voisé: Doktryna polityczno-prawna Jana Ostroroga, *Państwo i Prawo*, 1954, No. 6, p. 1037.

17. Monumentum pro comitiis generalibus regni . . . [in:] Starodawne prawa polskiego pomniki, *op. cit.*, vol. V, part II, p. 116: "Poloniae rex asserit (quod et verum est, nemini enim subiacet), nullum superiorem se, praeter Deum, recognoscere."

18. *Ibid.*, Chapter VIII, p. 120: "Dolendum etiam profecto et inhumanum facinus, Poloniae regnum alioqui liberum tantis Italorum in dies fraudari decipi astutiis, ut tam magna pecuniae summa ad Romanam ut vocant, curiam singulis efferatur annis sub specie pietatis falsaeque religionis, immo superstitionis potius in contribuenda ingenti pensione, quam Sacram sive Annatam vocant. . . ."

19. *Ibid.*, Chapter XIV, pp. 122–3: "Nec illud impostura caret, ut Romanus pontifex, quoties sibi videtur, etiam rege, proceribus invitis, bullas nescio quas, quae iubilaei dicuntur, in regnum mittere solet ad emungendam pecuniam sub praetextu remissionis peccatorum. . . . Interim heu quam multum illudimur o Poloni! . . . Satis superque indulgentiarum meretur, quisquis laborat, et habeat. . . ."

20. *Ibid.*, Chapter XIII, p. 122: ". . . quoties curtisanorum astu vel importunitate litigantium non appellationes solum sed etiam extraordinariae citationes ad curiam Romanam fiunt."

21. *Ibid*, Chapter XIII, p. 122: "Quare, domini Poloni! ne ultra patiamini vos ab astutis Italis decipi. Sunt in regno episcopi, extat metropolitanus et idem primas, illi causas discuntiant, in vero terminet et finiat, si quando opus erit."

22. *Ibid.*, Chapter VII, p. 120: "Quare propter maius malum melior videtur episcopi electio, quae fit a principe, ut is eligatur praesul, nedum qui doctus sit sed et gratus, ne ingrata vita et ingrata persona magis exacuat unum genus hominum contr aaliud odio perpetuo."

23. *Ibid.*, Chapter XXIV, p. 126: "O stupor, o ignavia nostra, o pudor et dedecus, opprobriumque ingens, quae necessitas, vel potius stultitia, tamdiu te in hoc inclito ac libero regno durare permisit, ut rege suo spreto proceribusque repudiatis omni denique optimatum universitate contempta, tamquam in universo regno hoc iustus et sagax non sit iudex, tamquam deficiant sapientes prudentesque ac litterati viri, in Maydemburg ius quaeratur. . . ."

24. *Ibid.*, Chapter XXII, p. 125: "O rem indignam, omnibus Polonis ignominiosam! In templis nostris lingua Theutonica multis in locis praedicatur, et quod iniquius, in loco suggesto ac digniori, ubi una tantum anus duaeve auscultant, plurimis Polonis in angulo quopiam cum suo concionatore constrictis."

25. J. Skoczek: *Legenda Kallimacha w Polsce*, Lwów, 1939, pp. 18–44 and 60–82.

26. The titles of Callimachus' works are: *Rhetorica; De vita et moribus Gregorii Sanocensis, archiepiscopi leopoliensis; Vita et mores Sbignei cardinalis; Historia de his, quae a Venetis tentata sunt,*

Persis ac Tartaris contra Turcos movendis; Historia de rege Vladislao, seu clade Varnensi; Ad Inno-centium Octavum . . . de bello inferendo Turcis oratio; Attila seu de gestis Attilae; Consilia Callimachi and metrical works, elegies, epigrams, letters and various materials.

27. S. Estreicher: Rady Kallimacha [in:] *Studia z dziejów kultury*, Warsaw, 1949, p. 172.

28. W. Sobociński: Kallimach o ideologii państwowo-prawnej polskiego Odrodzenia, *Państwo i Prawo*, 1953, No. 12, p. 790.

29. *Korespondencja Erazma z Rotterdamu z Polakami*, Transl. and Ed. M. Cytowska, Warsaw, 1965, p. 21.

30. Mowa Prawdomówcy Perypatetyka o postanowieniu sejmu zezwalającym na odbieranie mieszczanom wiejskich posiadłości, wypowiedziana w kole ludzi uczonych 1 kwietnia 1543 r. [in:] A. Frycz Modrzewski: *Dzieła wszystkie*, t. II: Mowy, Warsaw, 1954, s. 183.

31. A. Frycz Modrzewski: *Dzieła wszystkie*, t. I: O poprawie Rzeczypospolitej, ks. II: O prawach, rozdz. III, 10, Warsaw, 1953, p. 240.

32. Stanislaus Hosius Martino Cromero, Decembris 7 Heilsbergae [in:] *Stanislai Hosii . . . Epistolae tum etiam eius Orationes Legationes*, Tomus II, 1551–8, *Acta Historica res gestas Poloniae illustrata ab anno 1507 ad annum 1795*, Tomus IX, Cracow, 1886, p. 475, No. 1301: ". . . Libellus is non modo peccat contra religionem, verum etiam ubi de moribus deque legibus tractat, in patriam nostram est contumeliosum, praecipue vero in ordinem equestrem, non sine magna nostrae gentis ignomia editus, cuius et mores et leges vehementer in eo perstringuntur. Vel hoc solo nomine posset ei non parum exiberi negotii."

33. Jakub Przyłuski (Jacobo Prilusio): *Leges seu Statuta ac Privilegia Regni Poloniae*, Szczuczyn–Cracow, 1553.

34. *Ibid.*, lib. I, Praefatio.

35. Quoted after L. Kubala: *Stanisław Orzechowski*, Warsaw, 1906, p. 68.

36. Quoted after S. Kot: *Ideologia polityczna i społeczna braci polskich, zwanych arianami*, Warsaw, 1932, p. 20.

37. Quoted after S. Kot: *Ideologia polityczna . . . op. cit.*, p. 40.

38. Tractatus de natura iurium et bonorum regis. Et de reformatione regni ac eius Reipublicae regimine. Quem in lucem edidit Stanislaus Zaborowski regni Poloniae thesauri notarius [in:] Starodawne prawa polskiego pomniki, *op. cit.*, vol. V, part I, pp. 17–91.

39. Tractatus de natura iurium et bonorum regis . . . *op. cit.*, p. 78: "Naturale enim est (ut inquit Aegidius in de regimine principum) partem se exponere periculo pro toto, ut bracchium statim se exponit pro defensione corporis. Praeter ergo ordinem naturalem agit quillibet regnicola, maxime cuius interest, si non exponat se periculo pro defensione patriae, de qua ait Tulius in questionibus Tusculanis dicens: Tanta caritas est patriae, ut eam non sensu nostro sed salute ipsius metiamur. Itaque non deterret sapientem mors, quae propter incertos casus quotidie imminet, propter brevitatem vitae nunquam potest longe abesse, quominus in omne tempus reipublicae suisque consulat et posteritatem ipsam, cuius sensum habiturus non sit, ad se putet pertinere etc. Multo vero magis contra ordinem naturae et divinam legem agit, qui rem privatam non exponit pro republica. . . ."

40. See Kubala: *op. cit.*, pp. 73 ff.

41. *Quincunx*, (to jest): wzór Korony Polskiej na cynku wystawiony, przez Stanisława Orzechowskiego Okszyca z przemyskiej ziemi i na kolędę posłom koronnym do Warszawy na nowe lato roku pańskiego 1564 posłany, Ed. K. J. Turowski, Cracow, 1858, p. 40.

42. Mowa Zamojskiego za rodakiem [in:] *Rajnolda Hejdensztejna, sekretarza królewskiego "Dzieje Polski" od śmierci Zygmunta Augusta do roku 1594*, Ksiag XII, translated from Latin by M. Gliszczyński, with a biographical essay by W. Spasowicz, vol. I, St. Petersburg, 1857, pp. 215–16.

INDEX